DOCUMENTING
AMERICAN VIOLENCE

DOCUMENTING AMERICAN VIOLENCE

A SOURCEBOOK

Edited by

CHRISTOPHER WALDREP

AND MICHAEL BELLESILES

OXFORD
UNIVERSITY PRESS

2006

OXFORD

UNIVERSITY PRESS

Oxford University Press, Inc., publishes works that further
Oxford University's objective of excellence
in research, scholarship, and education.

Oxford New York
Auckland Cape Town Dar es Salaam Hong Kong Karachi
Kuala Lumpur Madrid Melbourne Mexico City Nairobi
New Delhi Shanghai Taipei Toronto

With offices in
Argentina Austria Brazil Chile Czech Republic France Greece
Guatemala Hungary Italy Japan Poland Portugal Singapore
South Korea Switzerland Thailand Turkey Ukraine Vietnam

Published by Oxford University Press, Inc.
198 Madison Avenue, New York, New York 10016

www.oup.com

Oxford is a registered trademark of Oxford University Press

Library of Congress Cataloging-in-Publication Data
Documenting American violence : a sourcebook / edited by Christopher Waldrep and
Michael Bellesiles.
    p. cm.
Includes bibliographical references and index.
ISBN-13 978-0-19-515003-2; 978-0-19-515004-9 (pbk.)
ISBN 0-19-515003-1; 0-19-515004-x (pbk.)
    1. Violence—United States—History—Sources. 2. United States—History—Sources.
I. Waldrep, Christopher, 1951– II. Bellesiles, Michael A.
HN90.V5D66 2006
303.6′0973—dc22   2005040642

9 8 7 6 5 4 3 2 1

Printed in the United States of America
on acid-free paper

For Alfred F. Young
a brilliant and inspiring scholar

Acknowledgments

The authors owe a debt of gratitude to Michael Mott and Daren Salter, the hardworking graduate students who read the entire manuscript, comparing the text to the original documents in a ceaseless effort to prevent error. William Hansen graciously assisted us with the James Farmer selection, and Martha Hunt Huie kindly aided us with the work of William Bradford Huie. Our special thanks go to Susan Ferber and Niko Pfund of Oxford University Press—two editors with the courage to act on their convictions.

CONTENTS

INTRODUCTION   3

1 CRIME AS SOCIAL DRAMA   11

Hugh Stone, a Convicted Murderer, on the Sin of Murder, 1698   17

Jereboam O. Beauchamp Confesses to Murdering
Solomon P. Sharp, 1825   21

Harry Thaw's Account of His Murder of Stanford White, 1906   27

Rev. Madison Peters Justifies the Murder of Stanford White, 1907   30

Jeffrey Toobin on the O. J. Simpson Trial, 1995   33

2 THE CONQUEST OF AMERICA   37

VIRGINIA'S CAPITAL LAWS
Laws of the Colony of Virginea, 1610–1611   43

THE PEQUOT WAR
Capt. John Underhill's Account of the Mystic Massacre, 1637   46

KIEFT'S WAR
David De Vries Describes the Beginnings of Kieft's War, 1642   49

BACON'S REBELLION
An Anonymous Account of the Rebellion in Virginia, 1676   52

THE PUEBLO UPRISING AND ITS SUPPRESSION
Governor Antonio de Otermín's Report on the Uprising in New
Mexico, 1680   55

Spanish Officials Question the Pueblo Indian Josephe, 1681   57

Don Carlos de Sigüenza y Góngora Describes the Reconquest
of New Mexico, 1692   58

THE SALEM WITCHCRAFT TRIALS
Thomas Brattle's Account of Witchcraft, 1692   62

THE PAXTON BOYS
Benjamin Franklin's Narrative of the Massacres, 1763   66

3 REVOLUTIONARY VIOLENCE   71

THE NORTH CAROLINA REGULATORS
The Petition from the Inhabitants of Orange County,
North Carolina, 1770   75

Judge Richard Henderson Confronts a Riot in Hillsborough,
North Carolina, 1770   76

The *Virginia Gazette* Reports on the Battle of Alamance, 1771   79

THE BOSTON MASSACRE
   The Town of Boston Presents Its Version of the Massacre, 1770   80

THE AMERICAN REVOLUTION BEGINS
   Reverend Jonas Clark Describes the Encounter at Lexington, 1775   85

   Ensign Henry De Bernicre Offers the British View of
      Lexington and Concord   87

REVOLUTIONARY INSTITUTIONS
   Major General Steuben on the Opportunities of War, 1779   91

   Colonel George Rogers Clark on the Conquest of the West, 1779   93

   General Nathanael Greene on the Difficulties of
      Sustaining the War, 1781   95

BATTLING DISSENT
   Rivington's Gazette on the Harassment of Loyalists, 1775   99

   Wm. Christian, Col. William Preston, Capt. Patrick Lockhart,
      and Col. Charles Lynch on the Revolutionary Origins of
      Lynching, 1779–1780   102

SHAYS'S REBELLION
   General William Shephard on the Confrontation at Springfield,
      Massachusetts, 1787   104

   The Town of Coleraine Petitions for Mercy for the Shaysites, 1787   106

   General Benjamin Lincoln Crushes Shays's Rebellion, 1787   107

   Thomas Jefferson on the Need for the Occasional Revolution,
      1787   109

4   SLAVERY   113

SLAVE LAW
   Colonial Virginia Slave Laws   115

   Mississippi's Slave Code, 1848   116

   North Carolina's Supreme Court Considers the Murder
      Conviction of the Slave Caesar, 1849   118

SLAVE REVOLT IN VIRGINIA
   Nat Turner Describes His Rebellion, 1831   124

A SLAVE INSURRECTION IN MISSISSIPPI
   The Vigilantes of Madison County, Mississippi,
      Justify Their Actions, 1835   128

DUELING
   White Mississippians Debate Dueling, 1844   133

THE DAILY EXPERIENCE OF CRUELTY
Frederick Douglass Searches for the Meaning of Violence
in a Slave Regime, 1855   135

5   THE CIVIL WAR   143

HARPERS FERRY
The National Intelligencer Describes Events at Harpers Ferry, 1859   148

THE EXPERIENCE OF BATTLE
Oliver Wendell Holmes Jr. on the Nature of Warfare,
1861, 1862, 1864   152

THE BATTLE OF GETTYSBURG
The British Officer James A. L. Fremantle Observes the
Battle of Gettysburg, 1863   157

THE NEW YORK CITY DRAFT RIOTS
David M. Barnes Records the Violence of the
New York City Riots, 1863   161

ANDERSONVILLE
Excerpts from the Diary of POW John L. Ransom, 1864   165

THE ASSASSINATION OF ABRAHAM LINCOLN
Thomas M. Harris Documents the Conspiracy to
Assassinate Lincoln, 1865   167

6   THE NEW SOUTH   171

BLACK CODES
Mississippi's Black Code, 1865   173

NEW ORLEANS RACE RIOT
J. D. O'Connell's Testimony before the House of
Representatives, 1866   175

THE KU KLUX KLAN
Henry Lowther's Testimony before a Congressional
Committee, 1871   177

THE VICKSBURG MASSACRE
James M. Batchelor Describes the Massacre, 1874   180

Testimony of Andrew Owen before the House of
Representatives, 1874   181

James M. Batchelor Writes of the Thrill of Violence, 1875   183

CALLS FOR A BLACK DEFENSE FORCE
Timothy Thomas Fortune's Speech Calling for
Self-Defense, 1884   185

THE CARROLLTON MASSACRE
James K. Vardaman Justifies the Carrollton Tragedy, 1886   186

LYNCHING
Ida B. Wells Documents the Violence against
Black Americans, 1895 189

WILMINGTON RACE RIOTS
Colonel Alfred M. Waddell Justifies a Race Riot, 1898 194

WHITE OPPOSITION TO MOB VIOLENCE
John Gordon Cashman Warns of the Danger of
Lawlessness, 1902, 1904 198

THE TULSA RACE RIOTS
The Oklahoma Commission to Study the Tulsa Race
Riot of 1921 Seeks Reparations, 2001 200

7 THE WILD WEST IN MYTH AND REALITY 207

THE MEXICAN WAR
A Group of Mexican Editors Blame U.S. Aggression
for an Unnecessary War, 1850 216

THE LITTLE BIGHORN MASSACRE
The *Chicago Tribune* Reports Custer's Defeat, 1876 221

Hamlin Garland Records the Cheyenne Two Moon's Version
of the Battle, 1876 223

BILLY THE KID
Pat Garrett's Version of the Lincoln County War, 1877 227

POPULAR TRIBUNALS
Hubert Howe Bancroft Defends Vigilance Committees, 1887 231

THE VIRGINIAN
Owen Wister Creates the Standard Image of the
Wild West, 1902 235

WOUNDED KNEE
James Mooney Documents the Ghost Dance Religion
and Its Consequence, 1890 239

8 THE INDUSTRIALIZATION OF VIOLENCE 245

THE STRIKE OF 1877
Allan Pinkerton on Putting Down the Great Strike of 1877 254

THE HAYMARKET TRIALS
Michael J. Schaack Remembers "the Red Terror"
in Chicago, 1886 262

CLASS WAR IN COEUR D'ALENE
The *Spokane Weekly Review* Reports on the Violence in
Coeur d'Alene, 1892 265

THE ASSASSINATION OF FRANK STEUNENBERG
Harry Orchard on Making a Bomb, 1905   268

THE LUDLOW MASSACRE
The United States Commission on Industrial Relations Charges
the Colorado National Guard with Inciting Violence, 1913   271

THE HAWK'S NEST TUNNEL
Philippa Allen, Arthur Peyton, Rush Dew Holt, and
John W. Finch Testify before the House of Representatives
on America's Worst Industrial Disaster, 1936   276

9   VIOLENCE AS A MEANS OF CRIME CONTROL   283

THE PROBLEM WITH DUE PROCESS
Justice David J. Brewer Downplays the Importance of
Due Process, 1903   286

THE PROBLEM OF CLASS
The Final Statements of Nicola Sacco and Bartolomeo
Vanzetti to the Court Sentencing Them to Death, 1927   288

THE PROBLEM WITH THE POLICE
The Wickersham Commission Documents Police Brutality, 1931   293

THE PROBLEM OF ORGANIZED CRIME
Testimony of Claude A. Follmer before a Congressional
Committee, 1950   299

THE PROBLEM OF RACE
The California Governor's Commission Looks for the
Causes of the Watts Riot of 1965   303

The Independent Commission on the Los Angeles Police
Department Looks for the Causes of the Los Angeles
Riot of 1992   307

THE DEATH PENALTY
The Supreme Court Considers the Electrocution of
Convicted Criminals, *In re Kemmler*, 1890   310

The Supreme Court Considers the Death Penalty in
Furman v. Georgia, 1972   313

10   CIVIL RIGHTS   319

A LAW AGAINST LYNCHING
Walter White Meets with Attorney General Homer
Cummings, 1936   322

Walter White Appeals to Eleanor Roosevelt, 1936   324

Victor Rotnem Argues for a Civil Right "Not to
    Be Lynched," 1943   326

Justice Frank Murphy's Notes on the Supreme Court
    Debate over a Right Not to Be Lynched, 1944   328

EMMETT TILL
    William Bradford Huie Describes "The Shocking Story of
    Approved Killing in Mississippi," 1956   330

FREEDOM RIDES
    James Farmer Leads the Freedom Riders, 1961   332

    FBI Informant Gary Thomas Rowe Jr. Participates in
    Klan Violence, 1961   335

CONFRONTATION AT OLE MISS
    The Mississippi National Guard Confronts Rioters at the
    University of Mississippi, 1962   339

JAIL AS A TEMPLE OF FREEDOM
    Aaron Henry's Testimony before the House Judiciary Committee,
    1963   343

A PRESIDENT SPEAKS IN FAVOR OF CIVIL RIGHTS
    President Lyndon B. Johnson Calls for an End to
    Racist Violence, 1965   350

THE SUPREME COURT PLACES CIVIL RIGHTS ABOVE STATES' RIGHTS
    The Supreme Court on the Murder of Michael Schwerner, James
    Goodman, and James Chaney, in United States v.
    Price, et al., 1966   352

II LOST TO HISTORY   355

LIVING WITH DOMESTIC VIOLENCE
    Abigail Bailey Describes Her Husband's Violent Ways,
    1767–1789   367

INCIDENTS IN THE LIFE OF A SLAVE GIRL
    Harriet Jacobs, a Slave, Is Raped by Her Owner, 1861   376

THE RIGHTS OF THE VICTIM
    Marla Hanson's Testimony before the Senate Judiciary
    Committee, 1990   384

INDEX   389

DOCUMENTING
AMERICAN VIOLENCE

INTRODUCTION

Violence is incoherent. It can seem, and often is, random, chaotic, anarchic. It takes many forms: a duel, a brawl, a shooting, a war, a feud, a riot. Some Americans consider abortion a form of violence, while others feel that preventing a desired abortion is violence. Has an industrial employee injured by unsafe machinery experienced violence? What about the victims of a drunken driver? When does intimidation become violence? Do images of violence provoke bloodshed, becoming themselves a form of violence? The definition itself remains elusive, describing behavior that is often ephemeral.

This book understands violence as being the physical injury of other human beings.[1] Our focus is on violence as a domestic tradition, not as an instrument of foreign policy. We seek to organize otherwise disjointed data while remaining, we hope, faithful to the often chaotic nature of American violence. Many brilliant scholars have looked carefully at the trend lines of American homicide and rioting.[2] This book has a different aim. It looks at violent events that have been sensationalized into metaphors, violent acts made to stand for some larger trend.[3] America has long had a "wound culture," a pornography of pain that

---

1. There are those who define violence expansively so as to include crimes against property, psychological damage, and even the use of hostile language.
2. Roger Lane, *Murder in America: A History* (Columbus: Ohio State University Press, 1997); Eric H. Monkkonen, *Murder in New York City* (Berkeley: University of California Press, 2001); Donald L. Horowitz, *The Deadly Ethnic Riot* (Berkeley: University of California Press, 2001).
3. Jeffory A. Clymer, *America's Culture of Terrorism: Violence, Capitalism, and the Written Word* (Chapel Hill: University of North Carolina Press, 2003); Murray Edelman, *Construing the Political Spectacle* (Chicago: University of Chicago Press, 1988); Joseba Zulaika and William A. Douglass, *Terror and Taboo: The Follies, Fables, and Faces of Terrorism* (New York: Routledge, 1996).

translates into a fascination with injured bodies.[4] Our first chapter examines four murder metaphors, starting with a colonial wife killer named Hugh Stone. Stone's conversation with a minister as he walked to his execution circulated in New England's pamphlet literature. Cotton Mather awarded Stone a measure of notoriety by including him in his 1699 collection of criminals' "Dying Speeches." Seventeenth-century technology would not allow Mather to attract an audience as large as the broadcasters of O. J. Simpson's trial could command. Stone never became as famous as O. J. Simpson; but Mather intended for Stone to become a metaphor for their time, just as Simpson may be for his. The rise of the penny press in the 1830s allowed journalists to transform murder metaphors into truly national phenomena.[5]

Violence forms a background for all American history, toppling British rule, creating and ending slavery, frustrating Reconstruction, and promoting civil rights. It is an element in the American character, a driving force that has defended privilege, challenged authority, advanced causes, and throttled hopes. Sensational murder investigations and trials often suggest a supposed tendency toward violence that is uniquely American. Americans allegedly have a murderous rage that comes from the ground up and not the top down. Such, for instance, was the case with lynching, which supposedly sprang from a force too powerful to control, the sovereign will of the public. Nazi Germany was certainly more violent than the United States, but the Holocaust emerged from an ideologically driven government program. The great horror story in American history was slavery, the subject of chapter 4. But that institution, though certainly sanctioned by the government, emerged from the behavior of ordinary people. Most of the violence necessary to maintain slavery came from individuals in situations involving two or three people. Many scholars have argued that American violence has a conservative, racial character as a result of its slave past.[6] Slavery taught white Americans to be violent outside of the law without fear of legal consequences.

The daily brutality of slavery has attracted considerable historical attention in the past few decades, but other violent chapters in America's past await further historical research. For instance, the violent nature of industrialization,

4. Mark Seltzer, *Serial Killers: Death and Life in America's Wound Culture* (New York: Routledge, 1998); Karen Halttunen, *Murder Most Foul: The Killer in the American Gothic Imagination* (Cambridge, MA: Harvard University Press, 1998).

5. Andie Tucher, *Froth and Scum: Truth, Beauty, Goodness, and the Ax Murder in America's First Mass Medium* (Chapel Hill: University of North Carolina Press, 1994).

6. See, for instance, John Hope Franklin, *The Militant South, 1800–1861* (Cambridge, MA: Harvard University Press, 1956); Edward L. Ayers, *Vengeance and Justice: Crime and Punishment in the Nineteenth-Century American South* (New York: Oxford University Press, 1984); Joel Williamson, *A Rage for Order: Black/White Relations in the American South since Emancipation* (New York: Oxford University Press, 1986).

the subject of chapter 8, is customarily disregarded. Another widespread form of violence that is generally lost to the historical record and constitutes the subject of this book's final chapter is domestic abuse. Most of this everyday violence goes unremarked, even if it finds its way into the courtroom. The press rarely covers yet another case of spousal abuse or an avoidable industrial accident. Occasionally some individual tragedy captures the American imagination in ways that routine acts of violence do not. These cases often become bywords for entire forms of violence, but they can also serve to divert attention from broader social issues and even persuade large segments of the population that it is better to remain silent for fear of provoking further violent outbursts. These dramatic public cases can mislead many into believing that the law is addressing serious social issues, or can be highly counterproductive by convincing segments of the population that the legal system is deeply flawed, as was the case with the O. J. Simpson and Rodney King trials.

Violence is not limited to the acts of individuals. Americans are excellent organizers, even when it comes to violence. In addition to vigilante movements, Americans have created a number of bloody organizations devoted to racial, religious, labor, and criminal goals. Industrialization accelerated this process.

Despite the obvious popular interest in violence, the history of American violence as a whole has attracted relatively little attention until recently. As Roger Lane wrote in 1999, "The relevant history is quite new." While the study of what Lane calls "sanctioned homicide"—war and other violent actions by the state—has long fascinated historians, they have only recently turned to a consideration of other forms of violence to discover "the attitudes and practices of the societies in which it occurs, their fears and sore spots, or the value they place on human life or on different kinds of human life."[7] In the late 1960s and early 1970s, a few general historical studies of violence appeared that were especially concerned with urban conflict, which many commentators felt was likely to increase in the years ahead and could destabilize the country. Beginning in the Watts area of Los Angeles in 1965, these riots highlighted the nation's racial and economic tensions in the midst of President Lyndon Johnson's major social reform effort, the War on Poverty. Millions of Americans watched on their televisions as poor African Americans battled the mostly white police forces of one city after another.

In the midst of these "long hot summers," President Johnson appointed the National Commission on the Causes and Prevention of Violence. Its report, published in 1969, exerted enormous influence on popular and scholarly perceptions of violence in American history and became the standard work cited

---

7. Roger Lane, "Murder in America: A Historian's Perspective," in Michael Tonry, ed., *Crime and Justice: An Annual Review of Research* 25 (1999): 192.

by historians who touched on the subject. The report's editors, Hugh Davis Graham and Ted Robert Gurr, set the tone for much of the historical discussion that followed by charging that the United States suffered from a "historical amnesia" when it came to violence. This refusal to face their violent past originated in "our historic vision of ourselves as a latter-day chosen people, a New Jerusalem."[8] Remarkably, "the Commission could find no significant work on violence in America, much less any that would relate it to that in other countries."[9] There were just some stories that the American people did not want to hear. As a consequence, the commission found it necessary to begin that historical process, calling upon a wide range of scholars to investigate America's violent past. The resulting volume was apparently "the first attempt to link the historical and comparative dimensions of research on the subject [of] group violence in America," with the editors emphasizing its "tentative" nature while calling for much more research.[10]

The commission's report included a number of significant essays that have continued to guide research to this day. Particularly important were the articles by Charles Tilly and Richard Maxwell Brown. Tilly's comparative study demonstrated that there was nothing unique about American violence, which he found fitting perfectly within a wider Atlantic context. The United States was therefore roughly consistent with the rest of the "Western world" until the end of World War II, when its level of violence accelerated and quickly surpassed that of any other industrial nation.[11] Such findings would appear to indicate some significant development in the recent past, but no conclusions were suggested by the report.

Brown's two essays chronicled a long tradition of collective violence, focusing especially on vigilante movements. Brown distinguished between "negative violence," such as criminal acts, and "positive violence," such as some vigilante actions: "Vigilante violence was used to establish order and stability on the frontier" and was therefore "widely accepted and applauded."[12] Vigilantism constituted just a small part of an unending story of brutality, for "violence has formed a seamless web with some of the noblest and most constructive chapters of American history."[13] While Brown denounced this constant resort to violence, he held that Americans are "an incorrigibly violent people," with violence an integral part of the "American value system."[14]

8. Hugh Davis Graham and Ted Robert Gurr, eds., *The History of Violence in America: Historical and Comparative Perspectives* (New York: Praeger, 1969), xiv; slightly different wording on p. 792.
9. Graham and Gurr, *History of Violence in America*, xv.
10. Graham and Gurr, *History of Violence in America*, 819.
11. Graham and Gurr, *History of Violence in America*, 798.
12. Graham and Gurr, *History of Violence in America*, 46.
13. Graham and Gurr, *History of Violence in America*, 75.
14. Graham and Gurr, *History of Violence in America*, 76.

Influenced by Brown's research, the editors sought the specific historical roots of American violence. They rejected entirely the notion that the United States is violent because people are violent. Human "cultural diversity" demonstrated, the editors concluded, that "man can through his intelligence so construct his cultural traditions and institutions as to minimize violence and encourage the realization of his humanistic goals."[15]

The commission's report had an immediate impact, especially on editorial writers, many of whom misread its findings as suggesting that the United States was somehow uniquely violent.[16] The historical report showed, in the words of John Herbers, "how deeply engrained in American life is the tradition, even the love, of violence."[17] It convinced many that, in the words of black militant H. Rap Brown, "violence is as American as cherry pie."[18] Because of its origins in the dramatic events of 1968, the committee was mostly concerned with what it called "civil strife," or collective forms of violence, and less troubled by individual acts of violence. It generalized that American violence was the result of "discontent," often but not solely in response to material circumstances.[19] But for discontent to turn violent, the majority of people must accept force as a legitimate means to an end. The United States fit this pattern by consistently rewarding, even if only with admiration, those who commit acts of violence.[20] The prevalence of violence, therefore, comes down to the degree of popular support.

The commission's report inspired a few books examining the role of violence in American history. Heavily influenced by events in the 1960s, these books uniformly read present conditions back into American history. Thus one writer could describe the Revolutionary-era Sons of Liberty as the equivalent of "the Students for a Democratic Society," a group of 1960s radicals.[21] Richard Hofstadter and Michael Wallace battled these anachronistic perceptions of the past in their 1970 documentary history of violence in America—the first, and until now last, of its kind. In his introductory essay, Hofstadter offered a carefully nuanced reading of America's past that was still very much a product of its time.[22] Hofstadter was no specialist in violence or its history; but, at that time violence seemed so pervasive, so threatening, that even a historian renowned for his work in more traditional fields could not ignore it.

---

15. Graham and Gurr, *History of Violence in America*, 802.
16. David Grimsted, "Making Violence Relevant," *Reviews in American History* 4 (1976): 331–38.
17. Graham and Gurr, *History of Violence in America*, xiii.
18. Graham and Gurr, *History of Violence in America*, xiii.
19. Graham and Gurr, *History of Violence in America*, 803.
20. Graham and Gurr, *History of Violence in America*, 808.
21. Ovid Demaris, *America the Violent* (Baltimore: Penguin, 1970), 13.
22. Richard Hofstadter and Michael Wallace, eds., *American Violence: A Documentary History* (New York: Knopf, 1970).

Hofstadter envisioned two futures for America. One was a nightmare scenario of a bloody spiral that began with an indefinite war in Vietnam or the
launching of another such military adventure, a continuing refusal by white
Americans to accept racial justice, more protest on college campuses, continuing
political polarization, the formation of armed groups along racial lines, mass
urban gunfights, the collapse of one or both political parties, and the capture
of the national government by a repressive and imperialistic national movement.[23] While this apocalyptic vision was possible, Hofstadter thought it the
least likely alternative. More realistically, the United States would fail to master
its afflictions as the mass of people lost interest; yet the country would somehow cope with its problems, blundering into an "uncertain future like some
huge inarticulate beast," wounded, "but too strong and resourceful to suc-
cumb."[24] Hofstadter based this latter prediction on the history of American
violence, but he suggested that historians could help the nation come to terms
with this lethal legacy if they but had the courage to study this difficult subject.[25] While considerable description of various assassinations, riots, and other
specific acts of violence had made its way into print, Hofstadter judged the
available analysis unsatisfactory. He found, for example, no real history of
lynching, "no great history of the subject that assesses its place in the political
culture of the South"; nor had anyone undertaken to explain "the peculiar
stubbornness with which Americans clung to their feeble and outmoded gun
control laws."[26] Hofstadter had no doubt that future historians, awakened by
the violence of the 1960s, would rectify this and several other notable omissions.

Hofstadter predicted that future historians would be attracted to the subject
of violence because it is "endemic," a constant running through the pages of
America's story.[27] Yet Hofstadter did not believe Americans exceptionally violent
and easily listed a variety of more violent cultures. Instead, he thought Americans had an exceptional talent for denial. More than the citizens of most
countries, Americans could be violent and at the same time see themselves as
orderly and well behaved. Hofstadter believed America to be both violent and
stable. In part, this was because most violence served conservative forces, carried
out by people with power against people without power to preserve the status
quo. Hofstadter rejected out of hand any explanation of violence as an attribute
of America's frontier heritage. It seemed obvious to Hofstadter that violence in
the United States had always been primarily a product of urban life. The ethnic

---

23. Hofstadter, "Reflections on Violence," 42, in Hofstadter and Wallace, eds., *American Vio-
    lence*.
24. Hofstadter, "Reflections on Violence," 43.
25. Hofstadter, "Reflections on Violence," 4.
26. Hofstadter, "Reflections on Violence," 4–5.
27. Hofstadter, "Reflections on Violence," 6.

and religious, though not the class, interactions of the city were "the funda-mental determinants of American violence."[28] What made the 1960s different, Hofstadter thought, was that the new violence emanated from the oppressed and the abused. This shift explained the sudden arousal of popular and gov-ernmental concern, as reflected in the National Commission on the Causes and Prevention of Violence. When established powers perpetrated the violence, it could be safely forgotten, hidden in obscure and unread histories; when Amer-ica's oppressed employed violence, it became a matter for political attention.

Buried within Hofstadter's shrewd and penetrating essay is another expla-nation for the failure of historians to adequately attend to American violence. American violence has taken a great many forms, and with a few notable ex-ceptions, these forms tend to be small- rather than large-scale. America has no tradition of violence, in the sense of a cohesive, ideologically driven force. In-stead, the nation has a history of violence, a lengthy and extensive history but not one that can easily constitute a chapter in a textbook. Hofstadter would likely have been amused had he lived to hear a well-educated and highly intel-ligent secretary of state, Colin Powell, assure Congress as the government pre-pared to launch a war on a distant nation that the United States always acted in the interest of peace and had never come as the conqueror.[29] Secretary Powell may have heard a different view had he stopped to ask the Sioux or Seneca, the Canadians or Mexicans, or the people of the Philippines or Puerto Rico. American violence does not lend itself to a concise narrative or sweeping gen-eralizations.

These are only the most public forms of violence. As the final chapter at-tempts to demonstrate, many types of violence occur behind closed doors and outside historical processes. Violence against women seems a constant, offering little evidence of the change over time that historians study. Nonetheless, surely few can deny that gendered violence is a major component of the American experience, and an ugly part of American history. The ignorance of hidden forms of violence affects the lives of thousands of people every year. Societies that turn a blind eye to some forms of violence give silent approval to its continuance, as American whites once did to the racial terrorism exerted to keep African Americans in a subservient status.

Ida B. Wells hoped that her careful documentation of southern lynchings would draw down the condemnation of the civilized world. She held a profound faith in the power of information and education to transform even the most warped culture. This conviction motivated many of the people discussed in this

---

28. Hofstadter, "Reflections on Violence," 12.
29. Secretary of State Colin Powell's statement to the House International Relations Commit-tee, February 12, 2003, www.cnn.com.

book to record the violence they saw. Obviously, and tragically, there are dozens of highly significant instances of violence that space limitations precluded from appearing in this collection. It is our hope that the material gathered here will allow each reader to formulate an individual understanding of America's historical experience of violence. Images of violence, sensational episodes woven into the national memory, have shaped our policies, our understanding of the possible and the impossible, our picture of who we are. The very definition of our character flows, at least in part, from our stored images of past violence. Violence is chaotic, incoherent, constant, and ephemeral, but historians ignore it at their peril. If we can only understand the historical roots of American violence, we may be able to address it more effectively in our own society.

Finally, a note on our editorial method: The documents in this book come from a wide variety of sources, both published and unpublished. As a consequence, and despite our best efforts, inconsistencies in editorial method may have inevitably crept in. Our guiding principle has been to reproduce the texts in a form as much like the originals as possible. We have, however, broken up long texts into paragraphs for ease of reading and we have removed the original reference notes. When reproducing handwritten documents, we have reproduced the author's corrections by using <angled brackets> for interlineations. Our own insertions appear in [square brackets].

ONE

CRIME AS SOCIAL DRAMA

O n June 16, 2000, Raynard Johnson's father came home from work to find his son's body hanging from a tree in his front yard in Kokomo, Mississippi. Since the Johnsons were African American, it seemed, for a moment, that a Mississippi lynch mob had claimed one more victim, on the eve of the twenty-first century. Jesse Jackson led a crowd of journalists to Kokomo, and Al Sharpton announced plans to make the trip himself. ABC, CBS, and NBC broadcast the story on their evening news programs. Through July, CNN analyzed the story, relying on panels of experts in the absence of hard news. Newspapers quoted Emmett Till's mother comparing Johnson to her son, killed by Mississippi racists in 1955.[1]

Americans die violently every day. The Federal Bureau of Investigation (FBI) keeps track of the body count through its Uniform Crime Report, begun in 1930. Very few of the deaths tallied by the FBI attract any special attention, and news accounts of the ups and downs of the crime rate do not always penetrate the national consciousness. Johnson's death came at a time when American violence had declined. Eric Monkkonen's careful study of New York homicides finds three waves in the murder rate. New York murders peaked in 1864, 1931, and 1991. After 1991, homicide plummeted not just in New York but across the nation.[2] And, yet, statistics are only part of the story. Many Americans form their opinions about the state of American violence through particular dramatic crimes and trials. One of the editors of this volume pointed out the statistical decline to his students only to be greeted with disbelief. The students had "seen"

---

1. Christopher Waldrep, *The Many Faces of Judge Lynch: Extralegal Violence and Punishment in America* (New York: Palgrave Macmillan, 2002), 152–53.
2. Eric Monkkonen, *Murder in New York City* (Berkeley: University of California Press, 2001), 7–54.

scores of homicides on television and read reports of murder trials in their newspapers without letup. They "knew" the murder rate was frighteningly high. Had Raynard Johnson really been lynched, most Americans would have seen his terrifying death as a "proof" of continuing racial violence. No statistic would have had the same impact. Civil rights leaders of national stature understood this symbolic power, and so did leading journalists. That's why they went to Kokomo.

But then, after July, the television networks abruptly dropped the story. Two autopsies, one sponsored by the Johnson family, found that the young man had most likely hanged himself. His death vanished from the national consciousness, becoming just another anonymous digit in the teen suicide tally. His family, and Jesse Jackson, lost their bid to make Raynard Johnson's "lynching" emblematic of continuing racial violence. This young man's death was no longer of interest to those who did not know him, yet the tragedy was not lessened for those who did.[3]

The trial of O. J. Simpson is a recent, sensational example of a single crime's power over public opinion. Millions watched the "trial of the century" unfold as a kind of real-life soap opera. Such trials educate. Viewers and readers gobbled up news and pictures about O.J. to watch a celebrity's downfall. In the process, they learned something about the influence of celebrity on a murder investigation and trial, domestic violence, and, finally, the racial influences on white police and black jurors. Black and white Americans drew dramatically different lessons from the O.J. trial, but all thought the case illustrated something fundamental, exposing either racist cops or feckless jurors.

Technology, and Judge Lance Ito, opened the Simpson trial to millions of viewers. But throughout American history, sensational trials have periodically attracted large audiences beyond the few witnesses, lawyers, and family members personally involved. The pamphlet carrying Hugh Stone's interrogation, en route to his execution, circulated to a large audience, albeit one only a tiny fraction of the numbers watching O. J. Simpson. Jereboam Beauchamp's confession, also published as a pamphlet, scandalized Kentuckians. By the twentieth century, though, technology allowed an entire nation to follow Harry Thaw through his various trials. We could have chosen other cases, but each of these trials excited a wide audience by contemporary standards. More than any statistic, the investigations of Hugh Stone, Jereboam Beauchamp, Harry Thaw, and O. J. Simpson each dramatized fundamental tensions in American society. The trials of these four defendants, like other sensational trials, used ordinary crimes to pose extraordinary questions. Can Christianity salvage a sinner's soul? How much power do women have in the South's honor culture?

3. Monkkonen, *Murder in New York City.*

Should society support an ordinary citizen who kills a misogynist, making New York "safe for virgins"? To what degree does race influence criminal justice? In powerful and important ways, each of these questions reflects its own time.

CELEBRITY

Violent, lawbreaking colonials, willing to repent—and legal and church records indicate most accused were eagerly penitent—escaped not only eternal damnation but anonymity. Ministers published their confessions, selling them as pamphlets for as little as two pence when they did not give them away. Readers especially valued the words of those poised on the precipice of the afterworld. In their final days these mostly disadvantaged, hopelessly obscure people knew their words would be preserved in print. For a fleeting moment, before they plunged into eternity, these authors could enjoy real celebrity.

But the ministers had far more power. In the seventeenth and early eighteenth centuries, clerics monopolized crime writing. They not only determined which of the condemned escaped obscurity but also revised, rewrote, and edited their final pleadings. The ministers had the power to bestow fame and the promise of salvation, or to consign the executed to an anonymous death with a grim guarantee of eternal damnation. In the case of Hugh Stone, an anonymous minister was able to elevate his confession into a popular pamphlet, making Stone a celebrity criminal.

By 1800, the clerical monopoly over crime literature had weakened. Accounts of trials began circulating, a genre that emphasized uncertainty and allowed the accused to plead their innocence rather than beg for salvation. When not denying their guilt, killers sometimes appealed for community sanction. Jereboam O. Beauchamp accused his victim, Solomon P. Sharp, of sexually exploiting Ann Cook. Beauchamp aimed to expose Sharp, a successful Kentucky lawyer, politician, and veteran of the U.S. Congress, and state attorney general, as a sexual deviant. More than a sense of honor or even a killer's self-justification may have motivated Beauchamp's *Confession*. It is surely relevant that Sharp died in the middle of his campaign for Kentucky's New Court Party or the Relief Party, a political movement aimed at assisting the debtor class through friendly legislation. These reformers wanted a "New Court" because the existing state supreme court, or "Old Court," had declared their proposed debtor relief legislation unconstitutional. Beauchamp passionately sided with the creditor class and with the old supreme court. Beauchamp's allegations of sexual impropriety may well have camouflaged his political motives in killing Sharp. There seems less doubt that politics motivated the publishers of Beauchamp's

Confession. Beauchamp achieved celebrity as the Old Court Party disparaged their New Court opponents by besmirching Sharp's reputation.

REVELATION

Crime literature has traditionally promised curious readers such shocking revelations of the sort contained in Beauchamp's *Confession.* Eighteenth-century execution sermons and confessions took readers vicariously into the heart of evil, delivering harrowing narratives of lives gone wrong, sin run amok, parents ignored, prayer neglected. Beauchamp's confession fashioned a most unflattering portrait of a successful politician's secret life. Eighteenth-century crime writers, like their nineteenth-century counterparts, allowed their readers to encounter an immorality usually hidden from public view.

After 1835, dramatic improvements in printing technology made cheap newspapers available to new classes of readers. The lower and middle classes could now purchase a newspaper for a penny. These new readers hungered for crime news. Like the readers of colonial execution sermons and conversion pamphlets, these new consumers of print wanted revelation. They expected the press to turn over flat rocks, revealing the squirming underside of the human condition. The penny press was more than willing to oblige.

Harry Thaw turned over one such rock in 1907. His trial for murdering the famed architect Stanford White became an inquiry into the victim's morality. Although Thaw also published his confession, it is his trial and published accounts of it that form the popular culture's record of the murder. Thaw's lawyers succeeded in putting the victim on trial. Like Beauchamp's *Confession,* newspaper reports of testimony at the Thaw trial unearthed a darker side of public life. Stanford White had designed Madison Square Garden and redesigned the University of Virginia. Famous for more than his architectural triumphs, White had lived a life of celebrity in a time of deep poverty and gilded excess. Testimony at Thaw's trial revealed that White, aged around fifty, enjoyed barely pubescent young girls. He delighted in their seduction, their "RUIN," in the language of the day. In fact, he is said to have invented the invitation "come up and see my etchings," a catchphrase for attempts by sexually hungry men to lure young victims into their lair for sexual puposes. (White, by the way, really did have etchings, some of a shocking nature, in his Madison Square Garden hideaway.) Thaw's lawyers turned White into the epitome of Gilded Age excess: his young women sat naked in velvet swings or popped out of pies at bacchanalian dinner parties. No wonder editorial writers and ministers insisted that Thaw must be freed, if only for having rid society of the scourge of Stanford White.

Unlike Beauchamp's charges against Sharp, Thaw's exposure of Whites' moral failings advanced no particular political agenda. Instead, Thaw's trial revelations threatened to undermine social Darwinist justifications for the privileged position of the wealthy elite. Social Darwinism, most famously articulated by Herbert Spencer, held that "the whole effect of nature" is to eliminate the weak and the ill disciplined "to make room for better" and stronger people. Successful individuals found Spencer's arguments seductive; Andrew Carnegie delighted in "the truth of evolution."[4] The Thaw trial revealed that one of the persons "naturally selected" for success, Stanford White, had flawed morals.

Perhaps if he had gone on trial in the Gilded Age, O. J. Simpson might have similarly exposed the lives of the famously rich. The raw material was certainly there. The "O. J. Trial" exposed the onetime sports hero and movie star as a poorly educated wife beater. His ex-wife and victim, Nicole Brown Simpson, emerged as a party animal so enamored of oral sex with strangers that one writer said she transformed casual sex into the "Brentwood hello." While such revelations titillated the millions who tuned in to watch O.J.'s trial, they never became the main point of the proceedings.

Simpson's lawyer Johnnie Cochran lobbied hard to make race the central focus of the trial, alleging that racist Los Angeles Police Department (LAPD) officers faked evidence against his client. Simpson, a famously successful black man, was charged with killing his ex-wife, a white woman, and her friend Ron Goldman, who was also white. Cochran likened the Simpson case to *Plessy v. Ferguson* and *Brown v. Board of Education*, though the comparison was generally lost on legal scholars. Both outside and inside court, Cochran promoted Simpson's case as a civil rights issue: the white establishment harassing a successful black man.[5] Prosecutor Marcia Clark wrote that the "bedrock issue" was not race "but race coupled with celebrity." Blacks, Clark understood, instinctively felt defensive, suspicious that whites sought to knock a successful black man off his pedestal.[6]

Though race and celebrity were undeniably at the core of the Simpson trial, ultimately the proceedings came to mean something even more than that. While Thaw put his victim on trial, the televised Simpson spectacle challenged the entire criminal justice system. Some observers, including the prosecutors, complained that Simpson's lawyers successfully put the LAPD on trial. The LAPD had a long history of racism and the violent abuse of minorities—as we shall see later in this book. The videotaped beating by police officers of motorist

4. Richard Hofstadter, *Social Darwinism in American Thought*, rev. ed. (Boston: Beacon Press, 1955), 41, 45.

5. Jeffrey Toobin, *The Run of His Life: The People v. O. J. Simpson* (New York: Random House, 1996), 410.

6. Marcia Clark with Teresa Carpenter, *Without a Doubt* (New York: Viking, 1997), 186.

Rodney King was only the most famous landmark on a densely packed land-scape of abuse. At Simpson's trial, detective Mark Fuhrman, sensationally ex-posed as a perjuring racist, came to symbolize the worst problems in the de-partment.

But viewers of the Simpson trial saw more than just the underside of the police laid open to public inspection. The televised trial revealed Judge Lance Ito as unable to control his courtroom. Even casual observers of the trial noted Ito's vanity and love of press attention. Simpson hired a "dream team" of the best lawyers in the country and their posturing dramatically illustrated that money could buy justice in American courts. In contrast, the government's evidence technicians seemed inept, and the overwhelmed assistant district at-torneys made serious mistakes.

Finally, there was the jury. In their memoirs of the trial, Simpson's prose-cutors universally condemned the jury. Marcia Clark grumbled that she had the "jury pool from hell," packed with pro-Simpson partisans willing to lie to get on the jury.[7] Christopher Darden wrote that the jurors "seemed to go out of their way to get a good look at Simpson, so they could smile at him." The jurors even "repeatedly expressed shock that he was a suspect."[8] Hank Goldberg remembered blurting out, "That's the worst looking jury I've every seen in my entire life."[9] For the prosecutors, the flawed jury pool largely explains Simpson's acquittal. The jury's rejection of DNA evidence—the same type of evidence that has freed dozens of convicted but innocent people from death row—led some to question the continuing value of the jury system. Others asked it the Simp-son jury had exercised a supposed right of "jury nullification" in a racist society. Either way, the U.S. criminal justice system suffered a serious blow to its rep-utation.

GENDER

In each of these murder cases, men killed to dominate women. David Court-wright has argued that "males of all mammalian species" are genetically pro-grammed to fight hard and mate often. Males are driven to compete violently "for access to the finite reproductive capacity of females."[10] The passage of time brings such male urges into sharper relief. Hugh Stone killed his wife in a

---

7. Clark with Carpenter, *Without a Doubt*, 192.
8. Christopher Darden with Jess Walter, *In Contempt* (New York: HarperCollins, 1996), 167.
9. Hank M. Goldberg, *The Prosecution Responds: An O. J. Simpson Trial Prosecutor Reveals What Really Happened* (Secaucus, NJ: Birch Lane, 1996), 42.
10. David T. Courtwright, *Violent Land: Single Men and Social Disorder from the Frontier to the Inner City* (Cambridge, MA: Harvard University Press, 1996), 16.

quarrel over land. While he acted in a patriarchal culture, the sparse details of Stone's action can only leave us wondering about the nature of their relationship. A patriarchal mind-set more clearly explains why Jereboam Beauchamp insisted he killed Sharp: he wanted to rehabilitate his wife's honor. Ann Cook's role in the affair, though, complicates our understanding of male honor and patriarchy. She manipulated her protector, demanding vengeance, or so wrote Beauchamp. Perhaps Evelyn Nesbit similarly manipulated Harry Thaw and Stanford White. Thaw killed White because White had once "had" his woman, Evelyn Nesbit. Nesbit incited Thaw to a murderous rage by telling him that after White seduced her, he had said, "Now you belong to me."[11]

By contrast, all accounts present Nicole Brown Simpson as an innocent victim. While Hugh Stone and his wife remain silent ciphers, by the end of the twentieth century, a storm of television programming, instant books, and magazine and newspaper articles were able to detail the lives of Simpson and his victims. We learned, for example, that O. J. Simpson once publicly grabbed his wife by her crotch and said, "This is where babies come from and this belongs to me."[12] Simpson abused Nicole Brown Simpson because he sought to dominate her. Watching Simpson sitting in court, prosecuted by a woman, Marcia Clark suspected that "being at the mercy of a woman had to be O. J. Simpson's personal idea of hell."[13]

It is far from sufficient to suggest that all or even most violence in American history is the result of male urges to dominate women, combined, sometimes, with female skill at manipulating such urges. On the other hand, historians and other scholars have often overlooked this fundamental explanation of a great deal of cruelty, as they look instead to the economic, religious, and ethnic roots of conflict. At least on the level of individual crimes of passion, there is much evidence that this will to sexual dominance plays a significant role in fostering male violence.

DOCUMENTS

Hugh Stone, a Convicted Murderer, on the Sin of Murder, 1698

The record of Hugh Stone's conversation with a minister as he walked to the gallows hardly seems like a modern criminal narrative. The condemned man does not protest his

11. Suzannah Lessard, *The Architect of Desire: Beauty and Danger in the Stanford White Family* (New York: Dial, 1996), 283.
12. Toobin, *The Run of His Life*, 276; Clark with Carpenter, *Without a Doubt*, 291.
13. Clark with Carpenter, *Without a Doubt*, 208.

innocence. Twenty-first-century Americans can more easily comprehend O. J. Simpson, who maintained his innocence despite DNA evidence, than someone like Hugh Stone, who is humbly pleading for salvation. Nonetheless, the elements of a conventional detective story are in place, though the mystery had nothing to do with Hugh Stone's guilt or innocence. In colonial murder stories, there are rarely doubts about the defendants' guilt; early American courts relied heavily on confessions, and most contemporaries accepted the courts' verdicts without question. In the absence of skepticism and appeals, there was no reason to provide details about the scene of the crime or the memories of witnesses. There are no clues and, thus, no need for detectives to interpret clues. The mystery for this society was whether Hugh Stone would achieve genuine salvation during his short walk from jail to his place of execution. This was high drama, with the minister probing a suspect's story. For most of those reading Stone's final confession, salvation was a far more important issue than any legal matter. The Reverend Cotton Mather, one of the most famous Puritan ministers, published the following account in 1698.

One *Hugh Stone*, upon a Quarrel, between himself & his Wife, about Selling a piece of Land, having some words, as they were walking together on a certain Evening, very barbarously reached a stroke at her Throat, with a Sharp knife; and by that *One Stroke* fetch'd away the Soul, of her, who had made him a Father of several Children, and would have brought yet another to him, if she had lived a few weeks longer in the world. The wretched man, was too soon Surprised by his Neighbours, to be capable of Denying the Fact; and so he pleaded, *Guilty*, upon his Tryal.

There was a *Minister* that walk'd with him to his *Execution*; and I shall insert the principal Passages of the Discourse between them; in which the Reader may find or make something *useful* to himself, what ever it were to the Poor man who was more immediately concerned in it.

> MINISTER. I am come to give you what Assistance I can, in you taking of the Steps, which your eternal *Weal* or *Woe*, now depends upon the well or ill taking of.
>
> HUGH STONE. *Sir, I thank you, and I beg you to do what you can for me.*
>
> MIN. Within a very few Minutes your immortal Soul must appear before God *the Judge of all*. I am heartily sorry you have lost so much time since your first Imprisonment: you had need use a wonderful Husbandry or the little piece of an *Inch* which now remains. Are you now prepared to stand before the Tribunal of God?
>
> H.S. *I hope I am.*
>
> MIN. And what *Reason* for that *Hope*?
>
> H.S. *I find all my Sins made so bitter to me, that if I were to have my life given*

me this Afternoon, to Live such a Life as I have Lived heretofore, I would not accept of it; I had rather Dy.

MIN. That is *well*, if it be *True*. But suffer me a little to search into the Condition of your Soul. Are you sensible, That you were *Born* a Sinner? That the Guilt of the *First Sin* committed by *Adam*, is justly charged upon *you*? And that you have hereupon a *Wicked Nature* in you, full of Enmity against all that is *Holy, and Just, and Good*? For which you deserved to be destroyed, as soon as you first came into this world.

H.S. *I am sensible of this.*

MIN. Are you further sensible, that you have lived, a very ungodly Life? That you are guilty of thousands of *Actual Sins*, every one of which *deserves the Wrath and Curse of God, both in this Life, and that which is to come*?

H.S. *I am sensible of this also.*

MIN. But are you sensible, That you have broken *all* the *Laws* of God? You know the *Commandments*. Are you sensible, That you have broken every one of *Them*?

H.S. *I cannot well answer to that. My answer may be liable to some Exceptions.— This I own, I have broken every Commandment on the Account mentioned by the Apostle* James; *that he who* breaks one is Guilty of all. *But not otherwise.*

MIN. Alas, That you know your self no better than so! I do affirm to you, that you have particularly broken *every one* of the Commandments, and you *must* be sensible of it.

H.S. *I cann't see it.*

MIN. But you must Remember, *That the Commandment is Exceeding Broad*; it reaches to the *Heart* as well as the *Life*: it excludes *Omissions* as well as *Commissions*, and it at once both *Requires* and *Forbids*. But I pray, make an experiment upon any *one* Commandment, in which you count your self most *Innocent*: and see whether you do not presently confess your self *Guilty* thereabout. I may not leave this point slightly passed over with you.

H.S. *That Commandment*, Thou shalt not make to thy self any Graven Image; *How have I broken it?*

MIN. Thus: You have had undue *Images* of God in your *Mind* a thousand times. But more than so; that Commandment not only *forbids* our using the *Inventions* of men in the worship of God, but it also *requires* our using all the *Institutions* of God. Now have not you many & many time turned your back upon some of those glorious *Institutions*?

H.S. *Indeed, Sir, I confess it: I see my sinfulness greater than I thought it was.*

MIN. You ought to see it. God help you to see it! There is a *boundless Ocean* of it. And then for that SIN, which has now brought a shameful Death upon you, 'tis impossible to Declare the Aggravations of it; hardly an Age will show the like. You have professed your self *Sorry* for it!

H.S. *I am heartily so.*

MIN. But your Sorrows must be *after a Godly Sort.* Not meerly because of the miseries which it has brought on your *outward Man*, but chiefly for the *Wrongs* and *Wounds* therein given to your own Soul; and not only for the *Miseries* you have brought on your self, but chiefly for the *Injuries* which you have done to the Blessed God. . . .

H.S. *What shall I do?*

MIN. . . . I would pray you to Vomit up all Sin with a very hearty detestation. You are going (if I may so speak) to disgorge your Soul; if you do not first cast up your Sin, if your Soul and your Sin come away together, you cannot but know something of the dismal condition which it must pass into. O, what cause have you to fall out with Sin for ever? it has been your only Enemy. Here is the only Revenge which you may allow in your self. You must not now bear any Malice against any one man in the World, but forgive even those that have done you the greatest Injuries. Only upon Sin be as revengeful as you can; I would have you, like *Sampson*, so to Dy, taking of a just Revenge.

H.S. *I hope I shall.*

MIN. Well, we are now but a very few paces from the place, where you must breathe your last. You are just going to take a most awful Step, which has this most Remarkable in it, *That it cannot be twice taken.* If you go wrong now, it cannot be Recalled throughout the Dayes of a long Eternity. I can but commit you into the Arms of a Merciful Redeemer, that he may keep you from a Miscarriage, which cannot be recall'd and redress'd throughout Eternal Ages. The Lord show unto you the *Path of Life*! Attend unto these, as the last words that I may speak before the Prayer, with which I am immediately to take a long *Farewell* of you. You are not just going to be *Confirmed* for ever. If the Great God presently find you under the power of *Prejudice* against any of His Truths and Wayes, or of *Enmity* against what has His blessed Name upon it, you shall be fixed, and settled, & confirmed in it, until the very Heavens be no more. But they are very terrible *Plagues* and *Pains*, which you may be sure will accompany this everlasting Disposition of your Soul. On the other side, if God now find your Soul, under the power of Inclinations to *Love Him, Fear Him, Serve Him*; & to esteem the Lord Jesus Christ above a thousand Worlds; you shall then be *Confirmed* in the perfection of such a Temper, and of all the *Joy*, that must Accompany it. Which of these is the Condition that I now leave you in.

H.S. *Sir, I hope the latter of them.*

MIN. The Good God make it so; and grant that I may find you at the Right hand of the Lord Jesus, *in the Day of his Appearing.* May this *Ladder* prove as a *Jacobs Ladder* for you, and may you find the *Angels* of the Lord Jesus ready here to convey your departing Soul into the Presence of the Lord.

After this Discourse; ascending the Ladder, *he made the following Speech.*

Young Men and Maids; observe the Rule of Obedience to your Parents; and Servants to your Masters, according to the will of God, and to do the will of your Masters: you take up the wicked ways, you set open a Gate to your *Sins*, to lead in bigger afterwards; thou can'st not do any thing but *God will see thee*, tho' thou thinkest thou shalt not be catched, thou thinkest to hide thy self in Secret, when as God in Heaven can see thee, though thou hast hid it from man. And when thou goest to *Thievery*, thy wickedness is discovered, and thou art found *Guilty*. O Young Woman, that is Married, and Young Man, look on Me here; be sure that in Solemn Engagement, you are obliged one to another; *Marriage* is an Ordinance of God, have a care of breaking that Bond of *Marriage-Union*; if the Husband provoke his Wife, and cause a Difference, he sins against God; and so does she, in such Carriage; for she is bound to be an *Obedient Wife*. O you Parents that give your Children in Marriage, remember what I have to say, you must take notice when you give them in Marriage, you give them freely to the *Lord*, and free them from that Service and Command you ought to have, yet you ought to have a tender regard to them. O thou that takest no care to lead thy life civilly and honestly, and then Committest that Abominable Sin of *Murder*, here is this *Murderer*, look upon him; and see how many are come with their eyes to behold this man, that abhors himself before God; *that* is the Sin that I abhor my self for, and desire you, take Example by *me*; there are here a great many Young People, and O Lord, *that they may be thy Servants!* Have a care, do not sin; I will tell you, that I wish I never had had the opportunity to do such a *Murder*; if you say, when a person has provoked you, *I will Kill him*: 'Tis a thousand to one, but the next time *you will do it*. Now I commit my self into the Hands of Almighty God.

Source: Daniel E. Williams, *Pillars of Salt: An Anthology of Early American Criminal Narratives* (Lanham, MD: Madison House, 1993), 78–83.

Jereboam O. Beauchamp Confesses to Murdering Solomon P. Sharp, 1825

Late on the night of November 6, 1825, Jereboam Beauchamp slipped through the streets of Frankfort, Kentucky, searching for the home of Colonel Solomon P. Sharp, the state's attorney general. Stopped by a slave patrol, Beauchamp explained his movements by

saying he intended to find some "judge breakers" and have "some fun out of them." The
patrol released Beauchamp; he was, after all, not a slave.

Beauchamp had not lied; he was intending to ill use a "judge breaker." As a fierce
partisan of the "Old Court Party," Beauchamp, who was just twenty-three years old,
opposed the "New Court Party," a political force that actually did want to "break" or
replace the existing state supreme court as a way of overturning their recent ruling
against debtor relief legislation. The man Beauchamp sought favored creation of a new
state Supreme Court, one that would uphold the state legislature's reform legislation,
and was scheduled to become Speaker of the House at its opening session on the very
next day.

But Beauchamp had an additional reason for seeking to harm Sharp, one that he
made the center of his legal defense. In 1818 Sharp had seduced, impregnated, and aban-
doned Ann Cooke, who was now married to Beauchamp, sixteen years his junior. In his
Confession, Beauchamp related that his beloved Ann drove him to the murder. Her
honor had been besmirched; his honor required action on her behalf. A jury, unimpressed,
sentenced Beauchamp to death. Ann Cooke committed suicide the day of her husband's
execution, joining him in a common grave. Beauchamp's last words were "Farewell, child
of sorrow! For you, I have lived; for you, I die."

Beauchamp wrote his confession in the three days before he was to be hung, leaving
instructions that it be published. His friends and family saw to its wide circulation. Yet
the assassination of Solomon P. Sharp ended up hurting the Old Court Party, which lost
to the Reformers, who would soon form the basis of the Jacksonian Democratic Party.

I am the second son, of a most worthy and respectable farmer. My parents at an early period of my life, became professors of the Christian religion,
and ever after lived quite piously up to its dictates. The early part of my education, which generally has a lasting impression upon the bent of the mind,
was of a most pious and salutary kind. I was much a favourite with my fond
father, although of a most wild eccentric and ungovernable temper of
mind....

I was placed quite early in the best schools within his reach. I was naturally of a most volatile, idle and wild disposition.... But feeling for the difficulties under which I saw my father labouring to do equal justice to others
of his numerous family, of younger children, who now began to claim more
of his exertions for their education, I resolved no longer to burthen him with
mine, but to thenceforth shift for myself and as well as I could complete my
education, by my own exertions....

...I made some money...and by the time I was eighteen years old, completed my education, so far as I thought it necessary or important to go, preparatory to the study of the law; which all my friends advised me to pursue.
Mingling with my acquaintances of the bar at Glasgow, and those attending

the courts there from Bowlinggreen, I was about this time attracted by a general burst of generous indignation amongst them, towards Col. Solomon P. Sharp, of the bar, from Bowling-Green, for the seduction of Miss Ann Cooke of that place. I was acquainted with Col. Sharp personally, and somewhat intimately too, for being greatly delighted with his eloquence, and designing to study the law myself, I had sought his acquaintance, and had expressed some thought of endeavoring to place myself in a situation, where I could study under his direction. I should have mentioned to him my wish, but for this very story about Miss Cooke. Now, I was not personally acquainted with Miss Cooke.—I knew however the Cook family by character, and I had heard the gentlemen of the bar of my acquaintance from Bowling-Green, speak often in high and enthusiastic terms of Miss Ann Cooke, for intelligence &c. And the more especially, when the execrations of Col. Sharp for her seduction, was in the high tone, to which it was at first carried amongst them. But there was a young gentleman from Bowling-Green at that time, a room mate and bosom friend of mine, who had been intimately acquainted with Miss Cooke, and much devoted to her.

Hearing the high account which he gave of her character, and the animated representation which an enthusiastic devotee would make of the dishonor to an injured female, to whom he was so much devoted; he much inflamed the indignation so infectious in the youthful bosom, for injuries of this kind, and which had been caught and kindled in my bosom, from those of the profession, with whom I then associated. My friend held Col. Sharp in utter contempt and abhorrence, and from him I imbibed somewhat of my personal dislike, in-so-much, that I felt a disinclination to enter into even those cordial salutations of friendship, which had heretofore characterized our intercourse. He was a man of the greatest penetration, and I think on one occasion, noticed this. For he had learned my design to enter the study of the law, and I suppose had heard some one speak of my thought of studying under him. For he asked me once, if I intended to go immediately to the study of the law. I replied, I should in a few months. He said he had learned I intended to go to Bowling-Green, and wished to study with him. I replied with rather more austerity than politeness, I should probably go to Bowling-Green, but I had not determined to study with *him*. The manner in which I spoke this, I saw startled some little surprise in his countenance, more from my impoliteness, than anything else. However, it passed off with his flattering me with auguring well of my success; and by saying, if I should come to Bowling-Green, he would be pleased to have it in his power to facilitate in any way, my progress. It may seem strange, that I should have been so easily infected with dislike, towards one I had heretofore admired; merely by the tale of his dishonour towards a female, to whom I was an utter stranger. But such was the enthusiasm of all my passions, that when I had a bosom friend, all his partialities were my partialities, all his antipathies mine. Besides, this was a species of dishonour, which, from my earliest recollection, had ever excited my most violent reprobation. I had ever said, I would as soon receive into my friendship, an horse thief, as a man, however high his standing, who had dishonoured and prostrated the hopes of a respectable and worthy female. And I still say, there is more intrinsic dishonour and baseness in it, than in stealing a man's horse; and should be received with less forgiveness, or countenance, by society.

Under these habitual feelings and sentiments, it is not so strange, that I should participate in a strong degree, with my friend in his contempt and dislike of Col. Sharp, for his dishonor towards a worthy orphan female, whom my friend represented in such high terms. With these prepossessions of sympathy for Miss Cooke, I retired to spend a few months in a country life with my father, previous to my entering the study of the law. . . . Miss Cooke had retired to a romantic little farm, within a mile of my father's, there to spend in seclusion the remainder of her days, with only her aged mother and a few servant's. Immediately on learning that, when I arrived at my father's, I determined to become acquainted with one I had heard so much talk about. . . . I told her that spending my life very lonesomely in the country, without either books or society, I had the more hope she would excuse my intrusion, and at least if she refused me her society, or to become acquainted with my sisters, who wished to visit her, she would favour me with the benefit of her library, whilst I remained in the country, as I had been told she had a very choice selection of books. . . .

On the approach of night when I spoke of taking my leave, I selected only one book, to take home with me; but she insisted on my taking several. I said I would read the one I had selected, and return for others. I saw from her smile she penetrated my design in that, to frame an excuse for another visit soon. . . .

I told her I would not break in upon her retirement, by presuming to address her as a lover; but that I only besought her society and conversation of an evening, occasionally as a friend. To this she at length so far assented as to meet me on my visits. . . . Thus passed as much as three months, during which time, scarce one week together escaped without my seeing her. And meantime, there was enkindled between us, a mutual friendship such as mortals seldom feel. I called it friendship, out of complaisance to her stoical philosophy. . . . But call it what we might, I was conscious there was kindled in my heart, a feeling and a flame, I had never felt before. In short I was in love. . . . At length I formally solicited her hand in marriage. She refused it, but with such a burst of feeling, as would have rendered her persisting in that refusal, tenfold more painful. But she told me there was an insuperable objection within her own bosom to marriage, but that her heart did not find that objection in me. In this, she long persisted, but would never tell me what that fatal barrier to my happiness was. At length, I resolved to take no denial, but to know this secret objection. She then told me, with a firmness, which spoke that it was the voice of fate, that the hand which should receive hers, would have to revenge the injury a vilian had done her. She said her heart could never cease to ache, till Col. Sharp should die through her instrumentality; that he had blighted all her hapiness; and while he lived, she would feel unworthy of my love. But she said, she would kiss the hand, and adore the person who would revenge her; but that no one else, save myself should do it.

No conditions, nor any earthly proposition she could have made me could have filled me with so much delight. Whenever I had contemplated a marriage with her, I had always esteemed the death of Col. Sharp a necessary consequence. I never for a moment could feel that I could suffer a vilain to live, who had been the seducer of one I pressed to my bosom as a wife. . . .

We therefore fell upon a scheme to turn the devotion of the administration to Col. Sharp to our advantage. I say we did, I mean my wife and myself. A great deal has been said about my wifes going on her knees to me to prevail with me not to kill Col. Sharp publicly. My wife never had to get on her knees to me to enforce her wishes. We reasoned together as intelligent beings on all occasions, neither assuming any superiority; but each confident of the others affections and confident the ideas of each would be duly weighed and appreciated by the other. I therefore, after the most mature deliberation, resolved if I should have to kill Col. Sharp, in Frankfort, to do it secretly. . . . I did not feel that I was bound to observe any law which regulates the reciprocal conduct of men of honor, in my conduct towards Col. Sharp, or to risque my own life, by shooting him publicly, any more than I would have felt bound to go publicly into an Indian town and shoot down the savage who had secretly crept to my house and murdered my defenceless children. . . .

It is vain to say, the laws of society provide adequate redress for all injuries of one citizen towards another. Where is the father of any sensibility or honorable feelings, who would not infinitely rather a villian would silently put his daughter out of the world, than to seduce and leave her to drag out a wretched degraded existence tenfold more painful to the father than her death? And yet what remedy had the law provided, which would be the least consolation to the unhappy father for the injury?

. . . Never was a murder planned with such studied precaution since the world began. I knew well it was impossible to avoid being arrested for the murder. I therefore planed every thing with a view to the evidence which I

should be able to bring forward in my favour. Three weeks before the meeting of the Legislature, I made a sale of my property, and gave out publickly,
on all occasions, I should start to Missouri the very Sunday on which I really
intended to kill Col. Sharp at night. . . .

I had business of consequence in Frankfort, and such as I would render it
very reasonable and even necessary I should go there before I should move
away. But I had never intimated the least intention to do so. For I wished it
to appear quite a casual thing, and wholly unexpected to me, that I should
ever be in Frankfort before my removal.

. . . I put on a mask of black silk which gave me, at five steps distance, in
the clearest moonlight, the exact appearance of a negro. So well had my wife
constructed and fitted it to my face. I put on two pair of yarn socks, to preserve my feet in running, and to avoid my being pursued by the direction in
which I might be heard running in the dark, if I had worn my shoes. . . .

I drew my dagger and proceeded to the door. I knocked three times, loud
and quick! Col. Sharp said,

"Who'se there?"

"Covington" I replied. Quickly Col. Sharp's foot was heard on the floor. I
saw under the door he approached without a light! I drew my mask from my
face, and immediately Col. Sharp opened the door, I advanced into the room
and with my left hand I grasped his right wrist, as with an iron hand. The
violence of the grasp made Col. Sharp spring back and trying to disengage
his wrist, he said,

"What Covington is this?"

I replied, "John A. Covington, sir."

"I do'nt know you," said Col. Sharp. "I know John W. Covington."

"My name" said I "is John A. Covington," about the time I said that Mrs.
Sharp, whom I had seen appear in the partition door as I entered the outer
door, disappeared. She had become alarmed I imagine, by the little scuffle
Col. Sharp made when he sprang back to get his wrist loose from my grasp.
Seeing her disappear, I said to Col. Sharp in a tone as though I was deeply
mortified at his not knowing me:

"And did you not know me sure enough."

"Not with your handkerchief about your face," said Col. Sharp. For the
handkerchief with which I had confined my mask upon my forehead was still
round my forehead.

I then replied in a soft conciliating and persuasive tone of voice, "Come
to the light Col. and you will know me." And pulling him by the arm he
came readily to the door. I ste[p]ped with one foot back upon the first step
out at the door, and still holding his wrist in my left hand, I stri[p]ped my
hat and handkerchief from over my forehead and head, and looked right up

in Col. Sharp's face. He knew me the more readily I imagine, by my long bushy curly suit of hair. He sprang back and exclaimed in the deepest tone of astonishment, dismay, horror and despair I ever heard, "Great God!! It's him!!!" And as he said that he fell on his knees, after failing to jerk loose his wrist from my grasp. As he fell on his knees I let go his wrist and grasped him by the throat, and dashing him against the facing of the door, I choked him against it to keep him from hallowing, and muttered in his face, "Die you villian!" And as I said that, I plunged the dagger to his heart. . . .

Source: Robert D. Bamberg, ed., *The Confession of Jereboam O. Beauchamp, Who Was Hanged at Frankfort, KY.* (Bloomfield, KY: Robert D. Bamberg, 1826), 3-13, 29-32, 35, 39-41.

Harry Thaw's Account of His Murder of Stanford White, 1906

On June 25, 1906, Stanford White dined with his son and a friend at Cafe Martin, a trendy New York restaurant, elegant with white linen and chandeliers. After dinner, White went to Madison Square Garden and sat at his reserved table near the stage. He watched Mamzelle Champagne *not so much for the quality of the performance but because he had his eye on one of the chorus girls. Harry K. Thaw, married to Evelyn Nesbit, one of White's former conquests, also watched the play. Thaw left his table, making his way across the floor to White. As one of the singers began crooning "I'd Love a Million Girls," three gunshots startled the audience.*

Thaw did not resist capture. "He deserved it," he told the arresting officer. "He ruined my wife." Thaw maintained this attitude through both his trials, even as his attorneys urged jurors to find him not guilty by reason of insanity. Ten thousand New Yorkers crowded around the city's courthouse when Evelyn Nesbit testified at Thaw's first trial, in 1907. The popular press pronounced White a moral monster, and many spectators cheered Nesbit as she fended off District Attorney William Travers Jerome's cross-examination.

After Thaw's first trial ended in a hung jury, Jerome tried again in 1908. The second jury delivered the expected verdict. The judge ordered Thaw dispatched to the Asylum for the Criminal Insane at Matteawan. In 1913 Thaw walked out the front door of Matteawan and stepped into a car sent by his mother, driving to Quebec, where cheering crowds greeted his arrival. Canadian authorities extradited Thaw, who now faced a third trial in New York. At this final trial, Thaw triumphed, winning an acquittal and a clean bill of mental health. He immediately divorced Nesbit, reneging on a deal to give her a million dollars. Thaw enjoyed the life of a wealthy socialite until his death in 1947; Nesbit survived by playing minor roles in theater and in films, dying in Hollywood in 1967.

The agony of Evelyn in the years of her girlhood formed the prelude to a long continuous drama of sorrow, the murk and gloom of which was never illuminated by a ray of sunshine until what occurred on the roof of Madison Square Garden and Stanford White fell dead. Then for the first time came to her and me hope for home and children and a cheerfulness we had never known. . . .

After ten years during which a crew of moneyed libertines had made life almost as unsafe for virgins as did the Minotaur, a revolver made New York safer for other girls. They are safe. . . .

We had dinner at Martin's Restaurant, Evelyn, Tommy McCaleb and I and Truxton Beale. We intended to go to Sherry's, but Beale, when we met by accident, was not dressed, so we changed. We were cheerful, very, and it happened that a number of friends had tables around us. Some of us moved over and talked, they came to us, then Mr. and Mrs. Clement Griscom, of the American Steamship Line, towards the end crossed over and were very kind in so doing, for they were much older than we.

It might be a half-hour after we reached our table I saw a tremor in Evelyn; I asked if she was ill. She told me no, and in a moment she tried to be more cheerful even than the rest. I nearly forgot her shuddering.

Then Evelyn asked for a piece of paper and McCaleb had one. This was some time after. She wrote, and I remember she held a menu card so she could write on that small bit of paper. She gave the message to McCaleb or to Beale for only me to see. I read these words: "The B. was here a minute ago but went out again." I smiled reassuringly as it was I who must see him, not Evelyn now, and asked her: "Are you all right?" She nodded: "Yes." We did not ask more; the others never were aware. This was no place for me, wild at missing him: how did that blackguard enter, how was I unaware of his presence? He had got out, how did he get out?

I had to cheer up poor Evelyn, too. She was cheerful, but I knew what she had seen for she had shuddered and grown white at the sight of him merely passing in a carriage; here she saw the "B" unexpectedly in this dining room. Still he was gone. We simply forgot him. We could talk after a dinner that had been cheerful, except that damned spot. All our different friends went away, their tables vacant; still I preferred to wait, for going to a theatre is usually a bore. "We are having a good time here," I said, "why not stay?" But Evelyn wanted action, and we had tickets at a *premier* at the Madison Square Garden Roof; in fact, Captain Wharton was in one of our chairs. We all had to go.

. . . [N]one of us knew that there was a girl in that cast, Maude Fulton, Evelyn-like, and seventeen years of age. It was her first appearance and her beauty, young and fresh, captivated White. He saw her and wrote asking her to supper. She refused, not knowing him. He knew her manager and he wrote again, and during the intermission he went behind the scenes to see the manager, Lionel Lawrence, who asked him, "Please wait until afterwards, we are so troubled this first night." He came out and waited. Worse for him.

So White was to die in the very act of trying to debauch another girl hardly past childhood. Had he not been waiting for her, he might not have come to his death that night. Of all this we knew nothing, nor did we know of another girl the following night. Miss Fulton learned of this second victim, whom my revolver saved, and long afterward when she had become celebrated both on the stage and as an author she told about it. On the night following White's death she and some members of the Company entered the elevator, when in came a mere slip of a girl.

A bit of a girl, a mere child to be exact, hardly more than thirteen (Miss Fulton knew, for she was then only seventeen) with her hair down her back, a shop girl type, shamefacedly approached.

"I shall never forget what happened. The elevator boy, his name was Arthur, seemed for an instant at a loss: 'Where do you want to go?' She hung her head still further. 'I want to go to Mr. White's rooms.'

"We were stunned," Miss Fulton said. "A deathlike silence prevailed. We girls looked at one another foolishly, helplessly. The kid didn't know. She had a rendezvous with White in his apartment and was trying to keep it. Finally Arthur broke the suspense. Without so much as a tremor he said: 'Mr. White is not here tonight,' and gently helped the child out of the car. The lever was moved, the elevator went up and we prepared to put on our make-up."

Just another little victim headed for hell.

I had looked at the stage and now I looked to my left to see if there were any I knew, a thing I always did. I saw the "B" and I said, "Excuse me" to McCaleb, the others being ahead some yards. I saw a path from the stage to his table; going directly he would not have seen me. I walked to the stage and turned towards him so that he must see me coming.

There I saw him thirty feet in front of me, and as he watched the stage he saw me. I walked towards him and about fifteen feet away I took out my revolver. He knew me and he was rising and held his right hand towards, I think, his gun, and I wanted to let him try, but who was next? A man, a dozen men might have maimed me, cut off the light, allowed him to escape and rape more American girls as he had; too many, too many, as he ruined Evelyn.

Half-rising he gazed at me malignantly. I shot him twelve feet away. I felt sure he was dead. But I wanted to take no chances, I walked toward him, and fired two more shots. He dropped.

I looked to see if any fool should attack me; there were two bullets left, if needed. Instead all the people moved and moved so far, surging to the end of the roof, that I feared some might be forced to fall, toppling to the street eighty feet below, so I slowly raised the gun above my head, and turned rather fast, yet not enough to alarm anyone, and went back the same way as I had taken.

Some men observing that they were safe, I walked and handed the pistol to one of them. Then straight to Evelyn. She uttered a cry: "My God, Harry, what have you done?" I held her close and told her: "It is all right, dearie, I have probably saved your life." Then I kissed her.

Source: Harry K. Thaw, *The Traitor: Being the Untampered With, Unrevised Account of the Trial and All That Led to It* (Philadelphia: Dorrance, 1926), ii, 141–45.

Rev. Madison Peters Justifies the Murder of Stanford White, 1907

If any man had cause for taking the law into his own hands, that man's name is Harry K. Thaw.

For a quarter of a century, I have been pastor of fashionable churches, most of which time has been spent in this city, and throughout these years I have not walked blindfolded through the streets nor shut my eyes when I mixed with so called society, nor have I closed my ears to the awful tales of human sin and disgrace which have been poured into them by lips that were wronged, voicing the promptings of broken hearts and ruined souls.

I have seen and heard and read many chapters in the book of sin, and so it was that the one relating to the Thaw-White tragic comedy interested me but little, for I considered it merely a stereotyped edition of others which had gone before.

I looked on White then as I do now, in the crimson light of a scoundrel, a menace to society, whose best interests are built on the sacredness and purity of our women, but at the same time I viewed Thaw in the yellow, sickening glare of an irresponsible, money-cursed degenerate whom the world could well spare and be none the poorer for his loss.

My general impression of him was gleaned from the popular idea that he was an unbalanced youth who squandered in the wildest dissipation and sinful carousals money he never earned, and I believed that on general principles he should be locked up for the good of society.

As to the woman, I did not then dignify her by the title of wife.

I believed her a type of the too common kind in New York.

I thought of the mother who allowed the child to enter the environments of temptation and was in fact fain to believe what many averred and what some still maintain, that Evelyn Nesbit's mother sold her for White's gold.

As time wore on after the tragedy on the Madison Square Roof Garden and both press and public still continued to blacken the characters of Thaw and his wife, I reserved judgment until I would be able to judge for myself when the time arrived and I could hear the testimony.

I have heard the testimony given by a willing heart but reluctant lips in a public court and after its . . . harrowing recital the preconceived opinion I had of Harry Thaw fell like a house of cards and I stood ready to absolve and acquit him on the spot.

If ever a man had cause for taking the law into his own hands that man's name is Harry K. Thaw.

Harry Thaw, instead of being behind prison bars today, should be free, holding the honor and respect of all who stand up for moral manliness.

Before I heard the testimony I saw and talked with Thaw in the Tombs.

He talked to us in the most rational manner and in every way showed that he had no fear of ultimate results, a demeanor which has characterized him all along, and which, to my mind, is a proof that his wife told the truth on the witness stand, for Thaw looks to that story to acquit him, and it will acquit him, and Jerome knows it.

He knows that not a jury on earth would convict after hearing the wife's story, hence the district attorney is prepared to seek cover under any subterfuge that will save him from an inglorious defeat.

So it is now rumored that he will apply for a commission in lunacy to bound Thaw to Matteawan rather than let him go free and be beaten himself.

If Jerome by any possibility could do this it would be but a poor sop of consolation to throw to himself, for it would be tantamount to a failure to convict.

Let the district attorney be manly, let him be honorable, let him not show the white feather before he is beaten. He's a poor specimen of a man who cannot accept defeat gracefully when he knows he is "down and out for keeps."

If Jerome cannot shake little Evelyn's story, and I think he cannot; if he cannot bring forward testimony in rebuttal; if he cannot make the jury believe that Stanford White was a saint and Harry Thaw a devil, let him retire gracefully and sustain the reputation of his manhood, but let him not fly at the poor child and badger her and torment her by useless and unnecessary cross-examination into a state of mental lassitude and physical collapse.

If such should happen on the witness stand would the sight reflect any luster on his shield.

Jerome knows he is handicapped, and well handicapped, by public sentiment, and he knows all that is best in the manhood and womanhood in this city will resent any torture of the frail girl who has already suffered so much.

Moreover, he knows he can never put a white mantle on the ghost called the memory of Stanford White—the more he tries to do it the black garments thereon cling the tighter. Harry Thaw will never be convicted, but Jerome must keep up his standing as prosecutor by any means, so now he will probably ask for a commission in lunacy, but I fail to see how he will attain his object according to law.

If Jerome should ask for a commission in lunacy and should such be granted it would be a travesty of justice, a mockery of law, an outrage on equity and an everlasting stain on the history of criminal jurisprudence in this city. Thaw, has suffered enough to make him insane. It is a wonder that he has kept his equipoise so well through it all, the strain has been so great.

Surely it is time to make up for the absurdity and foolishness of "expert" testimony. Think of the expenditure, too, the waste of public and private money involved; think of old fogies getting $100 a day for sitting owl like until they are called!

I would rather have one ounce of good, honest opinion from a keen, hard headed layman of experience regarding the sanity or insanity of a suspect than a ton of "expert" testimony given in jaw-breaking Latin medico phrases which the experts do not understand, nor the general public.

Away with these humbugs of science—give us honest men, true men, experienced men and let them decide.

Such men are the Thaw jury—let them decide the fate of Thaw. I believe the sorrow that has come unto Mr. Bolton's life will not prevent him from doing his full duty and that no fear of a mis-trial will give Jerome an opportunity to ask for a lunacy commission.

Source: *Vicksburg Evening Post*, February 20, 1907.

O. J. SIMPSON

On June 12, 1994, Orenthal James Simpson, celebrity actor and retired sports hero, cut the throats of his former wife, Nicole Brown Simpson, and her companion Ron Goldman. Goldman's body showed stab wounds to the left thigh and abdomen, as well as gashes to the head and a monstrous throat wound. Goldman had put up a fight, trapped in a corner of metal fencing. Simpson had a history of abusing Nicole, a history recorded in a 911 call and photographs. Simpson apparently acted out of sexual jealousy shortly after Nicole had pointedly declared her independence from her former husband. He also acted after his latest girlfriend, Paula Barbieri, had left a message breaking off their relationship on his answering machine that same day.

Investigating officers at first could not believe that Simpson, the famous O. J., could have committed such a crime. The police only reluctantly arrested Simpson after the evidence became overwhelming. Blood evidence, DNA tests, and his footprints placed

Simpson at the scene of the crime. Witnesses introduced by prosecutors Marcia Clark and Christopher Darden proved that Simpson could not be accounted for during the time of the murders. Nonetheless, the jury acquitted Simpson. Subsequently, in a civil suit, another jury looking at the same evidence found Simpson liable for the deaths for which he had been found innocent.

The prosecution of O. J. Simpson failed because Johnnie Cochran, F. Lee Bailey, and other defense lawyers attacked the Los Angeles Police Department as a bastion of racism, its officers willing to fake evidence to bring down a successful black man. A police detective named Mark Fuhrman seemed to confirm defense allegations when he testified that he had never used the word "nigger" in the previous ten years. In fact, Fuhrman has been tape-recorded using that racial epithet, and others, extensively with a would-be screen-writer. Having to rely on such witnesses, the prosecution could not persuade the jury to accept the evidence on its own terms. In a sense, Los Angeles's history of racism freed O. J. Simpson.

Jeffrey Toobin on the O. J. Simpson Trial, 1995

From the day he was hired in the case, Cochran teased the press with the possibility of Simpson testifying in his own defense. The lawyer said repeatedly the he *wanted* O. J. to testify and that O. J. himself *wanted* to testify, but these comments were just public relations. With the exception of Bailey, who actually did want Simpson to take the stand, no one on the defense team ever took the idea very seriously. Bailey thought, with good reason, that Simpson would have no chance of resuming anything like his former life unless he addressed the charges from the witness stand. Cochran and Shapiro were more worried about losing the case, and their view prevailed.

Still, even in jail, Simpson was as obsessed as ever by his image, and Cochran found an opportunity for him to put his point across. As part of the formalities of ending the case, [Judge Lance] Ito had to ask Simpson on September 22 whether he waived his right to testify. Cochran, in turn, requested that Simpson be allowed to make "a brief statement" as part of his waiver. Even though the jury was not present, Clark objected, saying that "this is a very obvious defense bid to get material admitted through these conjugal visits that is not admitted in court. . . . Please don't do this, Your Honor, I beg you."

Cochran replied with great indignation. "There seems to be this great fear of the truth in this case," he said. "This is still America. And we can talk. We can speak. Nobody can stop us." (A rather odd complaint on behalf of a client who had already written a best-selling book from jail.) Ito caved, and Simpson rose to deliver a sound bite for the evening news.

"Good morning, Your Honor," he said. "As much as I would like to address some of the misrepresentations made about myself and Nicole concerning our life together, I'm mindful of the mood and the stamina of the jury. I have confidence, a lot more it seems than Ms. Clark has, of their integrity, and that they'll find—as the record stands now—that I did not, would not, and could not have committed this crime. I have four kids—two kids I haven't seen in a year. They asked me every week, 'Dad, how much longer?' "

This was more than even Ito could take, and he cut Simpson off with a curt, "All right."

Simpson said, "I want this trial over."

Even this brief monologue offered a useful insight into Simpson's character. Throughout the trial, his obsession remained the "misrepresentations" about his relationship with Nicole, especially the notion that he was imploring Nicole to come back to him. Typically, too, he attributed his decision not to testify to the "mood and stamina" of the jury, when the real reason had more to do with his lead lawyers' belief in his guilt. The statement was, in short, another snapshot of Simpson's narcissism.

. . . Even before she uttered her first words to the jury, Marcia Clark was exhausted, with large half moons of purple under each eye. She looked emaciated beneath her simple beige jacket. The chicken salads delivered to her office every lunch hour had often gone untouched. Not so her silver cigarette lighter, the one inscribed with the words TRUTH AND JUSTICE. For all these months, she had fueled herself with an unending relay of Dunhills.

First, Clark thanked the jury, which was customary but not, for her, heartfelt. She and her colleagues had traveled a long way since the optimistic close to jury selection. Over the course of the trial, Clark had felt no warmth from this group, no sympathy for the victims, no core of emotional revulsion at the murders. Clark's instincts about juries had not entirely deserted her, even if enlightenment came far too late. She had come to see that these were fearful jurors, more concerned about the reaction to their verdict than about reaching the right one. They took few notes; they never smiled or frowned; they gave no sense of themselves away—they were too frightened to reveal anything. As the race issue took over the case, the prosecutors knew above all that they needed a courageous jury, and they sensed—correctly, as it turned out—that they didn't have one.

Clark's first words about the facts of the case included a revealing slip of the tongue. "Let me come back to Mark Fuhrman for a minute," she said. Actually, she had not mentioned him before, so she was not really coming "back" to him. It just seemed that way, for the defense had succeeded so completely in making Fuhrman the center of this case. Like it or not, everyone in this trial was always coming back to Mark Fuhrman.

"Did he lie when he testified here in this courtroom saying that he did not use racial epithets in the last ten years?" Clark continued. "Yes. Is he a racist? Yes. Is he the worst LAPD has to offer? Yes. Do we wish that this person was never hired by LAPD? Yes. Should LAPD have ever hired him? No. In fact, do we wish there were no such person on the planet? Yes.

"But the fact that Mark Fuhrman is a racist and lied about it on the witness stand does not mean that we haven't proven the defendant guilty beyond a reasonable doubt, and it would be a tragedy if, with such overwhelming evidence, ladies and gentlemen, as we have presented to you, you found the defendant not guilty in spite of all that, because of the racist attitudes of one police officer."

This immediate and categorical denunciation of Fuhrman was probably the best Clark could have done under the circumstances, but it also underlined how the racial issue paralyzed the prosecution. Yes, Fuhrman was racist, but Simpson was still guilty. The yes/but formulation represented the dominant motif of the summation that followed over the next five hours. Yes, the investigation had been imperfect; yes, the criminalists made mistakes—but the evidence led only to this defendant. Clark was rushed and a little scattered as she attempted to pull all the complex strands of evidence together, but still she delivered an adequate, professional summation—and a persuasive one for a jury willing to listen.

In one passage, Clark drew on the vast changes the trial had wrought in her own life. She thought the jurors might wonder just what Simpson had been doing in the narrow passageway behind Kaelin's room, the place where he knocked into the air conditioner and dropped the glove. "You are thinking, why not drop it in a Dumpster on the way home?" she said. But Clark suggested that this wasn't possible. "He can't. He can't, because he is famous. If someone sees him hanging around near a Dumpster on that night of all nights, they are going to recognize him, and he is going to have a witness." Clark came up with this theory because now she, too, was noticed everywhere she went, and she believed that Simpson, who had far more experience in being famous, had even factored his celebrity into his plans for murder. . . .

There was one hint of what was to come. Bill Hodgman had spent much of the previous month working on an elaborate chart entitled "Unrefuted Evidence," a summary of all the non-DNA non-Fuhrman-related evidence in the case. It was arranged in the form of a big pyramid, and Clark saved it for her conclusion. The chart was extremely impressive, and it listed things like Nicole's purchase of the gloves, Park's fruitless buzzing for Simpson, the blood to the left of the shoe prints and the cut on Simpson's left hand. It was a rather complicated graphic, and Clark did not discuss every point on it, so she offered the jurors an option.

"If you would like to take notes on this," Clark said, "I can leave it up for a little while."

Not one juror wrote down a thing.

Source: Jeffrey Toobin, *The Run of His Life: The People v. O. J. Simpson* (New York: Random House, 1996), 415–18, 422. Reprinted with the author's permission.

FURTHER READINGS

Daniel A. Cohen, *Pillars of Salt, Monuments of Grace: New England Crime Literature and the Origins of American Popular Culture, 1674–1860* (New York: Oxford University Press, 1993); Karen Halttunen, *Murder Most Foul: The Killer and the American Gothic Imagination* (Cambridge, MA: Harvard University Press, 1998); Daniel E. Williams, ed., *Pillars of Salt: An Anthology of Early American Criminal Narratives* (Madison, WI: Madison House, 1993).

For Jereboam O. Beauchamp: Robert D. Bamberg, ed., *The Confession of Jereboam O. Beauchamp* (Philadelphia: University of Pennsylvania Press, 1966); J. Winston Coleman, *The Beauchamp-Sharp Tragedy* (Frankfort, KY: Roberts Print, Co., 1950). Robert Penn Warren fictionalized the case in *World Enough and Time* (New York: Random House, 1950).

For Harry K. Thaw: Gerald Langford, *The Murder of Stanford White* (London: Victor Gollancz, 1963); Suzannah Lessard, *The Architect of Desire: Beauty and Danger in the Stanford White Family* (New York: Dial, 1996); Michael Macdonald Mooney, *Evelyn Nesbit and Stanford White: Love and Death in the Gilded Age* (New York: Morrow, 1976); Harry K. Thaw, *The Traitor* (Philadelphia: Dorrance, 1926).

For O. J. Simpson: Marcia Clark with Teresa Carpenter, *Without a Doubt* (New York: Viking, 1997); Christopher Darden with Jess Walter, *In Contempt* (New York: HarperCollins, 1996); Hank M. Goldberg, *The Prosecution Responds: An O. J. Simpson Trial Prosecutor Reveals What Really Happened* (Secaucus, NJ: Birch Lane, 1996); Jeffrey Toobin, *The Run of His Life: The People v. O. J. Simpson* (New York: Random House, 1996).

TWO

THE CONQUEST OF AMERICA

When it comes to the origins of violence in America, the classic nature versus nurture debate persists. Many commentators maintain that violence is inherent to men, and that any efforts to ameliorate violent conduct must come to terms with male character.[1] Others go further and insist that violent behavior is genetic, and that sufficient research can isolate these hereditary factors.[2] On the other side are a great number of scholars who argue that violence is learned conduct, and that any comparative examination demonstrates that in the absence of positive reinforcement violent actions become aberrant.[3]

In terms of American history, scholars debate the extent to which violent Europeans brought savage traditions with them to American shores. There is no doubt that the European conquerors and their white American successors launched a series of vicious wars against the Native American population, exterminating several peoples in the process.[4] But was that violence unavoidable, inherent to Western culture and therefore an immutable part of the resulting American culture? Or, alternatively, was this violence a temporary aberration forced on the settlers by their confrontation with a violent foe, the American

1. Richard Wrangham and Dale Peterson, *Demonic Males: Apes and the Origins of Human Violence* (Boston: Houghton Mifflin, 1996).
2. Albert J. Reiss Jr. and Jeffrey A. Roth, eds., *Understanding and Preventing Violence*, vol. 2, *Biobehavioral Influences* (Washington, DC: National Academy Press, 1994).
3. Dave Grossman, *On Killing: The Psychological Cost of Learning to Kill in War and Society* (Boston: Little, Brown, 1995).
4. See, for example, Francis Jennings, *The Invasion of America: Indians, Colonialism, and the Cant of Conquest* (Chapel Hill: University of North Carolina Press, 1975); Colin G. Calloway, *The American Revolution in Indian Country: Crisis and Diversity in Native American Communities* (Cambridge: Cambridge University Press, 1995); Robert M. Utley, *The Last Days of the Sioux Nation* (New Haven, CT: Yale University Press, 1963).

Indian, and would it fade with the advance of civilization? Frederick Jackson Turner, the great theoretician of the American frontier, held an ambiguous position on the role of violence in American life, perceiving it directed solely at the Indians, and therefore good: "The Indian was a common danger, demanding united action." The frontier served "as a military training school, keeping alive the power of resistance to aggression, and developing the stalwart and rugged qualities of the frontiersman." On the other hand, warfare was far from the primary task of the pioneer; clearing the land, tilling the soil, building institutions, these demanded the energy of western settlers, who were known for their enterprise rather than their violence.[5] Turner was certain that violence, like individualism, would vanish with the frontier; other scholars find evidence that the frontier crafted a culture and a set of myths and metaphors that make violence an inescapable part of American life.[6] The question for scholars has been to determine to what extent that frontier experience promoted a permanent culture of violence in North America.

In 1612 George Percy wrote "A Trewe Relacyon" of the events he had witnessed in the new English colony of Jamestown. The English had encountered a previously unknown people on the coast of North America. To Europeans they were "Indians," based on Christopher Columbus's misperception of his location. One of these Indian nations, the Powhatan, opposed the efforts of the English to expand out from their initial settlement at Jamestown. The English responded ruthlessly. "We Beate the Salvages outt of the Island burned their howses Ransaked their Temple Tooke down the Corpes of their deade kings from [out] of their Toambes And caryed away their pearles." And yet, Percy reported, "The Salvages still contineweinge their mallice Ageinste us."[7]

Percy and most of the other English worked on the assumption that a convincing show of strength would awe the Indians into submission. Some Indians did give in, only to be destroyed anyway. For instance, the Westos initially accepted the presence of the English in South Carolina, becoming trade partners, returning runaway slaves, and selling other Indians to the whites as slaves. But in the 1680s the government of South Carolina feared that the Westos might be getting too powerful, and so armed the Savannah Indians for a preemptive war that wiped out the Westos. Years later it would be the Savan-

5. Frederick Jackson Turner, "The Significance of the Frontier in American History" (1893), in Michael Bellesiles, ed., *BiblioBase* (Boston: Houghton Mifflin, 1993), 3, 13.

6. See especially Richard Slotkin's powerful triology, *Regeneration through Violence: The Mythology of the American Frontier, 1600–1860* (Middletown, CT: Wesleyan University Press, 1973); *The Fatal Environment: The Myth of the Frontier in the Age of Industrialization, 1800–1890* (New York: Atheneum, 1985); *Gunfighter Nation: The Myth of the Frontier in Twentieth-Century America* (New York: Atheneum, 1992).

7. George Percy, " 'A Trewe Relacyon,' Virginia from 1609 to 1612," *Tyler's Quarterly Historical and Genealogical Magazine* 3 (1922): 271.

nahs' turn, as they followed the Westos into extinction at the hands of a new Indian ally of the English in South Carolina. Similarly, the Pueblo Indians of the Southwest had initially welcomed the Spanish as allies who helped protect their lands from the hostile Apaches and Navajos. When Juan de Oñate and his small band of soldiers, settlers, and Franciscan priests arrived in 1598, the Pueblo Indians may not have understood that the Spanish claimed sovereignty over them. But the Spanish soon made their intention to stay and rule evident, punishing resistance with ferocity. When Francisco Coronado attacked Tiguex pueblo in retaliation for the killing of some Spanish horses, he burned both the town and its inhabitants. In 1599 Don Juan de Oñate responded to the murder of thirteen Spaniards at Acoma by attacking the pueblo, killing most of its inhabitants, and condemning the survivors to slavery, after ordering a foot cut off of all the men.

Though Spanish settlements in what they called New Mexico remained small, the Spanish rulers demanded a great deal from the Indians, including their labor and religious devotion. As the decades passed, the Spanish convinced themselves that the Pueblos were content to be part of the Spanish Empire and to accept its cultural values and religion. In 1680 they got a rude shock when the Pueblos rose up and cast the Spaniards out of New Mexico.

Other Indians doubted Europeans' motives from the start. They feared that if they once gave in to these aggressive newcomers, there would be no stopping them. These justified suspicions fed a number of bloody wars between the natives and the European conquerors. Some of these conflicts were ruthless and brutal, as the documents on Kieft's War and the Pequot War demonstrate. But that brutality should not give the impression that the colonial period was one of unrelieved violence. Entire generations passed in peace, and some regions, even in time of war, avoided conflict completely. Pennsylvania had the best record in this regard, avoiding warfare for its first eighty years of white settlement, not even bothering to create a militia system. By the late seventeenth century, even Virginia found itself at peace, going seventy years with only a single significant, brief military encounter. As George Washington wrote Lord Loudoun in 1757, "Virginia is a country young in war." Until the Seven Years' War, Virginia had "remained in the most profound and tranquil peace; ne'er studying war nor warfare."[8] Trade and cooperation marked Indian relations with the Europeans as much as warfare; but when the English launched a war against the Indians, they tended to fight it until their enemy ceased to exist.

Though uniformly Christian, the Europeans had little trouble legitimating

8. Washington to Loudoun, January 10, 1757, in John C. Fitzpatrick, ed., *The Writings of George Washington from the Original Manuscript Sources, 1745–1799*, 39 vols. (Washington, DC: Government Printing Office, 1931–44), 1:18–19.

their violent conquest of the Americas. Their Christianity not only did not interfere with the use of violence but actively encouraged it, for it was the perceived duty of most Christians at this time to spread the Gospels throughout the world. From the European perspective, they were conquering the Americas not just for their own nation but for Christ. In offering the heathen Americans the opportunity to come to Jesus, the European conquerors fulfilled a religious duty. And those who refused to accept the cross were justly punished for choosing Satan.

Many Europeans thus felt that they had a divine right to conquer and settle the Americas. Despite the presence of millions of American natives, and ignoring their own arguments that their conquest was justified for bringing Christianity to these natives, the Europeans often maintained that they were moving to an empty continent or "virgin land." In doing so they fulfilled the biblical injunction to multiply and spread over the earth. In 1630 a group of deeply religious English known as the Puritans began their "Great Migration" to North America. Before leaving from Southampton, one of these convoys of Puritans heard a sermon from their leading minister, John Cotton, who argued that this New England was a gift from God to his chosen people. Drawing on Psalm 80, Cotton argued that God "preparedst room for them" in America by making the land "void of inhabitants." "Where there is a vacant place," Cotton argued, "there is liberty for the sons of Adam or Noah to come and inhabit, though they neither buy it nor ask their leave." And any who resist this divine arrangement are clearly moved by the devil and may be destroyed by "lawful war."[9] In short, by going to New England, the Puritans spread Christianity to unoccupied territory; but should the occupants of that territory resist them, the Puritans might destroy them.

Racism lurked behind this sense of sacred duty. The Europeans, whether English or Spanish, French or Dutch, did not falter in their conviction that they were the superior race. Most Europeans granted little respect to the people they displaced in America, and they generally agreed that those who stood in their way could be killed with a clear conscience. On occasion that attitude could spill over into stunning acts of brutality and even genocide. Hundreds of thousands of deaths were unintentional; the Europeans did not mean to give America smallpox, influenza, and measles, but they did. But from the first contact a significant portion of the destruction was entirely intentional. Columbus did not hesitate to put thousands of Taino to death when they failed to deliver gold or when they resisted his authority. Intended or not, the impact of the Europeans on the Americas was devastating. The figures, staggering as they are, can only hint at the horrific level of suffering and death. When Columbus

9. *Old South Leaflets* (Boston: Directors of the Old South Work, n.d.), doc. 53.

landed on Hispaniola in 1492, there may have been half a million people living there. Fifty years later the Spanish government could only locate five hundred Taino still alive. The estimates of Mexico's population in 1519 vary widely from seven million to twenty-five million people; by 1600 the Spanish placed the population at two million.

Most European colonies began as military encampments. Even Puritan New England had a reputation for militarism in the colonial period. The colonists had experienced stiff resistance to their settlement from the native people, fighting two especially savage though brief wars in the seventeenth century, the Pequot War in 1636-37 and King Philip's War in 1675-76. In the eighteenth century, New England was raided on several occasions by France, which occupied Quebec to the north, and its Indian allies. On many occasions whites were taken into captivity by the Indians and made part of their tribe. Whites had trouble understanding this notion of "adoption," especially in light of the Indian practice of gruesome torture. To many whites it made no sense that one prisoner would have his skin flailed, his eyes ripped out, and his still living body then burned at the stake, while another person captured in the same attack would become a permanent member of an Indian family, being treated with kindness and inheriting the goods and even the name of an Indian who had often been killed by whites. The English usually took neither of these courses—brutal torture or adoption—making the Indians seem all the more exotic and unknowable.

Yet the English colonists were themselves capable of extreme cruelty. For instance, in July 1677, following some violent exchanges between whites and Indians along the Maine coast, fishermen from Marblehead, Massachusetts, captured two hostile Indians who had tried to seize their boat. One of the fishermen, Robert Roules, described how, upon their return to Marblehead, "the whole town flocked about" the Indians, "beginning first to insult them, and soon after, the women surrounded them and drove us by force from them." The women beat the Indians to death. Roules "found them with their heads off and gone, and their flesh in a manner pulled from their bones."[10]

Within white society, violence was common but hardly routine. There were occasional beatings and homicides, but such events, should they become public, were generally treated as highly significant events. Officially there was little tolerance for domestic violence, and little reference to such in the court records. Elizabeth Pleck found "only six indictments for family murder in the seventeenth-century Massachusetts Bay and Plymouth colonies."[11] But there are

10. Christine L. Heyrman, *Commerce and Culture: The Maritime Communities of Colonial Massachusetts, 1690–1750* (New York: Norton, 1984), 225-26.
11. Elizabeth Pleck, *Domestic Tyranny: The Making of Social Policy against Family Violence from Colonial Times to the Present* (New York: Oxford University Press, 1987), 19.

hints in church records that such violence was common in some families, and just as commonly ignored. A husband who beat his wife could avoid a court hearing by confessing his transgression before his congregation and begging for forgiveness, and many did so repeatedly. No one expected a parent to beg forgiveness for striking a child, since children were expected to receive regular beatings.

The colonists accepted a great deal of violence when it was directed at those in subservient positions. Indentured servants and slaves were subject to regular and often fatal beatings, both routinely justified as necessary for the mainte-nance of social order. Virginia's courts did nothing to prevent John Proctor from abusing his servants in the 1630s, even after he beat Elizabeth Abbott to death by whipping her five hundred times. A little later he beat servant Elias Hinton to death. If a servant complained, his or her term of service was gen-erally extended. Slaves, however, could not be punished by extending their pe-riod of enforced labor.[12] Virginia did not pass any slave laws until 1661, but when it did so, it struggled with the best way of controlling a large population that had no incentive to remain obedient. Clearly, in the minds of the slave owners, slavery required violence with the threat of death always hovering in the background. In 1669 the assembly passed a law regulating "the casuall kill-ing of slaves." The legislature noted that "the only law in force for the punish-ment of refractory servants resisting their master . . . [is] violent meanes." If, therefore, a slave "by the extremity of the correction should chance to die, that his death shall not be [accounted a] Felony." The logic behind this legislation was that no master would willingly "destroy his own estate" by killing a slave.[13] It is not surprising that Virginia's legislature consistently passed laws to the benefit of those who owned servants and slaves, for the legislature remained a gathering of masters throughout the colonial period.

The defense of society's existing structures allowed some of the most dra-conian laws in American history. As Virginia's capital laws of 1612 indicate, a wide range of criminal behavior could lead to a death sentence, as was the case in England. But American juries hesitated to impose the death penalty, espe-cially for any crime other than murder; and by the mid–eighteenth century a significant number of Americans had come to feel that it was time to reform America's legal system.

Judicial execution was most notoriously applied in the Salem witchcraft trials of 1692. The only major witchcraft trial in colonial America, the nineteen executions in Salem paled in comparison to the contemporary hysteria in Eu-

12. Edmund S. Morgan, *American Slavery, American Freedom: The Ordeal of Colonial Virginia* (New York: Norton, 1975), 127.
13. William W. Hening, ed., *The Statutes at Large, Being a Collection of All the Laws of Virginia*, 13 vols. (Richmond, VA, 1809-23), 2:270.

rope, where thousands of people, mostly women, were gruesomely put to death for being witches. Nonetheless, they continue to loom large in the consciousness of Americans as a terrible example of the dangers of hysteria.

Repeatedly in the colonial period we see that the state itself sanctioned violence, as in the witchcraft trials. Those in authority felt that they had no alternative if they were going to secure their society from external and internal dangers. That power could certainly be misused, as was the case in early Virginia and New Netherlands, but the perceived threat from the Indians and the evidence of popular uprisings such as Bacon's Rebellion evidenced the peril of a weak state unwilling to use force in the maintenance of social order. But the colonial governments were feeble, lacking police forces and standing armies, and relying on religion and public values to prevent violence. They put their faith in these cultural factors and were occasionally, as with the Paxton Boys, grievously disappointed. The Spanish were certain that once they had converted the Indians to Christianity they would need little force to maintain their authority. But coerced conversions often do not have much depth, as the Pueblo Indians demonstrated. Given the willingness of the Spanish themselves to violate Christian precepts in the name of the state, the willingness of the Indians to commit acts of violence should not have been too surprising. The law itself is often a form of violence, as Virginia's laws amply demonstrated. In a few instances, such as in Salem in 1692, religion joined with the state's authority to craft a grave injustice, leading even those in power to doubt the wisdom of granting the state unhindered legal authority to put people to death.

DOCUMENTS

VIRGINIA'S CAPITAL LAWS

Jamestown, the first English colony in North America to survive, was settled by the Virginia Company in 1607. Though acting under the authority of England's King James, the company was a private enterprise that enjoyed enormous power to determine the nature of its colony. Above all else, the Virginia Company sought to maintain its own control free of dissent. It therefore cast any opposition into the category of treason, punishable by death. In addition to these capital crimes, the first Virginia laws included a number of harsh and grotesque punishments for lesser transgressions, such as boring a hole through the tongue of a gossip. The company's managers did not hesitate to use the law and violence to make a profit. Young Englishmen who hoped to become landowners or to conquer imagined Indian nations as Hernando Cortés had done found themselves reduced to the position of agricultural laborers, often coerced labor without wages. In

practice, a common punishment for the powerless—white, black, and Indian—was en-
forced labor for the benefit of one of the colony's elite. Workers who misbehaved had
years added to their term of service and were literally worked to death.

  The tyranny of early Virginia proved counterproductive, the colony's death rate rising
to astronomical heights. Seven hundred people, for instance, lived in Jamestown at the
beginning of 1619, and 1,400 more arrived that same year. One year later the population
was 867. Although 8,000 English came to Virginia between 1607 and 1624, the colony had
a population of just 1,300 in 1624. In the latter year King James I revoked the company's
charter and made Virginia a royal colony under his direct control.

Laws of the Colony of Virginea, 1610–1611

Articles, Lawes, and Orders, Divine, Politique, and Martiall for the Colony in Virginea:
first established by Sir Thomas Gates Knight, *Lieutenant Generall, the 24. of May*
1610. exemplified and approved by the Right Honourable Sir Thomas West Knight,
Lord Lawair, Lord Governour and Captaine Generall the 12. of June 1610. Againe
exemplified and enlarged by Sir Thomas Dale *Knight, Marshall, and Deputie Gover-*
nour, the 22nd of June 1611. . . .

2. That no man speake impiously or maliciously, against the holy and
   blessed Trinitie, or any of the three persons, that is to say, against God
   the Father, God the Son, and God the holy Ghost, or against the knowne
   Articles of the Christian faith, upon paine of death.

3. That no man blaspheme Gods holy name upon paine of death, or use unlawful oathes, taking the name of God in vaine, curse, or banne, upon
   paine of severe punishment for the first offence so committed, and for
   the second, to have a bodkin thrust through his tongue, and if he continue the blaspheming of Gods holy name, for the third time so offending, he shall be brought to a martiall court, and there receive censure of
   death for his offence.

4. No man shall use any traiterous words against his Majesties Person, or
   royall authority upon paine of death. . . .

14. No man shall give any disgracefull words, or commit any act to the dis-
    grace of any person in this Colonie, or any part thereof, upon paine of
    being tied head and feete together, upon the guard everie night for the
    space of one moneth, besides to bee publikely disgraced himselfe, and be
    made uncapable ever after to possesse any place, or execute any office in
    this imployment.

15. No man of what condition soever shall barter, trucke, or trade with the
    Indians, except he be thereunto appointed by lawful authority, upon
    paine of death. . . .

31. What man or woman soever, shall rob any garden, publike or private, being set to weed the same, or wilfully pluck up therein any roote, herbe, or flower, to spoile and wast or steale the same, or robbe any vineyard, or gather up the grapes, or steale any eares of the corne growing, whether in the ground belonging to the same fort or towne where he dwelleth, or in any other, shall be punished with death.

THE MARSHALL LAWES

1. No man shall willingly absent himself, when hee is summoned to take the oath of Supremacy, upon paine of death. . . .
21. He that draweth his sword upon the Court of Guard, shall suffer death by the Armes which he weareth.
22. Hee that should draw his sword in a towne of Garrison, or in a Campe shall lose his right hand.
23. That souldier that shall goe out of the Fort, Towne or Campe, other then by the ordinary guards, issues, waies, or ports, shall suffer death by the Armes which he carrieth. . . .
31. No man shall depart from his guard without leave of his officer, upon paine of punishment: and who so shall be set Centinell, shall not depart from it untill he be relieved, nor sleepe thereof upon paine of death. . . .
38. No Souldier may speake or have any private conference with any of the salvages, without leave of his Captaine, nor his Captaine without leave of his chiefe Officer, upon paine of death.

Source: *For the Colony of Virginea Britannia. Lawes Divine, Morall and Martiall, etc.* (London: for Walter Burre, 1612).

THE PEQUOT WAR

The English established their first permanent settlement in New England at Plymouth in 1620. Just over a hundred settlers, generally called the Pilgrims, sought isolation from the evils of Europe to practice their religion undisturbed by other faiths. Only half of the Pilgrims lived through the first winter, the remainder surviving through the kind offices of Squanto and a number of other local Indians. The Pilgrims were followed in the late 1620s by the Puritans, thirty thousand of them arriving in just twelve years.

The Puritans, who also fled the perceived corruptions of Europe, hoped to serve as an example to the rest of the world. Setting themselves up first at Boston and Salem, they thrived, quickly expanding along the coast and then into the Connecticut River Valley. This tendency to seek ever more lands brought them into conflict with several Indian nations starting with the Pequot. In 1636 the Puritans sought to rid themselves of the Pequots. Over the few months of the Pequot War, the English soldiers succeeded in killing a thousand Pequots, selling the survivors into slavery in Bermuda. The pretext for the attack on Mystic was the execution of two pirates, Norton and Stone, by the Pequot for having killed one of their chiefs. Captain John Underhill, a professional soldier trained in the Netherlands, commanded the Massachusetts troops, while Captain John Mason led the Connecticut forces in the attack on the Pequot village of Mystic, described here. Their governments expected them to exterminate the Pequot. Underhill's Indian allies were so disgusted with the slaughter that they fled the scene. Governor William Bradford of Plymouth wrote, "It was a fearful sight to see them thus frying in the fire and the streams of blood quenching the same.... [We] praised God for a speedy victory over so proud and insulting an enemy." As the great Puritan minister John Robinson wrote Bradford on "the killing of those poor Indians": "Oh, how happy a thing had it been, if you had converted some before you had killed any!"[14]

Capt. John Underhill's Account of the Mystic Massacre, 1637

. . . The *Pequeats* having slaine one Captaine *Norton*, and Captaine *Stone*, with seven more of their company, order was given us to visit them, sayling along the *Nahanticot* shore with five vessels, the Indians spying of us came running in multitudes along the water side, crying, what cheere Englishmen, what cheere, what doe you come for? They not thinking we intended warre went on cheerefully untill they come to Pequeat river. . . .

That night the *Nahanitcot* Indians, and the *Pequeats*, made fire on both sides of the River, fearing we would land in the night. They made most dolefull, and wofull cryes all the night, (so that wee could scarce rest) hollowing one to another, and giving the word from place to place, to gather their forces together, fearing the English were come to warre against them.

The next morning they sent early aboard an Ambassadour. . . . They being a witty and ingenious Nation, their Ambassadour laboured to excuse the matter, and answered, we know not that any of ours have slaine any English: true it is, saith he, we have slaine such a number of men, but consider the ground of it; . . . we distinguish not betweene the *Dutch* and *English.* . . .

Our answer was, they were able to distinguish betweene *Dutch* and *English,* having had sufficient experience of both Nations, and therefore seeing you have slaine the king of *Englands* subjects, we come to demand an account of their blood, for we our selves are lyable to account for them. . . .

But wee seeing their drift was to get our Armes, we rather chose to beat up the Drum and bid them battell, marching into a champion field we dis-

14. William Bradford, *Of Plymouth Plantation, 1620–1647*, ed. Samuel Eliot Morison (New York: Knopf, 1963), 296, 374–75.

played our colours, but none would come neere us, but standing remotely off did laugh at us for our patience, wee suddenly set upon our march, and gave fire to as many as we could come neere, firing their Wigwams, spoyling their corne, and many other necessaries that they had buried in the ground we raked up, which the souldiers had for bootie. Thus we spent the day burning and spoyling the Countrey, towards night imbarqued our selves the next morning, landing on the *Nahanticot* shore, where we were served in like nature, no *Indians* would come neere us, but runne from us, as the Deere from the dogges; but having burnt and spoyled what we could light on, wee imbarqued our men, and set sayle for the *Bay*, having ended this exploit came off, having one man wounded in the legge; but certaine numbers of theirs slaine, and many wounded; this was the substance of the first yeares service: now followeth the service performed in the second yeare. . . .

Having imbarqued our souldiers, wee weighed ankor at *Seabrooke* Fort, and set sayle for the *Narraganset Bay*, deluding the *Pequeats* thereby, for they expected us to fall into *Pequeat* River; but crossing their expectation, bred in them a securitie: wee landed our men in the *Narraganset Bay*, and marched over land above two dayes journey before wee came to *Pequeat*; quartering the last nights march within two miles of the place, wee set forth about one of the clocke in the morning, having sufficient intelligence that they knew nothing of our comming:

Drawing neere to the Fort yeelded up our selves to God, and intreated his assistance in so waightie an enterprize. We set on our march to surround the Fort, Captaine *John Mason*, approching to the West end, where it had an entrance to passe into it, my selfe marching to the Southside, surrounding the Fort. . . .

[H]aving our swords in our right hand, our Carbins or Muskets in our left hand, we approched the Fort. Master *Hedge* being shot thorow both armes, and more wounded; though it bee not commendable for a man to make mention of any thing that might tend to his owne honour; yet because I would have the providence of God observed, and his Name magnified, as well for my selfe as others, I dare not omit, but let the world know, that deliverance was given to us that command, as well as to private souldiers. Captaine *Mason* and my selfe entring into the Wigwams, hee was shot, and received many Arrowes against his head-peece, God preserved him from any wounds; my selfe received a shotte in the left hippe, through a sufficient Buffe coate, that if I had not beene supplyed with such a garment, the Arrow would have pierced through me; another I received betweene necke and shoulders, hanging in the linnen of my Head-peece, others of our souldiers were shot some through the shoulders, some in the face, some in the head, some in the legs. Captaine *Mason* and my selfe losing each of us a man, and had neere twentie wounded: most couragiously these *Pequeats* behaved themselves: but seeing the Fort was to hotte for us, wee devised a way how wee might save our selves and prejudice them, Captaine *Mason* entring into a Wigwam, brought out a fire-brand, after hee had wounded many in the house, then hee set fire on the West-side where he entred, my selfe set fire on the South end with a traine of Powder, the fires of both meeting in the center of the Fort blazed most terribly, and burnt all in the space of halfe an houre; many couragious fellowes were unwilling to come out, and fought most desperately through the Palisadoes, so as they were scorched and burnt with the very flame, and were deprived of their armes, in regard the fire burnt their very bowstrings, and so perished valiantly. . . .

Source: Albert Bushnell Hart, ed., *American History Told by Contemporaries* (New York: Macmillan, 1898), 1:439–44.

KIEFT'S WAR

In the early seventeenth century "merchant adventurers" from several European countries sought wealth in North America. Spanish, Portuguese, English, French, Swedes, and Dutch traders all established trading posts, hoping to tap into America's natural resources. In 1623 the Dutch West India Company opened its trading station on Manhattan Island. Dutch merchants aimed particularly to access the American fur trade. But, as with most European settlements, the settlers of New Netherlands quickly exhausted local fur supplies and soon found themselves seeking sources of fur ever farther from the coast, expanding up the Hudson River as far north as Fort Orange (present-day Albany). In the process they came into conflict with other Europeans and Native Americans.

The Dutch ruthlessly abused the Indians. William Kieft, governor of New Netherlands during the 1640s, operated in the style of a modern drug lord, using the Mohawk as enforcers to extract tribute from the other Indians. When the "River Indians" who lived along the southern Hudson River refused to pay this protection money, Kieft decided to make an example of them. The ensuing war lasted three years, with the Dutch and Indians trading massacres, and ended in a peace enforced by the Mohawk. Kieft's War, as it is known, not only removed most Indians from the lower Hudson River but also destroyed Dutch trade networks, reducing New Netherlands to an insignificant European outpost that was easily conquered by the English in 1664. Racism enabled Kieft to use his political position to pursue his personal ambition with the power of the state. That same racism led many Dutch soldiers and settlers to commit acts of stunning brutality against those they deemed inferior.

One of the merchant adventurers who helped establish New Netherlands was David De Vries. He had made a living as a soldier and merchant in the Mediterranean, the Caribbean, Indonesia, and India before coming to America in 1633 with hopes of becoming a patroon—a landed gentleman. But De Vries's property was destroyed in the early stages of Kieft's War, a conflict he blamed entirely on the governor. Abandoning New Netherlands and returning to Amsterdam, De Vries published his memoirs in 1655, from which the following account of the beginning of the war is extracted.

David De Vries Describes the Beginnings of Kieft's War, 1642

ANNO 1642. . . . [A] harmless Dutchman, named Claes Rademaker, was murdered by a savage. He lived a short league from the fort by the Denselbay, where he had built a small house, and had set up the trade of wheelwright. It was on the Wickquasgeck road over which the Indians passed daily. It happened that a savage came to this Claes Rademaker for the purpose of trading beavers with him for duffels cloth, which goods were in a chest. This chest he had locked up, and had stooped down in order to take his goods out, when this murderer, the savage, seeing that the man had his head bent over into the chest, and observing an axe standing behind him, seized the axe, and struck Claes Rademaker on the neck therewith, so that he fell down dead by the chest. The murderer then stole all the goods and ran off.

The Commander sent to them and made inquiry in Wickquasgeck why this Dutchman had been so shamefully murdered. The murderer answered that, while the fort was being built, he came with his uncle and another savage to the freshwater, bringing beavers, in order to trade with the Dutchmen, that some Swannekes (as they call the Netherlanders) came there, took away from his uncle his beavers, and then killed him. He was then a small boy, and resolved that, when he should grow up, he would revenge that deed upon the Dutch, and since then he had seen no better chance to do so than with this Claes Rademaker. . . .

Commander Kieft then submitted the proposition whether or not we should avenge the murder of Claes Rademaker and make war upon the savages. We answered that time and opportunity must be taken, as our cattle were running at pasture in the woods, and we were living far and wide, east, west, south, and north of each other; that it was not expedient to carry on a war with the savages until we had more people, like the English, who make towns and villages. I told Commander Kieft that no profit was to be derived from a war with the savages; that he was the means of my people being murdered at the colony which I had commenced on Staten Island in the year forty; and that I well knew that the directors did not desire a war waged against the savages. . . . This I related to Commander Kieft, but he would not listen to it, so it becomes the managers to take care what persons they appoint as Directors, for thereon depends the welfare of the country. . . . [I]n the

East Indies they make no person commander of a fort, if he be not well acquainted with the country, and [they] have knowledge of the person's competence. But commanders are sent here whether they be fit or not. . . .

The 24th of February, sitting at a table with the Governor, he began to
state his intentions, that he had a mind to *wipe the mouths* of the savages; that
he had been dining at the house of Jan Claesz. . . . Damen, together with Jacob Planck, had presented a petition to him to begin this work.

I answered him that they were not wise to request this; that such work
could not be done without the approbation of the *Twelve Men*; that it could
not take place without my assent, who was one of the Twelve Men; that
moreover I was the first patroon, and no one else hitherto had risked there
so many thousands, and also his person, as I was the first to come from Holland or Zeeland to plant a colony; and that he should consider what profit
he could derive from this business, as he well knew that on account of trifling with the Indians we had lost our colony in the South River . . . with
thirty-two men, who were murdered in the year 1630. . . . But it appeared that
my speaking was of no avail. He had, with his co-murderers, determined to
commit the murder. . . .

When I had expressed all these things in full, sitting at the table, and the
meal was over, he told me he wished me to go to the large hall, which he
had been lately adding to his house. Coming to it, there stood all his soldiers
ready to cross the river to Pavonia to commit the murder. . . .

I remained that night at the Governor's, sitting up. I went and sat by the
kitchen fire, when about midnight I heard a great shrieking, and I ran to the
ramparts of the fort, and looked over to Pavonia. Saw nothing but firing, and
heard the shrieks of the savages murdered in their sleep. I returned again to
the house by the fire. Having sat there awhile, there came an Indian with his
squaw, whom I knew well, and who lived about an hour's walk from my
house, and told me that they two had fled in a small skiff, which they had
taken from the shore at Pavonia; that the Indians from Fort Orange had surprised them; and that they had come to conceal themselves in the fort. I told
them that they must go away immediately; that this was no time for them to
come to the fort to conceal themselves; that they who had killed their people
at Pavonia were not Indians, but the Swannekens, as they call the Dutch, had
done it. They then asked me how they should get out of the fort. I took
them to the door, and there was no sentry there, and so they betook themselves to the woods.

When it was day the soldiers returned to the fort, having massacred or
murdered eighty Indians, and considering they had done a deed of Roman
valor, in murdering so many in their sleep; where infants were torn from
their mother's breasts, and hacked to pieces in the presence of the parents,

and the pieces thrown into the fire and in the water, and other sucklings, being bound to small boards, were cut, stuck, and pierced, and miserably massacred in a manner to move a heart of stone. Some were thrown into the river, and when the fathers and mothers endeavored to save them, the soldiers would not let them come on land but made both parents and children drown—children from five to six years of age, and also some old and decrepit persons. Those who fled from this onslaught, and concealed themselves in the neighboring sedge, and when it was morning, came out to beg a piece of bread, and to be permitted to warm themselves, were murdered in cold blood and tossed into the fire or the water. Some came to our people in the country with their hands, some with their legs cut off, and some holding their entrails in their arms, and others had such horrible cuts and gashes, that worse than they were could never happen. And these poor simple creatures, as also many of our own people, did not know any better than that they had been attacked by a party of other Indians—the Maquas [Mohawks].

After this exploit, the soldiers were rewarded for their services, and Director Kieft thanked them by taking them by the hand and congratulating them. . . .

Source: J. Franklin Jameson, ed., *Narratives of New Netherland 1609–1664* (New York: Scribner, 1909), 213–15, 226–28.

BACON'S REBELLION

Indian wars could spill over to disrupt white society, especially when governments moved to prevent further clashes by restricting the westward movement of white settlers. One of the first such Indian wars created by settlers acting contrary to the intentions of their government came in 1676 in Virginia.

The royal governor of Virginia, William Berkeley, hoped to avoid another costly war by stabilizing his colony's relations with the Algonquian. But land was wealth, and many colonists wanted ever more, some in hopes of rising from poverty, others to increase their wealth. A recent arrival, Nathaniel Bacon, spoke for the land-hungry in demanding a war to "extirpate all Indians in Generall." Though wealthy himself and a member of the Governor's Council, Bacon used the language of class conflict when he charged that the government treated the Algonquian better than the whites in order to maintain elite power at the expense of the poor. "Those whom wee call great men," he argued, are "juggling Parasites whose tottering Fortunes have been repaired and supported at the Publique chardg."[15]

Governor Berkeley did not believe that white Virginians truly wanted a war that

15. Morgan, *American Slavery, American Freedom*, 259–62.

could threaten the very stability of their society, one dependent on keeping a large slave population in subjugation. He therefore dismissed Bacon from the council and charged him with treason. But Berkeley miscalculated. The legislature overwhelmingly supported Bacon and his call for war. The ensuing months were a time of near chaos, as Bacon led an untrained army of volunteers in attacking peaceful Indians, creating enemies for Virginia all along the backcountry, while Berkeley worked to convince the colony's elite to join him in a war against Bacon.

Traditional political categories have little meaning in Bacon's Rebellion. On the one hand, he appears the worst sort of violent bigot as he pursued his genocidal war against the Algonquian. On the other hand, he seemed almost a democrat as he armed the poor, accepted free blacks into his forces, promised freedom to any male indentured servant or slave who joined him, and looted the estates of the elite. To the elite, who wanted to avoid further conflict with the Indians, Bacon was a dangerous man who threatened to destroy both the security and the social structure of Virginia. Bacon's power became apparent when the official militia forces fled before his little army, and Bacon ordered the capital of Jamestown burned in October 1676. Violence structured Bacon's ambition; his followers did not hesitate to use force against fellow whites, while the successful use of that force seduced Bacon into seeking ever more power, confident of his own leadership and apparently heedless of the probable response of the Crown. At the very moment that he seized control of the colony, Bacon died, probably of dysentery. English regulars arrived shortly thereafter, and the rebellion evaporated.

Bacon's Rebellion produced a new political order in Virginia, though not in the ways Bacon had promised. King Charles II was furious that this uprising had interfered with his tobacco revenue. He therefore sent a military governor and brought the colony more firmly under royal control, increasing his personal revenues in the process. Virginia's elite also moved successfully to expand their own authority and to limit the threat from poor whites by offering them more opportunities to attain a modicum of prosperity. Some historians have suggested that the elite moved in the aftermath of Bacon's Rebellion to increase the number of slaves, who were thought easier to control than poor whites, and through the promotion of racism to keep whites and blacks at a safe distance from each other. The following account, Strange News from Virginia, *was published in London in 1677. Many people who initially followed Bacon, as the anonymous author of this piece may have, found it embarrassing after the arrival of English troops to admit that support. It proved very convenient, as in this account, to transfer all blame to the deceased leader.*

An Anonymous Account of the Rebellion in Virginia, 1676

. . . Mr. *Bacon*, about the 25*th* of *June* last, dissatisfied that he could not have a Commission granted him to go against the *Indians*, in the night time departed the Town unknown to any body, and about a week after got together between four and five hundred men of *New-Kent* County, with whom he marched to *James-Town*, and drew up in order before the House of State; and there peremptorily demanded of the Governor, *Council* and *Burgesses* (there then collected) a Commission to go against the *Indians*, which if they should refuse to grant him, he told them that neither he nor ne're a man in his Company would depart from their Doors till he had obtained his request; whereupon to prevent farther danger in so great an exigence, the Council and Burgesses by much intreaty obtain'd him a Commission Signed by the *Governor*, an Act for one thousand men to be Listed under his command to go against the *Indians*, to whom the same pay was to be granted as was allowed to them who went against the *Fort*. But *Bacon* was not satisfied with this, but afterwards earnestly importuned, and at length obtained of the *House*, to pass an Act of Indemnity to all Persons who had sided with him, and also Letters of recommendations from the Governor to his Majesty in his behalf; and moreover caused Collonel *Claybourn* and his Son Captain *Claybourn*, Lieutenant Collonel *West*, and Lieutenant Collonel *Hill*, and many others, to be degraded for ever bearing any Office, whether it were Military or Civil.

Having obtained these large Civilities of the *Governor*, *&c.* one would have thought that if the Principles of honesty would not have obliged him to peace and loyalty, those of gratitude should. But, alas, when men have been once flusht or entred with Vice, how hard is it for them to leave it, especially [if] it tends towards ambition or greatness, which is the general lust of a large Soul, and the common error of vast parts, which fix their Eyes so upon the lure of greatness, that they have no time left them to consider by what indirect and unlawful means they must (if ever) attain it.

This certainly was Mr. *Bacon's* Crime, who after he had once launched into Rebellion, nay, and upon submission had been pardoned for it, and also restored, as if he had committed no such hainous offence, to his former honour and dignities (which were considerable enough to content any reasonable mind) yet for all this he could not forbear wading into his former misdemeanors, and continued his opposition against that prudent and established Government, ordered by his Majesty of Great *Brittain* to be duely observed in that Continent.

In fine, he continued (I cannot say properly in the Fields, but) in the Woods with a considerable Army all last Summer, and maintain'd several Brushes with the Governors Party: sometime routing them, and burning all before him, to the great damage of many of his Majesties loyal Subjects there resident; sometimes he and his Rebels were beaten by the Governor, *&c.* and forc't to run for shelter amongst the Woods and Swomps. In which lamentable condition that unhappy Continent has remain'd for the space of almost a Twelve-month, every one therein that were able being forc't to take up Arms for security of their own lives, and no one reckoning their Goods, Wives, or Children to be their own, since they were so dangerously expos'd to the doubtful Accidents of an uncertain War.

But the indulgent Heavens, who are alone able to compute what measure of punishments are adequate or fit for the sins or transgressions of a Nation, has in its great mercy thought fit to put a stop, at least, if not a total period and conclusion to these *Virginian* troubles, by the death of this *Nat. Bacon*, the great Molestor of the quiet of that miserable Nation; so that now we who are here in *England*, and have any Relations or Correspondence with any of the Inhabitants of that Continent, may by the arrival of the next Ships from that Coast expect to hear that they are freed from all their dangers, quitted of all their fears, and in great hopes and expectation to live quietly under their own Vines, and enjoy the benefit of their commendable labours.

I know it is by some reported that this Mr. *Bacon* was a very hard drinker, and that he dyed by inbibing, or taking in two much Brandy. But I am informed by those who are Persons of undoubted Reputation, and had the happiness to see the same Letter which gave his Majesty an account of his death, that there was no such thing therein mentioned: he was certainly a Person [imbued] with great natural parts, which notwithstanding his juvenile extravagances he had adorned with many elaborate acquisitions, and by the help of learning and study knew how to manage them to a Miracle, it being the general vogue of all that knew him, that he usually spoke as much sense in as few words, and delivered that sense as opportunely as any they ever kept company withal: Wherefore as I am my self a Lover of Ingenuity, though an abhorrer of disturbance or Rebellion, I think fit since Providence was pleased to let him dye a Natural death in his Bed, not to asperse him with saying he kill'd himself with drinking.

Source: Albert Bushnell Hart, ed., *American History Told by Contemporaries* (New York: Macmillan, 1898), 1:245–46.

THE PUEBLO UPRISING AND ITS SUPPRESSION

While the Dutch and English often seemed intent on exterminating neighboring Indians, the Spanish preferred to exploit their labor. Harsh rulers, the Spanish drafted the Pueblo Indians into a form of coerced labor little different from slavery and attempted to destroy the native religion and culture. In 1680 the Pueblos attacked the Spanish in New Mexico in a well-coordinated surprise attack on their settlements. Within a few days the Pueblos had killed four hundred Spanish, including most of the priests, burned their churches and towns, and forced the survivors to flee New Mexico, leaving the re-

gion once more under Pueblo control. The governor, Antonio de Otermín, described these events in a letter to one of his superiors in Mexico City once he had reached the safety of El Paso.

One aspect of the rebellion that particularly shocked the Spanish was the fact that most of the Indians who rose against them had converted to Catholicism. The Spanish believed that they had offered Christianity to the Pueblo people, and that this gift had been graciously accepted. But from the point of view of many Indians, the Spanish had forced them into accepting conversion as part of a concerted effort to destroy their way of life. It was this desire to reclaim their culture and autonomy that led the Pueblo people to ally with their traditional enemies, the Apache, against the Spanish. In El Paso, Spanish officials attempted to determine how converted Indians could rise in rebellion, questioning a number of captives, including a Spanish-speaking Pueblo named Josephe.

Twelve years after the Spanish expulsion from New Mexico, in 1692, the viceroy of Mexico, the Count de Galva, determined to reconquer the province. He placed General Diego de Vargas Zapata in command of a small army with instructions to use any means to restore New Mexico to the Spanish empire. General de Vargas succeeded through intimidation and diplomacy in persuading the Pueblo to accept the restoration of Spanish rule. Carlos de Siguenza y Gongora accompanied de Vargas and published an account of the expedition in Mexico City in 1693. New Mexico remained part of the Spanish empire until the Mexican Revolution of 1821.

Governor Antonio de Otermín's Report on the Uprising in New Mexico, 1680

The time has come when, with tears in my eyes and deep sorrow in my heart, I commence to give an account of the lamentable tragedy, such as has never before happened in the world, which has occurred in this miserable kingdom and holy custodia. His divine Majesty having thus permitted it because of my grievous sins. . . .

. . . I received information that a plot for a general uprising of the Christian Indians was being formed and was spreading rapidly. . . . [T]hough I immediately, at that instant, notified the lieutenant general on the lower river and all the other alcaldes mayores [local officials]—so that they could take every-care and precaution against whatever might occur, and so that they could make every effort to guard and protect the religious ministers and the temples—the cunning and cleverness of the rebels was such, and so great, that my efforts were of little avail. . . .

On Tuesday [August 13, 1680] . . . at about nine o'clock in the morning, there came in sight of us in the suburb of Analco, in the cultivated field of the hermitage of San Miguel, and on the other side of the river from the villa, all the Indians of the Tanos and Pecos nations and the Queres of San Marcos, armed and giving war whoops. . . .

With this, seeing after a short time that they not only did not cease the pillage but were advancing toward the villa with shamelessness and mockery, I ordered all the soldiers to go out and attack them. . . . Advancing for this purpose, they joined battle, killing some at the first encounter. Finding themselves repulsed, they took shelter and fortified themselves in the said hermitage and the houses of the Mexicans, from which they defended themselves a part of the day with the firearms they had and with arrows. . . . Many of the rebels remained dead and wounded, and our men retired to the cases reales [trade store] with one soldier killed and . . . fourteen or fifteen soldiers wounded. . . .

. . . Friday, the nations of the Taos, Pecuríes, Jemez, and Queres having assembled during the past night, when dawn came more than 2,500 Indians fell upon us in the villa, fortifying and intrenching themselves in all its houses and at the entrances of all the streets, and cutting off our water. . . .

On the next day, Saturday, they began at dawn to press us harder and more closely with gunshots, arrows, and stones, saying to us that now we should not escape them, and that, besides their own numbers, they were expecting help from the Apaches whom they had already summoned. They fatigued us greatly on this day, because all was fighting, and above all we suffered from thirst. . . . At nightfall, because of the evident peril in which we found ourselves by their gaining the two stations where the cannon were mounted, which we had at the doors of the casas reales, aimed at the entrances of the streets, in order to bring them inside it was necessary to assemble all the forces that I had with me. . . . Instantly all the said Indian rebels began a chant of victory and raised war whoops, burning all the houses of the villa, and they kept us in this position the entire night, which I assure your reverence was the most horrible that could be thought of or imagined, because the whole villa was a torch and everywhere were war chants and shouts. What grieved us most were the dreadful flames from the church and the scoffing and ridicule which the wretched and miserable Indian rebels made of the sacred things, intoning the alabado and the other prayers of the church with jeers.

Finding myself in this state, with the church and the villa burned, and with the few horses, sheep, goats, and cattle which we had without feed or water for so long that many had already died, and the rest were about to do so, . . . I determined to take the resolution of going out in the morning to fight with the enemy until dying or conquering. Considering that the best strength and armor were prayers to appease the divine wrath, though on the preceding days the poor women had made them with such fervor, that night

I charged them to do so increasingly, and told the father guardián and the other two religious to say mass for us at dawn, and exhort all alike to repentance for their sins and to conformance with the divine will, and to absolve us from guilt and punishment. These things being done, all of us who could mounted our horses, and the rest went on foot.... On coming out of the entrance to the street it was seen that there was a great number of Indians. They were attacked in force, and though they resisted the first charge bravely, finally they were put to flight, many of them being overtaken and killed. Then turning at once upon those who were in the streets leading to the convent, they also were put to flight with little resistance.... The deaths of both parties in this and the other encounters exceeded three hundred Indians....

Spanish Officials Question the Pueblo Indian Josephe, 1681

[O]n the 19th day of the month of December, 1681, for the said judicial proceedings of this case, his lordship caused to appear before him an Indian prisoner named Josephe, able to speak the Castilian language, a servant of Sargento Mayor Sebastián de Herrera who fled from him and went among the apostates....

Being asked why he fled from his master ... and went to live with the treacherous Indian apostates of New Mexico ... he said that the reason why he left was that he was suffering hunger ... and a companion of his named Domingo urged [Josephe] to go to New Mexico for a while.... They did not come with the intention of remaining always with the apostate traitors and rebels, and after they arrived [the rebels] killed Domingo, his companion, because of the Pecos Indians having seen him fighting in the villa [of Santa Fe] along with the Spaniards....

Asked what causes or motives the said Indian rebels had for renouncing the law of God and obedience to his Majesty, and for committing so many kinds of crimes, and who were the instigators of the rebellion, ... he said that the prime movers of the rebellion were two Indians of San Juan, one named El Popé and the other El Taqu, and another from Taos named Saca, and another from San Ildefonso named Francisco. He knows that these were the principals, and the causes they gave were alleged ill treatment and injuries received from the present secretary, Francisco Xavier, and the [military commander] Alonso García, and from the sargentos mayores, Luis de Quintana and Diego López, because they beat them, took away what they had, and made them work without pay....

Asked if he has learned ... why the apostates burned the images, churches, and things pertaining to divine worship, making a mockery and a trophy of them, killing the priests and doing the other things they did, he said that he knows and has heard it generally stated that while they were besieging the villa the rebellious traitors burned the church and shouted in loud voices, "Now the God of the Spaniards, who was their father, is dead, and Santa María, who was their mother, and the saints, who were pieces of rotten wood," saying that only their own god lived. Thus they ordered all the temples and images, crosses and rosaries burned, and this function being over, they all went to bathe in the rivers, saying that they thereby washed away the water of baptism. For their churches, they placed on the four sides and in the center of the plaza some small circular enclosures of stone where they went to offer flour, feathers, and the seed of maguey, maize, and tobacco, and performed other superstitious rites, giving the children to understand that they must all do this in the future. The captains and chiefs ordered that the names of Jesus and of Mary should nowhere be uttered, and that they should discard their baptismal names, and abandon the wives whom God had given them in matrimony, and take the ones that they pleased. He saw that as soon as the remaining Spaniards had left, they ordered all the estufas erected, which are their houses of idolatry, and danced throughout the kingdom the dance of the cazina, making many masks for it in the image of the devil. . . .

[Asked to describe one attack] Alonso Catití, a leader of the uprising, . . . planned to deceive the Spaniards with feigned peace. He had arranged to send to the pueblo of Cochití all the prettiest, most pleasing, and neatest Indian women so that, under pretense of coming down to prepare food for the Spaniards, they could provoke them to lewdness, and that night while they were with [the women], . . . Catití would come down with all the men of the Queres and Jemez nations, . . . to kill the said Spaniards. . . . [Josephe] being present during all these proceedings, and feeling compassion because of the treason they were plotting, he determined to come to warn the Spaniards, as he did, whereupon they put themselves under arms and the said Indians again went up to the heights of the sierra, and the Spaniards withdrew. Thus he replies to the question.

Don Carlos de Sigüenza y Góngora Describes the Reconquest of New Mexico, 1692

At three o'clock the next day [September 10, 1692], with only 40 Spaniards and 50 Indians, all men of resolution and well armed, the General left his ranch of Mexia to strike a day break blow to the pueblo of Cochití, distant 18 leagues from that point. . . .

It must have been four o'clock in the morning of the 13th of September when they came in sight of the villa and at this hour they, the Indians, doubtless had sentries for they had already sounded the alarm. The whole place was found walled and with intrenchments, and especially the place used by them as a fortress, *which was the ancient palace of the governors*; and raising a frightful yell in order to give themselves courage the wall was crowned, on every part with an infinite multitude of Indians. While they were employed in this, and in bringing thick beams and logs and large stones to prevent our men from getting near to them, the water was cut off to them, which was carried in through a ditch. Having accomplished this, which was no small thing, a trumpeteer was sent to assure them of pardon and to offer them great conveniences if they would give themselves up; they all answered in one voice; and with derisions repeatedly thanked the Spaniards for coming into their houses, like madmen, saying without much trouble, we would all perish, therein. . . .

The next day dawned, being the 14th on which the Catholic church celebrates the feast of the Exaltation of the Cross, and having come out of the Villa, a good throng of the principal Indians, with demonstrations of peace, greeted the General, and the Religious and those who were there, with courteous words; and as they added that he (the General) could enter into it (the Villa) when he pleased, it did not seem convenient to the General to delay long in doing that. He arrived at the gate that is on the wall (which is a single one) and found it fastened on all sides with iron bars followed by a gangway with various loopholes which looked like a fort or half-moon for greater defense.

They proposed here tenaciously and with obstinacy, but also obsequiously and submissively, that, in order that their people might not become restless, the General and the Rev. Father President with six soldiers, and without handguns should enter.

"That is nothing," said the intrepid General. "Who will not risk himself in order to obtain with perpetual glory an illustrious name?" And calling upon the most Holy Mary with devout efficacy he stepped forward. He arrived with the Father President and the six soldiers to a great square where the Indians had just planted a beautiful cross. When the noise of the great crowd that was there had subsided, he proposed to them, in the Castilian language which many of them understood well, that: Our Monarch and Lord Charles II, their legitimate King, having forgotten the apostacy with which they had renounced the Catholic religion; the sacrilege whereby they had deprived the Religious of their lives; desecrated the temples, broken the images and contaminated the sacred vessels; of the cowardice with which they had knifed the Spaniards without sparing the women and tender children; of the barbarity with which they had burned the farms of the latter and ruined the pueblos; of the consequences that had followed from such abominations; he (His Majesty) had sent him with full authority, to pardon them without any other condition than their return to the fold of the Holy Church which would receive them as a pious mother if they solicited pardon with penance and tears and with the understanding that they should swear obedience to his Catholic Majesty as their legitimate King.

With pleasure they conceded both demands, the General then commanded the Royal Ensign, who was at his side, to unfurl his standard. The General then said in ringing and intelligible tones: "The Villa of Santa Fé, Capital of the Kingdom of New Mexico, I now take possession of, and with her, her provinces and all the pueblos, for the Catholic Majesty of the King, Our Lord Charles II, long live him for the protection of all his vassals and of his dominions many long years." "Long live, long live, long live, that we may all serve him, as we ought," the rest answered and prostrating themselves before the Holy Cross, and the Father President sang the Te Deum Laudamus. . . .

While this was happening in the Villa of Santa Fé there was at the pueblo of San Juan which is not very far from here, Don Luis Tupatú, an Indian of mature age, whose qualities and valor . . . gained for him the government of the whole kingdom, without any opposition from anyone. . . .

With the assurance that the General would be pleased to have him come when it should be his pleasure, he came the next day, the neighbors of the Villa having gone out to receive him after the usage of war, Don Luis arrived accompanied by 200 Indian soldiers well prepared. He came mounted on a fine horse, had a fire–lock, powder and ammunition, and on the forehead a nacarine shell like a crown and was dressed after the Spanish fashion, but with deer skins. At a distance of seventy steps from the General's tent he halted and the guard of 200 Indians formed into a square, and after dismounting he stepped forward with gravity, and making three bows, he bent the knee to Don Diego, who was outside, and kissed his hand. Don Diego returned all this with an embrace, and this first visit was continued to the customary salutations, Don Luis showing in his countenance his pleasure. After having presented the General gifts of marine wolf skins . . . and buffalo robes, and receiving (in return) a reward of a fine horse, which he accepted appreciatively, he took leave to return the next day. . . .

With a larger body of Spanish and Indian troops, and with more efficient military apparatus than what we had before, the General now started in a northerly direction and entered the pueblo of Tesuque the same day. . . . All who lived in the pueblos came out of them, all with crosses, and along the roads the most curious arches of cypresses and flowers were to be seen. These apostates reconciled themselves with the church, asked for baptism for their children with great anxiety, and their requests were granted after which we took new possession of them all, for and in the name of the Catholic Majesty, our Monarch and Lord, Charles II; all this was done amid great and general rejoicing and festive dances.

Sources: Charmion C. Shelby, ed. and trans., *Revolt of the Pueblo Indians of New Mexico and Otermín's Attempted Reconquest, 1680–1682* (Albuquerque: University of New Mexico Press, 1942), 1:94–103, 2:238–42; Benjamin M. Read, *Illustrated History of New Mexico* (Santa Fe: New Mexican Printing Company, 1912), 274–87.

THE SALEM WITCHCRAFT TRIALS

In 1692 witchcraft hysteria swept through the town of Salem, Massachusetts. The crisis began with some teenage girls complaining of mysterious pains and convulsions. The local minister, Samuel Parris, fed the crisis by encouraging the girls to make accusations of witchcraft against other members of the community. Authorities created a special court to hear these cases and sentenced many people to death, executing twenty alleged witches before the governor put a halt to the trials.

In a procedure that would reappear later in American history, the court forgave accused witches who would confess and name coconspirators, saving their own lives at the expense of others. Thus Margaret Jacobs admitted to witchcraft, claiming that her grandfather, already accused, had inducted her into the dark arts. After testifying against her grandfather and several others, Jacobs withdrew her confession, telling the court that the prosecutors "told me, if I would not confess, I should be put down into the dungeon and would be hanged, but if I would confess I should have my life." But it was too late; the others had already been executed. Jacobs was set free, but as she wrote her father, "through the Magistrates Threatenings, and my own Vile and Wretched Heart, [I] confessed several things contrary to my Conscience and Knowledg, tho to the Wounding of my own Soul, the Lord pardon me for it."[16] Thomas Brattle, a prominent local merchant and opponent of the trials, supplied the following description to an unknown British minister. Brattle saw himself as a friendly critic, not questioning the wisdom of the legal system, except in these cases. Yet he could not escape the conclusion that the witchcraft trials had called the law itself into disrepute.

---

16. Paul Boyer and Stephen Nissenbaum, eds., *The Salem Witchcraft Papers: Verbatim Transcripts of the Legal Documents of the Salem Witchcraft Outbreak of 1692*, 3 vols. (New York: DaCapo Press, 1977), 2:490–91.

Thomas Brattle's Account of Witchcraft, 1692

October 8, 1692.

Reverend Sir,

... First, as to the method which the Salem justices do take in their examinations, it is truly this: A warrant being issued out to apprehend the persons that are charged and complained of by the afflicted children, as they are called; said persons are brought before the justices, the afflicted being present. The justices ask the apprehended why they afflict those poor children; to which the apprehended answer, they do not afflict them. The justices order the apprehended to look upon the said children, which accordingly they do; and at the time of that look, (I dare not say *by* that look, as the Salem gentlemen do), the afflicted are cast into a fit. . . . The afflicted persons then declare and affirm, that the apprehended have afflicted them; upon which the apprehended persons, though of never so good repute, are forthwith committed to prison, on suspicion for witchcraft. One of the Salem justices was pleased to tell Mr. Alden, (when upon his examination), that truly he had been acquainted with him these many years, and had always accounted him a good man; but indeed now he should be obliged to change his opinion. . . . He saw reason to change his opinion of Mr. Alden, because that at the time he touched the poor child, the poor child came out of her fit. I suppose his Honour never made the experiment, whether there was not as much virtue in his own hand as there was in Mr. Alden's, to cure by a touch. . . .

I cannot but condemn this method of the justices, of making this touch of the hand a rule to discover witchcraft; because I am fully persuaded that it is sorcery, and a superstitious method, and that which we have no rule for, either from reason or religion. . . . [T]he account they give of it is this; that by this touch, the venomous and malignant particles, that were ejected from the eye, do, by this means, return to the body whence they came, and so leave the afflicted persons pure and whole. . . .

Secondly, with respect to the confessors, as they are improperly called, or such as confess themselves to be witches, . . . there are now about fifty of them in prison; many of which I have again and again seen and heard; and I cannot but tell you, that my faith is strong concerning them, that they are deluded, imposed upon, and under the influence of some evil spirit; and therefore unfit to be evidences either against themselves, or any one else. . . .

These confessors, as they are called, do very often contradict themselves, as inconsistently as is usual for any crazed, distempered person to do. This the S[alem] G[entlemen] do see and take notice of; and even the judges themselves have, at some times, taken these confessors in flat lies, or contradictions, even in the courts; by reason of which, one would have thought, that the judges would have frowned upon the said confessors, discarded them, and not minded one tittle of any thing that they said: but instead thereof, as sure as we are men, the judges vindicate these confessors, and salve their contradictions, by proclaiming, that the devil takes away their memory, and imposes upon their brain. . . .

These confessors then, as least some of them, even in the judges' own account, are under the influence of the devil; and the brain of these confessors is imposed upon by the devil, even in the judges' account. But now, if, in the judges' account, these confessors are under the influence of the devil, and their brains are affected and imposed upon by the devil, so that they are not their own men, why then should these judges, or any other men, make such account of, and set so much by, the words of these confessors, as they do? In short, I argue thus:

If the devil does actually take away the memory of them at some times, certainly the devil, at other times, may very reasonably be thought to affect their fancies, and to represent false ideas to their imagination. But now, if it be thus granted, that the devil is able to represent false ideas (to speak vulgarly) to the imaginations of the confessors, what man of sense will regard the confessions, or any of the words, of these confessors? . . .

It is true, that over and above the evidences of the afflicted persons, there are many evidences brought in, against the prisoner at the bar; either that he was at a witch meeting, or that he performed things which could not be done by an ordinary natural power; or that she sold butter to a sailor which proving bad at sea; and the seamen exclaiming against her, she appeared, and soon after there was a storm, or the like. But what if there were ten thousand evidences of this nature; how do they prove the matter of indictment? And if they do not reach the matter of indictment, then I think it is clear, that the prisoner at the bar is brought in guilty, and condemned, merely from the evidences of the afflicted persons. . . .

As to the late executions, I shall only tell you, that in the opinion of many unprejudiced, considerate and considerable spectators, some of the condemned went out of the world not only with as great protestations, but also with as good shews of innocency, as men could do. . . .

I do admire that some particular persons, and particularly Mrs. Thatcher of Boston, should be much complained of by the afflicted persons, and yet that the justices should never issue out their warrants to apprehend them, when as upon the same account they issue out their warrants for the apprehending and imprisoning many others.

This occasions much discourse and many hot words, and is a very great scandal and stumbling block to many good people; certainly distributive justice should have its course, without respect to persons; and although the said Mrs. Thatcher be mother in law to Mr. Curwin, who is one of the justices and judges, yet if justice and conscience do oblige them to apprehend others on the account of the afflicted their complaints, I cannot see how, without injustice and violence to conscience, Mrs. Thatcher can escape, when it is well known how much she is, and has been, complained of. . . .

A person from Boston, of no small note, carried up his child to Salem, near 20 miles, on purpose that he might consult the afflicted about his child; which accordingly he did; and the afflicted told him, that his child was afflicted by Mrs. Cary and Mrs. Obinson. The man returned to Boston, and went forthwith to the justices for a warrant to seize the said Obinson, (the said Cary being out of the way); but the Boston justices saw reason to deny a warrant. The Rev. Mr. I[ncrease] M[ather] of Boston, took occasion severely to reprove the said man; asking him, whether there was not a God in Boston, that he should go to the devil in Salem for advice; warning him very seriously against such naughty practices; which, I hope, proved to the conviction and good of the said person; if not, his blood will be upon his own head.

. . . Deacon Fry's wife, Capt. Osgood's wife, and some others, remarkably pious and good people in repute, are apprehended and imprisoned; and that which is more admirable, the forementioned women are become a kind of confessors, being first brought thereto by the urgings and arguings of their good husbands, who, having taken up that corrupt and highly pernicious opinion, that whoever were accused by the afflicted, were guilty, did break charity with their dear wives, upon their being accused, and urge them to confess their guilt; which so far prevailed with them as to make them say, they were afraid of their being in the snare of the devil. . . .

Now, that the justices have thus far given ear to the devil, I think it may be mathematically demonstrated to any man of common sense: And for the demonstration and proof hereof, I desire, only, that these two things may be duly considered, viz.

1. That several persons have been apprehended purely upon the complaints of these afflicted, to whom the afflicted were perfect strangers, and had not the least knowledge of imaginable, before they were apprehended.

2. That the afflicted do own and assert, and the justices do grant, that the devil does inform and tell the afflicted the names of those persons that are thus unknown unto them. Now these two things being duly considered, I think it will appear evident to any one, that the devil's information is the fundamental testimony that is gone upon in the apprehending of the aforesaid people. . . .

Nineteen persons have now been executed, and one pressed to death for a mute: seven more are condemned; two of which are reprieved, because they pretend their being with child. . . .

What will be the issue of these troubles, God only knows; I am afraid that ages will not wear off that reproach and those stains which these things will leave behind them upon our land. I pray God pity us, humble us, forgive us, and appear mercifully for us in this our [moment] of distress. . . .

Source: *Collections of the Massachusetts Historical Society* (Boston: Samuel Hall, 1798), 61–73, 76, 79.

THE PAXTON BOYS

As with Bacon's Rebellion eighty-five years earlier, the Paxton Boys crisis began with the perception among many poor whites that their government was not doing enough to push back the Indians. Shortly after the war between the English colonies and Pontiac's Confederation began in 1763, some frontier settlers in Lancaster County, Pennsylvania, calling themselves the Paxton Boys, murdered an entire village of twenty Indians, including the children. The Conestoga Indians had long been friendly with the whites, and their murder shocked and disgusted a great many white Americans, while persuading many Indians that the whites could not be trusted. After killing these unarmed Indians, the Paxton Boys marched on Philadelphia to demand that the government of Pennsylvania protect them from hostile Indians. Benjamin Franklin, probably the most famous and influential man in the British colonies, led the delegation which promised the Paxton Boys that their grievances would be addressed by the assembly.

The Paxton Boys created a crisis for a province that had enjoyed peace with the Indians for most of its history and that included a large number of pacifist Quakers in its elite. The latter held to the conviction that there was no need for an organized militia, though that faith was shaken less by an Indian threat than by the violence of the Paxton Boys. The assembly finally voted further funds for defense and organized a militia, but they also joined in negotiating a peace treaty with the western Indians. Franklin published the following account of the Conestoga Massacre, condemning the Paxton Boys as dangerous barbarians. Though not himself a Christian, Franklin expressed a popular opinion in feeling that Christianity, or at least the standards of European culture as they were

then understood, should have restrained the Paxton Boys. The Paxton massacre led many
of Franklin's contemporaries to join him in doubting the wisdom of extending political
power to such common people.

Benjamin Franklin's Narrative of the Massacres, 1763

. . . These *Indians* were the Remains of a Tribe of the *Six Nations*, settled at
Conestogoe, and thence called *Conestogoe Indians*. On the first Arrival of the *En-*
glish in *Pennsylvania*, Messengers from this Tribe came to welcome them, with
Presents of Venison, Corn, and Skins; and the whole Tribe entered into a
Treaty of Friendship with the first Proprietor, William Penn, which was to
last "as long as the Sun should shine, or the Waters run in the Rivers."

This Treaty has been since frequently renewed, and the *Chain brightened*, as
they express it, from time to time. It has never been violated, on their Part or
ours, till now. As their Lands by Degrees were mostly purchased, and the Settlements of the White People began to surround them, the Proprietor assigned them lands on the Manor of *Conestogoe*, which they might not part
with; there they have lived many years in Friendship with their White
Neighbours, who loved them for their peaceable inoffensive Behaviour.

It has always been observed, that *Indians*, settled in the Neighbourhood of
White People, do not increase, but diminish continually. This Tribe accordingly went on diminishing, till there remained in their Town on the Manor,
but 20 persons, viz. 7 Men, 5 Women, and 8 Children, Boys and Girls.

Of these, *Shehaes* was a very old Man, having assisted at the second Treaty
held with them, by Mr. Penn, in 1701, and ever since continued a faithful and
affectionate Friend to the *English*; He is said to have been an exceeding good
Man, considering his Education, being naturally of a most kind, benevolent
Temper.

Peggy was *Shehaes's* Daughter; she worked for her aged Father, continuing
to live with him, though married, and attended him with filial Duty and Tenderness.

John was another good old Man; his Son *Harry* helped to support him.

George and *Will Soc* were two Brothers, both young Men.

John Smith, a valuable young Man of the *Cayuga* Nation, who became acquainted with *Peggy*, *Shehaes's* Daughter, some few Years since, married her,
and settled in that Family. They had one Child, about three Years old.

Betty, a harmless old Woman; and her son *Peter*, a likely young Lad.

Sally, whose *Indian* name was *Wyanjoy*, a Woman much esteemed by all
that knew her, for her prudent and good Behaviour in some very trying situations of Life. She was a truly good and an amiable Woman, had no Children

of her own, but, a distant Relation dying, she had taken a Child of that Relation's, to bring up as her own, and performed towards it all the Duties of an affectionate Parent.

The Reader will observe, that many of their Names are *English*. It is common with the *Indians* that have an affection for the *English*, to give themselves, and their Children, the Names of such *English* Persons as they particularly esteem.

This little Society continued the Custom they had begun, when more numerous, of addressing every new Governor, and every Descendant of the first Proprietor, welcoming him to the Province, assuring him of their Fidelity, and praying a Continuance of that Favour and Protection they had hitherto experienced. They had accordingly sent up an Address of this Kind to our present Governor, on his Arrival; but the same was scarce delivered, when the unfortunate Catastrophe happened, which we are about to relate.

On *Wednesday*, the 14th of *December*, 1763, Fifty-seven Men, from some of our Frontier Townships, who had projected the Destruction of this little Commonwealth, came, all well mounted, and armed with Firelocks, Hangers and Hatchets, having travelled through the Country in the Night, to *Conestogoe* Manor. There they surrounded the small Village of *Indian* Huts, and just at Break of Day broke into them all at once. Only three Men, two Women, and a young Boy, were found at home, the rest being out among the neighbouring White People, some to sell the Baskets, Brooms and Bowls they manufactured. . . . These poor defenceless Creatures were immediately fired upon, stabbed, and hatcheted to Death! The good *Shehaes*, among the rest, cut to Pieces in his Bed. All of them were scalped and otherwise horribly mangled. Then their Huts were set on Fire, and most of them burnt down. When the Troop, pleased with their own Conduct and Bravery, but enraged that any of the poor Indians had escaped the Massacre, rode off, and in small Parties, by different Roads, went home.

The universal Concern of the neighbouring White People on hearing of this Event, and the Lamentations of the younger *Indians*, when they returned and saw the Desolation, and the butchered half-burnt Bodies of their murdered Parents and other Relations, cannot well be expressed.

The Magistrates of *Lancaster* sent out to collect the remaining *Indians*, brought them into the Town for their better Security against any farther Attempt; and it is said condoled with them on the Misfortune that had happened, took them by the Hand, comforted and *promised them Protection*. They were all put into the Workhouse, a strong Building, as the Place of greatest Safety. . . .

There are some, (I am ashamed to hear it,) who would extenuate the enormous Wickedness of these Actions, by saying, "The Inhabitants of the

Frontiers are exasperated with the Murder of their Relations, by the Enemy *Indians*, in the present War." It is possible;—but though this might justify their going out into the Woods, to seek for those Enemies, and avenge upon them those Murders, it can never justify their turning into the Heart of the Country, to murder their Friends. . . .

But it seems these People think they have a better Justification; nothing less than the *Word of God.* With the Scriptures in their Hands and Mouths, they can set at nought that express Command, *Thou shalt do no Murder;* and justify their Wickedness by the Command given *Joshua* to destroy the Heathen. Horrid Perversion of Scripture and of Religion! To father the worst of Crimes on the God of Peace and Love! Even the *Jews*, to whom that particular Commission was directed, spared the *Gibeonites*, on Account of their Faith once given. The Faith of this Government has been frequently given to those *Indians;* but that did not avail them with People who despise Government.

We pretend to be *Christians*, and, from the superior Light we enjoy, ought to exceed *Heathens, Turks, Saracens, Moors, Negroes* and *Indians*, in the Knowledge and Practice of what is right. . . .

Source: Albert Henry Smyth, ed., *The Writings of Benjamin Franklin* (New York: Macmillan, 1906), 4:289–92, 297–99.

FURTHER READINGS

On the European conquest of North America and native resistance: Ramón A. Gutiérrez, *When Jesus Came, the Corn Mothers Went Away: Marriage, Sexuality, and Power in New Mexico, 1500–1846* (Stanford, CA: Stanford University Press, 1991); Francis Jennings, *The Invasion of America: Indians, Colonialism, and the Cant of Conquest* (Chapel Hill: University of North Carolina Press, 1975); Edmund S. Morgan, *American Slavery, American Freedom: The Ordeal of Colonial Virginia* (New York: Norton, 1975); Helen Rountree, *Pocahontas's People: The Powhatan Indians of Virginia through Four Centuries* (Norman: University of Oklahoma Press, 1990); Ian K. Steele, *Warpaths: Invasions of North America* (New York: Oxford University Press, 1994); Richard R. White, *The Middle Ground: Indians, Empires, and Republics in the Great Lakes Region, 1650–1815* (Cambridge: Cambridge University Press, 1991).

On witchcraft in colonial America: Paul Boyer and Stephen Nissenbaum, *Salem Possessed: The Social Origins of Witchcraft* (Cambridge, MA: Harvard University Press, 1974); John Demos, *Entertaining Satan: Witchcraft and the Culture of Early New England* (New York: Oxford University Press, 1982); Richard Godbeer, *The Devil's Dominion: Magic and Religion in Early New England* (Cambridge: Cambridge University Press, 1992); Carol F. Karlsen, *The Devil in the Shape of a Woman: Witch-*

craft in Colonial New England (New York: Norton, 1987); Mary Beth Norton, *In the Devil's Snare: The Salem Witchcraft Crisis of 1692* (New York: Knopf, 2002).

On violence within colonial society: Lawrence M. Friedman, *Crime and Punishment in American History* (New York: Perseus, 1994); Eric H. Monkkonen, ed., *Crime and Justice in American History: The Colonies and Early Republic*, 2 vols. (Westport, CT: Meckler, 1991); Elizabeth Pleck, *Domestic Tyranny: The Making of Social Policy against Family Violence from Colonial Times to the Present* (New York: Oxford University Press, 1987); Wilcomb E. Washburn, *The Governor and the Rebel: A History of Bacon's Rebellion in Virginia* (Chapel Hill: University of North Carolina Press, 1957).

THREE

REVOLUTIONARY VIOLENCE

Though founded by a revolution, the United States does not have a significantly revolutionary history in the ensuing two centuries. By revolutionary, we mean the desire to challenge and transform existing social and/or political structures. Crowds would take over the streets, but generally with very immediate goals. Slaves would rise in rebellion in hopes of attaining their freedom, though there is little evidence to suggest that anyone until John Brown in the late 1850s hoped thereby to transform the country.[1] Political campaigns and ideas could inspire thousands, but often just to take part in barbeques and parades, as would be the case in the election of 1840. These actions had little long-term impact.

The American colonies inherited a tradition of crowd action from England. Violence was not integral to this tradition, at least not violence against persons. Attacks on property were a very different matter. By the seventeenth century, assaults on the property of prominent individuals by angry crowds seemed almost an accepted part of English life. Those menacing the perceived "customary rights" of the common people were particular targets. For instance, rural crowds tore down the fences and walls of aristocrats attempting to enclose common land or traditional tenancies, and in the towns they occasionally smashed the windows of the gentry. Courts were favored targets in both England and America, as crowds sought to prevent the serving of warrants, the collection of debts, and the punishment of other members of their communities.

In England at least, violence against persons remained the preserve of the

---

1. Though David Walker hinted at such a strategy in his controversial pamphlet *To the Colored Citizens of the World* (Boston, 1829). Walker vanished mysteriously shortly after the publication of this work.

state. The government accepted a certain level of crowd activity: protests, public displays of dissatisfaction, burning of effigies, and even damage to private property. But if a crowd showed any sign of getting out of control, of extending its actions beyond a single event or community, or if officials became the target of their ire, then the government sent in the army to clarify the lines of authority in England.

Yet the elite understood that they could not push back too hard. On most occasions prior to the 1760s, crowds dispersed when the army appeared. If they did not, the army would seize a few "leaders" of the mob and occasionally even execute them. But the sort of wholesale slaughter of protesters that would become common in the aftermath of the French Revolution was unknown. The English government always had before it the example of Charles I, whose efforts to extract even more profit from his royal forests had raised popular opposition and, combined with other factors, eventually led to his beheading. When Queen Caroline, the wife of George II, wanted to close St. James Park to the public, she "asked Sir Robert Walpole what it would cost her to do it. He replied, 'Only a *crown*, Madam.' "[2] The park remained public.

Fortunately for the elite, English crowds, either rural or urban, behaved with a notable lack of violence. For the gentry, as E. P. Thompson noted, "the insubordination of the poor was an inconvenience; it was not a menace."[3]

These same standards made their way across the Atlantic. There were a few significant differences between England and North America, though, chief among these being that the local governments generally had to rely on the militia rather than the army to quiet any crowd actions that got out of hand. There was, however, a core problem with that reliance: too often the *militia was* the crowd. On numerous occasions local authorities called out the militia only to discover that most of its membership, including the officers, were in the crowd the officials sought to pacify. And often the local officials themselves were leading the crowds, if for no other reason than because it was safer to be on the side of the majority of one's community than to serve a distant government with which one did not have to live day after day. As Michael Zuckerman has written, a rural crowd "was most clearly the ultimate expression of a community consensus, for no mob could have existed for more than a moment in those towns without the toleration of the people."[4] As a consequence, the Amer-

---

2. Horace Walpole, *Memoirs of the Reign of King George II*, 3 vols. (London: H. Colburn, 1847), 2: 220-21; Robert Shoemaker, *The London Mob: Violence and Disorder in Eighteenth-Century England* (London: Hambledon and London, 2004).

3. E. P. Thompson, "Patrician Society, Plebian Culture," *Journal of Social History* 7 (1974): 387.

4. Michael Zuckerman, *Peaceable Kingdoms: New England Towns in the Eighteenth Century* (New York: Knopf, 1970), 245.

ican crowd could pretty much do as it pleased, so long as it did not slip over into anything approximating a revolutionary threat.

What is notable, therefore, is how seldom that happened. American crowds, like those in England, relied primarily on intimidation to effect their ends, on the aggressive display of social power rather than on destructive injury. There would be a great deal of shouting and posturing, threats and denunciations, public humiliations and some breaking of windows, but almost no physical violence. On a few occasions, however, that accepted barrier broke down. We have already seen one example with Bacon's Rebellion, where divisions within the elite aggravated political dissent and almost led to the overthrow of the colonial government.

For the next ninety years the American colonies witnessed only the most minor tremors of political dissatisfaction. There were a few anti-inoculation riots, some battles between powerful landowners in the Chesapeake, and, the direst threat of all, the Stono Rebellion in South Carolina in 1739 and 1740, in which sixty slaves slaughtered whites and made a break for freedom. While the white demonstrations were treated mildly, with no more than a broken bone or two involved, slave uprisings, real or imagined, evoked an immediate and brutal response from the colonial governments. This history indicates two larger aspects of American violence in the colonial period. First, American crowds were not mindless, violent mobs, as they were often portrayed by critics within the contemporary elite and by many later historians. Rather, they were focused and direct, with a fine sense of the uses of aggression and the limits of their own power. Second, whites tended to reserve lethal violence for nonwhites.

The first indication that the traditional way of conducting crowd action might be changing came with the Stamp Act crisis of 1765. The British government, seeking to pay off its enormous debt from the Seven Years' War, passed a number of new taxes, including one on the American colonies requiring that all documents—defined to include nearly everything from marriage certificates to newspapers—carry a government stamp. What followed was far from the traditional, short-lived, and geographically isolated protest over some local matter. Instead, opposition to the Stamp Act was sustained, organized, and wideranging. There were demonstrations in every colony over several months, coordinated by ad hoc committees of correspondence. The British Empire had never seen anything quite like this resistance, which verged dangerously, from the point of view of the imperial government, on revolution.

Yet one way in which the crowds protesting the Stamp Act did not differ from traditional standards was in their avoidance of personal violence. Crowds burned prime ministers in effigy, threw stones through the windows of British officials, and intimidated every stamp officer but one into resigning his office;

but there were only a few scuffles and no deaths in these extensive political protests. That reticence to commit acts of deadly violence showed evidence of slipping in 1770. When personal violence ensued, as it did in North Carolina and Boston in 1770, it was as a consequence of the intransigence of government officials rather than as a result of disorder from below. After all, American protesters had every reason to avoid a military confrontation, for England had the most powerful and effective military in the world—as had been abundantly demonstrated in the Seven Years' War that ended in 1763. Yet the same fact led the British government to act with extreme confidence, certain that its military could defeat a bunch of poorly armed American peasants. It was an understandable assurance, but one that could easily spill over into a debilitating arrogance.

DOCUMENTS

THE NORTH CAROLINA REGULATORS

The Regulator movement, as it is known, spread quickly through the western areas of the Carolinas. The residents of this region were denied both fair representation in the legislature, which was dominated by the great "tidewater families," and the most essential services of government. The court system posed a particular grievance, as it rarely met and operated primarily in the interest of those connected to government. One result of this perceived bias in the system was a failure to prosecute criminals. The Regulators claimed that they had to act because the government would not.

The South Carolina Regulators posed no visible threat to government. Demanding more law enforcement is not very revolutionary, especially when the request came in such a polite fashion. Their only confrontation with the government came in early 1769 at the Musgrove Plantation on the Saluda River. But the battle was canceled when both sides proved unwilling to fight. Instead, they agreed that "the name of Regulators should be abolished, and that, for the future, the law should take its course without opposition."[5]

The Regulator movement caused much more concern for the government of North Carolina, largely because Governor William Tryon was unwilling to compromise. In April 1768 the sheriff of Orange County seized a horse from a farmer for failure to pay taxes, only to have a crowd of one hundred liberate the horse from the county seat in Hillsborough. A government officer, Edmund Fanning, who also happened to be a close friend of Governor Tryon, called out the militia, but they refused to appear for duty, though many of them were already present in the crowd. Instead, the crowd fired a few shots through Fanning's windows as a warning.

5. Richard Maxwell Brown, *The South Carolina Regulators* (Cambridge, MA: Harvard University Press, 1963), 94.

The North Carolina Regulators had almost nothing in common with the brutal Paxton Boys of Pennsylvania, and they showed little desire for violence. Herman Husband, the most visible Regulator leader, was a pacifist who relied on nonviolent methods of protest. The local sheriff arrested Husband and another leader, putting them in the Hillsborough jail. In response, an estimated seven hundred people surrounded the jail, demanding the release of the prisoners. The sheriff, who also hoped to avoid violence if only because he was terribly outnumbered, released his prisoners.

Governor Tryon accused the Regulators of "assuming to themselves Powers and Authorities unknown to the Constitution of calling Publick Officers to a settlement"—which is to say, of holding officials responsible for the fulfillment of their duties.[6] But when Tryon called out the Orange County militia to confront the Regulators, only four hundred men responded to his summons. In contrast, more than one thousand men responded to the Regulators' call. Tryon wisely negotiated a compromise that led to the resolution of most of the existing court cases. Declaring that order had been restored, Tryon disbanded the militia and returned east.

With a sense of certainty that they spoke for their communities, the leaders of the Regulators drafted petitions to the Superior Court of North Carolina setting out their grievances. Above all else they wanted fair courts that met regularly and within a day's journey of their settlements. It has been estimated that between six and seven thousand of the eight thousand adult white males in the three western counties of Orange, Anson, and Rowan supported the Regulators.[7] The following petition is from Orange County. To its authors this petition evidenced no challenge to established authorities, but rather a desire to spread government more extensively. The authorities themselves felt differently, Governor Tryon especially seeing the petition as a direct challenge to his rule.

The Petition from the Inhabitants of Orange County, North Carolina

[Undated but probably early September 1770]

... [W]e have labored honestly for our Bread and studied to defraud no man nor live on the spoils of other mens labors nor snatched the Bread out of other mens hands. Our only crime with which they can charge us is vertue in the very highest degree namely to risque our all to save our Country from Rapine and Slavery in our detecting of practices which the Law itself allows to be worse than open Robbery—It is not one in a hundred or a thousand of

6. William L. Saunders et al., eds., *The Colonial Records of North Carolina*, 30 vols. (Raleigh: State of North Carolina, 1886–1914), 7:792.
7. Marvin L. Michael Kay, "The North Carolina Regulation, 1766–1776: A Class Conflict," in Alfred F. Young, ed., *The American Revolution: Explorations in the History of American Radicalism* (De Kalb: Northern Illinois University Press, 1976), 73.

us who have broke one Law in this our struggle for only common Justice which it is even a shame for any Government or any set of Men in the Law once to have denied us off—Whereas them as has acted the most legally are the most torn to pieces by the Law through malicious prosecutions parried against them.

To sum up the whole matter of our Petition in a few words it is namely these that we may obtain unprejudiced Jurys, That all extortionate Officers Lawyers and Clerks may be brought to fair Tryals—That the Collectors of publick money may be called to proper settlements of their accounts. . . . If We cannot obtain this that we may have some security for our properties more than the bare humour of officers, we can see plainly that we shall not be able to live under such oppressions and to what extremities this must drive us you can as well judge of as we can ourselves, we having no other determination but to be redressed and that to be in a legal and lawful way. . . .

Signed by 174 Subscribers

Source: William L. Saunders, ed., *The Colonial Records of North Carolina*, 30 vols. (Raleigh, NC: J. Daniels, 1886–1914), 8:234.

Judge Richard Henderson, associate justice of the North Carolina Superior Court, was one of the recipients of this petition, and the first to encounter its words translated into action. Henderson was riding circuit when he arrived in Hillsborough, in the western part of North Carolina. There a mob confronted him with the unusual demand that the court hear cases, but without lawyers. In the following report addressed to Governor Tryon, Henderson describes his exchanges with the Regulators, whom he estimates as 150 in number. The type of weapons used by each side and the level of violence employed are of considerable significance, as is the failure of the officials to respond more aggressively.

Judge Richard Henderson Confronts a Riot in Hillsborough, North Carolina, 1770

September 29, 1770

. . . On Monday last being the second day of Hillsborough Superior Court, early in the morning the Town was filled with a great number of these people shouting[,] hallooing & making a considerable tumult in the streets. At about 11 o'clock the Court was opened, and immediately the House filled as close as one man could stand by another, some with clubs others with whips and switches, few or none without some weapon. When the House had become so crowded that no more could well get in, one of them (whose name I think is called Fields) came forward and told me he had something to say before I proceeded to business. . . . Thus I found myself under a necessity of attempting to soften and turn away the fury of this mad people, in the best manner in my power, and as much as could well be, pacifie their rage and at the same time preserve the little remaining dignity of the Court. The consequence of which was that after spending upwards of half an hour in this disagreeable situation the mob cried out "Retire, retire, and let the Court go on." Upon which most of the regulators went out and seemed to be in consultation in a party by themselves.

The little hopes of peace derived from this piece of behaviour were very transient, for in a few minutes Mr. Williams an Attorney of that Court was coming in and had advanced near the door when they fell on him in a most furious manner with Clubs and sticks of enormous size and it was with great difficulty he saved his life by taking shelter in a neighbouring Store House. Mr. [Edmund] Fanning was next the object of their fury, him they seized and took with a degree of violence not to be described from off the bench where he had retired for protection and assistance and with hideous shouts of barbarian cruelty dragged him by the heels out of doors, while others engaged in dealing out blows with such violence that I made no doubt his life would instantly become a sacrifice to their rage and madness. However Mr. Fanning by a manly exertion miraculously broke holt and fortunately jumped into a door that saved him from immediate dissolution. During the uproar several of them told me with oaths of great bitterness that my turn should be next. I will not deny that in this frightful affair my thoughts were much engaged on my own protection, but it was not long before James Hunter and some other of their Chieftains came and told me not to be uneasy for that no man should hurt me on proviso I would set and hold Court to the end of the term.

I took advantage of this proposal and made no scruple at promising what was not in my intention to perform for the Terms they would admit me to hold Court on were that no Lawyer, the King's Attorney excepted, should be admitted into Court, and that they would stay and see justice impartially done.

It would be impertinent to trouble your Exc[ellenc]y with many circumstances that occurred in this barbarous riot, Messrs. Thomas Hart, Alexander Martin, Michael Holt, John Litterell (Clerk of the Crown) and many others were severely whipped. Col. Gray, Major Lloyd, Mr. Francis Nash, John Cooke, Tyree Harris and sundry other persons timorously made their escape or would have shared the same fate. In about four or five hours their rage seemed to subside a little and they permitted me to adjourn Court and conducted me with great parade to my lodgings. Col. Fanning whom they had made a prisoner of [war] was in the evening permitted to return to his own House on his word of honour to surrender himself next day. At about ten o'clock that evening, I took an opportunity of making my escape by a back way, and left poor Col. Fanning and the little Borough in a wretched situation.

. . . They soon after to consummate their wicked designs, broke and entered his Mansion House, destroyed every article of furniture with axes & other instruments laid the Fabrick level with its foundation, broke and entered his Cellar and destroyed the contents, his Papers were carried into the streets by armfulls and destroyed, his wearing apparel shared the same fate; I much fear his Office will be their next object. . . . The merchants and Inhabitants were chiefly run out into the Country & expect their Stores and Houses without distinction will we [be] pillaged and laid waste. . . .

Source: William L. Saunders, ed., *The Colonial Records of North Carolina*, 30 vols. (Raleigh, NC: J. Daniels, 1886–1914), 8:241–43.

Up until this point, everything happened in accordance with established modes of behavior. The legislature even refused to compensate Fanning for his losses, determining that he was guilty of most of the charges made against him. In such ways did local elites traditionally attempt to mute dissent, acknowledging flaws in the system by pinning them on a single corrupt individual rather than calling the whole political structure into question. As a consequence, most Regulators felt that they had reached a compromise with the government and that they could expect most of their demands to be met in the near future.

But then Governor Tryon changed the procedure by calling out the eastern *militia. Tryon held that the province could not have competing centers of power and that the Regulators threatened to destabilize government. His first effort to use eastern militia against the Regulators in the spring of 1769 collapsed when a group of Regulators disguised as slaves destroyed most of his gunpowder. He tried again the following spring, marching toward Hillsborough with twelve hundred men. On May 15, 1770, a group of Regulators beat two militia officers loyal to Tryon. The governor resolved to do battle near the Alamance River, where the two forces met the following day. Initially Tryon's militia refused his order to fire. But once they started, they found it difficult to stop. Tryon enjoyed some significant advantages: more guns and gunpowder, several cannon, and a willingness to use lethal force. Finally Tryon ordered a charge and chased the Regulators off, his forces then setting the nearby woods on fire, the flames claiming several lives. The coastal militia suffered nine deaths, the Regulators between ten and twenty. The Regulator movement came to an almost immediate end. The* Virginia Gazette *of Williamsburg provided the following account.*

The *Virginia Gazette* Reports on the Battle of Alamance, 1771

May 16, 1771

Governour Tryon had under him a Thousand Men, and that the Regulators amounted to three and twenty Hundred; that his Excellency was much insulted by them, particularly one Fellow, whom he shot dead on the Spot, as he was approaching him; that this happened but a very short Time before the Expiration of the two Hours allowed them by the Governour [to surrender], upon which the Engagement began; that both Parties fought with great Animosity, for two Hours and upwards; that the Artillery was discharged six and thirty Times, and that one Shot struck a Tree, which in its Fall killed thirty odd of the Regulators; that the Governour had his horse killed under him, and the Breech of the Gun he had in his Hand shot away; that a Hundred and sixty of the Regulators were killed, and two Hundred wounded, forty of whom were taken Prisoners; that the Regulators were badly conducted, and fought in the utmost Confusion, their Ranks being, in some Places, a Hundred Men deep, and that many of them were unarmed; that the Governour had only two Men killed, and sixty wounded. . . .

The Families of these poor deluded People are much to be pitied, as they must be reduced to very great Distress. The Province likewise, in general, is in the greatest Disorder. And however faulty those who stile themselves Regulators may have been, as we learn that the Cause of their Complaints has been removed (their Leaders, it is probable, being bad Counsellors, . . . urged them on from one Step of Rebellion to another) it ought to be a Lesson for all good Governments to suffer no Set of Men, under the Sanction of Authority, to fleece the People.

Source: *Virginia Gazette* (Williamsburg), June 6, 1771.

THE BOSTON MASSACRE

Americans took to the streets often between 1765 and 1775, with a slow acceleration in the levels of violence. American crowds, rural and urban, moved from humiliating to beating to tarring and feathering their enemies, but they still refrained from killing them, with the single exception of the Battle of Alamance, where the government's troops had fired first. But even then, for a crowd to return fire was without precedent, and the confrontation at Alamance should have served as a warning to officials, had they been paying closer attention.

In the late 1760s British soldiers and artisans fought a series of violent street battles in New York, with both sides suffering many injuries. But fists and sticks had been the weapons used, limiting the level of injury to bruises and contusions. The worst incident of violence in these political upheavals of the 1760s in Boston came when customs collector John Robinson beat patriot leader James Otis unconscious with a cane, Otis suffering mental problems for the rest of his life. But on March 5, 1770, British soldiers ratcheted up the level of violence by opening fire on an angry crowd and killing five men.

The crowd gathered outside the Customs House had come to protest British policies, specifically the presence of British regulars in Boston. There was some disagreement over the behavior of the crowd. Did their hurling of insults give way to stones or snowballs? Were those snowballs wrapped around rocks? Did the British commander order his troops to fire, or was it all a terrible accident? The soldiers had clearly been provoked, yet their use of firearms shocked the American public. Paul Revere issued a famous woodcut showing massed troops firing a volley at a perceptibly nonviolent crowd while an officer raises his sword giving the order to fire.

The people of Boston were outraged by the "Massacre," called the "King Street Riot" by supporters of the Crown. They responded, however, not with a lynch mob but by bringing the soldiers to justice, charging them with murder in a civilian court. John Adams, a leader of the resistance, defended them brilliantly. Adams felt not only that the soldiers deserved the ablest legal defense they could get—and Adams felt he was best qualified in that regard—but also that the crowd had acted inappropriately by hurling stones at the soldiers without cause. In this instance, it had been the crowd that violated tradition. That perceived standard of conduct helps to explain why a Boston jury found the soldiers innocent.

The following account was published "by Order of the Town of Boston" shortly after the event, becoming the standard patriot perspective of the "Massacre."

The Town of Boston Presents Its Version of the Massacre, 1770

. . . Capt. Wilson, of the 59th, exciting the negroes of the town to take away their masters' lives and property, and repair to the army for protection, which was fully proved against him—the attack of a party of soldiers on some of the magistrates of the town—the repeated rescues of soldiers from peace officers—the firing of a loaded musket in a public street, to the endangering of a great number of peaceable inhabitants—the frequent wounding of persons by their bayonets and cutlasses, and the numerous instances of bad behavior in the soldiery, made us early sensible that the troops were not sent here for any benefit to the town or province, and that we had no good to expect from such conservators of the peace.

It was not expected, however, that such an outrage and massacre, as happened here on the evening of the fifth instant, would have been perpetrated. There were then killed and wounded, by a discharge of musketry, eleven of his majesty's subjects, viz.:

Mr. Samuel Gray, killed on the spot by a ball entering his head.

Crispus Attucks, a mulatto, killed on the spot, two balls entering his breast.

Mr. James Caldwell, killed on the spot, by two balls entering his back.

Mr. Samuel Maverick, a youth of seventeen years of age, mortally wounded; he died the next morning.

Mr. Patrick Carr mortally wounded; he died the 14th instant.

Christopher Monk and John Clark, youths about seventeen years of age, dangerously wounded. It is apprehended they will die.

Mr. Edward Payne, merchant, standing at his door; wounded.

Messrs. John Green, Robert Patterson, and David Parker; all dangerously wounded.

The actors in this dreadful tragedy were a party of soldiers commanded by Capt. Preston of the 29th regiment. This party, including the captain, consisted of eight, who are all committed to jail. . . .

Benjamin Frizell, on the evening of the 5th of March, having taken his station near the west corner of the Custom-house in King street, before and at the time of the soldiers firing their guns, declares (among other things) that the first discharge was only of one gun, the next of two guns, upon which he the deponent thinks he saw a man stumble; the third discharge was of three guns, upon which he thinks he saw two men fall; and immediately after were discharged five guns, two of which were by soldiers on his right hand; the other three, as appeared to the deponent, were discharged from the balcony, or the chamber window of the Custom-house, the flashes appearing on the left hand, and higher than the right hand flashes appeared to be, and of which the deponent was very sensible, although his eyes were much turned to the soldiers, who were all on his right hand. . . . [Six more depositions follow]

What gave occasion to the melancholy event of that evening seems to have been this. A difference having happened near Mr. Gray's ropewalk, between a soldier and a man belonging to it, the soldier challenged the ropemakers to a boxing match. The challenge was accepted by one of them, and the soldier worsted. He ran to the barrack in the neighborhood, and returned with several of his companions. The fray was renewed, and the soldiers were driven off. They soon returned with recruits, and were again worsted. This happened several times, till at length a considerable body of soldiers was collected, and they also were driven off, the ropemakers having been joined by their brethren of the contiguous ropewalks. By this time Mr. Gray being alarmed inter[p]osed, and with the assistance of some gentlemen prevented any further disturbance. To satisfy the soldiers and punish the man who had been the occasion of the first difference, and as an example to the rest, he turned him out of his service; and waited on Col. Dalrymple, the commanding officer of the troops, and with him concerted measures for preventing further mischief. Though this affair ended thus, it made a strong impression on the minds of the soldiers in general, who thought the honor of the regiment concerned to revenge those repeated repulses. For this purpose they seem to have formed a combination to commit some outrage upon the inhabitants of the town indiscriminately; and this was to be done on the evening of the 5th instant or soon after; as appears by the depositions of the following persons, viz.:

William Newhall declares, that on Thursday night the 1st of March instant, he met four soldiers of the 29th regiment, and that he heard them say, "there were a great many that would eat their dinners on Monday next, that should not eat any on Tuesday."

Daniel Calfe declares, that on Saturday evening the 3d of March, a camp-woman, wife to James McDeed, a grenadier of the 29th, came into his father's shop, and the people talking about the affrays at the ropewalks, and blaming the soldiers for the part they had acted in it, the woman said, "the soldiers were in the right;" adding, "that before Tuesday or Wednesday night they would wet their swords or bayonets in New England people's blood." . . . [Seven more depositions follow]

By the foregoing depositions it appears very clearly, there was a general combination among the soldiers of the 29th regiment at least, to commit some extraordinary act of violence upon the town. . . .

The outrageous behaviour and the threats of the [soldiers] occasioned the ringing of the meeting-house bell near the head of King street, which bell ringing quick, as for fire, it presently brought out a number of the inhabitants, who being soon sensible of the occasion of it, were naturally led to King street. . . . [T]here was much foul language between them [the soldiers and the public], and some of them, in consequence of [a sentry] pushing at them with his bayonet, threw snowballs at him, which occasioned him to knock hastily at the door of the Custom-house. . . . The officer on guard was Capt. Preston, who with seven or eight soldiers, with fire-arms and charged bayonets, issued from the guard house, and in great haste posted himself and his soldiers in front of the Custom-house, near the corner. . . . In passing to this station the soldiers pushed several persons with their bayonets, driving through the people in so rough a manner that it appeared they intended to create a disturbance. This occasioned some snowballs to be thrown at them, which seems to have been the only provocation that was given. . . .

The [soldiers] formed into a half circle; and within a short time after they had been posted at the Custom-house, began to fire upon the people.

Captain Preston is said to have ordered them to fire, and to have repeated that order. One gun was fired first; and then others in succession, and with deliberation, till ten or a dozen guns were fired. . . . By which means eleven persons were killed and wounded. . . .

One happy effect has arisen from this melancholy affair, and it is the general voice of the town and province . . . [that] all the troops are removed from the town. They are quartered for the present in the barracks at Castle island; from whence it is hoped they will have a speedy order to remove entirely out of the province, together with those persons who were the occasion of their coming hither.

Source: Frederic Kidder, ed., *History of the Boston Massacre* (Albany, NY: J. Munsell, 1870), 29–35, 39–42.

THE AMERICAN REVOLUTION BEGINS

Historians have long debated just how revolutionary was the American Revolution. As Alfred F. Young has written, "Those who took a radical stand against Great Britain were not necessarily radical on internal matters; quite the contrary. And conversely, those who were radical on internal matters were not necessarily radical towards Britain or even part of the patriot movement."[8] For instance, many former Regulators sided with the British during the Revolution, since the coastal elite who had oppressed them for so long led the movement for independence. But as the opposition to England moved from, in Pauline Maier's words, "resistance to revolution,"[9] most of those who hoped to effect significant political change came around to the cause of American independence. Those who hoped for some more fundamental alteration in society were largely disappointed.

Throughout the first decade of their political battle with England, Americans had adhered to traditional ways of protesting government policies. With the possible exception of the Boston Massacre, the government had responded to these protests in a customary manner, often by giving in. The Stamp Act crisis witnessed the types of public gatherings, petitions to Parliament, and even the intimidation of officials that anyone in England would have recognized. None of that was new, nor was the fact that the Crown repealed the Stamp Act, though it insisted it was doing so at the request of British merchants rather than because of American protests. Even the Boston Tea Party can be understood as an extravagant form of traditional modes of protest through the destruction of property,

8. Alfred F. Young, "Introduction," in Young, *American Revolution*, x.
9. Pauline Maier, *From Resistance to Revolution: Colonial Radicals and the Development of American Opposition to Britain, 1765–1776* (New York: Knopf, 1972).

albeit with a surprising panache. Provoked by the Tea Party, the government should have responded with a show of force, and perhaps the trial of some obvious leaders as an example to His Majesty's subjects in Massachusetts. At least that is what custom demanded.

But by 1773 the British government feared that the distance to North America was so great and the colonists so out of control that the normal political discourse had collapsed. Guided by Prime Minister Lord North, Parliament attempted to both punish Massachusetts and limit the ability of the Americans to move beyond traditional forms of nonviolent protest. In addition to revoking the charter of Massachusetts, thus shutting down its political institutions, and closing the port of Boston until it paid the East India Company £10,000 for the destroyed tea, Parliament also lay an embargo on all firearms and their accessories, lead, and gunpowder in October 1774. By these measures Parliament hoped to both isolate Massachusetts and keep the radical Americans from launching an effective resistance to the British government. Instead, it precipitated the American Revolution.

Through the winter of 1775 New Englanders prepared for a conflict they knew was coming. Munitions were collected and purchased—even from England in violation of the embargo—and militia units trained more seriously than they had at any time in the eighteenth century. The British sent spies through the countryside while Americans hostile to the government attempted to close the roads out of Boston, where most of the British troops were stationed. General Thomas Gage, commander of British forces in North America and military governor of Massachusetts, decided that he could put a quick halt to the emerging rebellion if he arrested a few prominent leaders such as Samuel Adams and John Hancock, and seized or destroyed the American munitions stockpiles. On the night of April 18 he ordered British regulars to slip quietly across the Charles River out of Boston and to march on Concord, the site of a large store of arms and powder. His intelligence also indicated that Hancock and Adams might be present in Concord.

Gage thought he could launch a surprise attack, but every movement of his troops was observed and reported. As the British rowed across the Charles River in the predawn hours of April 19, 1775, riders beat them across to spread the warning to the towns on the way to Concord, including the little village of Lexington.

The Reverend Jonas Clark was the minister of Lexington and a recent convert to the opposition to the British government. He arrived on the green just a moment after the brief firing that marked the encounter between British troops and American farmers. The following description of events began as a sermon and ended as a political pamphlet demanding vengeance. Clark carefully and repeatedly insists that the Americans had no desire to begin the war.

Reverend Jonas Clark Describes the Encounter at Lexington, 1775

Between the hours of *twelve* and *one*, on the morning of the NINE-TEENTH OF APRIL, we received intelligence, by express, from the Honorable JOSEPH WARREN, Esq., at *Boston*, "that a large body of the *king's troops* (supposed to be a brigade of about 12 or 1500) were embarked in boats from *Boston*. . . . And that it was shrewdly suspected, that they were ordered to seize and destroy the *stores, belonging to the colony, then deposited at Concord.*" . . .

. . . [T]he *militia* of the town were alarmed, and ordered to meet on the usual place of parade; not with any design of *commencing hostilities* upon the *king's troops*, but to consult what might be done for our own and the people's safety: And also to be ready for whatever service providence might call us out to, upon this alarming occasion, in case *overt acts* of *violence, or open hostilities* should be committed by this *mercenary band of armed and blood-thirsty oppressors.*

About the same time, two persons were sent express to *Cambridge*, if possible, to gain intelligence of the motions of the troops. . . .

The *militia* met according to order; and waited the return of the messengers. . . . Between 3 and 4 o'clock, one of the expresses returned, informing, that there was no appearance of the troops, on the roads, either from *Cambridge* or *Charlestown*; and that it was supposed that the *movements in the army* the evening before, were only a *feint* to alarm the people. Upon this, therefore, the *militia company* were dismissed for the present, but with orders to be within call of the drum,—waiting the return of the other messenger. . . . But he was prevented by their [the British] silent and sudden arrival at the place where he was, waiting for intelligence. So that, after all this precaution, we had no notice of their approach,'till the *brigade was actually in the town*, and upon a quick march within about a mile and a quarter of the *meeting house* and *place of parade*.

However, the commanding officer thought best to call the company together,—not with any design of opposing so superior a force, *much less of commencing hostilities*; but only with a view to determine what to do. . . .

Accordingly, about half an hour after four o'clock, *alarm guns were fired, and the drums beat to arms*; and the *militia* were collecting together.—Some, to the number of about 50, or 60, or possibly more, were on the parade, others were coming towards it.

In the mean time, the troops, having thus stolen a march upon us, and to prevent any intelligence of their approach, having seized and held prisoners several persons whom they met *unarmed* upon the road, seemed to come *determined* for MURDER and BLOODSHED; and that whether provoked to it, or not!

When within about half a quarter of a mile of the *meeting-house*, they halted, and the command was given to *prime* and *load*, which being done, they marched on 'till they came up to the east end of said meeting-house, in sight of our *militia* (collecting as aforesaid) who were about 12 or 13 rods distant.—

Immediately upon their appearing *so suddenly*, and *so nigh*, Capt. *Parker*, who commanded the *militia company*, ordered the men to disperse, and take care of themselves; and *not to fire*. Upon this, our men dispersed;—but, many of them, not so speedily as they might have done. . . .

For, no sooner did they [the British] come in sight of our company, but one of them, supposed to be an officer of rank, was heard to say to the troops, "*Damn them; we will have them!*"—Upon which the troops shouted aloud, huzza'd, and rushed furiously towards our men.—

About the same time, three officers (supposed to be Col. *Smith*, Major *Pitcairn* and another officer) advanced, on horse back, to the front of the body, and coming within 5 or 6 rods of the *militia*, one of them cried out, "*ye villains, ye Rebels, disperse; Damn you, disperse!*"—or words to this effect. One of them (whether the same, or not, is not easily determined) said, "*Lay down your arms; Damn you, why don't you lay down your arms!*"—The second of these officers, about this time, fired a pistol towards the *militia*, as they were dispersing.—The foremost, who was within a few yards of our men, brandishing his sword, and then pointing towards them, with a loud voice said, to the troops, "Fire!—By God, fire!"—which was instantly followed by a discharge of arms from the said troops, succeeded by a very heavy and close fire upon our party, dispersing, so long as any of them were within reach.—*Eight were left dead upon the ground! Ten were wounded.*—The rest of the company, through divine goodness, were (to a miracle) preserved unhurt in this *murderous* action! . . .

After the *militia company* were dispersed and the firing ceased, the troops drew up and formed, in a body on the common, *fired a volley* and *gave three huzzas*, by way of *triumph*, and as expressive of the *joy of VICTORY* and *glory of CONQUEST*!—Of this transaction, I was a witness, having at that time, a fair view of their motions, and being at the distance of not more than 70 or 80 rods from them. . . .

Source: Jonas Clark, *The Fate of Blood-thirsty Oppressors, and God's Tender Care of His Distressed People* (Boston: Powars and Willis, 1776), "A Narrative," 2–5.

Ensign Henry De Bernicre had a slightly different version of these events. In February 1775 General Gage sent De Bernicre and a Captain Brown out to secretly reconnoiter the roads and terrain of the countryside outside of Boston "as he expected to march troops through that country the ensuing Spring."[10] *The British were almost entirely ignorant of the territory in which they were to operate. De Bernicre and Brown traveled "disguised like countrymen, in brown cloaths and reddish handkerchiefs round our necks."*[11] *A black woman waiting on table recognized them for British officers at their first stop in Charlestown. Almost everywhere they went the locals realized they were spies. Nonetheless, they returned to Boston unmolested. Gage sent them out again in late March to examine the roads to Concord.*

In British eyes, the vast majority of Americans were already rebels, though the war had not yet begun. Once Gage decided to move against the Americans, it seemed obvious that De Bernicre should guide the British troops on their march to Concord on April 19. Ensign De Bernicre, like the wider British public, was shocked that the Americans resisted His Majesty's regulars and actually returned fire. Such behavior defied all customary expectations. He could not imagine what inspired the Americans to fight back so vigorously. De Bernicre's notes were discovered in Boston after the British retreat in 1776 and published by J. Gill of Boston in 1779.

Ensign Henry De Bernicre Offers the British View of Lexington and Concord

On the night of the 18th of April 1774, at nine o'clock, the grenadiers and light infantry of the army at Boston, received orders to embark immediately under the command of Col. Smith, in the men of war's boats, and proceed according to his directions. They embarked at the common in Boston, and crossed to the shore lying between Charlestown and Cambridge, where they landed and received a day's provisions:

They began their march about twelve o'clock for Concord, that being the place they were ordered to go to, for the purpose of destroying some military stores laid up there by the rebels.

The troops received no interruption in their march until they arrived at Lexington, a town eleven miles from Boston, where there were about 150 rebels drawn out in divisions, with intervals as wide as the front of the divisions; the light infantry who marched in front halted, and Major Pitcairn came up immediately and cried out to the rebels to throw down their arms and disperse, which they did not do; he called out a second time, but to no purpose; upon which he ordered our light-infantry to advance and disarm them, which they were doing, when one of the rebels fired a shot, our soldiers returned the fire and killed about fourteen of them; there was only one

10. Henry De Bernicre, "Notes," *Collections of the Massachusetts Historical Society*, 2nd ser., 4 (1816): 203.
11. Ibid.

of the 10th light-infantry received a shot through his leg; some of them got into the church and fired from it, but were soon drove out.

We then continued our march for Concord, and arrived there between nine and ten o'clock in the morning of the 19th April, the light-infantry marched on the hills that lay the length of the town, and the grenadiers took the lower road immediately on our arrival; Capt. Parsons of the 10th, was dispatched with six light-companies to take possession of a bridge that lay three quarters of a mile from Concord, and I was ordered to shew him the road there, and also to conduct him to a house where there was some cannon and other stores hid; when we arrived at the bridge, three companies under the command of Capt. Lowry of the 43d, were left to protect it, these three companies were not close together, but situated so as to be able to support each other; we then proceeded to Col. Barrett's, where these stores were, we did not find so much as we expected, but what there was we destroyed;

[I]n the mean time Capt. Lowry and his party were attacked by about 1500 rebels and drove from the bridge, three officers were wounded and one killed, three soldiers were killed and a number wounded, notwithstanding they let Capt. Parsons with his three companies return, and never attacked us; they had taken up some of the planks of the bridge, but we got over; had they destroyed it we were most certainly all lost; however, we joined the main body.

Col. Smith during our absence, had sent Capt. Pole of 10th regiment, to destroy some provisions and cannon that were lodged in another part of the town, he knock'd the trunnions off three iron 24 pound cannon and burnt their carriages; they also destroyed a quantity of flour, and some barrels of trenchers and spoons of wood for their camp.

Upon the different detachment's joining the main body, and after getting some horses and chaises for the wounded, we began the march to return to Boston, about twelve o'clock in the day, in the same order of march, only our flankers were more numerous and further from the main body; all the hills on each side of us were covered with rebels—there could not be less than 5000; so that they kept the road always lined and a very hot fire on us without intermission; we at first kept our order and returned their fire as hot as we received it, but when we arrived within a mile of Lexington, our ammunition began to fail, and the light companies were so fatigued with flanking they were scarce able to act, and a great number of wounded scarce able to get forward, made a great confusion;

Col. Smith (our commanding officer) had received a wound through his leg, a number of officers were also wounded, so that we began to run rather than retreat in order—the whole behaved with amazing bravery, but little order, we attempted to stop the men and form them two deep, but to no purpose, the confusion increased rather than lessened:

At last, after we got through Lexington, the officers got to the front and presented their bayonets, and told the men if they advanced they should die: Upon this they began to form under a very heavy fire; but at that instant, the first brigade joined us, consisting of the 4th, 23d, and 47th regiments, and two divisions of marines, under the command of Brigadier-General Lord Percy; he brought two field pieces with him, which were immediately brought to bear upon the rebels, and soon silenced their fire—

After a little firing the whole halted for about half an hour to rest. Lord Percy then made the light-infantry march in front, the grenadiers next, and the first brigade brought up the rear and sent out flankers; the rebels still kept firing on us, but very lightly until we came to Menotomy, a village with a number of houses in little groups extending about half a mile, out of these houses they kept a very heavy fire, but our troops broke into them and killed vast numbers; the souldiers shewed great bravery in this place, forcing houses from whence came a heavy fire, and killing great numbers of the rebels.

At about seven o'clock in the evening we arrived at Charlestown, they kept up a scattering fire at us all the way; at Charlestown we took possession of a hill that commanded the town, the Selectmen of which sent to Lord Percy to let him know that if he would not attack the town, they would take care that the troops should not be molested, and also they would do all in their power for to get us across the ferry; the Somerset man of war lay there at that time, and all her boats were employed first in getting over the wounded, and after them the rest of the troops; the piquets of 10th regiment, and some more troops, were sent over to Charlestown that night to keep every-thing quiet, and returned next day. The rebels shut up the neck, placed senti-nels there, and took prisoner an officer of the 64th regiment that was going to join his regiment at Castle William.—

So that in the course of two days, from a plentiful town, we were reduced to the disagreeable necessity of living on salt provisions, and fairly blocked up in Boston.

Return of the killed, wounded and missing, on the 19th of April, 1775, as made to General Gage. . . .

	Killed.	Wounded.	Missing.
Officers	2	13	3
Serjeants	2	7	1
Drummers	1	0	1
Rank and file	68	154	21
Total	73	174	26

Source: Henry De Bernicre, "Notes," *Collections of the Massachusetts Historical Society*, 2nd ser., 4 (1816): 215–19.

REVOLUTIONARY INSTITUTIONS

There were many revolutions in the 1770s and 1780s, and many distinctive perceptions of how best to attain the desired political ends. At first revolutionary leaders hoped that a demonstration of unity and virtue on the part of the Americans would persuade the British government to respect American rights. When they realized that they had a war on their hands, there was a great deal of disagreement over how to fight it. Many felt that the Americans should conduct a purely defensive war, with the militia rising to resist the British army wherever it went. Others ridiculed this idea as a certain route to failure. The militia performed well on a few occasions in a purely defensive capacity, but they did not sustain their commitment to service beyond a few days. They also showed a willingness to run away at the first sign of real combat. And at the start of the war Britain had only ten thousand troops in all of North America. What would happen when the mightiest empire in the world brought its full resources to bear? The colonies had to have a standing army, these leaders insisted, or the British would crush the revolution. This argument persuaded the Continental Congress to appoint George Washington of Virginia, in June 1775, to lead the Continental army, transforming a rebellion into a war of revolution.

Washington was consistently shocked by the difficulty of finding adequate numbers of troops and supplies. In a prosperous young country of nearly three million people, he was never able to field an army of more than twelve thousand men—though he did place a limit on himself by initially refusing to enlist black troops. Recruiters consistently found that Americans lacked enthusiasm for military service. Captain Alexander Graydon described as typical of those he was able to lure into Continental service in 1776, "A fellow . . . who would do to stop a bullet as well as a better man, and as he was a truly worthless dog, . . . that the neighborhood would be much indebted to us for taking him away."[12]

From such unlikely recruits did George Washington hope to construct a professional army capable of defeating the well-trained British regulars. The initial problem was that the Continental army contained very few officers with experience at training soldiers. In January 1778 Washington received invaluable assistance from a most unlikely figure, Friedrich Wilhelm, Baron von Steuben. Steuben inspired those he drilled and put his ideas on the proper training of troops into a book that served as the guide for the Continental army, Regulations for the Order and Discipline of the Troops of the United States *(which Steuben originally called "Infantry and Cavalry Tactics"). Steuben's letters and experiences point to the opportunities created for many people, including self-created Prussian aristocrats, by any revolution. Steuben left Europe a former captain of artillery and within a year was one of the most famous generals in America. Opportunities appeared for those included in its citizenry: white males.*

---

12. Alexander Graydon, *Memoirs of His Own Time* (Philadelphia: Lindsay and Blakiston, 1846), 136.

Major General Steuben on the Opportunities of War, 1779

Major-General Steuben to Privy-Counsellor Baron de Frank . . . July 4, 1779

. . . My services as a volunteer lasted no longer than five weeks, during which I drilled the army and made various dispositions in it which met with such approbation that I received my commission as a major-general on the 26th of April. This was also accompanied at the same time with another commission of inspector-general of all the armies of the United States. . . .

Flattering as these decided marks of distinction have been, it only, my friend, makes me the more desirous to merit them. As far as my mental faculties and bodily vigor will allow, I shall unremittingly devote them to fulfilling the demands of a nation which has honored me with such great confidence. No difficulties, no troubles, no danger, shall, nor can they, prevent my success. My department is extensive, and one eighth of the world seem to think that my talents may be of service to them. Thank God that up to the present they have been; and cheerfully will I die for a nation that has so highly honored me with its confidence. Up to the present time all of my undertakings have progressed successfully, and I can say that the trust reposed in me by the army increases daily. I commanded the left wing in the first engagement of the battle of Monmouth last year, and was so fortunate as to turn the day in our favor. . . . Last winter I completed the "Infantry and Cavalry Tactics," which were at once printed and promulgated. . . .

I am at present on a tour of inspection for the purpose not only of reviewing all the regiments, but of introducing the system laid down in my tactics. Indeed, my friend, I have been fortunate in everything I have here undertaken. I am now fifth in rank as general; and if my career be not ended by a fever or by half an ounce of lead, the possibilities are vast enough to satisfy the most ambitious. . . . Two years of work—if one is not afraid of toil and danger—can make a man successful. . . .

What a beautiful, what a happy country this is! Without kings, without prelates, without blood-sucking farmer-generals, and without idle barons! Here everybody is prosperous. Poverty is an unknown evil.

. . . I must candidly admit to you that six foreign officers cause more trouble to me here than two hundred American ones; and indeed most of the foreigners have so utterly lost their credit, that it is daily becoming more difficult to employ foreign officers. A large number of German barons and French marquises have already sailed away; and I am always nervous and apprehensive when a baron or marquis announces himself.

While here we are in a republic; and Mr. Baron does not count a farthing more than Mister Jacob or Mister Peter. Indeed, German and French noses can hardly accustom themselves to such a state of things! Our general of artillery [Henry Knox], for instance, was a bookbinder in Boston. He is a worthy man, thoroughly understands his trade, and fills his present position with much credit. . . .

I will finish the war here, or it will finish me. Without doubt England, at the utmost, can continue the game but two years longer. It will then be my care to put the army and the militia in the thirteen provinces on a uniform and solid footing. . . . Congress has promised me, not gifts, but a landed estate either in New Jersey or Pennsylvania, two of the best provinces. A considerable pension from France, after the (successful) termination of the war, was pledged to me by the French court. . . . To acquire all this requires on my part only three years, at the farthest, of life, health, steadfastness of purpose and courage. The first two conditions do not depend upon me: the last two are within my power and control. . . .

When you write to me, my best of friends, address your letters . . .

"To His Excellence, the honorable Baron of Steuben, Inspector-General and Major-General of the Armies of the United States of North America."

Source: William L. Stone, ed. and trans., *Letters of Brunswick and Hessian Officers during the American Revolution* (Albany, NY: J. Munsell, 1891), 245–49, 252–55.

The American Revolution was also expansive. The former colonies used the war to move aggressively westward, bypassing the barriers put in their way by the British Empire, which had sought to preserve peace along the frontier. The new American nation cared little for peace when it came to pushing Indians aside in order to acquire ever more territory. In 1779 George Rogers Clark led a successful campaign into the Ohio River Valley, pressing U.S. claims to the entire region. At the Paris peace talks in 1782 and 1783, Benjamin Franklin made good on those claims as the British abandoned their former Indian allies to the United States. As Colin Calloway has written, "The American revolutionaries who fought for freedom from the British Empire in the East also fought to create an empire of their own in the West." There was just no place for the Native Americans in this American empire. The expansive violence of the white Americans guaranteed that "the American Revolution was a disaster for most American Indians."[13] The fury of Clark's troops compounded that disaster.

13. Colin G. Calloway, *The American Revolution in Indian Country: Crisis and Diversity in Native American Communities* (Cambridge: Cambridge University Press, 1995), xv, 291.

Colonel George Rogers Clark on the Conquest of the West, 1779

The Journal of Colonel George Rogers Clark, 1779

23rd Feby. [1779] Sett off very early, waded better than three miles on a stretch, our people prodigious, yet they keep up a good heart in hopes of a speedy sight of our enemys. At last about two o'clock we came in sight of this long sought town and enemy, all quiet, the spirits of my men seemed to revive we marched up under cover of a wood called the Warriours Island where we lay concealed untill sunset. . . .

I sent out two men to bring in one [of the town's inhabitants] who came and I sent him to town to inform the inhabitants I was near them ordering all those attached to the King of England to enter the Fort and defend it, those who desired to be friends to keep in their houses. . . .

At sun down I put the divisions in motion to march in the greatest order and regularity and observe the orders of their officers—above all to be silent. . . . [W]e entered the town on the upper part leaving detached Lt. Bayley and 15 riflemen to attack the Fort and keep up a fire to harrass them untill we took possession of the town and they were to remain on that duty till relieved by another party, the two divisions marched into the town and took possession of the main street, put guards &c without the least molestation[.] I continued all night sending parties out to annoy the enemy and caused a trench to be thrown up across the main street about 200 yds from the Fort Gate. . . .

24th As soon as daylight appeared the enemy perceived our works and began a very smart fire of small arms at it, but could not bring their cannon to bear on them, about 8 o'clock I sent a flag of truce with a letter desiring Lt. Gov. [Henry] Hamilton in order to save the impending storm that hung over his head immediately to surrender up the Garrison, Fort, Stores &c. &c. and at his peril not to destroy any one article now in the said Garrison—or to hurt any house &c. belonging to the Inhabitants for if he did by Heaven, he might expect no mercy—his answer was Gov. H. begs leave to acquaint Col. C. that he and his Garrison were not disposed to be awed into any action unworthy of British subjects—I then ordered out parties to attack the Fort and the firing began very smartly on both sides one of my men thro' a bravery known but to Americans walking carlesly up the main street was slightly wounded over the left eye but no ways dangerous—About 12 o'clock the firing from the Fort suspended a Flag coming out I order'd my people to stop firing till further orders. I soon perceived it was Capt. [Leonard] Helm [one of Clark's officers taken prisoner by the British] who after salutations inform'd me that the purport of his commission was, that Lt. Gov. Hamilton was willing to surrender up the Fort and Garrison provided Col. Clarke would grant him honourable terms. . . . [M]y answer to Gov. H was that I should not agree to any other terms than that Lt Gov. H should immediately surrender at discretion and allowed him half an hour to consider thereof. . . . Capt. Helm came back with Lieut. Gov. H's second proposals . . . [of] a truce for three days, during which time there shall be no defensive works . . . carried on in the Garrison. . . .

This moment received intelligence that a party of Indians were coming up from the falls with Pris[one]rs or Scalps, which party was sent out by G. Hamilton for that purpose, my people were so enraged they immediately intercepted the party which consisted of 8 Indians and a french man of the Garrison. [T]hey killed three on the spot and brought 4 in who were tomahawked in the street oposite the Fort Gate and thrown into the river—the frenchman we shewd mercy as his aged father had behaved so well in my party—I relieved the two poor Pris[one]rs who were French hunters on the Ohio, after which Ct. Helm carried my answer thus—Col. Clarks comp[limen]ts to G. H. and begs leave to inform him that Col. Clarke will not agree to any other terms than of G. H. surrendering himself and Garrison prisoners at discretion—if G. H. desires a conference with Col. Clarke, he will meet him at the church with Capt. Helm. . . .

I imediately repaired there to confer with G. Hamilton . . .

Gov. Hamilton then begd I would consider the situation of both parties that he was willing to surrender the Garrison but was in hopes that Col. Clark would let him do it with Honour. . . . I am Sir (replied I) well acquainted with your strength and force and am able to take your Fort, therefore I will give no other terms but to submit yourself and Garrison to my discretion and mercy—he reply'd Sir my men are brave and willing to stand by me to the last, if I can't surrender upon Hon[ora]ble terms I'll fight it out to the last—Answered, Sir this will give my men infinite satisfaction and pleasure for it is their desire. . . . I told Capt Helm Sir you are a prisoner on your parole, I desire you to reconduct G. H. into the Fort and there remain till I retake you. Lt Gov. Hamilton then returned saying, Col. Clarke why will you force me to dishonour myself when you cannot acquire more honor by it—I told him could I look on you as a Gentleman I would do to the utmost of my power, but on you Sir who have embrued your hands in the blood of our women and children, Honor, my country, everything calls on me alloud for Vengeance. . . . [T]herefore repair to your Fort and prepare for battle on which . . . Capt. Helm says Gentlemen don't be warm, strive to save many lives which may be usefull to their country which will unavoidably fall in case you don't agree[,] on which we again conferd—G. Hamilton said, is there nothing to be done but fighting—Yes, Sir, I will send you such arti-

cles as I think proper to allow, if you accept them, well—I will allow you half
an hour to consider on them. . . .

1st Lt. Gov. Hamilton engages to deliver up to Col. Clark Fort Sackville as it
      is at present with all the stores, ammunition, provisions, &c.
2nd. The Garrison will deliver themselves up Prisrs of War to march out with
      their arms accoutrements, Knapsacks &c.
3.   The Garrison to be delivered up tomorrow morning at 10 o'clock.
4th. Three days to be allowed to the Garrison to settle their accounts with the
      traders of this place and inhabitants.
5.   The officers of the Garrison to be allowed their necessary baggage &c. . . .

Within the limited time Capt. Helm returned with the articles signed
thus, vizt.

Agreed to for the following reasons, remoteness from succours, the state
and quantity of Provisions &c. the unanimity of officers and men on its expe-
diency, the Hon[ora]ble terms allowd and lastly the confidence in a generous
Enemy. (signed) H. Hamilton . . .

Source: "Journal of Colonel Clark," *American Historical Review* 1 (1895): 91–94.

*Finding supplies for the Continental army was hindered not just by the weakness of
Congress and the various state governments but also by the self-interest of suppliers who
hoped to reap great profits, as General Nathanael Greene discovered when he attempted
to rebuild the southern army after its disastrous defeat at Camden. Though to General
Steuben and most foreign observers, white Americans appeared uniformly prosperous,
they generally avoided giving support to the very army fighting to win their independence.*

General Nathanael Greene on the Difficulties of Sustaining the War, 1781

General Nathanael Greene to President Joseph Reed, January 9th, 1781
On my journey [south to take command of the army] I visited the Maryland
and Virginia Assemblies, and laid before them the state of this army, and
urged the necessity of an immediate support. They both promised to do everything in their power, but such was their poverty, even in their Capitals, that
they could not furnish forage for my horses. I have also written to the States
of Delaware and North Carolina, neither of which have taken any measures
yet for giving effectual aid to this army. . . .

All the way through the country, as I passed, I found the people engaged in matters of interest and in pursuit of pleasure, almost regardless of their danger. Public credit totally lost, and every man excusing himself from giving the least aid to Government, from an apprehension that they would get no return for any advances. This afforded but a dull prospect, nor has it mended since my arrival.

I overtook the army at Charlotte. . . . The appearance of the troops was wretched beyond description, and their distress, on account of provisions, was little less than their sufferings for want of clothing and other necessities. General Gates had lost the confidence of the officers, and the troops all their discipline, and so addicted to plundering, that they were a terror to the inhabitants. The General and I met upon very good terms, and parted so. The old gentleman was in great distress, having but just heard of the death of his son before my arrival.

The battle of Camden is spoken of very differently here to what it is to the Northward, and as for a regular retreat, there was none; every man got off the ground in the best manner he could. This is the account Colonel Williams gives, who was one of the last on the field. Indeed, the whole business was a short fight and then a perfect flight, and the greatest loss happened after the troops broke, and attempted to make their escape. . . .

The General (Smallwood) is gone to the Northward, having declared, for reasons, that he could not think of submitting to the command of Baron Steuben, and that if justice was done him and the State, his commission would be dated at least two years earlier than his appointment. I expostulated with him upon the impossibility of the thing, let his private merit be ever so great, but it was all to no purpose. . . .

The wants of this army are so numerous and various, that the shortest way of telling you is to inform you that we have nothing. . . .

The loss of our army in Charleston, and the defeat of General Gates has been the cause of keeping such vast shoals of militia on foot, who, like the locusts of Egypt, have eaten up everything, and the expense has been so enormous, that it has ruined the currency of the State. It is my opinion there is no one thing upon the Continent that wants regulating so much, as the right which the States exercise of keeping what militia on foot they please at the Continental expense. I am persuaded North Carolina has militia enough to swallow up all the revenues of America, especially under their imperfect arrangements, where every man draws and wastes as much as he pleases. The country is so extensive and the powers of Government so weak, that everybody does as he pleases. The inhabitants are much divided in their political sentiments, and the Whigs and Tories pursue each other with little less than savage fury. . . . The ruin of the State is inevitable if there are such large bodies of militia kept on foot. No army can subsist in the country long if the ravages continue. Indeed, unless the army is better supported than I see any prospect of, the Country is lost beyond redemption....

Source: William B. Reed, *Life and Correspondence of Joseph Reed*, 2 vols. (Philadelphia: Lindsay and Blakiston, 1847), 2:344–45.

General Greene rebuilt the southern Continental army and conducted a brilliant campaign that lured the British forces under Lieutenant-General Cornwallis farther inland and away from British lines of supplies. Completely outmaneuvered, his forces exhausted and supplies running low, Cornwallis made for the coast and the safety of the British fleet. Washington, who finally had his professional army, moved briskly with his French allies to corner Cornwallis near the mouth of the Chesapeake at a place called Yorktown. With Admiral de Grasse's victory over the British fleet, the situation was hopeless for Cornwallis. On October 19 he surrendered his army to General Washington, effectively ending the military struggle.

BATTLING DISSENT

The United States won its independence and, to a degree, transformed its society by violent means. Not all Americans favored the Revolution—far from it. Those who did not go along with the majority often found themselves the target of more than disapproval. The people who had the most to gain from a complete social revolution, the slaves, found little on offer from those fighting for American independence. When Lord Dunmore, the last royal governor of Virginia, offered freedom to any slave who joined his forces, hundreds made the perilous break for British lines. If the British had expanded on that policy, they could have launched a fundamental social revolution throughout North America. But that was probably precisely the reason the British government withdrew Dunmore's offer and did little to encourage slaves to rise up in revolution against their masters. Few white people in either England or the new United States wanted to take the chance on a complete alteration in social arrangements. A political revolution was frightening enough in the forces unleashed and the uncertainty of how matters would develop; a total overturn of the social structures of America could lead anywhere. As a result, far more slaves ran away than ever joined the British. Virginia's Governor Thomas Jefferson estimated that thirty thousand Virginia slaves had taken advantage of the upheaval of the Revolution to seek freedom in the single year of 1778. To combat this voting with their feet, the southern states condemned slaves caught in the act of seeking freedom to harsh punishment, often torture and death.

The majority of slaves saw little advantage in the Revolution, no matter how it turned out. There were also those who questioned the use of violence as a means to a political end. Mostly members of pacifist denominations, these dissenters often found themselves the target of patriot animosity. The Quakers constituted the largest religious group who, in the words of Samuel Allison of New Jersey, "desire not war or any of its consequences, nor do we apprehend any benefit arising from it."[14] In January 1775 the Philadelphia yearly meeting issued a "Testimony" against violence. "We deeply lament that contrary modes of proceeding have been pursued, which have involved the colonies in confusion, appear likely to produce violence and bloodshed, and threaten the subversion of the constitutional government, and of . . . liberty of conscience."[15] As always when there was a war on, Quakers faced a crisis by their refusal to support a government waging war. Further complicating matters, the new American government had usurped legitimate authority, which they felt themselves beholden to obey. As one Quaker asked another who thought of supporting the war, "If thou canst not justify war from the doctrines and example of our Savior, His apostles and the primitive Christians, would it not be a dangerous innovation, to set up thy own judgment in opposition to the highest authorities?"[16]

Sincere pacifists not only refused to participate as soldiers; they would not work to aid the war effort in any way, whether selling goods to combatants or undertaking the most minor task. When a German officer ordered Joseph Townsend, a young Quaker with a farm close to the Brandywine, to help in removing a fence to make more room for the German troops to march to battle, Townsend initially complied. But on the "removal of the second rail I was forcibly struck with the impropriety of being active in assisting to take the lives of my fellow beings and therefore desisted in proceeding any further in obedience to his commands" despite the sword waved in his face by the officer.[17] In September 1776 Philadelphia's Quakers resolved to neither vote nor hold public office while the war continued. Many pacifists who refused to serve were sent off to jail or forced to labor for the military.

An even larger group—the loyalists—opposed revolutionary change outright. Those loyal to the Crown of England, called Tories by their enemies, equated liberty with the stability offered by the English government and monarchy. For the loyalists, a British victory would ensure freedom, an exact inversion of the patriot position. At one level they were absolutely correct, for the supporters of the Revolution had no intention of extending the rights for which they were fighting to their political opponents. The various state legislatures and local committees of safety disarmed the loyalists, confiscated and sold their property, sent them into exile, beat or imprisoned without trial those who dared to return, and basically treated them as not subject to the law.

14. Peter Brock, *Pacifism in the United States from the Colonial Era to the First World War* (Princeton, NJ: Princeton University Press, 1968), 217.

15. Thomas Gilpin, ed., *Exiles in Virginia: With Observations on the Conduct of the Society of Friends during the Revolutionary War* (Philadelphia: C. Sherman, 1848), 283.

16. Brock, *Pacifism in the United States*, 204.

17. Isaac Sharpless, *A Quaker Experiment in Government: History of Quaker Government in Pennsylvania, 1682–1783*, 2 vols. (Philadelphia: Ferris and Leach, 1902), 2:189.

The following selection is from a letter signed "Plain English" addressed to the Mas-sachusetts Provincial Congress, originally published in a New York City loyalist news-paper six weeks before the battles at Lexington and Concord. In May the paper's editor, James Rivington, was forced to apologize for publishing such articles; in November a patriot mob destroyed his printing press, and Rivington fled to England. The revolution-aries found war sufficient justification for denying the rights they claimed to other Amer-icans who did not share their views.

Rivington's Gazette on the Harassment of Loyalists, 1775

Rivington's Gazette, March 9, 1775

Your assuming the government of Massachusetts Bay, makes it unneces-sary for me to make any apology for addressing you in this public manner, further, than by acquainting you that it is to represent to you the distresses of some of those people, who, from a sense of their duty to the king, and a reverence for his laws, have behaved quietly and peaceably; and for which rea-son they have been deprived of their liberty, abused in their persons, and suf-fered such barbarous cruelties, insults, and indignities, besides the loss of their property, by the hands of lawless mobs and riots, as would have been disgraceful even for savages to have committed.

The courts of justice being shut up in most parts of the province, and the justices of those courts compelled by armed force, headed by some who are members of your Congress, to refrain from doing their duties, at present it is rendered impracticable for those sufferers to obtain redress, unless it be by your interposition, or the aid of military force, which will be applied for in case this application fails.

A particular enumeration of all the instances referred to, is apprehended unnecessary, as many of your members are personally knowing to them, and for the information of any of you who may pretend ignorance of them, the following instances are here mentioned. In August last, a mob in Berkshire forced the justices of the court of Common Pleas from their seats, and shut up the court-house. They also drove David Ingersoll from his house, and damaged the same, and he was obliged to leave his estate; after which his en-closures were laid waste. At Taunton, Daniel Leonard was driven from his house, and bullets fired into it by the mob, and he obliged to take refuge in Boston, for the supposed crime of obeying his Majesty's requisition as one of his council for this province. Colonel Gilbert, of Freetown, a firm friend to government, in August last being at Dartmouth, was attacked at midnight by a mob of about an hundred, but by his bravery, with the assistance of the family where he lodged, they were beaten off. The same night Brigadier Ruggles was also attacked by another party, who were routed after having painted and cut the hair off of one of horse's mane and tail. Afterwards he had his arms taken from his dwelling-house in Hardwick, all of which are not yet returned. He had at another time a very valuable English horse, which was kept as a stallion, poisoned, his family disturbed, and himself obliged to take refuge in Boston, after having been insulted in his own house, and twice on his way, by a mob.

The chief justice of the province [Thomas Hutchinson] in Middleborough, was threatened to be stopped on the highway in going to Boston court, but his firmness and known resolution, supporting government in this as well as many other instances, intimidated the mob from laying hands on him; he was also threatened with opposition in going into court, but the terror of the troops prevented. The whole bench were hissed by a mob as they came out of court. In September, Mr. Sewall, his Majesty's Attorney-General for Massachusetts Bay, was obliged to repair to Boston for refuge. His house at Cambridge was attacked by a mob, and his windows were broken, but the mob was beaten off by the gallant behavior and bravery of some young gentlemen of his family. About the same time the Lieutenant-Governor Oliver, president of his Majesty's council, was attacked at Cambridge, by a mob of about four thousand, and was compelled to resign his seat at the board, since which, upon further threats, he has been obliged to leave his estate, and take refuge with his family in Boston. . . .

Colonel Phips, the very reputable and highly esteemed sheriff of the county of Middlesex, by a large mob was obliged to promise not to serve any processes of courts, and to retire to Boston for protection from further insults. Colonel Saltonstall, the very humane sheriff of the county of Essex, has been obliged to take refuge in Boston, to screen himself from the violence of the mob. The court of Common Pleas was forbidden to sit at Taunton, by a large mob, with a justice acting as one of their committee. . . .

Thomas Foster, Esq., an ancient gentleman, was obliged to run into the woods, and had like to have been lost, and the mob, although the justices, with Mr. Foster, were sitting in the town, ransacked his house, and damaged his furniture. He was obnoxious as a friend to government, and for that reason they endeavored to deprive him of his business, and to prevent even his taking the acknowledgement of a deed. . . .

Jesse Dunbar, of Halifax, in Plymouth county, bought some fat cattle of Mr. Thomas the counsellor, and drove them to Plymouth for sale; one of the oxen being skinned and hung up, the committee came to him, and finding he bought it of Mr. Thomas, they put the ox into a cart, and fixing Dunbar in his [the oxen's] belly, carted him four miles, and there made him pay a dollar, after taking three more cattle and a horse from him. The Plymouth mob delivered him to the Kingston mob, which carted him four miles further, and forced from him another dollar, then delivered him to the Duxborough mob, who abused him by throwing the tripe in his face, and endeavoring to cover him with it to the endangering his life. They then threw dirt at him, and after other abuses carried him to said Thomas's house, and made him pay another sum of money, and he not taking the beef, they flung it in the road and quitted him. Daniel Dunbar, of Halifax, an ensign of militia there, had his colors demanded by the mob, some of the selectmen being the chief actors. He refused; they broke into his house, took him out, forced him upon a rail, and after keeping him for two or three hours in such abuses, he was forced to give his colors up to save his life. . . .

In February, at Plymouth, a number of ladies attempted to divert themselves at their assembly room, but the mob collected . . . and flung stones which broke the shutters and windows, and endangered their lives. They were forced to get out of the hall, and were pelted and abused to their own homes. After this the ladies diverted themselves by riding out, but were followed by a mob, pelted and abused, with the most indecent Billingsgate language. . . .

The Honorable Israel Williams, Esq., one who was appointed of his Majesty's new council, but had declined the office through infirmity of body, was taken from his house by the mob in the night, carried several miles, put into a room with a fire, the chimney at the top [and] the doors of the room closed, and kept there for many hours in the smoke, till his life was in danger; then he was carried home, after being forced to sign what they ordered, and a guard placed over him to prevent his leaving the house.

To recount the suffering of all from mobs, rioters, and trespassers, would take more time and paper than can be spared for that purpose. It is hoped the foregoing will be sufficient to put you upon the use of proper means and measures for giving relief to all that have been injured by such unlawful and wicked practices.

Source: Frank Moore, ed., *Diary of the American Revolution*, 2 vols. (New York: Scribner, 1860), 1:37–42.

As the Revolution proceeded, the treatment of loyalists became ever harsher, ever more violent. In some frontier regions the conflict between patriots and loyalists became a civil war, with each side committing acts of terror and executing prisoners. The letters that follow concern campaigns in western Virginia and along the upper Ohio River. Colonel Charles Lynch arrested and tried anyone the least bit suspicious, whipping many, forcing others to enlist in the Continental army, and hanging some.

Wm. Christian, Col. William Preston, Capt. Patrick Lockhart, and Col. Charles Lynch on the Revolutionary Origins of Lynching, 1779–1780

Wm. Christian to Col. William Fleming, July 23, 1779

Dear sir:

... We have news here that Col Wm Campbell with a Body of Washington Militia, hearing that a Number of Tories up this River about the Carolina Line had embodied in order to take the Mines ... with a Body from this County, in the whole about 130 Men they Marched from the Mines up the River & found that the greater Part had scattered, but some still kept together. Our People shot one, Hanged one, and whipt several, and next Monday are to have a Sale of the Tories Estates. The one who was Hanged has twice Deserted & is also a noted Thief. I expect this Affair will settle the Tories for a While. I expect Col. Campbell will return Home next Week, after this Service is Done. Let us know when when [*sic*] you will be along.

Col. William Preston to Gov. Thomas Jefferson. August 8, 1780

Sir:

A most horrid Conspiracy amongst the Tories in this Country being Providentia[l]ly discovered about ten days ago obliged me not only to raise the militia of the County but to care for so a large Number from the Counties of Washington and Botetourt that there are upwards of four hundred men now on Duty exclusive of a Party which I hear Col Lynch marched from Bedford towards the Mines yesterday. Col Hugh Crocket had sent two young men amongst the Tories as tory officers, with whom they agreed to Embody to a very great Number near the Lead Mines the 25th Instant, and after securing that Place to over run the Country with the assistance of the british Troops, who they were made to believe would meet them, and to relieve the Convention Prisoners [taken at Saratoga]. These they were to Arm & then subdue the whole State. A List of a Number of Officers was given to our Spies.—This Deception gave our Militia an Opportunity of fixing on many of them who have been taken and I believe there are near sixty now in confinement.—A number of Magistrates were called together from this County and Botetourt to examine Witnesses and enquire fully into the Conduct of those deluded Wretches In which we have been Engaged three Days; & I am convinced the Enquiry will continue at least a fortnight, as there are Prisoners brought in every hour and new Discoveries making. One has been enlarged on giving Security in £100,000 to appear when called for, some have been whipped & others, against whom little can be made appear, have enlisted to serve in the Continental Army. There is yet another Class who comes fully within the Treason Law, that we cannot Punish otherwise than by sending to the best Prisons in the Neighbouring Counties, until they can be legally tried according to an Act of the last Session of Assembly to which however we are strangers, as we have not been able to procure a Copy of the Act & have only heard of it.

Some of the Capital offenders have disappeared whose personal Property has been removed by the soldiers & which they insist on being sold & divided as Plunder to which the Officers have submitted otherwise it would be almost impossible to get men on those pressing Occasions. I would beg your Excellency's Opinion on this head; as also what steps you Judge necessary to be taken by the Officers & Magistrates with the Prisoners, other than what I have mentioned.

Capt. Patrick Lockhart to Col. William Preston, August 12, 1780
Sir:
The Officers from this County forgot to Consult you Relative to giving Credit at the sale of the Tories Effects. [I] shall be Obliged for your Advice in the Matter for I think whatever Measures is Adopted in regard to their Effects sold in your County ought to be here. We brought all the prisoners &c. safe[. A]s I came home I took a Young Man Named Stewart on Suspicion of being Connected with those Disaffected on the North Fork . . . [he] gladly agreed to inlist. Capt May seems displeased because he was one of his Company & demands him as a Recruit for his Division[.] I told him I would Submit it to the Officers &c appointed to lay off the County in Divisions to say who was entitled.

Col. Charles Lynch to Col. William Preston, August 17, 1780
Dr. Sir:
I was Honour'd with yours a few days past, in which you Desire Me to Desist in trying torys &c &c—What sort of tryals you have been inform'd I have given them I know not, but I can assure you I only Examine them strictly & such as I believe not Very criminal I set at Liberty. Others I have for a proper tryal, some I have kept for soldiers, some as witnesses, some perhaps Justice to this Country May require they shou'd be Made Exampels of. [I]t may also appear Very Od to you at first View that I shou'd be in your county apprehending some of those you have had Before you & nothing appear'd against them, all which Dificultrys I hope to reconcile to you Esspetially and to Every good Man. . . .

[I] soon Discover'd the Conspiracy to be so great as well in Bedford as in your parts, I thought it best to have something Done in Bedford, without Delay.

Source: Louise Phelps Kellogg, ed., *Frontier Retreat on the Upper Ohio, 1779–1781,* vols. 23 and 24 of the Wisconsin Historical Society Collections (Madison: State Historical Society of Wisconsin, 1916–17), 23:405, 24:241–42, 244, 250–52.

SHAYS'S REBELLION

Economic crisis gripped much of the new United States after the Revolution. In New England, creditors sued to seize the property of their debtors. The wealthiest of these creditors had powerful connections with the courts and state governments, and found local authorities only too willing to auction the property of small farmers and to imprison those whose land proved insufficient to cover their debts. In western Massachusetts in the fall of 1786, farmers held rallies protesting high taxes and the heavy-handed use of the courts to the benefit of creditors. When the state legislature ignored their petitions, these protesters acted in traditional ways by closing down the local courts and freeing imprisoned debtors. When Governor James Bowdoin called out the militia to reopen the courts, he found that most of the western militia was either on the side of the protesters or dared not oppose their neighbors. Calling themselves "Regulators"—making an explicit connection to the Southern Regulators of twenty years earlier—the protesters formed a military force under the leadership of Daniel Shays, a farmer and former captain in the Continental army. They claimed that they wanted nothing more than to protect their land and reclaim their government from the eastern elite. The Massachusetts legislature responded with a riot act outlawing unauthorized assemblies, suspended habeas corpus, granted Governor Bowdoin emergency powers, and raised what amounted to a private army through contributions from Boston merchants.

The Massachusetts Regulators or Shaysites, needing guns and ammunition for their rebellion, moved first to capture the Springfield arsenal. A state force under the command of General William Shepard, well armed from the arsenal stores, stood guard. General Shepard describes the impact of that initial round of cannon fire that constituted this brief "battle."

General William Shephard on the Confrontation at Springfield, Massachusetts, 1787

General Shepard to Governor Bowdoin, Springfield, January 26, 1787
Sir,
The unhappy time is come in which we have been obliged to shed blood. Shays, who was at the head of about twelve hundred men,

marched yesterday afternoon about four o'Clock, towards the public buildings in battle array. He marched his men in an open column by plattoons. I sent several times by one of my aids, and two other gentlemen, Captains Buffington and Woodbridge, to him to know what he was after, or what he wanted. His reply was, he wanted barracks, and barracks he would have and stores. The answer returned was he must purchase them dear, if he had them.

He still proceeded on his march until he approached within two hundred and fifty yards of the arsenal. He then made a halt. I immediately sent Major Lyman, one of my aids, and Capt Buffington to inform him not to march his troops any nearer the Arsenal on his peril, as I was stationed here by order of your Excellency and the Secretary at War, for the defence of the public property, in case he did I should surely fire on him and his men.

A Mr. Wheeler, who appeared to be one of Shays' aids, met Mr. Lyman, after he had delivered my orders in the most peremptory manner, and made answer, that that was all he wanted. Mr. Lyman returned with his answer.

Shays immediately put his troops in motion, and marched on rapidly near one hundred yards. I then ordered Major Stephens, who commanded the Artillery, to fire upon them. He accordingly did. The two first shott he endeavoured to overshoot them, in hopes they would have taken warning without firing among them, but it had no effect on them. Major Stephens then directed his shott thro' the center of his column. The fourth or fifth shot put their whole column into the utmost confusion. Shays made an attempt to display the column, but in vain. We had one howitz which was loaded with grape shot, which when fired, gave them great uneasiness. Had I been disposed to destroy them, I might have charged upon their rear and flanks with my Infantry and the two field pieces, and could have killed the greater part of his whole army within twenty five minutes.

There was not a single musket fired on either side. I found three men dead on the spot, and one wounded, who is since dead. One of our Artillery men by inattention was badly wounded. Three muskets were taken up with the dead, which were all deeply loaded. . . . I have received no reinforcement yet, and expect to be attacked this day by their whole force combined.

I am, Sir, with great respect, Your Excellency's most obedient h[um]ble Servt. W. Shepard.

Source: "Documents Relating to the Shays Rebellion, 1787," *American Historical Review* 2 (1897): 694–95.

Shays's forces fled in terror, and towns throughout the state petitioned their government to go easy on the rebels, arguing that a policy of conciliation was best in the long run. One such petition from the town of Coleraine requesting the avoidance of violence follows. The state chose to ignore these petitions.

The Town of Coleraine Petitions for Mercy for the Shaysites, 1787

Petition from Coleraine to the Governor and Council, January 29, 1787
May it please your Excellency and your honorable Council[,]

Your petitioners inhabitants of the town of Colrain in the County of Hampshire beg leave to represent to your Excellency and Council our sense of the present alarming situation of public affairs and of the Horrors which we Justly entertain of a general effusion of human blood, which from what has already happened is justly to be dreaded and of which if it further proceeds none knows either the extent or end.

Your petitioners pretend not to Justify the practice of flying to arms to obstruct the [s]itting of courts of Justice or of interfering in matters of civil government in any other way than what is pointed out by the Constitution. But as great numbers for some cause or other have had recourse to arms, many of them persons of reputable Characters in society; who have been by some means or other led into unfavourable sentiments of Civil Government as at present established, and as their views of personal danger (particularly that of their leaders who have taken their post by voluntary election) disposes them to continue in the same course and as these things are at present upon the point of involving our land in confusion and bloodshed and devastation:

Your petitioners from a realizing sense of the horrid Consequences of civil war most humbly beseech your Excellency and your honourable Council as the supreme executive of the state that a suspension of military force may immediately take place, and that with your Excellency's concurrence our desires may be presented to the Honorable Senate and House of Representatives at their next Session, that an act of indemnity for all past offences may take place. . . . [A]s in battle the sword devoureth one as well as another[,] devastation and ruin will probably fall upon the most innocent and valuable part of a community and the advantages to be gained will be[,] we conceive[,] in no wise answerable to the blood and treasure to be expended in the procuring of them, and we flatter ourselves that the body of the people now in arms upon the prospect of such an act will be willing to return to their allegiance; Or that if such measures should prove ineffectual with some they will at least strengthen the hands of a constitutional government by detaching from the opposite party the most valuable part of their numbers so as to render any future quelling of insurrections a matter of less difficulty, and future attempts to obstruct the courts of justice will be considered more inexcusable both in the sight of God and the world. . . .

Source: "Documents Relating to the Shays Rebellion, 1787," *American Historical Review* 2 (1897): 696–97.

Commanding General Benjamin Lincoln saw no reason to exercise restraint in crushing the rebellion. Lincoln's army hunted down the Shaysites a week after the confrontation at Springfield. The general describes the encounter at Petersham in the following document.

Following the crushing defeat of Shays's Rebellion, the state legislature required a loyalty oath. Generals Lincoln and Shepard traveled through the western counties, administering this "oath of allegiance." In disarming the people and imposing the oath, Lincoln wrote that those he encountered "yield with reluctance, yet they must be born down, & if they will not submit to government allured by the blessings of it they must bend to its force. This will be a yoke too galling for them long to bear; it will soon melt them into submission or induce them to leave the state."[18] To prove his point, Lincoln sentenced fourteen rebels to death. Samuel Adams, speaking as president of the Massachusetts Senate, bluntly stated that "the man who dares to rebel against the laws of a republic ought to die."[19] Benjamin Lincoln and Daniel Shays were both veterans of the Revolution, yet they had very different visions of what this revolution had meant.

General Benjamin Lincoln Crushes Shays's Rebellion, 1787

Benjamin Lincoln to George Washington, February 22, 1787.

I had constant applications from Committees and Selectmen of the several towns in the Counties of Worcester and Hampshire, praying that the effusion of blood might be avoided; while the real design, as was supposed, of these applications was to stay our operations until a new Court [legislature] should be elected. They had no doubt if they could keep up their influence until another choice of the Legislature and the Executive that matters might be moulded in General Court to their wishes. This to avoid was the duty of the government. As all these applications breathed the same spirit, the same answer was given to them. . . .

In this position I remained refreshing the troops who had suffered very severe fatigue. This also gave time for the several towns to use their influence

18. Lincoln to Bowdoin, Feb. 14, 1787, *Collections of the Massachusetts Historical Society*, 88 vols. (Boston: The Society, 1794–1992), 6:137.
19. John Lockwood et al., *Western Massachusetts: A History, 1636–1925*, 4 vols. (New York: Lewis Historical Publishing, 1926), 1:183.

with their own people to return, if they thought proper to urge it, and to circulate among Shays' men that they would be recommended for a pardon if they would come in, and lay down their arms. The 2d of February I was induced to reconnoitre Shays' post on his right, left, and rear. I had received information by General Putnam before, that we could not approach him in front. . . . This reconnoitering gave him an alarm. . . .

In the evening of [February 3], I was informed that Shays had left his ground, and had pointed his rout towards Petersham in the County of Worcester, where he intended to make a stand as a number of Towns in the vicinity had engaged to support him. Our troops were put in motion at 8 o'Clock. The first part of the night was pleasant, and the weather clement, but between two and three o'Clock in the morning, the wind shifting to the Westward, it became very cold and squally, with considerable snow. The wind immediately arose very high, and with the light snow which fell the day before and was falling, the paths were soon filled up, the men became fatigued, . . . and the cold was so increased, that they could not halt in the road to refresh themselves. Under these circumstances they were obliged to continue their march.

We reached Petersham about 9 o'Clock in the morning exceedingly fatigued with a march of thirty miles, part of it in a deep snow and in a most violent storm; when this abated, the cold increased and a great proportion of our men were frozen in some part or other, but none dangerously. We approached nearly the centre of the Town, where Shays had covered his men [in shelters]; and had we not been prevented from the steepness of a large hill at our entrance, and the depth of the snow, from throwing our men rapidly into it we should have arrested very probably one half this force; for they were so surprized as it was that they had not time to call in their out-parties, or even their guards. About 150 fell into our hands, and none escaped but by the most precipitate flight in different directions.

Thus that body of men who were a few days before offering the grossest insults to the best citizens of this Commonwealth, and were menacing even government itself, were now nearly dispersed, without the shedding of blood but in an instance or two where the Insurgents rushed on their own destruction. That so little has been shed is owing in a measure to the patience and obedience, the zeal and the fortitude in our troops. . . .

I at once threw detachments into different parts of the County, for the purpose of protecting the friends to government and apprehending those who had been in arms against it. This business is pretty fully accomplished, and there are no insurgents together in arms in the State.

Source: Albert Bushnell Hart, ed., *American History Told by Contemporaries* (New York: Macmillan, 1901), 3: 193–94.

*Massachusetts's reactionary policies following the suppression of Shays's Rebellion alien-
ated voters throughout the state, and Bowdoin was defeated for reelection in 1787 by a
margin of three to one. The new governor, John Hancock, pardoned the Shaysites, including those sentenced to death, and threw his weight behind debt relief.*

*Elsewhere in the country, Shays's Rebellion frightened the political leadership. George
Washington wrote James Madison, "We are fast verging to anarchy and confusion,"
finding the crisis in Massachusetts but a local variant of a national problem.*[20] *For Washington and Madison, Shays's Rebellion demonstrated that something needed to be done
to increase the power of the central government so that it could both support a stronger
economy and respond adequately to any future threats to national stability. The result,
many historians argue, was the Constitution of the United States.*

*It is certainly the case that the government created by the Constitution was far more
capable of dealing quickly and thoroughly with threats to internal security. When a new
set of Regulators closed courts and harassed officials in western Pennsylvania in 1794 in
what is known as the Whiskey Rebellion, their traditional approach to crowd action was
met in an innovative fashion. President Washington called out the militia from several
states and fashioned an army of fifteen thousand troops, larger than any force he led in
the Revolution. Simply by marching west, this army put an end to the rebellion. These
Regulators never even appeared to challenge the federal forces. By the time a similar
uprising known as Fries Rebellion occurred elsewhere in Pennsylvania in 1799, President
John Adams just needed to send in a force of five hundred federal troops, and the uprising
melted away with a whimper.*

*Shays's Rebellion was not the end of crowd action—far from it. Crowds would con-
tinue to gather and challenge local authority; it would be difficult, however, to frame
their actions as in any way revolutionary. The traditional valuation of crowd action was
dead. In the future the government would not hesitate to use troops to crush any movement that posed a threat to established order, and usually with widespread public support.
But the rhetoric lived on, thanks in part to the passionate language of Thomas Jefferson.
Jefferson, the third president of the United States, would not hesitate to use force to crush
a slave uprising; nor would he quell at using the full power of the federal government to
enforce his Embargo Acts of 1807 and 1808. He also proclaimed his own election the
"Revolution of 1800," because of the peaceful transference of power from the Federalists
to his Republicans. Nonetheless, Jefferson would always keep alive the language of violent
revolutionary action. The following letter is one of several in which Jefferson spoke of his
admiration for Shays's Rebellion as an indicator of political life. Fortunately for Jefferson,
he did not have to respond to a rebellion during his presidency.*

20. Washington to David Humphreys, October 22, to Henry Lee, October 31, to Madison, November 5, 1786, in John C. Fitzpatrick, ed., *The Writings of George Washington*, 39 vols. (Washington, DC: Government Printing Office, 1931–44), 29:26–28, 33–35, 50–52.

Thomas Jefferson on the Need
for the Occasional Revolution, 1787

DEAR SIR, . . . I do not know whether it is to yourself or Mr. Adams, I am to give my thanks for the copy of the new constitution. I beg leave through you to place them where due. It will yet be three weeks before I shall receive them from America. There are very good articles in it, and very bad. I do not know which preponderate. What we have lately read, in the history of Holland, in the chapter on the Stadtholder, would have sufficed to set me against a chief magistrate, eligible for a long duration, if I had ever been disposed towards one; and what we have always read of the elections of Polish Kings should have forever excluded the idea of one continuable for life. Wonderful is the effect of impudent and persevering lying. The British ministry have so long hired their gazetteers to repeat, and model into every form, lies about our being in anarchy, that the world has at length believed them, the English nation has believed them, the ministers themselves have come to believe them, and what is more wonderful, we have believed them ourselves. Yet where does this anarchy exist? Where did it ever exist, except in the single instance of Massachusetts? And can history produce an instance of rebellion so honorably conducted? I say nothing of its motives. They were founded in ignorance, not wickedness.

God forbid we should ever be twenty years without such a rebellion. The people cannot be all, and always, well informed. The part which is wrong will be discontented, in proportion to the importance of the facts they misconceive. If they remain quiet under such misconceptions, it is a lethargy, the forerunner of death to the public liberty. We have had thirteen States independent for eleven years. There has been one rebellion. That comes to one rebellion in a century and a half, for each State. What country before, ever existed a century and a half without a rebellion? And what country can preserve its liberties, if its rulers are not warned from time to time, that this people preserve the spirit of resistance? Let them take arms. The remedy is to set them right as to facts, pardon and pacify them. What signify a few lives lost in a century or two? The tree of liberty must be refreshed from time to time, with the blood of patriots and tyrants. It is its natural manure. Our convention has been too much impressed by the insurrection of Massachusetts; and on the spur of the moment, they are setting up a kite to keep the hen yard in order. I hope in God, this article will be rectified before the new constitution is accepted. You ask me if any thing transpires here on the subject of South America? Not a word. I know that there are combustible materials there, and that they wait the torch only. But this country probably will join the extinguishers. The want of facts worth communicating to you, has occasioned me to give a little loose to dissertation. We must be contented to amuse, when we cannot inform.

Source: Andrew A. Lipscomb, ed., *The Writings of Thomas Jefferson*, 13 vols. (Washington, DC: Thomas Jefferson Memorial Association, 1904), 6:371–73.

FURTHER READINGS

For the nature of crowd action and the early stages of the revolutionary struggle, see Edward Countryman, *A People in Revolution: The American Revolution and Political Society in New York, 1760–1790* (Baltimore: Johns Hopkins University Press, 1981); Pauline Maier, *From Resistance to Revolution: Colonial Radicals and the Development of American Opposition to Britain, 1765–1776* (New York: Knopf, 1972); William Pencak, Matthew Dennis, and Simon P. Newman, eds., *Riot and Revelry in Early America* (University Park: Pennsylvania State University Press, 2002); Alfred F. Young, ed., *The American Revolution: Explorations in the History of American Radicalism* (De Kalb: Northern Illinois University Press, 1976).

On the Regulator movement, see Richard Maxwell Brown, *The South Carolina Regulators* (Cambridge, MA: Harvard University Press, 1963); Marjoleine Kars, *Breaking Loose Together: The Regulator Rebellion in Pre-Revolutionary North Carolina* (Chapel Hill: University of North Carolina Press, 2002); Paul D. Nelson, *William Tryon and the Course of Empire: A Life in British Imperial Service* (Chapel Hill: University of North Carolina Press, 1990).

On the military aspects of the American Revolution, see E. Wayne Carp, *To Starve the Army at Pleasure: Continental Army Administration and American Political Culture, 1775–1783* (Chapel Hill: University of North Carolina Press, 1984); Robert Middlekauff, *The Glorious Cause: The American Revolution, 1763–1789* (New York: Oxford University Press, 1982); Charles Royster, *A Revolutionary People at War: The Continental Army and American Character, 1775–1783* (Chapel Hill: University of North Carolina Press, 1979).

For the political struggles that ensued after the Revolution, see Thomas P. Slaughter, *The Whiskey Rebellion: Frontier Epilogue to the American Revolution* (New York: Oxford University Press, 1986); David P. Szatmary, *Shays' Rebellion: The Making of an Agrarian Insurrection* (Amherst: University of Massachusetts Press, 1980); Alfred F. Young, ed., *Beyond the American Revolution: Explorations in the History of American Radicalism* (De Kalb: Northern Illinois University Press, 1993).

FOUR

SLAVERY

Though sanctioned by law, slavery was no government program. In 1855 Frederick Douglass got it exactly right when he wrote that "the plantation is a little nation of its own, having its own language, its own rules, regulations and customs." In this little nation, Douglass continued, "The laws and institutions of the state, apparently, touch it nowhere."[1] Former slave Harriet Jacobs wrote that "no shadow of law" protected slave women from lecherous white men.[2] Every slave state maintained a slave code, a set of laws intended to govern slavery. But legislators and the courts hesitated to interfere in the relationship between master and slave. In slavery, white men could do almost anything they wanted to their human property. At its core, slavery was a lawless institution.

Southern slave codes can be said to have begun in the colonies, where legislatures passed slave laws piecemeal. Virginia's earliest laws, enacted as slavery became profitable, put in place the essential elements of later codes. Slaves must never leave their plantations or farms without a pass from their owners. No slave should ever "presume to lift up his hand" against any white person. Many of these laws represented whites' fantasy rather than reality. In fact, slaves crafted their own culture, regularly undertook subversive actions against their masters, from work slowdowns to sabotage, and occasionally possessed weapons, from old swords to guns, that would have terrified their owners had they known of their existence. It is likely that few slaves ever confined their travel entirely to their owners' property; the South is still crisscrossed by the remnants

---

1. Frederick Douglass, *My Bondage and My Freedom* (New York: Miller, Orton and Mulligan, 1855), 64.
2. Harriet Jacobs with L. Maria Child, *Incidents in the Life of a Slave Girl* (Boston: published for the author, 1861), 27.

of slave trails connecting plantations. Some slaves lived virtually unsupervised for years, with no pass or certificate allowing them to do so.

Compared with other slaveholding regimes, the United States experienced few slave revolts. Perhaps the most tumultuous time in the annals of American slavery came between 1832 and 1835, when a religious zealot named Nat Turner fomented murderous rebellion in Virginia and panic swept down the Mississippi valley. Whites redoubled their patrolling and eyed heretofore faithful servants suspiciously. When whites in Madison County, Mississippi, suspected two whites of conspiring with local slaves, they organized vigilante tribunals. Whites sometimes subjected errant slaves to their criminal justice system. But threatened large-scale revolts seemed—to the whites—too urgent to be left to local courts and judges. Even though the slave power completely dominated law and law enforcement, slave owners did not trust the courts to guard their interests.

In the midst of slavery, dueling flourished. Dueling did occur outside the South, the first American duelists may have been Revolutionary army officers, eager to establish themselves as an elite class. Vice President Aaron Burr shot Alexander Hamilton in a duel in New Jersey in 1804. Yet, while dueling faded in the North early in the nineteenth century, white southerners continued their peculiar predilection for "affairs of honor" as necessary to maintain social order. Dueling, in other words, documented a fundamental lack of faith in law and institutional methods of maintaining order.

Slavery planted in the minds of whites a deep distrust of law and legal process. Southern whites came to believe that blacks could only be disciplined outside the law. This lack of faith in the law would have consequences that endured for a century after the fall of slavery, if not longer.

DOCUMENTS

SLAVE LAW

Dutch merchants brought the first slaves to Virginia in 1619, but for decades planters did not invest heavily in the institution, preferring indentured servants. In Virginia's coastal disease environment, field hands died so young that it made little economic sense to invest in slaves-for-life. Indentured servants were cheaper, and slaves lived no longer. This situation changed by 1660.

Virginia converted its labor force to slavery as disease abated, the colony's food supply stabilized, and the workers' life expectancy lengthened. Colonial legislators had allowed landlords considerable freedom to brutalize and abuse their indentured servants. They granted slave owners even more power. Indentured servants could be compelled to obe-

dience out of fear that their term might be extended. Since slaves had no expectation of ever achieving freedom, they could be reduced to obedience only through violence. Employers of slave labor felt they had to beat slaves harder than indentured servants to attain the same degree of discipline. Legislatures declared open season on runaways and sanctioned the deliberate maiming of recalcitrant slaves. In the new world of slave labor, white people learned to violently abuse black people without fear of government interference. Slave codes, the laws colonies and states passed to regulate slavery, remained mostly theoretical or applied to slaves off their masters' plantations.

The following laws were among the first adopted by the colony of Virginia intended to regulate the institution of slavery. They are followed by Mississippi's slave code of 1848, which was fairly typical for the Southern states in the years just before the Civil War. These slave codes served to institutionalize racial violence, granting white brutality against blacks the legitimacy of the law.

Colonial Virginia Slave Laws

At a Grand Assemblie, Holden at James Cittie by Prorogation from the Seaventeenth of September, 1668, to the twentieth of October 1669; in the twentie first yeare of the Raigne of our soveraigne Lord King Charles the Second.

ACT I *AN ACT ABOUT THE CASUALL KILLING OF SLAVES.*

WHEREAS the only law in force for the punishment of refractory servants resisting their master, mistris or overseer cannot be inflicted upon negroes, nor the obstinacy of many of them by other then violent meanes supprest, *Be it enacted and declared by this grand assembly,* if any slave resist his master (or other by his masters order correcting him) and by the extremity of the correction should chance to die, that his death shall not be accompted felony, but the master (or that other person appointed by the master to punish him) be acquit from molestation, since it cannot be presumed that prepensed malice (which alone makes murther felony) should induce any man to destroy his owne estate.

At a Generall Assemblie, Begunne at James Cittie the Eighth Day of June, Anno 1680, in the two and Thirtieth yeare of our Soveraigne Lord King Charles the Second.

ACT X *AN ACT FOR PREVENTING NEGROES INSURRECTIONS.*

WHEREAS the frequent meeting of considerable numbers of negroe slaves under pretence of feasts and burialls is judged of dangerous consequence; for prevention whereof for the future, *Bee it enacted by the kings most excellent ma-*

jestie by and with the consent of the generall assembly, and it is hereby enacted by the authority aforesaid, that from and after the publication of this law, it shall not be lawfull for any negroe or other slave to carry or arme himselfe with any club, staffe, gunn, sword or any other weapon of defence or offence, nor to goe or depart from of his masters ground without a certificate from his master, mistris or overseer, and such permission not to be granted but upon perticuler and necessary occasions; and every negroe or slave soe offending not haveing a certificate as aforesaid shalbe sent to the next constable, who is hereby enjoyned and required to give the said negroe twenty lashes on his bare back well layd on, and soe sent home to his said master, mistris or overseer. *And it is further enacted by the authority aforesaid* that if any negroe or other slave shall presume to lift up his hand in opposition against any christian, shall for every such offence, upon due proofe made thereof by the oath of the party before a magistrate, have and receive thirty lashes on his bare back well laid on. *And it is hereby further enacted by the authority aforesaid* that if any negroe or other slave shall absent himself from his masters service and lye hid and lurking in obscure places, comitting injuries to the inhabitants, and shall resist any person or persons that shalby any lawfull authority be imployed to apprehend and take the said negroe, that then in case of such resistance, it shalbe lawfull for such person or persons to kill the said negroe or slave soe lying out and resisting, and that this law be once every six months published at the respective county courts and parish churches within this colony.

Source: William Waller Hening, *The Statutes at Large; being a collection of all the Laws of Virginia from the First Session of the Legislature in the Year 1619* (New York: Bartow, 1823), 2:270, 481–82.

Mississippi's Slave Code, 1848

1. *What Persons deemed Slaves.* All persons lawfully held to service for life, and the descendants of the females of them, within this state, and such persons and their descendants, as hereafter may be brought into this state, pursuant to law, being held to service for life, by the laws of the state or territory from whence they were removed, and no other person or persons whatsoever, shall henceforth be deemed slaves. . . .

8. *Slaves not to go from Home without Pass.* No slave shall go from the tenements of his master, or other person with whom he lives, without a pass, or some letter or token whereby it may appear that he is proceeding by authority from his master, employer or overseer; if he does, it shall be lawful for any person to apprehend and carry him before a Justice of the Peace, to be by his order punished with stripes, or not, at his discretion,

not exceeding twenty stripes; and if any slave shall presume to come and
be upon the plantation of any person whatsoever, without leave in writing
from his or her master, employer or overseer, not being sent upon lawful
business, it shall be lawful for the owner or overseer of such plantation,
to give, or order such slaves ten lashes on his or her bare back, for every
such offense: and if any negro or mulatto, bond or free, shall furnish a
pass or permission, to any slave, without the consent of the master, employer or overseer of such slave, he or she so offending, shall on conviction thereof before any Justice of the Peace, of this state, receive on his or
her bare back, well laid on, any number of lashes not exceeding thirty-
nine, at the discretion of such Justice of the Peace. . . .

32. *Punishment of Negro or Mulatto for Abusive Language or Assaulting, a White Person.* If any negro, or mulatto, bond or free, shall, at any time use abusive
and provoking language to, or lift his or her hand in opposition to any
person, not being a negro or mulatto, he or she so offending, shall, for
every such offence, proved by the oath of the party, before a Justice of the
Peace, of the county or corporation, where such offence shall be committed, receive such punishment as the justice shall think proper, not exceeding thirty-nine lashes, on his or her bare back, well laid on; except in
those cases, where it shall appear to such justice, that such negro or mulatto was wantonly assaulted, and lifted his or her hand in his or her defense. . . .

52. *Punishment of Slave for Assault and Battery on a White Person with Intent to
Kill.* If any slave or slaves, shall, at any time commit an assault and battery, upon any white person, with intent to kill, every such slave or slaves,
so committing such assault and battery, with intent to kill, as aforesaid,
and being thereof convicted, in manner hereinafter directed, shall suffer
death. . . .

55. *Certain Capital Offenses.* If any slave shall maim a free white person, or
shall attempt to commit a rape on any free white woman, or female child
under the age of twelve years, or shall attempt to commit any capital
crime, or shall be voluntarily accessary before or after the fact, in any capital offence, or shall be guilty of the manslaughter of any free person, or
shall be guilty of burning any dwelling-house, store, cotton-house, gin or
out-house, barn or stable, or shall be accessary thereto, or shall be guilty
of any of the crimes aforesaid, or any other crime made capital by law, or
shall be accessary thereto, every such slave shall, on conviction, suffer
death. . . .

59. *Punishment of Negro or Mulatto for Perjury; Charge to Negro, &c., before sworn.*
If any negro or mulatto shall be found, upon due proof made to any
county or corporation Court of this State, to have given false testimony,

every such offender shall, without further trial, be ordered by the said Court, to have one ear nailed to the pillory, and there to stand for the space of one hour, and then the said ear to be cut off, and thereafter the other ear nailed in like manner, and cut off at the expiration of one other hour, and moreover to receive thirty-nine lashes on his or her bare back, well laid on, at the public whipping post, or such other punishment as the Court shall think proper, not extending to life or limb. And whenever it shall be necessary to examine any slave, free negro or mulatto, as a witness in any trial, it shall be the duty of the Court, or Justice sitting on such trial, before such witness shall be examined, to charge him to declare the truth, in the manner following, to wit: "You are brought here as a witness, and, by the direction of the law, I am to tell you before you give your evidence, that you must tell the truth, the whole truth, and nothing but the truth; and if it be found hereafter, that you tell a lie, and give false testimony in this matter, you must, for so doing, have both your ears nailed to the pillory, and cut off, and receive thirty-nine lashes on your bare back, well laid on, at the common whipping post."

Source: A. Hutchinson, comp., *Code of Mississippi; Being an Analytical Compilation of the Public and General Statutes of the Territory and the State* (Jackson, MS: E. Barksdale, 1848), 512–14, 517, 521–22.

North Carolina's Supreme Court Considers the Murder Conviction of the Slave Caesar, 1849

By the end of the antebellum era, southern states had begun to allow slaves greater access to circuit and appellate courts. Most state supreme court precedents involving slaves date to the 1840s or 1850s. Since slaves gained access to the due process protections of circuit courts only by committing the most serious, capital offenses, almost all these cases involve either rape, arson, or murder. Whites awarded slaves due process not out of a sense of justice to black people but as a way of protecting the property of slave owners. Violating the due process rights of a slave defendant threatened to destroy the property of a white man.

One of the most notorious antebellum slave murder cases concerned a North Carolina slave named Caesar. The case began in 1848, near the town of Jameston, when two drunken white men came across two slaves in a field near a storehouse. One of the white men, known only as Brickhouse, lied to the slaves, saying he and his friend were patrollers. Brickhouse and the other white man, Kenneth Mizell, hit the slaves with a board and asked if the blacks could "get some girls for them."

Caesar and Dick, the two slaves, must have realized that two drunks asking for

*"some girls" were not on county business. As they refused to do the whites' bidding,
another slave, Charles, approached. Brickhouse seized Charles and told Dick to get a whip
so he could beat Charles. Dick's refusal enraged Brickhouse and Mizell, and the two white
men began pummeling Dick with their fists. Caesar first looked on helplessly but then
announced that he "could not stand" it any longer and seized a fence rail, striking
Brickhouse and Mizell. Brickhouse survived the blow, but Mizell died. Authorities put
Caesar on trial for murder.*

*Everyone understood that if a white man had struck Mizell in such a spontaneous
fashion, he would be guilty of manslaughter rather than murder. But at Caesar's trial,
the judge instructed the jury that no black man could ever be allowed to strike any white
man, under any circumstances. Caesar must be guilty of murder, the judge decided. The
jury agreed.*

*Caesar appealed his death sentence to the state supreme court. The justices had to
decide if the common law could be made to apply to slaves. In essence, they had to decide
if a black man could ever strike a white man. Justice Richmond M. Pearson wrote the
opinion of the court, finding that, indeed, blacks could sometimes kill a white man and
be guilty only of manslaughter. Chief Justice Thomas Ruffin dissented, insisting that
slavery required absolute obedience on the part of slaves with no exceptions allowed. The
court's decision saved Caesar from death, as he was tried again, convicted of manslaughter, had his thumb branded with the letter M, and was returned to slavery.*

THE STATE V. CAESAR, a slave.

PEARSON, J. The prisoner, a slave, is convicted of murder in killing a *white
man*. The case presents the question, whether the rules of law, by which manslaughter is distinguished from murder, as between white men, are applicable,
when the party killing is a slave. If not, then to what extent a difference is to
be made?

. . . To present the general question by itself, and prevent confusion, it
will be well to ascertain, what would have been the offence, if all the parties
had been white men? Two friends are quietly talking together at night—two
strangers come up—one strikes each of the friends several blows with a board;
the blows are slight, but calculated to irritate—a third friend comes up—one
of the strangers seizes him, and orders one of the former to go and get a
whip that he might whip him. Upon his refusing thus to become an aider in
their unlawful act, the two strangers set upon him—one holds his hands,
while the other beats him with his fist upon the head and breast, he not ven-
turing to make resistance and begging for mercy—his friend yielding to a
burst of generous indignation, exclaims, "I can't stand this," takes up a fence
rail, knocks one down, and then knocks the other down, and without a *repetition of the blow*, the three friends make their escape. The blow given to one
proves fatal. Is not the bare statement sufficient? Does it require argument,

or a reference to adjudged cases to show, that this is not a case of *murder*? or, "of a black," diabolical heart, regardless of social duty and fatally bent on mischief? It is clearly a case of manslaughter in its most mitigated form. The provocation was grievous. The blow was inflicted with the first thing that could be laid hold of: it was *not repeated* and must be attributed, *not to malice*, but to a generous impulse, excited by witnessing injury done to a friend. . . .

As this would have been a case of manslaughter, if the parties had been white men; are the same rules applicable, the party killing being a slave? The lawmaking power has not expressed its will, but has left the law to be declared by the "courts, as it may be deduced from the primary principles of the doctrine of homicide." The task is no easy one, yet it is the duty of the court to ascertain and declare what the law is. . . .

I think it clearly deducible from . . . the common law, that, if a white man wantonly inflicts upon a slave, over whom he has no authority, a severe blow, or repeated blows under unusual circumstances, and the slave *at the instant* strikes and kills, without evincing, by the means used, great wickedness and cruelty, he is only guilty of manslaughter, giving due weight to motives of policy and the necessity for subordination.

This latter consideration, perhaps, requires the killing should be *at the instant*; for, it may not be consistent with due subordination to allow a slave, after he is extricated from his difficulty and is no longer receiving blows or in danger, to return and seek a combat. A wild beast wounded or in danger will turn upon a man, but he seldom so far forgets his sense of inferiority as to seek a combat. Upon this principle, which man has in common with the beast, a slave may, without losing sight of his inferiority, strike a white man, when in danger or suffering wrong; but he will not seek a combat after he is extricated.

If the witness, Dick, while one white man was holding his hands, and the other was beating him, had killed either of them, there would have been no difficulty in making the application of the above principles, and deciding, that the killing was but manslaughter, and of a mitigated grade, contrasted with *Will's case*, who, although he did not seek the combat, but was trying to escape, killed his *owner* with a knife, after being guilty of wilful disobedience; and the conclusion would derive confirmation from the reasoning of Judge Gaston, in *Jarrott's case*, where the prisoner had it in his power to avoid the combat, if he would, and struck *several blows, after the white man was prostrated*.

In making the application of the principles before stated to the case of the prisoner, another principle is involved. The prisoner was not engaged in the fight—he was the associate and friend of Dick, and was present and a witness to his wrongs and suffering.

We have seen, that had he been a white man, his offence would have been manslaughter; "because of the *passion*, which is *excited*, when one sees his friend assaulted."...But he is a slave, and the question is, does that benignant principle of the law, by which allowance is made for the infirmity of our nature, prompting a parent, brother, kinsman, friend, or even a stranger to interfere in a fight and kill, and by which it is held that, under such circumstances, the killing is ascribed to *passion* and not to *malice*, and is manslaughter not *murder*; does this principle apply to a slave? or is he commanded, under *pain of death*, not to yield to these feelings and impulses of human nature, under any circumstances? I think the principle does apply, and am not willing, by excluding it from the case of slaves, to extend the doctrine of constructive murder beyond the limits, now given to it by well-settled principles. The application of this principle will, of course, be restrained and qualified to the same extent and for the same reasons, as the application of the principle of legal provocation, before explained. A slight blow will not extenuate; but, if a white man wantonly inflicts upon a slave, over whom he has no authority, a severe blow, or repeated blows under unusual circumstances, and another, yielding to the impulse, natural to the relations above referred to, strikes at the instant and kills, without evincing, by the means used, great wickedness or cruelty, the offense is extenuated to manslaughter....

The prisoner was the associate or friend of Dick—his general character was shown to be that of an obedient slave, submissive to white men—he had himself received several slight blows, without offence on his part, to which he quietly submitted—he was present from the beginning—saw the wanton injury and suffering inflicted upon his helpless, unoffending and unresisting associate—he must either run away and leave him at the mercy of two drunken ruffians, to suffer, he knew not how much, from their fury and disappointed lust—the hour of the night forbade the hope of aid from white men—or he must yield to a generous impulse and come to the rescue. He used force enough to release his associate and they made their escape, without a *repetition* of the *blow*. Does this show he has a heart of a murderer? On the contrary, are we not forced, in spite of stern policy, to admire, even in a slave, the generosity, which incurs danger to save a friend? The law requires a slave to tame down his feelings to suit his lowly condition, but would it be savage, to allow him, under no circumstances, to yield to a generous impulse.

I think his Honor erred in charging the jury, that, under the circumstances, the prisoner was guilty of murder, and that there was no legal provocation. For this error the prisoner is entitled to a new trial. He cannot, in my opinion, be convicted of murder, without overruling *Hale's case* and *Will's case*. It should be borne in mind, that in laying down rules upon this subject, they must apply to white men as a class, and not as individuals; must be suited to the most *degraded*, as well as the most orderly. Hence great caution is required to protect slave property from wanton outrages, while, at the same time, due subordination is preserved.

It should also be borne in mind, that a conviction of manslaughter is far from being an acquittal; it extenuates on account of human infirmity, but does not justify or excuse. Manslaughter is a felony. For the second offense life is forfeited.

I think there ought to be a new trial.

RUFFIN, C.J. I am unable to concur in the judgment of the Court, and, upon a point of such general consequence, I conceive it to be a duty to state my dissent, and the grounds of it.

... The dissimilarity in the condition of slaves from anything known at the common law cannot be denied; and, therefore, as it appears to me, the rules upon this, as upon all other kinds of intercourse between white men and slaves, must vary from those applied by the common law, between persons so essentially differing in their relations, education, rights, principles of action, habits, and motives for resentment.

... There is nothing analogous to [the difference in condition of free white men and slaves] in the relations recognized by the common law. . . . It involves a necessity, not only for the discipline on the part of the owner requisite to procure productive labor from them, but for enforcing a subordination to the white race, which alone is compatible with the contentment of the slaves with their destiny, the acknowledged superiority of the whites, and the public quiet and security. The whites forever feel and assert a superiority, and exact an humble submission from the slaves; and the latter, in all they say and do, not only profess, but plainly exhibit a corresponding deep and abiding sense of legal and personal inferiority. Negroes—at least the great mass of them—born with deference to the white man, take the most contumelious language without answering again, and generally submit tamely to his buffets, though unlawful and unmerited. Such are the habits of the country. It is not now the question, whether these things are naturally right and proper to exist. They do exist actually, legally, and inveterately. Indeed, they are inseparable from the state of slavery; and are only to be deemed wrong upon the admission that slavery is fundamentally wrong. . . .

So, it follows, as certainly as day follows night, that many things, which drive a white man to madness, will not have the like effect, if done by a white man to a slave; and, particularly, it is true, that slaves are not ordinarily moved to kill a white man for a common beating. For, it is an incontestable fact, that the great mass of slaves—nearly all of them—are the least turbulent of all men; that, when sober, they never attack a white man; and seldom, very seldom, exhibit any temper or sense of provocation at even gross and violent injuries from white men. They sometimes deliberately murder; oftener at the instigation of others, than on their own motive. They sometimes kill each other in heat of blood, being sensible to the dishonor in their own caste of crouching in submission to one of themselves. That, however, is much less frequent than among whites; for they have a duller sensibility to degradation. But hardly such a thing is known, as that a slave turns in retaliation on a white man, and, especially, that he attempts to take life for even a wanton battery, unless it be carried to such extremity as to render resistance proper in defense of his own life. Crowds of negroes in public places are often dispersed with blows by white men, and no one remembers a homicide of a white man on such occasions. The inference is, that the generality of slaves—those who are well disposed towards the whites, as are almost all—do not in truth and fact find themselves impelled to a bloody vengeance, upon the provocation of blows with the fist or switch from a white man. That is the experience of the whole country. In the course of nearly forty-two years of personal experience in the profession and a very extensive intercourse with other members of the profession from every part of the State, I have not known or heard of half a dozen instances of killing or attempting to kill a white man by a negro in a scuffle, although the batteries on them by whites have been without number, and often without cause or excessive. Desperate runaways sometimes resist apprehension by a resort to deadly weapons. But the fact certainly is, negro slaves can hardly be said to be at all sensible to the provocation of an assault from a white man, as an incentive to spill blood. Such being the real state of things, it is a just conclusion of reason, when a slave kills a white man for a battery not likely to kill, maim, or do permanent injury, nor accompanied by unusual cruelty, that the act did not flow from generous and uncontrollable resentment, but from a bad heart—one, intent upon the assertion of an equality, social and personal, with the white, and bent on mortal mischief in support of the assertion. It is but the pretense of a provocation, not usually felt. Therefore, it cannot be tolerated in the law. . . .

. . . I believe, this is the very first instance in which a slave has ventured to interpose, either between white men, or between a white man and a slave, taking part against the white man. Why should he intermeddle upon the plea of resisting the unlawful power, or redressing the wanton wrong, of a white man, when he, to whom the wrong was done, is admitted to have been unresisting? Shall one slave be the arbiter of the quarrels witnessed by him between another slave and the whites? It seems to me to be dangerous to the last degree to hold the doctrine, that negro slaves may assume to themselves the judgment as to the right or propriety of resistance, by one of his own race, to the authority taken over them by the whites, and upon the notion of a generous sympathy with their oppressed fellow servants, may step forward to secure them from the hands of a white man, and much less to avenge their wrongs. First denying their general subordination to the whites, it may be apprehended that they will end in denouncing the injustice of slavery itself, and, upon that pretext, band together to throw off their common bondage entirely. The rule, which extenuates the assistance given by a white man to his friend, in a conflict between him and another white man—all being *in equali jure*—cannot, I think, be safely or fairly extended, so as to allow a slave, upon supposed generous impulses, to do the noble duty of killing a white man, because he tyrannizes over a negro man, so far as to give him a rap with a ratan and a few blows with his fists. I have never heard such a position advanced before, either as a doctrine of our law or as an opinion of any portion of our people.

For these reasons, the judgment, I think, ought to be affirmed.

Source: *The State v. Caesar,* 31 NC 391 (1849).

SLAVE REVOLT IN VIRGINIA

On August 21, 1831, in southeastern Virginia, Nat Turner led seventy fellow slaves in a revolt that sought to end their bondage. Turner began by killing his owner, Joseph Travis, and Travis's family; by the time the rebellion had been crushed just two days later, the rebels had killed fifty-seven whites. Local whites responded brutally in turn, executing two hundred slaves, many of whom had nothing to do with the uprising. The revolt unnerved Southern whites. Turner and his owner had gotten along well; Turner described Travis as a kind man who had encouraged Turner to learn to read and write and become a preacher. Before he was hanged with thirteen of his fellow rebels, Turner dictated the following narrative to his attorney, Thomas R. Gray, who published it as "The Confessions of Nat Turner," after Turner's execution. Many scholars have come to doubt the complete veracity of Gray's transcription, assuming that he had his own reasons for slanting the final document. Unfortunately, it is not possible to determine how true the "Confession" is to Turner's own voice. However it remains extremely useful as one of the few statements of the perceptions and intentions of a slave rebel in antebellum America.

Nat Turner Describes His Rebellion, 1831

Sir,—You have asked me to give a history of the motives which induced me to undertake the late insurrection, as you call it. To do so I must go back to the days of my infancy.... In my childhood a circumstance occurred which made an indelible impression on my mind, and laid the ground-work of that enthusiasm, which has terminated so fatally to many, both white and black, and for which I am about to atone at the gallows. . . . Being at play with other children, when three or four years old, I was telling them something, which my mother overhearing, said it had happened before I was born—

I stuck to my story, however, and related some things which went in her opinion to confirm it—others being called on were greatly astonished, knowing that these things had happened, [and] caused them to say in my hearing, I surely would be a prophet, as the Lord had shewn me things that had happened before my birth. . . .

Having soon discovered, that to be great, I must appear so, and therefore studiously avoided mixing in society, and wrapped myself in mystery, devoting my time to fasting and prayer—By this time, having arrived to man's estate, and hearing the scriptures commented on at meetings, I was struck with that particular passage which says: "Seek ye the kingdom of Heaven and all things shall be added unto you." I reflected much on this passage, and prayed daily for light on this subject—As I was praying one day at my plough, the spirit spoke to me, saying "Seek ye the kingdom of Heaven and all things shall be added unto you." . . .

[A]nd I was greatly astonished, and for two years prayed continually, whenever my duty would permit—and then again I had the same revelation, which fully confirmed me in the impression that I was ordained for some great purpose in the hands of the Almighty.

Several years rolled round, in which many events occurred to strengthen me in this my belief. At this time I reverted in my mind to the remarks made of me in my childhood, and the things that had been shown me—and as it had been said of me in my childhood by those by whom I had been taught to pray, both white and black, and in whom I had the greatest confidence, that I had too much sense to be raised, and if I was, I would never be of any use to any one as a slave. Now finding I had arrived at man's estate, and was a slave, and these revelations being made known to me, I began to direct my attention to this great object, to fulfill the purpose for which, by this time, I felt assured I was intended. Knowing the influence I had obtained over the minds of my fellow servants, (not by means of conjuring and such like tricks—for to them I always spoke of such things with contempt) but by the communion of the Spirit whose revelations I often communicated to them, and they believed and said my wisdom came from God. I now began to prepare them for my purpose, by telling them something was about to happen that would terminate in fulfilling the great promise that had been made to me. . . .

And about this time I had a vision—and I saw white spirits and black spirits engaged in battle, and the sun was darkened—the thunder rolled in the Heavens, and blood flowed in streams—and I heard a voice saying, "Such is your luck, such you are called on to see, and let it come rough or smooth, you must surely bare [in original] it."

I now withdrew myself as much as my situation would permit, from the intercourse of my fellow servants, for the avowed purpose of serving the Spirit more fully—and it appeared to me, and reminded me of the things it had already shown me, and that it would then reveal to me the knowledge of the elements, the revolution of the planets, the operation of tides, and changes of the seasons. After this revelation in the year 1825, and the knowledge of the elements being made known to me, I sought more than ever to obtain true holiness before the great day of judgment should appear, and then I began to receive the true knowledge of faith. And from the first steps of righteousness until the last, was I made perfect; and the Holy Ghost was with me, and said "Behold me as I stand in the Heavens" and I looked and saw the forms of men in different attitudes—and there were lights in the sky to which the children of darkness gave other names than what they really were—for they were the lights of the Savior's hands, stretched forth from east to west, even as they were extended on the cross on Calvary, for the redemption of sinners. And I wondered greatly at these miracles, and prayed to be informed of a certainty of the meaning thereof—and shortly afterwards, while laboring in the field, I discovered drops of blood on the corn as though it were dew from heaven—and I communicated it to many, both white and black, in the neighborhood—and I then found on the leaves in the woods hieroglyphic characters, and numbers, with the forms of men in different attitudes, portrayed in blood, and representing the figures I had seen before in the heavens. And now the Holy Ghost had revealed itself to me, and made plain the miracles it had shown me—For as the blood of Christ had been shed on this earth, and had ascended to heaven for the salvation of sinners, and was now returning to earth again in the form of dew—and as the leaves on the trees bore the impression of the figures I had seen in the heavens, it was plain to me that the Savior was about to lay down the yoke he had borne for the sins of men, and the great day of judgment was at hand. . . . And on the 12th of May, 1828, I heard a loud noise in the heavens, and the Spirit instantly appeared to me and said the Serpent was loosened, and Christ had laid down the yoke he had borne for the sins of men, and that I should take it on and fight against the Serpent, for the time was fast approaching when the first should be last and the last should be first.

QUES.. Do you not find yourself mistaken now?
ANS.. Was not Christ crucified?—

And by signs in the heavens that it would make known to me when I should commence the great work—and until the first sign appeared, I should conceal it from the knowledge of men—

And on the appearance of the sign, (the eclipse of the sun last February) I should arise and prepare myself, and slay my enemies with their own weapons. And immediately on the sign appearing in the heavens, the seal was removed from my lips, and I communicated the great work laid out for me to do, to four in whom I had the greatest confidence, (Henry, Hark, Nelson and Sam)—It was intended by us to have begun the work of death on the 4th of July last—Many were the plans formed and rejected by us, and it affected my mind to such a degree, that I fell sick, and the time passed without our coming to any determination how to commence—Still forming new schemes and rejecting them, when the sign appeared again, which determined me not to wait longer.

Since the commencement of 1830, I had been living with Mr. Joseph Travis, who was to me a kind master, and placed the greatest confidence in me; in fact, I had no cause to complain of his treatment to me. On Saturday evening, the 20th of August, it was agreed between Henry, Hark and myself, to prepare a dinner the next day for the men we expected, and then to concert a plan, as we had not yet determined on any. . . .

I saluted them on coming up; . . . it was quickly agreed we should commence at home (Mr. J. Travis') on that night, and, until we had armed and equipped ourselves, and gathered sufficient force, neither age nor sex was to be spared, (which was invariably adhered to.) . . .

It was then observed that I must spill the first blood. On which, armed with a hatchet, and accompanied by Will, I entered my master's chamber, it being dark, I could not give a death blow, the hatchet glanced from his head, he sprang from the bed and called his wife, it was his last word, Will laid him dead with a blow of his axe, and Mrs. Travis shared the same fate, as she laid in bed. The murder of this family, five in number, was the work of a moment, not one of them awoke; there was a little infant sleeping in a cradle, that was forgotten, until we had left the house and gone some distance, when Henry and Will returned and killed it; we got here four guns that would shoot, and several old muskets, with a pound or two of powder. We remained for some time at the barn, where we paraded; I formed them in a line as soldiers, and after carrying them through all the maneuvres I was master of, marched them off to Mr. Salathul Francis', about six hundred yards distant. . . .

During the time I was pursued, I had many hair-breadth escapes, which your time will not permit me to relate. I am here loaded with chains, and willing to suffer the fate that awaits me.

Source: Thomas R. Gray. *The Confessions of Nat Turner* (Baltimore: Thomas R. Gray, 1831), 7–12, 17–18.

A SLAVE INSURRECTION IN MISSISSIPPI

Madison County, Mississippi, lies just above Jackson, the state capital. In the nineteenth century, blacks vastly outnumbered whites in the county's remote plantation districts. Thus, when rumors of slave insurrections swept the Mississippi valley in 1835, Madison County residents eyed their slaves with suspicions driven by justified paranoia. Terrified whites organized vigilante committees to suppress the threatened slave rebellion and to forestall a lynch mob. The record Madison County whites published of their extralegal tribunals documents the South's lawlessness under slavery, revealing whites as poised on the brink of anarchy and mayhem.

The Vigilantes of Madison County, Mississippi, Justify Their Actions, 1835

About the middle of the month of June 1835, a rumor was afloat through Madison county, that an insurrection of the slaves was meditated; no authentic information however, having been obtained, how, or where the report originated; most of the citizens were disposed to treat it as unfounded, and consequently took no steps to ascertain its truth or falsehood, until within a few days previous to the 4th of July.

After ascertaining that the report had emanated from a lady resident at Beatie's Bluff, in this county, about 9 miles from Livingston, a number of gentlemen waited upon her, for the purpose of learning upon what grounds of suspicions, she had given publicity to it. The lady, in compliance with their request, informed them that she was induced to believe an insurrection of the negroes was in contemplation. . . .

. . . The report of the gentlemen of course, was, that they had good reason to believe that an insurrection of the negroes was contemplated by them, and warned their fellow citizens to be on their guard, and requested them to organize patroles, a matter which had been entirely neglected heretofore, and to appoint committees of vigilance throughout the county.

This report awakened the people in a measure from their lethargy: meetings were held in different parts of the county, for the purpose of taking into consideration the state of affairs.

On the 27th of June, at a large and respectable meeting of the citizens, held at Livingston, Col. H. D. RUNNELS in the chair; resolutions were adopted, appointing patroles and committees of investigation, who were requested to report the result of their inquiries and discoveries at an adjourned meeting to be holden at Livingston on the 30th June.

On the 30th June, pursuant to adjournment, the citizens again met at Livingston, Dr. M. D. Mitchell was called to the chair, when, Mr. William P. Johnson, a planter near Livingston, made a report of his investigation on his own plantation. He informed the meeting that he had instructed his driver, a negro man, in whom he had confidence, to examine all the negroes on his place and see if they knew any thing of the conspiracy. . . . [T]he driver had . . . learned from an old negro, who was in the habit of hauling water from Livingston, that there was to be (using his own language,) "a rising of the blacks soon, but did not know when; that he had learned it from a negro man belonging to Ruel Blake, who lived in Livingston." . . .

Mr. Johnson had the old negro brought to town and put into the hands of the committee of investigation for Livingston, whom he instructed to use as they might deem proper. The negro man was asked to confess what he had told the driver of Mr. Johnson the evening previous. He denied bitterly ever having any conversation with the driver; and the committee finding they could get nothing out of him by persuasion, ordered him to be whipped until he would tell what the conversation was, not being informed of what nature it was.

After receiving a more severe chastisement, he came out and confessed all he knew respecting the contemplated insurrection, and confirmed in every particular the statement of the driver, but could not tell what particular day was fixed upon for the insurrection. . . .

The citizens in the neighborhood of Beaties Bluff were not idle. . . . After two days of patient and scrutinizing examination of the negroes implicated at Beaties Bluff, their guilt was fully established, not only by their own confessions, but by other facts and circumstances, which could not leave a doubt on the mind. Each negro was examined separate and apart from the rest, neither knowing that another was suspected or in custody; each acknowledging his own guilt, and implicating all of the others; every one implicating the same *white men*, and the whole of their statements coinciding precisely with each other.

After ascertaining so fully the guilt of these negroes, and the time for the consummation of the designs being at hand; the situation of the country being such as to render consummation so easy; the whole community and the owners of the negroes in particular, demanded the immediate execution of the guilty, and they were accordingly hung on the 2d of July. . . .

The following white men, Cotton and Saunders, were arrested and in custody; and this, too, before the disclosures of the negroes at Beatties Bluff were known. The arrest being made upon circumstances of suspicion and facts, indicating in a very strong degree their agency and participation in the plans then hastening to their full development and consummation. And when the disclosures made at Beatties Bluff as above unfolded, were fully made known at Livingston, there seemed to be left no alternative but to adopt the most efficient and decisive measures.

The question became general—what should they do with the persons implicated? Should they hand them over to the civil authority? This, it would seem, under ordinary circumstances, to be the proper course. But should that be the course, it was well known that much of the testimony which established their guilt beyond all doubt, would under the *forms* of the law, be excluded; and, if admissible, that the witnesses were then no more. If, from our peculiar situation, the laws were incompetent to reach their case—should such acts go unpunished? Besides, from what had been seen and witnessed the day before, it was universally believed, and doubtless such would have been the fact, these persons would have been *forcibly* taken, even from the custody of the law, and made to suffer the penalty due to their crimes. Should they even be committed for trial, there was much reason to apprehend that they would be rescued by their confederates in guilt—if not by *perjury* at least by breaking the jail. They had an example of the dreadful excitement on the evening of the 2d July, at Livingston. Immediately after the execution of the negroes at Beatties Bluff was made known in Livingston, it created a most alarming excitement. The two old negro men who were in custody of the committee of examination at Livingston, were demanded by the citizens; and previous to a vote of condemnation and a full examination, they were forcibly taken by an infuriated people from the custody of those who intended to award them a fair trial, and immediately hung.

The time was near at hand when the intentions of the conspirators would inevitably be carried into effect, if some prompt and efficient means should not be adopted by the citizens to strike terror among their accomplices, and to bring the guilty to a summary and exemplary punishment. It was not believed that the execution of a few negroes, unknown and obscure, would have the effect of frightening their *white* associates from an attempt to perpetrate their horrid designs; which *association* was fully established by the confessions of the accused and other circumstances.

There was no time to be lost, and for the purpose of effecting their object, to arrest the progress of the impending danger, to extend to the parties implicated something like a *trial*, if not *formal* at least *substantial*, and to save them from the inevitable fate of a speedy and condign punishment, the citizens circulated a call for a general assemblage of the community on the day following, at Livingston, which call was obeyed; and, at an early hour the next day, July 3d, there collected a vast concourse of people from the adjoining neighborhoods.

This meeting, thus speedily assembled, (for it was full by 9 A.M.) was composed of at least 160 respectable citizens of Madison and Hinds counties, who then and there acting under the influence of the law of self preservation, which *is paramount to all law*, chose from among the assemblage thirteen of their fellow citizens, who were immediately organized, and styled a "Committee of Safety"—to whom they determined to commit what is emphatically and properly called the *supreme law*, the *safety* of the people, (or salus populi est summa lex,) and then pledged themselves to carry into effect any order which the committee might make. Which committee were invested, by the citizens, with the authority of punishing all persons found guilty, by them, of aiding and exciting the negroes to insurrection, as they might deem necessary for the safety of the community; all of which will more fully appear by the subjoined resolutions adopted at the meeting, which organized the committee. . . .

At 10 o'clock, A.M., on the 3d, the committee commenced their labours with the examination of the case of Joshua Cotton.

TRIAL OF JOSHUA COTTON.

This man had been in the State of Mississippi about twelve months; was a native of some one of the New England States, but last from the Western District of Tennessee. On his arrival in this State he settled at the Old Indian Agency, in Hinds county, where he married soon after. From the Agency he moved to Livingston, in Madison county, where he set up shop and hoisted a sign as "Steam Doctor." He was not liked by the citizens of Livingston: with whom he had no social intercourse. In his business transactions he had been detected in many low tricks, and attempts to swindle. It was in evidence before the committee that he had left Memphis, Tennessee, (soon after the conviction of the celebrated Murrel,) with a wife and child, who were *never afterwards heard of.* As an evidence of his want of feeling and affection for his second wife, Saunders stated to the committee that he, Cotton, had made a proposiiton to him to take Cotton's second wife to Red River, in Arkansas, and there leave her, with the promise that Cotton would meet her so soon as he should settle his affairs in this country; at the same time informing Saunders that his object was to abandon her.

William Saunders, at the meeting of the citizens held in Livingston, on the 30th June, stated that Cotton was in the habit of trading with negroes; would buy any thing they would steal and bring to him; that he believed Cotton had stolen John Slater's negroes, in connexion with Boyd—(afterwards ascertained Boyd had stolen them.)

This disclosure, and other evidence of his bad character, being generally known, led to his arrest on the 1st of July. But Saunders having left town, and no evidence being offered at his examination, sufficient to justify the citizens in detaining him, he was by their order discharged. Immediately after his dismission he returned to the house of his father-in-law, whither he had removed with his family a *few days* prior to the discovery of the insurrection. Saunders, in the mean time, was making off, as he said, for Texas; he informed a gentleman, on his way to Vicksburg, that a discovery of a conspiracy of negroes was made in Madison county, and disclosed to him all their plans, as subsequently developed, in the course of the investigations of the committee at Livingston, and said that Cotton *wanted him to join them but he would not.* He likewise stated that it was the intention of the conspirators (should *some* one of the *clan* fail, to rob one of the partners of the Commission house of Ewing, Maddux & Co., who was then on his way from New Orleans to Livingston,) to rob their house at Livingston. This part of their plans was to be attended to by Cotton and Blake. The gentleman believing Saunders to be one of the conspirators had him arrested and delivered into the hands of the Livingston guard, who were in search of him, and was brought back to Livingston on the 2d of July.

On the strength of Saunders' confessions, Cotton was again arrested and brought back to Livingston on the same evening. . . .

On the 4th of July the confessions of the negroes hung at Beatties Bluff were in evidence before the committee, as it was seen in the preceding report of the proceedings at Beatties Bluff. Cotton was said to be one of the ringleaders in exciting them to insurrection.

After having much other corroborating testimony the committee had Cotton removed from the committee room, in order that they might deliberate on this case.

Immediately after leaving the room he exclaimed to the guard "It's all over with me!" All I wish is, that the committee will have me decently buried, and not suffer me to hang long after I am dead. Great God!! was the exclamation of the bystanders—"Cotton, you do not know that you will be convicted?" He replied, despondingly, "that the testimony was so strong against him that they must convict him—that they *could* not avoid it." Some said "he must be a very guilty man to condemn himself, and if he was guilty to come out and tell the truth, that it would be some atonement for his guilt—and to tell them who were his accomplices;" there being a number of white men in custody at the time, in Livingston and elsewhere in the county. Cotton replied to their request by saying "if the committee would pledge themselves not to have him hung immediately, that he would come out and tell them all he knew about the conspiracy." The request of Cotton was communicated to the committee, who in answer said, through their chairman, "that they would not pledge themselves to extend any favor to him whatever; that they were satisfied as to his guilt, and that he might confess or not." In answer to the reply of the committee Cotton sent word to them "If they would hear what he had to say, he would make a confession." . . .

The committee after receiving his confession, condemned him to be hanged in an hour after sentence, in order that the news of his execution might be circulated extensively before night, thinking it would frighten his accomplices from the undertaking.

After his condemnation he made publicly some additional disclosures, which, unfortunately, were not reduced to writing. Under the gallows he acknowledged his guilt and the justness of his sentence, and remarked "it was nothing more than he deserved;" and likewise invoked the vengeance of his God, if every word he had written was not true; and that all those he had implicated were as actively engaged in the conspiracy as he was. And, lastly, in answer to some person who asked him "if he really thought there would be any danger that night," he said "he did, if they should not hear he was hung." His last words were "take care of yourselves to night and to morrow night," and swung off.

Source: Thomas Shackelford, *Proceedings of the Citizens of Madison County, Mississippi at Livingston, in July, 1835, in Relation to the Trial and Punishment of Several Individuals Implicated in a Contemplated Insurrection in This State* (Jackson, MS: Mayson and Smoot, 1836), 5–8, 12–13, 15–19.

DUELING

In 1844, citizens of Vicksburg, Mississippi, met to discuss how to end "duelling, street fights, violence, and other outrages upon civilized society." The meeting not only failed to end dueling, which continued until the end of the nineteenth century in Mississippi, but also prompted Joseph E. Davis, the older brother of Jefferson Davis, to denounce efforts to end the practice. It is striking how little faith the proponents of dueling placed in the law. Without "personal accountability," Davis said, white gentlemen would be subjected to a hellish anarchy of insult. Dueling maintained order, accomplishing what Davis believed the law could not. This lack of respect for their own laws underlay much of the violence that plagued Southern society.

White Mississippians Debate Dueling, 1844

Capt. Davis concluded by offering the following in lieu of the resolutions offered by the majority of the committee.

Resolved, That it is the sense of this meeting that the habit of wearing concealed weapons is injurious to the moral feeling, peace and reputation of this community.

Resolved, That the public broils and street rencontres endanger the safety of peaceable citizens, derogate from the character of the city, and should bring reprobation upon all who are concerned in either.

Resolved, That duelling, however irrational and immoral, can only be suppressed by the progress of intelligence, morality and good breeding; therefore, as the nearest approximation to the end we all desire, that the effort be made to prevent, *unnecessarily,* a resort to deadly weapons, and to regulate such a resort, when it cannot be prevented by principles of fairness, and as far as may be equality between the combattants.

Resolved, therefore, that a committee of—be appointed to prepare a constitution and bylaws for an association to be formed on these principles and to carry out these objects, and that said committee report to an adjourned meeting to be held on—day.

The resolutions of Capt. Davis awakened the roar of debate, and the meeting was addressed and readdressed by the voluminous and weary Jacob Shall Yerger, esq. He had just three ideas upon which he rung 333 changes. . . . His final sentiment was the reiteration that the duel was against the laws of God and man. We would advise this speaker and all of his name as Mr. Prentiss now does to read the scriptures. In them will be found the account of a splendid duel between David and Golia[t]h. This was a cool and premeditated affair, the challenge having been given every day for forty days, and taken up by David on the fortieth. The daughters and maidens of Israel and every body else rejoiced at the result of this duel. Who stood by and backed David? Was not the Lord himself at David's elbow, and his only second? We, in fact, recollect but one new idea in Mr. Yerger's speech. He called aloud upon all members, church and state to give their support, and pledged himself, that within five years a man would as quick think of challenging a person as to send a challenge to a member of the Vick (WEAK) society!

Mr. Yerger was followed by Capt. Walter Guion, late of the U.S. Army, who in pure language and diction, as well as high-toned Southern sentiments and chivalry was scarcely exceeded by the main speaker, J. E. Davis Esq., who then in his sixtieth year, stood forth in a strain of pure, upright, manly and chivalric feeling which put his Honor to the blush. He concluded by the remark that if he mistook not the signs of the times—if he mistook not the experience of forty years in a southern country, the responsibility of the duel could not now be abolished. He admitted the abuse of the code of honor to every southern man, and remarked to the chair that when men had become so just and enlightened as to do away with the necessity for personal accountability, that his Honor would be required no longer to sit upon the bench—that in point of fact circumstances and changes in the times had but increased the value of an Institution, without which the country would be little else than the land of insult and the abode of those closely approximating to highwaymen. He said, no, Mr. Chairman, let us correct the abuses, but, sir, let us, for all gross insults not properly atoned for, make it imperative upon the agressed to stand on equal terms and fight; make it so, sir, that he must fight atone, or leave the country. This sir, said he, is the way to put down insult and puppy fights, and in his humble opinion the only way.

Source: *Vicksburg Sentinel*, June 5, 1844.

THE DAILY EXPERIENCE OF CRUELTY

Frederick Douglass was just one of thousands of slaves who "stole himself," running away to freedom. A dynamic speaker and brilliant polemicist, Douglass became one of the most articulate opponents of slavery and published three versions of his autobiography, the first in 1845. My Bondage and My Freedom, *which came out in 1855, was the most complete exploration of his experience of slavery and brought home to thousands of readers in the North the daily sadism of slavery. For Douglass, slavery's violence began at birth, as the slave owner deprived the baby of that most basic social requirement, a family.*

Frederick Douglass Searches for the Meaning of Violence in a Slave Regime, 1855

In regard to the *time* of my birth, I cannot be as definite as I have been respecting the *place*. Nor, indeed, can I impart much knowledge concerning my parents. Genealogical trees do not flourish among slaves. A person of some-consequence here in the north, sometimes designated *father*, is literally abolished in slave law and slave practice. It is only once in a while that an exception is found to this statement. I never met with a slave who could tell me how old he was. Few slave-mothers know anything of the months of the year, nor of the days of the month. They keep no family records, with marriages, births, and deaths. They measure the ages of their children by spring time, winter time, harvest time, planting time, and the like; but these soon become undistinguishable and forgotten. Like other slaves, I cannot tell how old I am. This destitution was among my earliest troubles. I learned when I grew up, that my master—and this is the case with masters generally—allowed no questions to be put to him, by which a slave might learn his age. Such questions are deemed evidence of impatience, and even of impudent curiosity.. . . .

The practice of separating children from their mothers, and hiring the latter out at distances too great to admit of their meeting, except at long intervals, is a marked feature of the cruelty and barbarity of the slave system.

But it is in harmony with the grand aim of slavery, which, always and every-where, is to reduce man to a level with the brute. It is a successful method of obliterating from the mind and heart of the slave, all just ideas of the sacred-ness of *the family*, as an institution.

. . . My poor mother, like many other slave-women, had *many children*, but NO FAMILY!

. . . I say nothing of *father*, for he is shrouded in a mystery I have never been able to penetrate. Slavery does away with fathers, as it does away with families. Slavery has no use for either fathers or families, and its laws do not recognize their existence in the social arrangements of the plantation. When they *do* exist, they are not the outgrowths of slavery, but are antagonistic to that system. The order of civilization is reversed here. The name of the child is not expected to be that of its father, and his condition does not necessarily affect that of the child. He may be the slave of Mr. Tilgman; and his child, when born, may be the slave of Mr. Gross. He may be a *freeman*; and yet his child may be a *chattel*. He may be white, glorying in the purity of his Anglo-Saxon blood; and his child may be ranked with the blackest slaves. Indeed, he *may* be, and often *is*, master and father to the same child. He can be father without being a husband, and may sell his child without incurring reproach, if the child be by a woman in whose veins courses one thirty-second part of African blood. My father was a white man, or nearly white. It was sometimes whispered that my master was my father.

. . . [T]he fact remains, in all its glaring odiousness, that, by the laws of slavery, children, in all cases, are reduced to the condition of their mothers. This arrangement admits of the greatest license to brutal slaveholders, and their profligate sons, brothers, relations and friends, and gives to the pleasure of sin, the additional attraction of profit. . . . One might imagine, that the children of such connections, would fare better, in the hands of their mas-ters, than other slaves.

The rule is quite the other way; and a very little reflection will satisfy the reader that such is the case. A man who will enslave his own blood, may not be safely relied on for magnanimity. Men do not love those who remind them of their sins—unless they have a mind to repent—and the mulatto child's face is a standing accusation against him who is master and father to the child. What is still worse, perhaps, such a child is a constant offense to the wife. She hates its very presence, and when a slaveholding woman hates, she wants not means to give that hate telling effect. . . .

Masters are frequently compelled to sell this class of their slaves, out of deference to the feelings of their white wives; and shocking and scandalous as it may seem for a man to sell his own blood to the traffickers in human flesh, it is often an act of humanity toward the slave-child to be thus re-moved from his merciless tormentors. . . .

. . . I may remark, that, if the lineal descendants of Ham are only to be enslaved, according to the scriptures, slavery in this country will soon become an unscriptural institution; for thousands are ushered into the world, annually, who—like myself—owe their existence to white fathers, and, most frequently, to their masters, and master's sons. The slave-woman is at the mercy of the fathers, sons or brothers of her master. The thoughtful know the rest.

. . . The slaveholder, as well as the slave, is the victim of the slave system. A man's character greatly takes its hue and shape from the form and color of things about him. Under the whole heavens there is no relation more unfavorable to the development of honorable character, than that sustained by the slaveholder to the slave. Reason is imprisoned here, and passions run wild. Like the fires of the prairie, once lighted, they are at the mercy of every wind, and must burn, till they have consumed all that is combustible within their remorseless grasp. Capt. Anthony could be kind, and, at times, he even showed an affectionate disposition. Could the reader have seen him gently leading me by the hand—as he sometimes did—patting me on the head, speaking to me in soft, caressing tones and calling me his "little Indian boy," he would have deemed him a kind old man, and really, almost fatherly. But the pleasant moods of a slaveholder are remarkably brittle; they are easily snapped; they neither come often, nor remain long. His temper is subjected to perpetual trials; but, since these trials are never borne patiently, they add nothing to his natural stock of patience.

Old master very early impressed me with the idea that he was an unhappy man. Even to my child's eye, he wore a troubled, and at times, a haggard aspect. His strange movements excited my curiosity, and awakened my compassion. He seldom walked alone without muttering to himself; and he occasionally stormed about, as if defying an army of invisible foes. "He would do this, that, and the other; he'd be d——d if he did not,"—was the usual form of his threats. Most of his leisure was spent in walking, cursing and gesticulating, like one possessed by a demon. Most evidently, he was a wretched man, at war with his own soul, and with all the world around him. To be overheard by the children, disturbed him very little. He made no more of *our* presence, than of that of the ducks and geese which he met on the green. He little thought that the little black urchins around him, could see, through those vocal crevices, the very secrets of his heart. Slaveholders ever underrate the intelligence with which they have to grapple. I really understood the old man's mutterings, attitudes and gestures, about as well as he did himself. But slaveholders never encourage that kind of communication, with the slaves, by which they might learn to measure the depths of his knowledge.

Ignorance is a high virtue in a human chattel; and as the master studies to keep the slave ignorant, the slave is cunning enough to make the master think he succeeds. The slave fully appreciates the saying, "where ignorance is bliss, 'tis folly to be wise." When old master's gestures were violent, ending with a threatening shake of the head, and a sharp snap of his middle finger and thumb, I deemed it wise to keep at a respectable distance from him; for, at such times, trifling faults stood, in his eyes, as momentous offenses; and, having both the power and the disposition, the victim had only to be near him to catch the punishment, deserved or undeserved.

One of the first circumstances that opened my eyes to the cruelty and wickedness of slavery, and the heartlessness of my old master, was the refusal of the latter to interpose his authority, to protect and shield a young woman, who had been most cruelly abused and beaten by his overseer in Tuckahoe. This overseer—a Mr. Plummer—was a man like most of his class, little better than a human brute; and, in addition to his general profligacy and repulsive coarseness, the creature was a miserable drunkard. He was, probably, employed by my old master, less on account of the excellence of his services, than for the cheap rate at which they could be obtained. He was not fit to have the management of a drove of mules. In a fit of drunken madness, he committed the outrage which brought the young woman in question down to my old master's for protection.

This young woman was the daughter of Milly, an aunt of mine. The poor girl, on arriving at our house, presented a pitiable appearance. She had left in haste, and without preparation; and, probably, without the knowledge of Mr. Plummer. She had traveled twelve miles, bare-footed, bare-necked and bare-headed. Her neck and shoulders were covered with scars, newly made; and not content with marring her neck and shoulders, with the cowhide, the cowardly brute had dealt her a blow on the head with a hickory club, which cut a horrible gash, and left her face literally covered with blood. In this condition, the poor young woman came down, to implore protection at the hands of my old master. I expected to see him boil over with rage at the revolting deed, and to hear him fill the air with curses upon the brutal Plummer; but I was disappointed. He sternly told her, in an angry tone, he "believed she deserved every bit of it," and, if she did not go home instantly, he would himself take the remaining skin from her neck and back. Thus was the poor girl compelled to return, without redress, and perhaps to receive an additional flogging for daring to appeal to old master against the overseer.

Old master seemed furious at the thought of being troubled by such complaints. I did not, at that time, understand the philosophy of his treatment of my cousin. It was stern, unnatural, violent. Had the man no bowels of compassion? Was he dead to all sense of humanity? No. I think I now understand it. This treatment is a part of the system, rather than a part of the man.

. . . *Esther* . . . was a young woman who possessed that which is ever a curse to the slave-girl;—namely, personal beauty. She was tall, well formed, and made a fine appearance. The daughters of Col. Lloyd could scarcely surpass her in personal charms. Esther was courted by Ned Roberts, and he was as fine looking a young man, as she was a woman. He was the son of a favorite slave of Col. Lloyd. Some slaveholders would have been glad to promote the marriage of two such persons; but, for some reason or other, my old master took it upon him to break up the growing intimacy between Esther and Edward. He strictly ordered her to quit the company of said Roberts, telling her that he would punish her severely if he ever found her again in Edward's company. This unnatural and heartless order was, of course, broken. A woman's love is not to be annihilated by the peremptory command of any one. . . .

Had old master been a man of honor and purity, his motives, in this matter, might have been viewed more favorably. As it was, his motives were as abhorrent, as his methods were foolish and contemptible. It was too evident that he was not concerned for the girl's welfare. It is one of the damning characteristics of the slave system, that it robs its victims of every earthly incentive to a holy life. The fear of God, and the hope of heaven, are found sufficient to sustain many slave-women, amidst the snares and dangers of their strange lot; but, this side of God and heaven, a slave-woman is at the mercy of the power, caprice and passion of her owner. Slavery provides no means for the honorable continuance of the race. Marriage—as imposing obligations on the parties to it—has no existence here, except in such hearts as are purer and higher than the standard morality around them. It is one of the consolations of my life, that I know of many honorable instances of persons who maintained their honor, where all around was corrupt. . . .

. . . [Old master's] attentions were plainly brutal and selfish, and it was as natural that Esther should loathe him, as that she should love Edward. Abhorred and circumvented as he was, old master, having the power, very easily took revenge. I happened to see this exhibition of his rage and cruelty toward Esther. The time selected was singular. It was early in the morning, when all besides was still, and before any of the family, in the house or kitchen, had left their beds. I saw but few of the shocking preliminaries, for the cruel work had begun before I awoke. I was probably awakened by the shrieks and piteous cries of poor Esther. My sleeping place was on the floor of a little, rough closet, which opened into the kitchen; and through the cracks of its unplaned boards, I could distinctly see and hear what was going on, without being seen by old master.

Esther's wrists were firmly tied, and the twisted rope was fastened to a strong staple in a heavy wooden joist above, near the fireplace. Here she stood, on a bench, her arms tightly drawn over her breast. Her back and shoulders were bare to the waist. Behind her stood old master, with cowskin in hand, preparing his barbarous work with all manner of harsh, coarse, and tantalizing epithets. The screams of his victim were most piercing. He was cruelly deliberate, and protracted the torture, as one who was delighted with the scene. Again and again he drew the hateful whip through his hand, adjusting it with a view of dealing the most pain-giving blow. Poor Esther had never yet been severely whipped, and her shoulders were plump and tender. Each blow, vigorously laid on, brought screams as well as blood. *"Have mercy; Oh! have mercy"* she cried; *"I won't do so no more;"* but her piercing cries seemed only to increase his fury. His answers to them are too coarse and blasphemous to be produced here.

The whole scene, with all its attendants, was revolting and shocking, to the last degree; and when the motives of this brutal castigation are considered, language has no power to convey a just sense of its awful criminality. After laying on some thirty or forty stripes, old master untied his suffering victim, and let her get down. She could scarcely stand, when untied. From my heart I pitied her, and—child though I was—the outrage kindled in me a feeling far from peaceful; but I was hushed, terrified, stunned, and could do nothing, and the fate of Esther might be mine next. The scene here described was often repeated in the case of poor Esther, and her life, as I knew it, was one of wretchedness.

. . . [All day] the human cattle are in motion, wielding their clumsy hoes; hurried on by no hope of reward, no sense of gratitude, no love of children, no prospect of bettering their condition; nothing, save the dread and terror of the slave-driver's lash. So goes one day, and so comes and goes another.

Source: Frederick Douglass, *My Bondage and My Freedom* (New York: Miller, Orton and Mulligan, 1855), 34–38, 48, 51–52, 58–60, 80–88, 104–5.

FURTHER READING

On slave laws, see Timothy S. Huebner, "The Roots of Fairness: *State v. Caesar* and Slave Justice in Antebellum North Carolina," in Christopher Waldrep and Donald G. Nieman, eds., *Local Matters: Race, Crime, and Justice in the Nineteenth-Century South* (Athens: University Press of Georgia, 2001), 29–52; Paul Finkelman, *An Imperfect Union: Slavery, Federalism, and Comity* (Chapel Hill: University of North Carolina Press, 1981); Thomas D. Morris, *Southern Slavery and the Law, 1619–1860* (Chapel Hill: University of North Carolina Press, 1996); Philip J. Schwarz, *Twice Condemned: Slaves and the Criminal Laws of Virginia, 1705–1865* (Baton Rouge: Louisiana State University Press, 1988).

On the society of the South under slavery, see Edmund S. Morgan, *American Slavery, American Freedom: The Ordeal of Colonial Virginia* (New York: Norton,

1975); Eugene D. Genovese, *Roll Jordan Roll: The World the Slaves Made* (New York: Pantheon, 1974); James Oakes, *The Ruling Race: A History of American Slaveholders* (New York: Knopf, 1982); Bertram Wyatt-Brown, *Southern Honor: Ethics and Behavior in the Old South* (New York: Oxford University Press, 1982).

On slave rebellions, see David Robertson, *Denmark Vesey: The Buried History of America's Largest Slave Rebellion and the Man Who Led It* (New York: Knopf, 1999); Henry Irving Tragle, *The Southhampton Slave Revolt of 1831: A Compilation of Source Material* (Amherst: University of Massachusetts Press, 1971).

For personal narratives of slavery, see Frederick Douglass, *My Bondage and My Freedom* (New York: Miller, Orton and Mulligan, 1855); Gilbert Osofsky, ed., *Puttin' on Ole Massa: The Slave Narratives of Henry Bibb, William Wells Brown, and Solomon Northup* (New York: Harper and Row, 1969); Harriet Jacobs, edited by L. Maria Child, *Incidents in the Life of a Slave Girl, Written by Herself* (Boston: published for the author, 1861); Sterling L. Bland, ed., *African American Slave Narratives: An Anthology*, 3 vols. (Westport, CT: Greenwood Press, 2001).

FIVE

THE CIVIL WAR

C ivil wars tend to be the bloodiest conflicts in the history of nations. As a people turn on one another, they act with a viciousness and anger rarely demonstrated elsewhere. The American Civil War ripped the country apart. Americans killed each other to an extent not previously experienced. In pure numbers, more people died in battle on the single day of September 17, 1862, at Antietam than in all the military encounters in North America over the previous two centuries combined.

Historians have noted the ever-increasing levels of violence in the United States in the 1850s. In one of the most important studies of the subject, David Grimsted linked the perceived need of Southern slave owners to defend their racist system and their growing use of violence as a means of resolving political disputes. In their vicious assault on slaves suspected of questioning their bondage and upon abolitionists who rejected the entire system, Southern whites broke with the traditional forms of crowd actions that had almost always confined themselves to intimidation and property damage. Southern defenders of slavery even demanded that the North treat its abolitionists similarly. Violence in defense of slavery, Grimsted argues, drove frustrated Northerners to the increased use of force in the defense of freedom.[1]

The Southern leadership nullified constitutional protections of free speech by outlawing any questioning of slavery, even in private letters. Southern crowds reinforced this closure of public discussion of slavery with the greatest possible brutality. Alexander Stephens summarized the view of the Southern leadership perfectly: "I have no objection to the liberty of speech, when the liberty of the

---

1. David Grimsted, *American Mobbing, 1828–1861: Toward Civil War* (New York: Oxford University Press, 1998).

cudgel is left free to combat it."[2] Southern mobs beat, burned, and tortured their victims with a savagery unknown in other parts of the country, and with the support of local authorities. Northern and western crowds did not often burn their victims alive, or castrate them, or gouge out their eyes. Northern congressmen did not threaten to hang Southerners or cane them on the floor of the Senate. Nor could Northern crowds expect to be led in these activities by their local sheriffs, militia commanders, and governors, as was the case with Southern mobs. As Jefferson had warned in *Notes on the State of Virginia*, slavery warped every aspect of Southern society, intensifying levels of violence and the willingness of slaveholders to use violence in support of their opinions.[3]

One aspect of the changing attitudes toward violence in the 1850s is the willingness of whites to kill whites. In domestic relations, white Americans had long directed their violence against blacks and Indians, rarely against one another. Events in Kansas in the mid-1850s marked a dramatic shift in attitudes.

In 1854 Senator Stephen Douglas of Illinois thought he had the solution to the nation's division over slavery. His legislation for the organization of the territories of Kansas and Nebraska put forth the policy of "popular sovereignty," leaving the question of slavery to the white American settlers in the territories. Douglas's proposal overturned the Compromise of 1820, which had abolished slavery north of Missouri's southern border, while opening up these western territories to a rush of true believers who hoped to gain these territories for either slavery or freedom. Benjamin Stringfellow encouraged the citizens of Missouri to "mark every scoundrel . . . that is the least tainted with free-soilism or abolitionism, and exterminate him. . . . I advise you, one and all, to enter every election district in Kansas . . . and vote at the point of the bowie-knife and the revolver."[4] Kansas quickly became the literal battleground between these contending regional and ideological forces. Pro-slavery activists migrated to Kansas in great numbers, while Free-Soilers, those opposed to the expansion of slavery into the new territories, also moved into Kansas.

When the first territorial elections were held in 1855, hundreds of Missourians marched into Kansas, taking over polling places to ensure the victory of the pro-slavery forces. Though six thousand votes were cast in a territory that supposedly had only fifteen hundred inhabitants, Congress recognized the pro-

2. Stephens to Thomas H. Thomas, 25 May 1856, Stephens Papers, Emory University.

3. Andrew A. Lipscomb and Albert Ellery Bergh, eds., *The Writings of Thomas Jefferson*, 20 vols. (Washington, DC: Thomas Jefferson Memorial Association, 1904), 2:225–28; Grimsted, *American Mobbing*, 85–113.

4. Thomas H. Gladstone, *The Englishman in Kansas; or, Squatter Life and Border Warfare* (1857; Lincoln: University of Nebraska Press, 1971), 80; Grimsted, *American Mobbing*, 247–48, 259; Charles Robinson, ed., *The Kansas Conflict* (New York: Harper and Brothers, 1892), 265–67, 392–406.

slavery government of Kansas territory. The Free-Soilers, charging massive fraud, set up a competing government in Lawrence and demanded recognition from Congress. The pro-slavery forces responded in May 1856 by burning Lawrence to the ground. In retaliation, an intense and deeply religious abolitionist named John Brown led a small band of followers in killing five pro-slavery men who lived on Pottawatomie Creek.

Between 1855 and 1858, fifty-two people were murdered in the territory, which at the time appeared an unprecedented level of violence and earned the state its sobriquet of "Bleeding Kansas." The pro-slavery faction proved more prone to commit murder, thirty-six compared with the fourteen killed by the free-state faction (two pro-slavery men died accidentally while committing acts of violence). In the summer of 1857, the pro-slavery Lecompton government applied for statehood under a constitution that protected slavery. The Democratic Party split over the Lecompton constitution. President James Buchanan, a Democrat, favored admitting Kansas as a slave state, while the author of the system under which the pro-slavery constitution had been written, Senator Stephen Douglas of Illinois, opposed it. This division carried over into the election of 1860, with the Democratic Party dividing into northern and southern factions and a third splinter group called the Unionists, helping to elect the Republican, Abraham Lincoln, president.

The nation's deep polarization was evident in the election results. Lincoln earned 1,838,347 votes in the free states to 1,572,637 for his three opponents, carrying every free state except New Jersey, which he split with Douglas. Many of the slave states did not even allow the Republicans to appear on the ballot, with the result that Lincoln garnered just 26,388 votes to his opponents' 1,248,520 votes. That sharp polarization, which allowed little room for compromise or even dialogue, fed the violence that ensued.

The leadership of the Deep South had faced the election of 1860 as an all-or-nothing proposition. They insisted that if Lincoln won, they would lead their states out of the union. The Southern elite had become accustomed to dominating the nation's politics, having supplied most of the nation's presidents, cabinet officers, and congressional leadership. Despite the fact that the Democrats still controlled Congress and the Supreme Court, the loss of the executive branch unhinged the South's white leadership. A Northern president at the helm of a political party that insisted that the expansion of slavery must end persuaded the Southern political leadership that their region could no longer play by the traditional democratic rules.

Refusing to recognize the results of the election, eleven Southern states seceded from the Union, starting with South Carolina on December 20, 1860. These states rapidly formed themselves into a new union called the Confederate States of America with Jefferson Davis as their president. Thousands of Southern white men rushed to defend their "way of life" from a probable Northern attack aimed at preserving the Union. But the initial Northern reaction was more shocked than militant. The willingness of Southern whites to throw aside the union for the sake of slavery stunned many Northerners. What room for compromise was there when even a "moderate" pro-Douglas Atlanta paper could proclaim, "We regard every man in our midst an enemy to the institutions of the South, who does not boldly declare that he believes African slavery to be a social, moral, and political blessing"?[5]

Northern hesitation vanished when Southern volunteers fired on Fort Sumter in April 1861. With the Confederates now the aggressors, spontaneous demonstrations filled the streets of Northern cities and towns. Former Democratic presidential candidate Stephen Douglas captured Northern sentiment well when he told a huge crowd in Chicago: "The question is, Are we to maintain the country of our fathers, or allow it to be stricken down by those who, when they can no longer govern, threaten to destroy.... Every man must be for the United States or against it. There can be no neutrals in this war, only patriots and traitors."[6] When President Lincoln called for seventy-five thousand volunteers, tens of thousands of men turned out to enlist. Within a few weeks, enlistment had outstripped the ability of the states to handle recruits. Governors sent unarmed troops to Washington, hoping that the federal government would find guns for them while other states turned away volunteers. There was obviously wide popular enthusiasm for war throughout the country.

Through the spring of 1861, each side prepared for war, convinced of its own rectitude and certain that the war would be brief. The first major battle at Bull Run on July 21, 1861, showed otherwise, though only the most astute observers realized it. Many Southerners hoped that the federal troops who fled Virginia would learn their lesson and never return. Instead, over the next four years, the armies of North America fought and died in ever-increasing numbers. The tactics of both sides were ill suited for the technological changes in warfare. Officers on both sides had graduated from West Point, where they had learned the style of Napoleonic warfare that they put into practice, moving mass troops across open terrain in the face of entrenched enemy forces. Improved firearms and artillery mowed down advancing Americans in an approach to combat ably described as "attack and die."[7] The Civil War ended as the greatest slaughter in American history, with more than six hundred thousand dead and hundreds of thousands maimed and seriously injured veterans.

5. *Atlanta Confederacy* (1860), http://hometown.aol.com/jfepperson/quotes.html.
6. Clark E. Carr, *Stephen A. Douglas: His Life, Public Services, Speeches and Patriotism* (Chicago: A. C. McClurg, 1909), 137–38.
7. Grady McWhiney and Perry D. Jamieson, *Attack and Die: Civil War Military Tactics and the Southern Heritage* (University: University of Alabama Press, 1982).

DOCUMENTS

HARPERS FERRY

John Brown, the antislavery zealot who murdered pro-slavery Kansans in the infamous Pottawatomie massacre in 1855, continued to attack slaveholders in Kansas and Missouri. With President James Buchanan offering a personal reward for Brown's capture, John Brown became a national figure and symbol of abolitionism.

Brown felt that only bloodshed would cleanse America of the sin of slavery. Hoping to begin a national war against slavery, Brown traveled to Boston to meet with leading abolitionists. Frederick Douglass warned that Brown would damage the cause, but several abolitionists provided financial support, on condition that Brown not tell them what he planned to do with the money. In the summer of 1859, Brown moved to a Maryland farm near the Potomac River, from where he intended to launch an attack on the federal armory at Harpers Ferry with his army of twenty-three men, a group that included his sons and several free African Americans. The arsenal's guns would arm white supporters of his cause, while the slaves were to be armed at first with pikes. As more slaves joined their rebellion, they would create a free black republic in the Appalachians, supporting insurrections throughout the South until slavery collapsed. That, at least, was Brown's plan.

Brown's troops moved on Harpers Ferry in October 1859, capturing the arsenal with little resistance. The first person killed by Brown's forces was Heywood Shepherd, the free black baggage master at the Harpers Ferry train station. Brown had made no arrangement to spread word of the rebellion, just assuming that slaves would hear of it somehow. While no fresh recruits swelled Brown's ranks, U.S. Marines under the command of Brevet Colonel Robert E. Lee rushed to reclaim the arsenal. Using a makeshift battering ram, the marines broke into the armory fire—enginehouse where Brown and his men had retreated and bayoneted two inside, arresting the rest. Lieutenant Israel Green stabbed and slashed Brown with his sword.

Seen as a terrorist by most white Southerners, Brown became an instant hero for many Northerners, marking and accentuating the nation's polarization. The State of Virginia tried Brown and several coconspirators and sentenced them to hang. Certain that abolitionists would attempt to rescue Brown, the state surrounded the prisoners with hundreds of troops. Appeals for clemency poured in to the office of Virginia's governor Henry A. Wise, while Brown's attorneys attempted to show that he was mentally unstable. Brown rejected the insanity plea, as did much of the country. "John Brown may be a lunatic," the Boston Post *proclaimed, but if so, "then one-fourth of the people of Massachusetts are madmen."[8] Governor Wise shared that prognosis, refusing to commute Brown's sentence.*

On his way to the gallows on December 2, 1859, Brown passed a note to one of the

8. Quoted in Stephen B. Oates, *To Purge This Land with Blood: A Biography of John Brown* (New York: Harper and Row, 1970), 334.

guards. *"I John Brown am now quite* certain *that the crimes of this* guilty land will *never be purged* away; *but with Blood."*[9] *For thousands of opponents of slavery, John Brown was martyred in Virginia. That very reaction convinced many supporters of slavery that they had no future in the Union. The* Charleston Mercury, *a paper never known for its moderation, announced, "The day of compromise is past," and Brown's raid at Harpers Ferry must convince even "the most bigoted Unionist that there is no peace for the South in this Union."*[10]

The dramatic assault upon federal property transfixed the nation. The new method of "telegraphic correspondence" allowed the reporting of events as they were happening, with hourly dispatches posted in the windows of newspaper offices. The following account, which gives a sense of the confusion and disbelief that gripped much of the country in October 1859, is taken from the National Intelligencer, *the leading Washington newspaper.*

The *National Intelligencer* Describes Events at Harpers Ferry, 1859

TELEGRAPHIC CORRESPONDENCE
The Originators of the Conspiracy

The principal originator of the insurrection, and the chief leader in its short but bloody existence, was undoubtedly Captain John Brown, whose connexion with the scenes of violence and border warfare in Kansas then made his name familiarly notorious to the whole country. Captain Brown made his first appearance in the vicinity of Harper's Ferry more than a year ago, accompanied by his two sons, the whole party assuming the name of Smith. They inquired about land in the vicinity, made investigations as to the probability of finding ores, and for some time boarded at Sandy Hook, one mile east of Harper's Ferry. After an absence of some months, they re-appeared in the vicinity, and the elder Brown rented or leased a farm on the Maryland side, about four miles from Harper's Ferry. They bought a large number of picks and spades, and thus confirmed the belief that they intended to mine for ores. They were seen frequently in and about Harper's Ferry, but no suspicion seems to have existed that "Bill Smith" was Captain Brown, or that he intended embarking in a movement so desperate and extraordinary. Yet the development of the plot leaves no doubt that his visits to the Ferry and his lease of the farm were all parts of his preparation for an insurrection which he supposed was to be successful in exterminating slavery in Maryland and Western Virginia. Captain Brown's chief aid was John E. Cook,[11] a compara-

---

9. John Brown, Charlestown, Virginia, December 2, 1859, John Brown Papers, Chicago Historical Society.
10. *Charleston Mercury* November 29, 1859.
11. John E. Cook was the brother-in-law of Governor A. P. Willard of Indiana.

tively young man, who has resided in and near Harper's Ferry for some years. He was first employed in tending a lock on the canal. He afterwards taught school on the Maryland side, and, after a brief residence in Kansas, where it is supposed that he became acquainted with Brown, returned to the Ferry and married there. He was regarded as a man of some intelligence, known to be anti-slavery, but not so violent in the expression of his opinions as to excite any suspicions. . . .

The Commencement of the Insurrection

The first active movement in the insurrection was made about half-past ten o'clock on Sunday night. Wm. Williams, watchman on Harper's Ferry bridge, whilst walking across towards the Maryland side, was seized by a number of men, who said he was their prisoner and must come with them. He recognized Brown and Cook among the men, and, knowing them, treated the matter as a joke; but enforcing silence, they conducted him to the Armory, which he found already in their possession. He was retained till after daylight and then discharged. The watchman who was to relieve Williams at midnight found the bridge lights all out, and immediately was seized. Supposing it an attempt at robbery, he broke away, and his pursuers stumbling over the track, he escaped.

The next appearance of the insurrectionists was at the house of Col. Lewis Washington, a large farmer and slave owner, living about four miles from the Ferry. A party headed by Cook proceeded there, roused Col. W., and told him he was a prisoner. . . .

The Beginning of the Fight

As the day advanced, and the news spread around, and the people came into the Ferry, the first demonstrations of resistance were made to the insurrectionists. A guerrilla warfare commenced, chiefly led on by a man named Chambers, whose house commanded the Armory yard. The colored man, named Hayward, railroad porter, was shot early in the morning for refusing to join the movement. The next man shot was Joseph Burley, a citizen of Harper's Ferry. He was shot whilst standing in his own door. About this time also Samuel P. Young, Esq. was shot dead. He was coming into the town on horseback, carrying a gun, when he was shot from the Armory, receiving a wound of which he died during the day. He was a graduate of West Point, and greatly respected in the neighborhood for his high character and noble qualities.

The insurrectionists at this time, finding a disposition to resist them, had withdrawn nearly all within the Armory grounds, leaving only a guard on the bridge. About noon the Charlestown troops, under command of Col. Robert W. Baylor, arrived, crossing the Potomac river some distance up, and marching down the Maryland side to the mouth of the bridge. Firing a volley, they made a gallant dash across the bridge, clearing it of the insurrectionists, who retreated rapidly down towards the Armory. . . .

Arrival of the Military

At 10 o'clock on Monday night the train with the Baltimore military and United States marines arrived at Sandy Hook, where they waited for the arrival of Col. Lee, deputized by the War Department to take command. The reporters pressed on, leaving their military allies behind. They found the bridge in possession of the military, and entered the besieged and beleagured town without difficulty, the occasional report of a gun or the singing motion of a Sharp's rifle ball warning them that it was advisable to keep out of range of the Armory. Their first visit was to the bedside of Aaron Stevens, the wounded prisoner. They found him a large, exceedingly athletic man, a perfect Sampson in appearance. He was in a small room, filled with excited armed men, who more than once threatened to shoot him where he was, groaning with pain, but answering with composure and apparent willingness every question in relation to the foray in which he was engaged. He said he was a native of Connecticut, but had lately lived in Kansas, where he knew Captain Brown. He had also served in the United States army. The sole object of the attempt was to give the negroes freedom, and Captain Brown had represented that as soon as they seized the Armory the negroes would flock to them by thousands, and they would soon have force enough to accomplish their purposes. He believed that the freeing of the negroes was a proper purpose, one for which he would sacrifice his life, but thought that Captain Brown had been greatly deceived in relation to the movement. He said preparations had been making for some months for the movement, *but that the whole force consisted of seventeen white men and five free negroes.* This statement was repeated without variation by all the prisoners with whom we conversed. They all agreed as to the number in the movement, and as to its objects, which some of them called the work of philanthropy. Lewis Leary, the negro shot at the rifle mill, stated before he died that he enlisted with Captain Brown for the insurrection at a fair held in Lorraine county, Ohio. . . .

The Attack and Capture

Shortly after seven o'clock Lieut. J. E. B. Stuart, of the 1st cavalry, who was acting as aid for Col. Lee, advanced to parley with the besieged, Samuel Strider, Esq., an old and respectable citizen, bearing a flag of truce. They were received at the door by Captain Cook. Lieut. Stuart demanded an unconditional surrender, only promising them protection from immediate violence and trial by law. Capt. Brown refused all terms but those previously demanded, which were substantially: "That he should be permitted to march out with his men and arms, taking their prisoners with them; that they should proceed unpursued to the second toll-gate, when they would free their prisoners. The soldiers were then at liberty to pursue and they would fight if they could not escape." Of course this was refused, and Lieut. Stuart pressed upon Brown his desperate position, and urged a surrender. The expostulation, though beyond ear-shot, was evidently very earnest, and the coolness of the Lieutenant and the courage of his aged flag bearer won warm praise.

At this moment the interest of the scene was intense. The volunteers were arranged all around the building, cutting off escape in every direction. The marines, divided in two squads, were ready for a dash at the door. Finally, Lieut. Stuart, having exhausted all argument with the determined Captain Brown, walked slowly from the door.

Immediately the signal for attack was given, and the marines, headed by Colonel Harris and Lieutenant Green, advanced in two lines on each side of the door. Two powerful fellows sprang between the lines and with heavy sledge hammers attempted to batter down the door. The door swung and swayed, but appeared to be secured with a rope, the spring of which deadened the effect of the blows. Failing thus to obtain a breach, the marines were ordered to fall back, and twenty of them took hold of a ladder, some forty feet long, and advancing at a run brought it with tremendous power against the door. At the second blow it gave way, one leaf falling inward in a slanting position. The marines immediately advanced to the breach, Major Russell and Lieutenant Green leading. A marine in the front fell; the firing from the interior is rapid and sharp; they fire with deliberate aim, and for the moment the resistance is serious and desperate enough to excite the spectators to something like a pitch of frenzy. The next moment the marines pour in, the firing ceases, and the work was done, whilst the cheers rang from every side, the general feeling being that the marines had done their part admirably.

When the insurgents were brought out—some dead, others wounded—they were greeted with execrations, and only the precautions that had been taken saved them from immediate execution.

Source: *National Intelligencer*, October 20, 1859.

THE EXPERIENCE OF BATTLE

Supreme Court Justice Oliver Wendell Holmes, "the great dissenter," died on March 6, 1935. He had long maintained that the decisive moment in his life had come seventy-four years earlier, when he had been a senior at Harvard, and South Carolina volunteers had

*attacked and captured Fort Sumter, beginning the Civil War. Holmes responded with
resolute patriotism: he deserted his studies and enlisted.*

*His experiences as a young infantry officer can be traced through his letters home
and in surviving fragments from his diary. Holmes's wartime service exemplifies that of
many young men who marched off to the sound of trumpets only to find grisly carnage
and despair. Wounded in 1861, Holmes returned to service and was injured a second
time, at Antietam. In 1863, Holmes received his third and final wound near Fredericks-
burg. By 1863, the eager youth of 1861 had become sickened of war; Holmes told his
parents he wanted to resign his commission. In 1864, Holmes finally received his discharge,
retiring as a brevet lieutenant-colonel. He enrolled in Harvard Law School shortly
thereafter, while the war continued.*

*Holmes's Civil War service haunted him all his life. Many scholars feel that it hard-
ened him, toughening his attitude toward people and life. When he died in 1935, his safety
deposit box was opened. Among the contents were two musket balls wrapped in paper.
There was a note: "These were taken from my body in the Civil War."*[12]

*The First Battle of Bull Run demonstrated to both sides that the war would not be decided
quickly. The commander of the Union's Army of the Potomac, General George B. Mc-
Clellan, moved cautiously, as he attempted to transform his inexperienced volunteers into
a professional army. McClellan ordered General Charles P. Stone to "make a slight
demonstration" into Virginia. On October 21, 1861, near the town of Leesburg, Stone's
Massachusetts troops, commanded by Abraham Lincoln's old friend Colonel Edward
Baker, encountered the Confederates. When Baker was shot in the head and killed, the
Union forces crumbled and fled back toward the Potomac. Confederate troops on the
bluff fired down on the Union soldiers as they attempted to get back to Maryland. It was
a devastating defeat for the Union. The ensuing public outcry led to a congressional
inquiry and the imprisonment of General Stone, a precedent that would haunt the Union
war effort for years as officers refused to take chances for fear of ending up a scapegoat
like Stone. The following extract is from Holmes's diary and gives a sense of medical
care during the war, which tended to aggravate injury and increase the death rate.*

Oliver Wendell Holmes Jr. on the
Nature of Warfare, 1861, 1862, 1864

At Ball's Bluff, Tremlett's boy George told me, I was hit at 4 1/2 P.M., the
heavy firing having begun about an hour before, by the watch.

I felt as if a horse had kicked me and went over—1st Sergt Smith grabbed
me and lugged me to the rear a little way & opened my shirt and ecce! The

---

12. G. Edward White, *Justice Oliver Wendell Holmes: Law and the Inner Self* (New York: Oxford
    University Press, 1993), 488.

two holes in my breasts & the bullet, which he gave me. George says he
squeezed it from the right opening—Well—I remember the sickening feeling
of water in my face. I was quite faint—and seeing poor Sergt Merchant lying
near—shot through the head and covered with blood—and then the thinking
begun—(Meanwhile hardly able to speak—at least, coherently)—Shot through
the lungs? Let's see—and I spit—<Yes> already the blood was in my mouth.
. . . What should I do? Just then I remembered and felt in my waistcoat
pocket. Yes there it was, a little bottle of laudanum which I had brought
along—But I won't take it yet; no, see a doctor first—It may not be as bad as
it looks—At any rate wait till the pain begins—

When I had got to the bottom of the Bluff the ferry boat, (the scow,) had
just started <with a load> but there was a small boat there—Then, still in
this half conscious state, I heard somebody groan—Then I thought "Now
wouldn't Sir Philip Sydney have that other feller put into the boat first?" But
the question, as the form in which it occurred shows, came from a mind still
bent on a becoming and consistent carrying out of its ideals of conduct not
from the unhesitating instinct of a still predominant & <heroic> will—I am
not sure whether I propounded the question but I let myself be put aboard.

I never have been able to account for the fact that bullets struck in the
bank of the island over our heads as we were crossing. Well; the next question was how to get me from the ferry to the hospital—this I solved by another early recollection—the "Armchair"—Two men crossed their hands in
such a way that I could sit on 'em & put my arms round their necks—& so
they carried me—The little house was filled so I was taken into the large
building which served as a general hospital; and I remember the coup d'oeuil
on which I closed my eyes with the same sickening which I had felt on seeing
poor Merchant—Men lying round on the floor—the spectacle wasn't familiar
then—a red blanket with an arm lying on it in a pool of blood—it seems as if
instinct told me it was John Putnam's (then Capt. Comdg Co H)—and near
the entrance a surgeon calmly grasping a man's finger and cutting it off—
both standing—while the victim contemplated the operation with a very
grievous mug. Well presently old Hayward approached and inspected me—
"How does it look, Doctor, shall I recover? Tell me the truth for I really want
to know"—(It seemed then and does now as if I was perfectly rational but
Whittier says that when he saw me later I was very light headed—) Hayward
in his deliberate way—"We-ell, you *may* recover—Gen. Shields did"—Shields![13]
I'd thought of him before and got small comfort from that—we all thought

---

13. General James Shields had been hit in the chest by grapeshot at the Battle of Cerro Gordo
    in the war with Mexico. The shot passed through his body, just missing his spine, the
    wound being treated by "drawing a silk handkerchief through it on a ramrod."

that night that I had a couple of bullets in my lungs—& I bled from them (at the mouth) very freely—"That means the chances are against me, don't it?" "Ye-es, the chances are against you"—Meanwhile he picked something from the left opening—I thought it was bone till he told me it was a bit of flannel— again I felt for the laudanum and again determined to wait till pain or sink- ing strength warned me of the end being near—I didn't feel sure there was no chance—and watching myself did not feel the hand of death upon me beyond a hope—my strength seemed to hold out too well.

After this my recollection of events is confused. I remember poor Willy Putnam's groans—and his refusing to let the Dr. operate on him, saying he knew the wound was mortal and it would only be more pain for nothing—I remember hobnobbing with the man who lay near me, and when to my astonishment John O'Sullivan (Whit's & my servt) appeared telling him to help my neighbor too, and feeling very heroic after that speech—(By the way Hayward had turned me on my breast & this may have helped a good deal of the wound to heal almost by first intention)—I remember being very sleepy— (some enlisted man has since told me he gave me some coffee and my face flushed and I went right off—) & presently a Doctor of (Baxter's?) Fire Zou- aves[14] coming in with much noise & bluster, and oh, troops were crossing to the Virginia side, and we were going to lick, and heaven knows what not—I called him and gave him my address and told him (or meant <& tried> to) if I died to write home & tell 'em I'd done my duty—I was very anxious they should know that—and I then imparted to him my laudanum scheme—This he dissuaded and gave me a dose of some opiate—he said it wasn't lauda- num, but I guess that was a white lie—and when I slumbered I believe he prigged [stole] the bottle—

Pen[15] before I was moved came in & kissed me and went away again— Whittier came & saw me too, though I'm not sure if I remember it—and Sturgis[16] of whom anon—I think I remember the confusion when some bul- lets struck the house—and the story that the enemy would shell the island. But all these recollections are obscure and the order of their occurrence un- certain—

. . . Later I only can recall, in a general way, being carried across the Is- land in a blanket lying on the bank, comatose, being ferried across <to the [Maryland] shore> with some hitch (we came mighty near being upset I heard afterwards)—swearing terrifically as I've said—and finally after being put

---

14. The Seventy-second Regiment of Pennsylvania Volunteers, commanded by Colonel DeWitt Clinton Baxter, was famous for its bright red uniforms patterned on those of the Turkish Zouaves.
15. Lieutenant Norwood Penrose Hallowell.
16. Lieutenant Henry H. Sturgis.

in the hold of a canal boat and the hatches or scuttle or whatever you call it tumbling in and nearly <all but> smashing me & one or two others into sudden death, that I muzzed away the time till we got to Edwards Ferry. . . .

I was taken from the Canal boat and put into one of the two wheeled ambulances which were then in vogue as one form of torture—Captain Dreher was my companion—shot through the head & insensible, but breathing heavily—The Ambulance was broken—the horse baulked and the man didn't know how to drive—whenever we came to a hill, & there were several, there we stopped, head downward, till some of the men along the road gave us a boost & started our horse forward again—I suffered much in mind. . . .

[In this letter he addresses his father, Oliver W. Holmes Sr., as his "Governor."]

Dec. 20, 1862
My Dear Governor
    . . . The successes of wh. [which] you spoke were to be anticipated as necessary if we entered into the struggle—But I see no farther progress. I don't think either of you[17] realize the unity or the determination of the South.
    I think you are hopeful because (excuse me) you are ignorant. But if it is true that we represent civilization wh. is in its nature, as well as slavery, diffusive & aggressive, and if civn [civilization] & progress are the better things why they will conquer in the long run, we may be sure, and will stand a better chance in their proper province—peace—than in war, the brother of slavery—brother—it is slavery's parent, child and sustainer at once—At any rate dear Father don't, because I say these things imply or think that I am the meaner for saying them—I am, to be sure, heartily tired and half worn out body and mind by this life, but I believe I am as ready as ever to do my duty. . . .

May 16, 1864
Dear Parents
    Rec'd last night enclosed letters—Yesterday & today tolerably quiet, a quiet that you will easily believe was needed after the long series of collisions beginning on the 5th—Before you get this you will know how immense the butchers bill has been—And the labor has been incessant—I

17. The other being John Lothrop Motley, who had just published some open letters to Secretary of State Seward on the proper conduct of the war in the *Boston Daily Advertiser*.

have not been & am not likely to be in the mood for writing details. I have kept brief notes in my diary wh. I hope you may see some day— Enough that these nearly two weeks have contained all of fatigue & horror that war can furnish—The advantage has been on our side but nothing decisive has occurred & the enemy is in front of us strongly intrenched—I doubt if the decisive battle is to be fought between here & Richmond—nearly every Regimental off[icer] I knew or cared for is dead or wounded—

I have made up my mind to stay on the staff if possible till the end of the campaign & then if I am alive, I shall resign—I have felt for sometime that I didn't any longer believe in this being a duty & so I mean to leave at the end of the campaign as I said if I'm not killed before. . . .

The duties & thoughts of the field are of such a nature that one cannot at the same time keep home, parents and such thoughts as they suggest in his mind at the same time as a reality—Can hardly indeed remember their existence—and this too just after the intense yearning which immediately precedes a campaign[.] Still your letters are the one pleasure & you know my love
Your Aff. Son
OWH Jr.

Source: Oliver W. Holmes, Jr., diary entry no. 2, [undated] 1864; Oliver W. Holmes, Jr., to Oliver W. Holmes, Sr., addressed as "Governor," Dec. 20, 1862; Oliver W. Holmes, Jr., to his parents, May 16, 1864, the Oliver Wendell Holmes, Jr., Papers, Special Collections, Harvard Law School Library, microfilm reel 15.

THE BATTLE OF GETTYSBURG

There was a geographic component to the war, North versus South, but not strictly limited in that way. Many white Southerners remained loyal to the union, with thousands joining the national army and thousands more resisting the Confederacy. Tens of thousands of black Southerners also enlisted in the Union army, once Abraham Lincoln realized that he was ignoring an important source of manpower. By the beginning of 1863, it was clear that the longer the war lasted, the more the advantage lay with the Union. In 1860, the states that would form the Confederacy claimed only 15 percent of the factories in the United States, 39 percent of the population, 33 percent of the farm acreage, 30 percent of commodity output, and 34 percent of railroad mileage. The North, which remained open to massive influxes of new immigrants, saw its population increase steadily, while Southern manpower bled away. All forms of Northern industry developed at dramatic rates during the war. In 1860, for instance, private manufacturers produced fifty thousand firearms. By 1865, manufacturers in the United States—excluding the Confederate states— made more than one and a half million guns a year.

Despite the notable economic disparities, Confederate leaders remained convinced that they could overcome their material disadvantages. Even as the Civil War became America's first total war, the Southern leadership clung to traditional, even romantic, notions of warfare. Sometimes such attitudes paid off. In May 1863, Robert E. Lee took the dangerous gamble of splitting his army in half to attack General Joseph Hooker's Union forces from two directions. The Battle of Chancellorsville was a stunning victory for the Confederates, as the Union troops fled in disarray and northern Virginia was once more in Confederate hands. Lee felt that his only chance was one final great victory over the Union army, a crushing defeat that would disperse the Army of the Potomac and open the road to Washington.

Moving quickly, Lee launched his second invasion of the North. But this time he faced George Meade, a general willing to fight. On July 1, 1863, at the small Pennsylvania town of Gettysburg, the two armies collided: seventy-five thousand Confederates faced eighty-five thousand U.S. troops. Over three days of bitter fighting, the Union soldiers held their positions, even after the Confederates retreated—which drove Lincoln into a fury. Lee left the field of battle having lost one-third of his army.

At the beginning of April 1863, a twenty-eight-year-old British lieutenant-colonel named James A. L. Fremantle arrived in Brownsville, Texas, on leave from his army. He did not come as an official observer of the Confederacy, but solely out of private curiosity. He briefly visited the headquarters of General Braxton Bragg's Army of the Tennessee and then journeyed to Richmond, where he obtained permission to travel to Gettysburg. After the battle he crossed the lines to the Union forces, paid his respects, and headed to New York to catch a boat back home. Fremantle must have had charm, for he quickly found himself involved in every discussion, included in every meeting, and invited into everyone's mess. He also kept a diary, which he published in London at the end of the year. This book was published in both Mobile and New York in 1864, providing the North with one of its best views of the southern army.

The British Officer James A. L. Fremantle
Observes the Battle of Gettysburg, 1863

[1 July] At 4.30 P.M. we came in sight of Gettysburg, and joined General Lee and General Hill, who were on the top of one of the ridges which form the peculiar feature of the country round Gettysburg. We could see the enemy retreating up one of the opposite ridges, pursued by the Confederates with loud yells. The position into which the enemy had been driven was evidently a strong one. His right appeared to rest on a cemetery, on the top of a high ridge to the right of Gettysburg, as we looked at it.

General Hill now came up and told me he had been very unwell all day, and in fact he looks very delicate. He said he had had two of his divisions engaged, and had driven the enemy four miles into his present position, capturing a great many prisoners, some cannon, and some colors. . . .

. . . The firing ceased about dark, at which time I rode back with General Longstreet and his Staff to his headquarters at Cashtown, a little village eight miles from Gettysburg. At that time troops were pouring along the road, and were being marched towards the position they are to occupy to-morrow.

In the fight to-day nearly 6,000 prisoners had been taken, and 10 guns. About 20,000 men must have been on the field on the Confederate side. . . . This day's work is called a "brisk little scurry," and all anticipate a "big battle" to-morrow. . . .

2d July (Thursday).— . . . At 2 P.M. General Longstreet advised me, if I wished to have a good view of the battle, to return to my tree of yesterday. I did so, and remained there with Lawley and Captain Schreibert during the rest of the afternoon. But until 4.45 P.M. all was profoundly still, and we began to doubt whether a fight was coming off to-day at all. At that time, however, Longstreet suddenly commenced a heavy cannonade on the right. Ewell immediately took it up on the left. The enemy replied with at least equal fury, and in a few moments the firing along the whole line was as heavy as it is possible to conceive. . . .

At 5.45 all became comparatively quiet on our left and in the cemetery; but volleys of musketry on the right told us that Longstreet's infantry were advancing, and the onward progress of the smoke showed that he was progressing favorably; but about 6.30 there seemed to be a check, and even a slight retrograde movement. Soon after 7, General Lee got a report by signal from Longstreet to say *"we are doing well."* A little before dark the firing dropped off in every direction, and soon ceased altogether. We then received intelligence that Longstreet had carried every thing before him for some time, capturing several batteries, and driving the enemy from his positions; but when Hill's Florida brigade and some other troops gave way, he was forced to abandon a small portion of the ground he had won, together with all the captured guns, except three. His troops, however, bivouacked during the night on ground occupied by the enemy this morning. . . .

3d July (Friday).— . . . At noon all Longstreet's dispositions were made; his troops for attack were deployed into line, and lying down in the woods; his batteries were ready to open. The general then dismounted and went to sleep for a short time. The Austrian officer and I now rode off to get, if possible, into some commanding position from whence we could see the whole thing without being exposed to the tremendous fire which was about to commence. After riding about for half an hour without being able to discover so desirable a situation, we determined to make for the cupola, near Gettysburg, Ewell's headquarters. Just before we reached the entrance to the town, the cannonade opened with a fury which surpassed even that of yesterday.

Soon after passing through the toll-gate at the entrance of Gettysburg, we found that we had got into a heavy cross-fire; shells both Federal and Confederate passing over our heads with great frequency. At length two shrapnel shells burst quite close to us, and a ball from one of them hit the officer who was conducting us. We then turned round and changed our views with regard to the cupola—the fire of one side being bad enough, but preferable to that of both sides. A small boy of twelve years was riding with us at the time: this urchin took a diabolical interest in the bursting of the shells, and screamed with delight when he saw them take effect. I never saw this boy again, or found out who he was.

The road at Gettysburg was lined with Yankee dead, and as they had been killed on the 1st, the poor fellows had already begun to be very offensive. We then returned to the hill I was on yesterday. But finding that, to see the actual fighting, it was absolutely necessary to go into the thick of the thing, I determined to make my way to General Longstreet. It was then about 2.30. After passing General Lee and his Staff, I rode on through the woods in the direction in which I had left Longstreet. I soon began to meet many wounded men returning from the front; many of them asked in piteous tones the way to a doctor or an ambulance. The further I got, the greater became the number of the wounded. At last I came to a perfect stream of them flocking through the woods in numbers as great as the crowd in Oxford-street in the middle of the day. Some were walking alone on crutches composed of two rifles, others were supported by men less badly wounded than themselves, and others were carried on stretchers by the ambulance corps; but in no case did I see a sound man helping the wounded to the rear, unless he carried the red badge of the ambulance corps. They were still under a heavy fire; the shells were continually bringing down great limbs of trees, and carrying further destruction amongst this melancholy procession. I saw all this in much less time than it takes to write it, and although astonished to meet such vast numbers of wounded, I had not seen *enough* to give me any idea of the real extent of the mischief.

When I got close up to General Longstreet, I saw one of his regiments advancing through the woods in good order; so, thinking I was just in time to see the attack, I remarked to the General that "*I wouldn't have missed this for any thing.*" Longstreet was seated at the top of a snake fence at the edge of the wood, and looking perfectly calm and imperturbed. He replied, laughing, "*The devil you wouldn't! I would like to have missed it very much; we've attacked and been repulsed: look there!*"

For the first time I then had a view of the open space between the two positions, and saw it covered with Confederates slowly and sulkily returning towards us in small broken parties, under a heavy fire of artillery. But the fire where we were was not so bad as further to the rear; for although the air seemed alive with shell, yet the greater number burst behind us.

. . . No person could have been more calm or self–possessed than General Longstreet under these trying circumstances, aggravated as they now were by the movements of the enemy, who began to show a strong disposition to advance. I could now thoroughly appreciate the term bulldog, which I had heard applied to him by the soldiers. Difficulties seem to make no other impression upon him than to make him a little more savage. . . .

Source: Lieut.-Col. James A. L. Fremantle, *Three Months in the Southern States, April–June, 1863* (New York: John Bradburn, 1864), 254–56, 259–66.

THE NEW YORK CITY DRAFT RIOTS

James Fremantle arrived in New York City on July 13, 1863, the very day that the bloodiest riot in American history swept through the city. He was enjoying a brisk walk to his hotel on Fifth Avenue when "I found all the shopkeepers beginning to close their stores, and I perceived by degrees that there was great alarm about the resistance to the draft." As he reached his hotel, he saw "a whole block of buildings on fire close by: [fire] engines were present, but were not allowed to play by the crowd." Not content to stay in his hotel, Fremantle "walked about in the neighborhood, and saw a company of soldiers on the march, who were being jeered at and hooted by small boys, and I saw a negro pursued by the crowd." Fremantle was baffled, believing that the North was fighting for the blacks. "I inquired of a bystander what the negroes had done that they [the crowd] should want to kill them? He replied civilly enough—'Oh sir, they hate them here; they are the innocent cause of all these troubles.'" Fremantle added that it was to the advantage of white workers to maintain the system of slavery and to see "that the free Northern negroes who compete with them for labor should be sent to the South also." When the crowd attacked the black seamen on a British merchant ship, the commander of a French man-of-war took them aboard for their safety. Fremantle concluded that "the terror and anxiety were universal," and then boarded a ship for Britain.[18]

The riot Fremantle witnessed had its roots in the South. In 1862 the Confederacy ignored its stated hostility to central authority and passed a conscription act, the first in American history. The U.S. Congress followed suit early the following year. No longer able to maintain their war efforts with volunteers, both sides instituted class-based drafts

18. Lieut.-Col. James A. L. Fremantle, *Three Months in the Southern States, April–June, 1863* (New York: John Bradburn, 1864), 299–302.

that allowed wealthier men to buy replacements. Not surprisingly, both conscription acts aroused popular anger. In the South, opposition mostly took the form of avoidance and desertion—some regiments lost as much as a fifth of their number to desertion by 1864. The Union also experienced higher rates of desertion starting in 1863, but the real crisis came in active resistance to draft officers in many Northern cities. Adding a racial component to the crisis, New York's Democratic mayoral candidate, Fernando Wood, warned that the government planned to bring freed slaves north to replace drafted workers. On July 13, 1863, angry New York workers, mostly Irish, started the worst riot in American history by destroying the building that housed conscription headquarters. Over the next three days the rioters turned their anger on the homes of the wealthy and, most violently, upon individual blacks. As the crowds crossed into black neighborhoods and burned the Colored Orphan Asylum to the ground, city officials frantically called upon first the militia, and then the U.S. Army to restore order. It took the arrival of forces straight from the battlefield at Gettysburg to end the riots on July 17. No one can determine the total number of casualties, as so many bodies were destroyed by fire or thrown into the river, but the total was between three hundred and one thousand dead.

David M. Barnes Records the Violence
of the New York City Riots, 1863

MURDER OF COL. O'BRIEN.

The murder of Col. H. J. O'BRIEN, by the mob, on the afternoon of Tuesday of Riot Week, was characterized by appalling barbarities. After the battle between the police under Inspector CARPENTER, in the Second Avenue, and after the police had left, Col. O'BRIEN, in command of two companies, 11th Regiment, N.Y. Vols., arrived at Thirty-fourth Street and Second Avenue. The rioters had reassembled, a collision ensued, and the military opened fire. The mob dispersed, and Col. O'BRIEN, leaving his command, walked up the avenue a short distance, entering a drug store. Returning to the street in a few moments, he was instantly surrounded by a vengeful and relentless crowd, which had re-collected, at once knocked down, beaten and mutilated shockingly till insensible. He thus lay for upwards of an hour, breathing heavily, and on any movement receiving kicks and stones. He was then taken by the heels, dragged around the street, and again left lying in it. For some four hours did he thus lay, subjected to infamous outrages, among them the occasional thrusting of a stick down his throat when gasping for breath. No one who did not seek to feed his brutality upon him was allowed to approach him. One man who sought to give him a drop of water was instantly set upon and barely escaped with his life. While still breathing, he was taken into the yard of his own house, near the scene, and there the most revolting atrocities were perpetrated, underneath which the life, that had so tenaciously clung to him, fled. No one could have recognized his remains. The murderers, satiated with their excess of fiendishness, left, and the body was allowed to be removed to Bellevue Hospital.

COLORED VICTIMS OF THE RIOT.

WM. HENRY NICHOLS (colored). Resided at No. 147 East Twenty-eighth St. Mrs. STAAT, his mother, was visiting him. On Wednesday, July 15th, at 3 o'clock, the house was attacked by a mob with showers of bricks and stones. In one of the rooms was a woman with a child but three days old. The rioters broke open the door with axes and rushed in. NICHOLS and his mother fled to the basement; in a few moments the babe referred to was dashed by the rioters from the upper window into the yard, and instantly killed. The mob cut the water pipes above, and the basement was being deluged; ten persons, mostly women and children, were there, and they fled to the yard; in attempting to climb the fence Mrs. STAATS fell back from exhaustion; the rioters were instantly upon her; her son sprang to her rescue, exclaiming, "Save my mother, if you kill me." Two ruffians instantly seized him, each taking hold of an arm, while a third, armed with a crow-bar, calling upon them to hold his arms apart, deliberately struck him a savage blow on the head, felling him like a bullock. He died in the N.Y. Hospital two days after.

JAMES COSTELLO (col'd).— . . . No. 97 West Thirty-third Street, killed on Tuesday morning, July 14th. COSTELLO was a shoe-maker, an active man in his business, industrious and sober. He went out early in the morning upon an errand, was accosted, and finally was pursued by a powerful man. He ran down the street; endeavored to make his escape; was nearly overtaken by his pursuer; in self-defence he turned and shot the rioter with a revolver. The shot proved to be mortal; he died two days after. COSTELLO was immediately set upon by the mob. They first mangled his body, then hanged it. They then cut down his body and dragged it through the gutters, smashing it with stones, and finally burnt it. The mob then attempted to kill Mrs. COSTELLO and her children, but she escaped by climbing fences and taking refuge in a police station-house.

ABRAHAM FRANKLIN (colored).—This young man, who was murdered by the mob on the corner of Twenty-seventh Street and Seventh Avenue, was a quiet, inoffensive man, of unexceptionable character. He was a cripple, but supported himself and his mother, being employed as a coachman. A short time previous to the assault, he called upon his mother to see if anything could be done by him for her safety. The old lady said she considered herself perfectly safe; but if her time to die had come, she was ready to die. Her son then knelt down by her side, and implored the protection of Heaven in behalf of his mother. The old lady said that it seemed to her that good angels were present in the room. Scarcely had the supplicant risen from his knees, when the mob broke down the door, seized him, beat him over the head and face with fists and clubs, and then hanged him in the presence of his parent. While they were thus engaged the military came and drove them away, cutting down the body of FRANKLIN, who raised his arm once slightly and gave a few signs of life. The military then moved on to quell other riots, when the mob returned and again suspended the now probably lifeless body of FRANKLIN, cutting out pieces of flesh, and otherwise shockingly mutilating it. . . .

PETER HEUSTON.—Sixty-three years of age, a Mohawk Indian, dark complexion, but straight hair, and for several years a resident of New York, proved a victim to the riots. HEUSTON served with the New York Volunteers in the Mexican war. He was brutally attacked and shockingly beaten, on the 13th of July, by a gang of ruffians, who thought him to be of the African race because of his dark complexion. He died within four days, at Bellevue Hospital, from his injuries.

JEREMIAH ROBINSON (colored).—He was killed in Madison near Catharine Street. His widow stated that her husband, in order to escape, dressed himself in some of her clothes, and, in company with herself and one other woman, left their residence and went toward one of the Brooklyn ferries. ROBINSON wore a hood, which failed to hide his beard. Some boys, seeing his beard, lifted up the skirts of his dress, which exposed his heavy boots. Immediately the mob set upon him, and the atrocities they perpetrated are so revolting that they are unfit for publication. They finally killed him, and threw his body into the river. His wife and her companion ran up Madison street, and escaped across the Grand Street Ferry to Brooklyn. . . .

JOSEPH REED (colored).—This was a lad of seven years of age, residing at No. 147 East Twenty-eighth Street, with an aged grandmother and widowed mother. On Wednesday morning of the fearful week, a crowd of ruffians gathered in the neighborhood, determined on a work of plunder and death. They attacked the house, stole everything they could carry with them, and, after threatening the inmates, set fire to it. The colored people, who had the sole occupancy of the building, fled in confusion into the midst of the gathering crowd. And then the child was separated from his guardians. His youth and evident illness, even from the devils around him, it would be thought, should have insured his safety. But no sooner did they see his unprotected, defenceless condition, than a gang of fiendish men seized him, beat him with sticks, and bruised him with heavy cobble-stones. But one, ten-fold more the servant of Satan than the rest, rushed at the child, and with the stock of a pistol struck him on the temple and felled him to the ground. A noble young fireman, by the name of JOHN F. GOVERN, of No. 39 Hose Company, instantly

came to the rescue, and, single-handed, held the crowd at bay. Taking the
wounded and unconscious boy in his arms, he carried him to a place of
safety. The terrible beating and the great fright the poor lad had undergone
was too much for his feeble frame; he died on the following Tuesday....

——WILLAMS (colored).—He was attacked on the corner of Le Roy and
Washington Streets, on Tuesday morning, July 14th, knocked down, a number
of men jumped upon, kicked, and stamped upon him until insensible. One
of the murderers knelt on the body and drove a knife into it; the blade being
too small he threw it away and resorted to his fists. Another seized a huge
stone, weighing near twenty pounds, and deliberately crushed it again and
again on to the victim. A force of police, under Captain DICKSON, arrived and
rescued the man, who was conveyed to the New York Hospital. He was only
able to articulate "WILLIAMS" in response to a question as to his name, and
remained insensible thereafter, dying in a few days.

ANN DERRICKSON.—This was a white woman, the wife of a colored man,
and lived at No. 11 York Street. On Wednesday, July 15th, the rioters seized a
son of [the] deceased, a lad of about twelve years, saturated his clothes and
hair with camphene, and then procuring a rope, fastened one end to a lamppost, the other around his neck, and were about to set him on fire, and hang
him; they were interfered with by some citizens and by the police of the First
Ward, and their diabolical attempt at murder frustrated. While Mrs. DERRICK-
SON was attempting to save the life of her son she was horribly bruised and
beaten with a cart rung. The victim, after lingering three or four weeks, died
from the effects of her injuries.

Sources: David M. Barnes, *The Draft Riots in New York, July, 1863* (New York: Baker and
Godwin, 1863), 113–16.

ANDERSONVILLE

*Both sides treated prisoners of war horribly. The death rate accelerated in 1864 as General
Ulysses S. Grant put an end to prisoner exchanges as part of his policy of bleeding the
Confederacy of its manpower. The Confederates, suffering a terrible food shortage, often
allowed prisoners to slowly starve to death, keeping the prisoners in horrendously over-
crowded camps. Only disease flourished in the prison camps, north and south. Of 194,000
Union soldiers held in Confederate camps, 36,400 died in captivity; 30,150 of the 220,000
Confederates captured died in prison camps.*

*John L. Ransom of the Ninth Michigan Cavalry was taken prisoner in Tennessee in
November 1863 at the age of twenty. Sent to the notorious Andersonville Prison in southern Georgia, Ransom battled to stay alive as disease swept through the camp, with almost
no food, preyed upon by other Union prisoners, and threatened with being shot should*

he pass the "dead line." Andersonville held 49,485 Union soldiers during the war, 13,000 of whom died. Its commandant, Henry Wirz, was the only Confederate convicted of war crimes and was hanged in November 1865. After the war Ransom returned to his home in Jackson, Michigan, where he slowly recovered and became a printer. He published his diary in 1881, shortly after he moved to Chicago, where he lived until his death in 1919.

Excerpts from the Diary of POW John L. Ransom, 1864

April 13.—Jack Shannon, from Ann Arbor, died this morning. The raiders [thieves among the prisoners] are the stronger party now, and do as they please; and we are in nearly as much danger now from our own men as from the rebels. Capt. Moseby, of my own hundred, figures conspicuously among the robberies, and is a terrible villain. During the night some one stole my jacket. Have traded off all superfluous clothes, and with the loss of jacket have only pants, shirt, shoes, (no stockings,) and hat; yet I am well dressed in comparison with some others. Many have nothing but an old pair of pants which reach, perhaps, to the knees, and perhaps not. . . .

April 14.—At least twenty fights among our own men this forenoon. It beats all what a snarling crowd we are getting to be. The men are perfectly reckless, and had just as soon have their necks broken by fighting as anything else. . . . Van Tassel, a Pennsylvanian, is about to die. Many give me parting injunctions relative to their families, in case I should live through[.] Have half a dozen photographs of dead men's wives, with addresses on the back of them. Seems to be pretty generally conceded that if any get through, I will. Not a man here now is in good health. An utter impossibility to remain well. . . .

April 27. . . . A man caught stealing from one of his comrades and stabbed with a knife and killed. To show how little such things are noticed here, I will give the particulars as near as I could get them. There were five or six men stopping together in a sort of shanty. Two of them were speculators, and had some money, corn bread, &c., and would not divide with their comrades, who belonged to their own company and regiment. Some time in the night one of them got up and was stealing bread from a haversack belonging to his more prosperous neighbor, and during the operation woke up the owner, who seized a knife and stabbed the poor fellow dead. The one who did the murder spoke out and said: "Harry, I believe Bill is dead; he was just stealing from me and I run my knife into him." "Good enough for him," says Harry. The two men then got up and straightened out "Bill," and then both lay down and went to sleep. An occupant of the hut told me these particulars and they are true. This morning poor Bill lay in the hut until eight or nine o'clock, and was then carried outside. The man who did the killing made no secret of it, but told it to all who wanted to know the particulars, who were only a few, as the occurrence was not an unusual one. . . .

July 6.—Boiling hot, camp reeking with filth, and no sanitary privileges; men dying off over a hundred and forty per day. Stockade enlarged, taking in eight or ten more acres, giving us more room, and stumps to dig up for wood to cook with. Mike Hoare is in good health; not so Jimmy Devers. Jimmy has now been a prisoner over a year, and poor boy, will probably die soon. Have more mementoes than I can carry, from those who have died, to be given to their friends at home. At least a dozen have given me letters, pictures &c., to take North. Hope I shan't have to turn them over to some one else.

July 8. . . . Over a hundred and fifty dying per day now, and twenty six thousand in camp. Guards shoot now very often. Boys, as guards, are the most cruel. It is said that if they kill a Yankee, they are given a thirty days furlough. . . . The swamp now is fearful, water perfectly reeking with prison offal and poison. Still men drink it and die. . . . The prison is a success as regards safety; no escape except by death, and very many take advantage of that way.

Source: John L. Ransom, *Andersonville Diary* (Auburn, NY: for the author, 1881), 51, 53, 77–78.

THE ASSASSINATION OF ABRAHAM LINCOLN

Today Abraham Lincoln is a beloved figure, an American icon. Yet, in his lifetime, many Americans despised him. Southerners offered rewards for his murder, and many Northerners blamed him for the Civil War. Even many of his fellow Republicans disliked Lincoln's policies as too soft on the Confederates; on the day of his assassination, Republican leaders met on Capitol Hill to discuss how to turn the murder to their advantage. John Wilkes Booth, a prominent actor, had conspired with a small group to shoot the president and much of his cabinet as a last desperate effort to forestall the collapse of the Confederacy. Booth was shot and killed while trying to escape; military authorities tried the remaining members of his conspiracy before a special tribunal. Some Republicans used evidence gathered by the commission to argue that Booth's conspirators had been part of a wider network that reached to the upper echelons of the Confederate government. For decades after Lincoln's death, conspiracy buffs published books arguing that leading Confederates, perhaps operating out of Canada, had plotted Lincoln's death, as in the following excerpt. One hundred years later, conspiracy theories would similarly flourish in the wake of President John F. Kennedy's assassination.

Thomas M. Harris Documents the Conspiracy
to Assassinate Lincoln, 1865

The evidence which will be hereafter referred to shows that John Wilkes Booth and John H. Surratt had, as early as the latter part of October, or early in November, 1864, entered into a contract with Davis's Canada Cabinet to accomplish the assassinations they had planned, and that they immediately entered upon their work of preparation. It would seem from the evidence, that at that time the purpose was to execute their designs at a much earlier date than they did; and that this delay was occasioned by the Canada conspirators. . . .

They were stimulated by their intense hostility to the administration of President Lincoln and desire for the establishment of the Southern Confederacy, and also by the delusive idea of winning enduring fame and the lasting gratitude of their countrymen of the South for being thus the instruments of retrieving the fortunes of their dying cause. But in addition to these considerations, they had large promises of pecuniary reward. They were, in fact, the hired assassins of Jefferson Davis and his Canada Cabinet. . . .

On the morning of the 14th of April 1865, the President's messenger went to Ford's Theatre in Washington City and engaged a private box for the President and General Grant, with their wives, to witness the play of "Our American Cousin," which was to be rendered there that night. The heavy burden of responsibility, the weight of cares and anxieties which had for four long years rested on the head of President Lincoln in his official position of President of the United States and Commander-in-Chief of its army and navy . . . had been partially lifted by the signal success of the Union arms at Appomattox, and the surrender of Lee's army. . . . When we think of what President Lincoln had endured through all these years of the war; of his unfaltering purpose to discharge all the duties of his official oath, by protecting, defending and preserving the constitution of his country; of the formidable difficulties that had to be met and overcome—difficulties thrown across his pathway often by friends, always by foes; when we remember his largeness of soul, his unbounded love of, and sympathy with, mankind; his all controlling love of his country and her institutions of freedom; his patient toleration of opposing views of martial and political policy; his self-poise, and almost infallible appreciation of the situation and its demands, in whatever circumstances he might be placed; his kindness of nature and goodness of heart, we can well conceive what must have been his fullness of joy on this the last day of his sojourn on earth. . . .

During the day General Grant received a telegram that called him to Philadelphia on business, and owing to this apparently providential circumstance he was prevented from accompanying the President to the theatre on that eventful night, and also in all probability, from being, with the President, a victim of the plot, in which there is good reason to conclude, from all the evidence, his life was included, and that for him an assassin had been provided.

In lieu of General and Mrs. Grant, President Lincoln had taken Major Rathbone and Miss Harris, the step-son and daughter of Senator Harris, of New York, into the Presidential party. On reaching the theatre at a somewhat late hour, and after the play had commenced, as soon as the presence of the President became known, the actors stopped playing, the band struck up "Hail to the Chief," and the audience rose and received him with vociferous cheering. . . .

About ten o'clock Booth rode up the alley back of the theatre where he had been accustomed to keep his horse, and having reached the rear entrance, called for Ned three times, each time a little louder than before. At the third call Ned Spangler answered to his summons by appearing at the door. Booth's first salutation was in the form of a question: "Ned, you will help me all you can, won't you?" To which Spangler replied, "Oh, yes!" Booth then requested him to send "Peanuts" (a boy employed about the theatre), to hold his horse. Spangler gave the boy orders to do this, and upon the boy making the objection that he might be out of place at the time he had a duty to perform, Spangler bade him go, saying that he would stand responsibility for him. The boy then took the reins, and held the horse for about half an hour, until Booth returned to reward him with a curse and a kick, as he jerked the rein from him preparatory to remounting for his flight. After entering the theatre, Booth passed rapidly across the stage, glancing at the box occupied by his intended victim, and looking up his accomplices, he passed out of the front door on to the walk where he was met by two of his fellow conspirators. One of these was a low, villainous-looking fellow, whilst the other was a very neatly-dressed man. Booth held a private conference with these by the door where he and the vulgar-looking fellow had stationed themselves. The neatly-dressed man crossed the walk to the rear of the President's carriage and peeped into it. One of the witnesses, who was sitting on the platform in front of the theatre, had his attention arrested by the manner and conduct of these men, and so watched them very closely.

It was at the close of the second act that Booth and his two fellow conspirators appeared at the door. . . . Taking a hasty, but careful, look through the hole which he had made in the door for the purpose of assuring himself of the President's position, and cocking his pistol and with his finger on the trigger, he pulled open the door, and stealthily entered the box, where he stood right behind and within three feet of the President. The play had advanced to the second scene of the third act, and whilst the audience was intensely interested Booth fired the fatal shot—the ball penetrating the skull on the back of the left side of the head, inflicting a wound in the brain (the ball passing entirely through and lodging behind the right eye), of which he died at about half-past seven o'clock on the morning of the fifteenth. [Lincoln] was unconscious from the moment he was struck until his spirit passed from earth. An unspeakable calm settled on that remarkable face, leaving the impress of a happy soul on the casket it had left behind.

Thus died the man who said, "Senator Douglas says he don't care whether slavery is voted up, or voted down; but God cares, and humanity cares, and I care."

Source: Thomas M. Harris, *Assassination of Lincoln: A History of the Great Conspiracy* (Boston: American Citizen Company, 1892), 24, 25, 34–39.

FURTHER READINGS

On the accelerating sectional crisis, see Michael Holt, *The Political Crisis of the 1850s* (New York: Norton 1978); David Grimsted, *American Mobbing, 1828–1861: Toward Civil War* (New York: Oxford University Press, 1998); David M. Potter, *The Impending Crisis, 1848–1861* (New York: Harper and Row, 1976); Gerald Leonard, *The Invention of Party Politics: Federalism, Popular Sovereignty, and Constitutional Development in Jacksonian Illinois* (Chapel Hill: University of North Carolina Press, 2002); Richard H. Sewell, *Ballots for Freedom: Antislavery Politics in the United States, 1837–1860* (New York: Oxford University Press, 1976); William J. Cooper Jr., *The South and the Politics of Slavery, 1828–1856* (Baton Rouge: Louisiana State University Press, 1978); James A. Rawley, *Race and Politics: "Bleeding Kansas" and the Coming of the Civil War* (Philadelphia: Lippincott, 1969); David S. Reynolds, *John Brown, Abolitionist: The Man who Killed Slavery, Sparked the Civil War and Seeded Civil Rights* (New York: Knopf, 2005).

On military aspects of the Civil War, see Emory M. Thomas, *The Confederate Nation, 1861–1865* (New York: Harper and Row, 1979); Phillip Shaw Paludan, *People's Contest: The Union and Civil War, 1861–1865* (Baton Rouge: Louisiana State University Press, 1988); Grady McWhiney and Perry D. Jamieson, *Attack and Die: Civil War Military Tactics and the Southern Heritage* (University: University of Alabama Press, 1982); Paddy Griffith, *Battle Tactics of the Civil War* (New Haven, CT: Yale University Press, 1989); Edward L. Ayers, *In the Presence of mine enemies: The Civil War in the Heart of America, 1859–1863* (New York: Norton, 2003); James M. McPherson, *Battle Cry of Freedom: The Civil War Era* (New York: Oxford University Press, 1988).

For more information on the treatment of prisoners of war, see William Marvel, *Andersonville: The Last Depot* (Chapel Hill: University of North Carolina Press, 1994); George Levy, *To Die in Chicago: Confederate Prisoners at Camp Douglas, 1862–1865* (Evanston, IL: Evanston Publishing, 1994); Lonnie R. Speer, *Portals to Hell: Military Prisons of the Civil War* (Mechanicsburg, PA: Stackpole Books, 1997).

On the assassination of Abraham Lincoln, see Theodore Roscoe, *The Web of Conspiracy: The Complete Story of the Men Who Murdered Abraham Lincoln* (Englewood Cliffs, NJ: Prentice-Hall, 1960); Thomas Reed Turner, *Beware the People Weeping: Public Opinion and the Assassination of Abraham Lincoln* (Baton Rouge: Louisiana State University Press, 1982); Edward Steers, *Blood on the Moon: The Assassination of Abraham Lincoln* (Lexington: University Press of Kentucky, 2001).

SIX

THE NEW SOUTH

Reconstruction began for much of the American South in the summer of 1863, after General Ulysses S. Grant's Union army swept through the lower Mississippi River Valley, conquering vast plantation districts, freeing tens of thousands of African American slaves. Grant's army ruled its captured territory only briefly, returning control of courthouses, jails, and state capitols to white southerners in the summer of 1865.

Some in the North wanted to remake southern society, to "reconstruct" its economy and race relations. The most determined of these reformers were called "Radicals," a name that implied criticism in that popular views held a radical as someone who wants to move too fast. In the case of post–Civil War Reconstruction, most Radicals merely wanted to allow freed slaves access to the ballot box. While this hardly seems radical to us now, it inspired determined and violent resistance on the part of white southerners, the defeated Confederates.

This resistance first took the form of statutory enactments. Southern legislatures intended to substitute law for the lash as a means of racial control; lawmakers hoped to use courts and lawyers to accomplish what had once been done informally on plantations by slave owners and their overseers. Within a short time, white southerners, who doubted that blacks could be effectively disciplined through law in the first place, lost faith in this process.

After Congress took control of Reconstruction policies, allowing black voting, whites organized vigilante organizations, most notably the Ku Klux Klan. The Klan and other vigilante groups acted in secret, wearing masks and riding at night. They did not dare act openly because they feared legal prosecution and extralegal retaliation. In some districts, the Klan mounted powerful resistance to congressional reconstruction policies.

The Klan sought to prevent the implementation of democracy in the South by establishing uncontested white Democratic rule. Attaining that goal did not mean just keeping Republicans from the polls, though the Klan proved very good at that practice as well. Members of the Klan spread terror by destroying every manifestation of African Americans' new civil and political status. The Klan targeted prosperous African Americans, white and black Republican political leaders, members of black militia companies, and anyone who appeared willing to cross racial barriers.

Republican leaders throughout the South pleaded for more federal troops, but the government refused to comply. Congressional Republicans investigated incidents of political violence—several of the documents here are drawn from those inquires—but hesitated to respond with force for fear of losing their northern constituents. Congressional Republicans insisted that individuals could protect their own rights by turning to the legal system. As it became evident that southern courts were too often in the thrall of white Democrats, and antiblack violence escalated in the South, Congress passed a series of antiterrorism laws that made efforts to prevent a citizen from exercising his civil rights a federal offense. Federal marshals used this legislation to arrest hundreds of Klan members, but very little came of their efforts, and the U.S. Supreme Court severely limited most of these civil rights laws.[1]

In the 1880s, white racial violence became more public and less secretive. Even after Congress abandoned its efforts to reconstruct southern society, leaving every state in the South to one-party white rule, white terror groups continued to employ the most savage forms of violence to prevent African Americans from enjoying the rights of citizenship. Mobs hanged and burned their black victims in daylight, no longer afraid of retaliation. That these lynch mobs enjoyed wide popular support in the white community is evidenced not only by the failure of the police to intervene and the legal system to punish those responsible but also by the popularity of postcards picturing grinning crowds standing around their gruesomely tortured victims. With time, the justification for these acts of violence shifted from enforcing white supremacy to protecting white women from ravaging black males. As Senator Ben Tillman of South Carolina declared on the floor of the U.S. Senate in 1907: "As governor of South Carolina I proclaimed that, although I had taken the oath of office to support the law and enforce it, I would lead a mob to lynch any man, black or white, who had ravished a woman, black or white." Though he could provide no examples of a white man lynched for rape, Tillman felt "justified by my conscience in the sight of God" in violating the law. "Civilization peels off us," when confronted with a tale of rape, Tillman concluded, "and we revert to the original savage type whose impulses under any and all such circumstances has

---

1. Civil Rights Cases (1883), *United States Reports* 109:3–62; US v. Cruikshank (1876), *United States Reports* 92:542; US v. Harris (1882), *United States Reports* 106:629.

always been to 'kill! kill! kill!' "[2] Southern whites had achieved consensus: blacks could be legitimately killed outside the law.

DOCUMENTS

BLACK CODES

Though they had lost the Civil War, southern racists intended to win the peace. The policies of President Andrew Johnson placed in office conservative whites determined to maintain racial hegemony even after the fall of slavery. In November 1865, the Mississippi legislature began passing the first laws that northern newspapers would dub "black codes." Lawmakers hoped these brutally discriminatory statutes would keep African Americans in a slavelike status. Mississippi's black codes, copied by other southern states, allowed white capital to violently discipline black labor. Admonitions against "cruel and unusual" punishments aped slavery-era prohibitions and seemed to have as little application. Master and apprentice laws returned black youngsters to the supervision of their former masters and permitted the white supervisors of black labor to administer corporal punishment. Another law established legal tribunals intended to discipline blacks: the new county courts would meet the expected tidal wave of black crime by hearing cases all the time, rather than twice a year as did circuit courts, and could hang defendants by their thumbs for the sorts of minor crimes whites thought blacks, freed from slavery, would likely commit.

Mississippi's Black Code, 1865

CHAPTER II AN ACT TO ESTABLISH COUNTY COURTS

Section 1. *Be it enacted by the Legislature of the State of Mississippi,* That a court to be styled the County Court of   county, shall be and is hereby established in each and every county of this State, with inferior criminal and civil jurisdiction to the circuit courts of this State, and shall be held once in every month, at the court house of the county, at such times as the judges of said court may from time to time appoint, and shall continue in session from day to day until the business therein . . . shall require. The county court of each county shall have all the powers and authority, and shall be governed and controlled by the same laws, rules and practice of the circuit court of this State, as far as the same can be applied and extended to the matters and jurisdiction confided to said county court, except that no grand jury or dis-

2. *The Congressional Record—Senate,* 59th Cong., 2nd sess., vol. 41, pt. 2 (January 1907): 1440–1441.

trict attorney shall be necessary, but may be dispensed with, and all cases in said county court may be tried by the court upon the laws and facts upon information in writing in the name of the State of Mississippi, made out and certified by the attorney or clerk of the court, under the supervision and direction of the court, containing the substance of the charges, the nature and character of the offence, in what county committed, and the person, and property, if either, against whom or which committed, and about; the date thereof, giving in a plain and simple way, notice to the accused what he or she is arrested and to be tried for, and the same shall be read to the accused before trial. . . .

Sec. 3. Be it further enacted, That the county court shall have full and complete jurisdiction of all cases of petit larceny, assaults, assaults and batteries, riots, affrays, routes, unlawful assemblies, words of insult made indictable by our statute, violations of the Sabbath of every kind against law, disturbances of religious worship or persons assembled for that purpose . . . defaulting road overseers, . . . unlawful exhibition of deadly weapons, gaming, racing or shooting upon any public road, street or square, obtaining goods, money or other property by false pretences, under the value of one hundred dollars, and all other common law and statutory offences below the grade of felony, not specially designated above . . . and to impose such fines and punishments as are provided by law for such offences, or may inflict corporeal punishment, by suspending the party convicted by the thumbs, not more than two hours in twenty-four, nor more than ten days, and so as not to permanently injure the party so punished. . . .

CHAPTER V AN ACT TO BE ENTITLED, "AN ACT TO REGULATE THE RELATION OF MASTER AND APPRENTICE, AS RELATES TO FREEDMEN, FREE NEGROES, AND MULATTOES."

SECTION 1. *Be it enacted by the Legislature of the State of Mississippi,* That it shall be the duty of all sheriffs, justices of the peace, and other civil officers . . . to report to the probate courts . . . all freedmen, free negroes and mulattoes, under the age of eighteen . . . who are orphans, or whose parent or parents have not the means, or who refuse to provide for and support said minors, and thereupon it shall be the duty of said probate court, to order the clerk of said court to apprentice said minors to some competent and suitable person . . . : Provided, that the former owner of said minors shall have the preference, when in the opinion of the court, he or she shall be a suitable person for that purpose. . . .

Sec. 3. Be it further enacted, That in the management and control of said apprentices, said master or mistress shall have power to inflict such moderate corporeal chastisement as a father or guardian is allowed to inflict on his or her child or ward at common law: Provided that in no case shall cruel or inhuman punishment be inflicted. . . .

Approved November 22, 1865.

Source: 1865 Miss. 66–68, 86–87, 90.

NEW ORLEANS RACE RIOT

In Louisiana, Republicans tried to win control of the state government from the traditional elite President Johnson had returned to power. Supposedly backed by the federal government, Louisiana Republicans convened a new constitutional convention at the Mechanics Institute in New Orleans on July 30, 1866. As the meeting came to order, angry white Democrats attacked the building, leading to the death of 38 people and the wounding of 150 others. Police, most of whom held their position as patronage from the local Democratic political machine, participated in the violence; in reality, the affair was a police riot. The House of Representatives investigated this riot and other acts of violence in the South, their findings persuading Congress to take control of the former Confederate states and end Johnson's Reconstruction policies.

J. D. O'Connell's Testimony before the House of Representatives, 1866

NEW ORLEANS, December 24, 1866.

J. D. O'CONNELL sworn and examined.

By the CHAIRMAN: . . .

914. Were you where you could see what took place, or any part of what took place, on the 30th of July? [A.] . . . I heard some shots fired in the direction of Canal street about that time, and saw people retreating towards Common street. As the mass of people were retreating towards Common street they came in view from the windows of the hall. I saw a policeman follow the crowd and discharge his revolver towards them. The people on the street were principally colored, and they took possession of a pile of brickbats on the street, quite close to the hall, and commenced firing them at the police and citizens acting with them, who were shooting their revolvers towards the negroes.

As the crowd were driven further back towards Common street I saw two colored men have long pistols, which appeared to be horse-pistols, and discharge them towards the police. These were the only arms I saw discharged toward the police. The police became very numerous about this time. I suppose there were no less than 2,000 police and citizens who assembled to attack this crowd of colored people. The colored people defended themselves until they were driven on towards Common street. They then rallied again, and drove the police towards Canal street. I believe they drove each other first towards Common and then towards Canal street twice or three times, when the colored people were dispersed. During this time some shots were fired at the hall from the street by people coming from the direction of Canal street. . . .

Persons lying right alongside me were shot by the police, and I saw that it was no more safe there than to stand. I got up, and advanced upon the door. About the same time Mr. Fish and Mr. Horton advanced to the door. At this time a policeman levelled his pistol at me and fired, but the ball did not hit me. I asked Mr. Horton not to come to the door. He was holding a white handkerchief, and asking the men for God's sake not to murder them, saying they were not armed. . . .

The second attack they entered again, and the police came up to negroes and white men indiscriminately taking no prisoners, but shooting them as rapidly as possible. I saw one policeman, while a negro was kneeling before him and begging for mercy, shoot into his side. I saw another discharge his revolver into a negro lying flat on the floor. All this time I was anxiously hoping the military would arrive and quell the riot . . . , and I suggested that we barricade the hall, and hold it until the military should come. It was the only chance we had.

. . . I pulled the chairs down and drove the colored people from the door, so that their presence should not provoke the police to any further acts of violence. They very submissively went toward the other end of the hall. As the police entered the hall, one in the rear of the one I had spoken to advanced, calling out, "Yes, you G——d d——d sons of bitches, we'll protect you." I had confidence that they would protect us, but when they entered the hall, even this man who had tendered me his hand rushed forward with the others, discharging their pistols indiscriminately. One of the police, pointing his pistol towards me, said, "So you will surrender, you G——d d——d son of a bitch," and discharging his revolver towards my head, said, "Take that and go to hell, will you?" I was standing close to him and had the presence of mind to throw up his hand, and the ball passed through my hat both in front and rear. I retired towards the door, and another policeman approached me with a long knife and struck at me. I defended myself against him with the leg of a chair and got back into the room.

Those inside again rallied with broken chairs and whatever they could get hold of, and drove the police out. I suppose this was about twenty-five minutes of three o'clock. The fight had gone on continuously up to this time. I assisted in driving them out, and followed them to the top of the stairs.. . . .When I found the crowd had again nearly reached the top of the stairs, seeing a vacancy near the foot of them, I jumped. . . . As I got on to the street I saw a line of police standing like soldiers across Dryades street; towards Canal street. . . . I went to two of them and tried to get their numbers, so that I could know who they were, but their hat-bands, on which they wore the letters "police" and the number, were turned wrong side out. I then spoke to them, and told them if they wanted anything of the people in the hall why not enter the room like men; that it was cowardly to shoot into a building that way. Two of them left, but eight or ten of them kept on discharging their revolvers.

Source: House of Representatives Report no. 16, 39th Cong., 2d sess., 1866–67, pp. 77–79.

THE KU KLUX KLAN

In 1866 Tennessee whites organized the Ku Klux Klan as a social fraternity in the little town of Pulaski, on the Alabama border. After Congress wrested control of Reconstruction from President Johnson, ordering the southern states to write new constitutions to be submitted to all voters, black and white, the Ku Klux Klan morphed into a vigilante organization, an arm of the white conservative Democratic political party. Congress investigated the Klan, taking testimony from Klansmen and their victims. The testimony of Henry Lowther, a black political leader, illustrates the gendered nature of Klan violence. There was nothing in Lowther's testimony to suggest that he sexually threatened women of any color; nonetheless, whites castrated him. White racists, apparently, associated political power with male potency.

Henry Lowther's Testimony before a Congressional Committee, 1871

Atlanta, Georgia, October 20, 1871
Henry Lowther, (colored,) sworn and examined.

. . . I was put in jail Saturday evening; my son was put in there with me. They said they had a warrant for him, but they did not have any. They arrested him twelve miles from home. When they got to the jail-house and locked the door and started out, my son said to me: "Father, they are not after me, they are after you. To-morrow I am going to ask Captain Thomas to turn me out of jail." Sure enough, he did so. I asked him to turn me out, for I was in there for nothing. He said I could not get out without a trial. I said, "Captain, I want a trial." He said, "If you want one you must have it; but to-day is Sunday, and if you will take my advice you will put it off until to-morrow. Monday morning I will take you out early and give you a fair trial."

Monday morning came; they went around and arrested about sixteen persons; about six of them were engaged in a company to protect me. We had a company to protect me after they first went to my house. They arrested about eight more besides them, and brought them to town; they carried them to the court-house and examined about half of them. They did not take me out of jail at all. It was about 2 o'clock in the day when they got through with them. They dealt with them all, either by making them pay $2.70 costs, or giving bonds for appearance at court. Of course they gave the $2.70. My son, a grown young man, was up there. He said, "Father, Rack Bell says he is satisfied you did not have this company of men to take him out and kill him. They say it is left with him whether you get out of jail or not." I said, "Tell Rack Bell to come here to the jail." He came; and I said to him, "What does this mean? We have ate together and slept together, and we have helped each other. It is with you whether I get out of jail or not." He said, "Captain Eli Cummins and Lewis Peacock say you cannot get out of jail." I said, "Tell Captain Cummins to come here." A gentleman came with him by the name of Beaman. Captain Cummins sat down and talked with me about an hour, but there was nothing he said that I thought had any substance in it, only when he went to leave he said, "Harry, are you willing to give up your stones to save your life?" I sat there for a moment, and then I told him, "Yes." . . .

There were supposed to be one hundred eighty of them. When they first took me out they tied me and carried me off from the jail-house about a hundred yards; they then divided into four parties, and about twenty of them carried me off into a swamp about two miles. Well, within a hundred yards of the swamp they all stopped and called numbers, began with number one, and went up as high as number ten. When they got to number ten they went for a rope, and I was satisfied they were going to hang me. I begged for my life. They told me if they did not kill me I would shoot into the Ku-Klux again. I told them I had not done it. They asked me who it was; I told them who I heard it was, but I did not know. One of them who was standing by told the other who was talking to me to hush up and ask no questions, because he knew more about it than I did. They went on then into the swamp, and came to a halt again, and stood there and talked awhile. There were eight men walking with me—one hold of each arm, three in front of me with guns, and three right behind me.

After some conversation, just before they were ordered to march, or something was said, every man cocked his gun and looked right at me. I thought they were going to shoot me, and leave me right there. The moon was shining bright, and I could see them. I was satisfied they were going to kill me, and I did not care much then. They asked me whether I preferred to be altered or to be killed. I said I preferred to be altered. After laying me down and getting through, they said: "Now, as soon as you can get to a doctor go to one; you know the doctors in this country, and as soon as you are able to leave do it, or we will kill you next time." I asked how long it would take to get well, and they said five or six weeks. I was naked and bleeding very much. It was two miles and a quarter to a doctor's. The first man's house I got to was the jailer's. I called him up and asked him to go to the jail-house and get my clothes. He said he could not go; I said, "You must; I am naked and nearly froze to death." That was about 3 o'clock in the night. He had a light in the house, and there was a party of men standing in the door. I told him I wanted him to come out and give me some attention. He said he could not come. I could hardly walk then. I went on about ten steps further and I met the jailer's son-in-law. I asked him to go and get my clothes; and he said, "No," and told me to go up and lie down. I went right on and got up to a store; there were a great many men sitting along on the store piazza; I knew some of them, but I did not look at them much. They asked me what I wanted; I said I wanted a doctor. They told me to go on and lie down. I had then to stop and hold on to the side of the house to keep from falling. I staid there a few minutes, and then went on to a doctor's house, about a quarter of a mile, and called him aloud twice. He did not answer me.

The next thing I knew I was lying on the sidewalk in the street—seemed to have just waked up out of a sleep. I thought to myself, "Did I lie down here and go to sleep?" I wanted some water; I had to go about a quarter of a mile to get some water; I was getting short of breath, but the water helped me considerably. I went to a house about fifty yards further. I called to a colored woman to wake my wife up; she was in town. I happened to find my son there, and he went back for a doctor. When he got there the doctor answered the first time he called him. The reason he did not answer me was that he was off on this raid. I asked the doctor where he was when I was at his house, and he said he was asleep. I said, "I was at your house." The men kept coming in and saying to me that I did not get to the doctor's house, and I said that I did. After two or three times I took the hint, and said nothing more about that. But I told my son the next morning to go there and see if there was not a large puddle of blood at the gate. They would not let him go. But some colored woman came to see me and told me that the blood was all over town; at the doctor's gate, and everywhere else. It was running a stream all the time I was trying to find the doctor, and I thought I would bleed to death. My son tended me until I got so I could travel.

Source: *Report of the Joint Select Committee to Inquire into the Condition of Affairs in the Late Insurrectionary States*, 13 vols. (Washington, DC, 1872), House Reports, 42d Cong., 2nd sess., vol. 6, 356–57.

THE VICKSBURG MASSACRE

Congressional control of Reconstruction emboldened southern blacks. In Warren County, Mississippi, a black majority county, Republicans had made political gains by 1874, winning control of some county offices. In the face of continued white violence, freed blacks organized themselves into protective militia companies. By the summer of 1874, Warren County whites were themselves organizing for the coming race war. James Madison Batchelor, called "Mad" by his family, was a Civil War veteran who had fought at Gettysburg. In 1874, Mad was a planter living near Vicksburg. His letters to his brother, Albert, revealed Mississippi whites excitedly preparing for war.

James M. Batchelor Describes the Massacre, 1874

LETTER FROM JAMES MADISON BATCHELOR TO ALBERT A. BATCHELOR, SEPTEMBER 6, 1874.

I have been so engaged in war like preparation and political organization that I have had no time in the last thirty days to devote to the pleasant duty of letter writing.... We have had ever since the 1st Aug even three weeks before that. The greatest excitement caused by the *negros* arming drilling & making numerous threats. At one time about 5th Aug a collision seemed inevitable. And being that they intended killing us all on or about a certain day we called a meeting of the citizens in our neighborhoods to prepare for them. Where upon we organized in to a company. They doing me the honor to select me as their Captain. And requiring assistance from abroad, I sent into Hinds Co & got the promise of three hundreds men about two hundreds of whom came over & went into camp near the "Baldwins Ferry" about five miles distant. Put out our scouts <& pickets> & kept a sharp look out generally. Finally about 12 oc <at night> one night, I received the intelligence that a thousand negroes intended to attack us in camp at daylight. We were overjoyed at the prospect of a good *killing* & prepared to give them a *warm* reception. But we waited in vain until twelve oc, in the mean time they were still *collecting* <from every direction> and sending us defiant & insulting messages. Finding them slow to attack—And being reinforced by 100 rebel *Confeds* from Vicksbg and with *sixteen shooters* we concluded to make the attack our selves. But alas for our hopes for marching to the place of rendezvous we could only find the *tracks* where they had *lastly* dispersed on hearing of our approach & scattered in *every direction*. So we had the mortification to return to our respective homes without a fight not before however we went to the cabins of a few (which we could only find) and gave them orders if they *ever* placed themselves in such a defiant attitude again we would *shoot* and *hang* the last one of them. The leaders were sharp enough to keep out of sight or we would have made an example anyhow (In this section of county we have about *thirty* (30) negro men to one white man). . . . We have since learned they are waiting to sell their crops to provide themselves with the proper guns and ammunitions. We are still keeping up organizations all over *both counties* Warren & Hinds & regard a war of races as *inevitable*. It only being a question of time and the slightest excitement may plunge us into it at anytime. If you ever see anything from our city you can see we are renovating nothing and are furnishing *Jail* accommodations almost daily to some (one more) radical official. We are about to get our sheriff <(a negro)> for the next man and as he has considerable influence in the county among the 4000 negro votes & as they have now an opportunity to supply themselves with the material of war I am in hopes they will "*show their hands*[.]" While upon the subject allow me to say I never saw a people *so* united in my life as are the white people. We have adopted the [ ] of a "*white line*" to the *very letter* have organized clubs all over the county and are preparing for the election for next fall a year off. Which we intend to carry *against* an overwhelming majority or run every negro out of the county, we propose *every man* to discharge & drive out of the county on the 1st day of Jan every objectionable negro or *everyone* who has been conspicuous in this disturbance. Every man will be published in the papers & no man being in the *county* will or *dare* hire or allow them to stay on their places.

Source: Folder 36, box 2, Albert A. Batchelor Papers, Special Collections, Hill Memorial Library, Louisiana State University.

Testimony of Andrew Owen before the House of Representatives, 1874

The violence Batchelor lusted after came in December 1874, when armed whites drove the black sheriff, Peter Crosby, from office. On the morning of Monday, December 7, white Vicksburgers sounded the alarm, fearing that armed blacks from the rural precincts intended to return Crosby to office. Excited and armed white men quickly assembled. The mayor put the assembled mob under the command of former Confederate Horace H. Miller. Miller ordered Crosby arrested and then took to the field to confront a body of black men approaching town under Andrew Owen's command. Owen described what happened next in his testimony before congressional investigators.

Andrew Owen (colored) sworn.
By Mr. Hurlbut: . . .

> Q.: State whether or not you came in toward this city with any number of colored people on the 7th of December; and if so, on which road you came in?— A.: I did, sir; I came in on the Baldwin's Ferry road.

Q.: How many colored people were with you?— A.: I suppose I might have had about one hundred and twenty men. . . .

Q.: Have you any military organization in this county?— A.: No, sir.

Q.: The men that you started with, did you organize in any form; did you make them up into squads, or put any officers over them?— A.: No, sir. We had none but the one. We went marching along in one line.

Q.: Were they all armed?— A.: No, sir; not one-half of them.

Q.: Those who were armed, how were they armed?— A.: With a few shot-guns, and some of them old muskets that they had here in the United States armory. Some had pistols. . . .

Q.: Did Colonel Miller come up and have a conversation with you?— A.: Yes, sir.

Q.: State what that conversation was. . . . — A.: He rode up and said, "Owen, go back home." I says, "Colonel, I do not feel disposed to go back home until I see Crosby." "Well," says he, "I advise you to go back." I says, "Colonel, will you do one thing?" He says "What is that, Owen?" I said, "Submit Crosby out to see me or me to see him." He did so, took me in to see Crosby with Dr. Hunt. . . .

Q.: What occurred between you and Crosby?— A.: I says to him, "I am here, and what is to be done?" He said, "Disband your men and let them go home." I said, "All right," and goes back to my men with Doctor Hunt. On the way back I saw cavalry just beyond my men. I asked Colonel Miller to get the cavalry out of the way and let my men go back. I says, "Men, go right back home." They marched along back, and when I got across the first bridge . . . the firing began. My men says, "Let us form in line of battle." I says, "You shall not do it if I can prevent it." They said they would. I said, "If you do it you will have to put a bullet in me. Everything is settled, let us go home." I did not want any trouble. Well, they [the whites] kept on firing. I said, "Perhaps they are only firing to scare you; you march along." The firing got stronger and stronger, three or four formed into a line, I pulled out my revolver; I says, "If you return the fire I will give you the next volley." That squashed them. They marched on after the balance, and I saw one of them in a few minutes fall upon the hill. I thought my time was getting close, and I fell into a ditch there and staid until they captured me. . . .

Q.: Now, was there any firing on either side until you had retreated through that Point Lookout cut?— A.: No, sir.

Q.: Was the firing commenced by Colonel Miller's infantry party or by the cavalry, the mounted men.— A.: I could not say now what party at all; but I went over the thing since and I think it was by the cavalry, because they were near us. . . .

By Mr. Speer: . . .

Q.: Were any men hurt on that side before your men fired?— A.: My men
never fired a gun.

Q.: How do you know?— A.: Because I fell right back in the rear of them
when the very first gun was fired. . . .

By Mr. O'Brien: . . .

Q.: You were walking facing the county?— A.: Yes, sir; right toward the Big
Black [River].

Q.: Do you mean to tell this committee that when you had crossed the
bridge and were going out in the country with a large body of men
behind you of your command, that they might not have fired?— A.: After
they yelled I fell back to the rear, and no firing had been done then on
the other side. I said, "I wish you to go back quiet and peaceable, or you
may raise the minds of the people behind us. You should not do that."
And then in about a minute a gun was fired, and they then said they were
going to fight us. I said, "No they ain't; that is to hurry you off, perhaps.
Do not get scared. Do not go and run, because if you do they may get
after you." And then they began a regular fire, and I told my men to
scatter. . . .

Q.: Were you injured?— A.: I do not know whether they shot me or struck
me, sir.

Q.: At what time did you first feel that injury to your face?— A.: I do not
think I felt it until after they captured me, and after we had got fifty or
sixty yards, when I saw the blood falling on my shoulder.. . . .

Source: House of Representatives Report no. 265, 43rd Cong., 2nd sess., 1875, pp. 108, 109,
110, 117, 121.

James M. Batchelor Writes of the Thrill of Violence, 1875

After the Vicksburg riot, "Mad" Batchelor wrote his brother again.

JAMES MADISON BATCHELOR TO
ALBERT A. BATCHELOR, JANUARY 4, 1875.

In regard to our recent troubles, I am happy to state (with the exception
of George shooting *himself* thro the foot) we all escaped any other injury. Of
course, we were greatly excited & suffered somewhat from mental anxiety for
some time as regards the final results & ending of our troubles. The ladies
and old men especially. But I think all of the younger *men*, who were on the

"war path" with me for *about ten days* rather enjoyed the excitement, especially as our neighborhood was never duller than about that time. As to the causes &c. I would refer you to our papers [ ] which you have doubtless seen. Twas the same spirit which caused the excitement last summer which came so near resulting in blows. The *conservation* element among us, checked us from punishing them as we *should have done* which in my opinion we will *yet* have reason to regret. Had we done our DUTY, we would have taught them a lesson which would have lasted a life time. Not *having done* so, we are *all ready* expecting—in fact have information of another attempt to over throw the whites, which will prove a *hundred times* more serious than the other. In fact so long as we have such an infamous scoundrel for Gov as Ames we must expect *at any and all* times a WAR of races. The whites throughout all the counties where the negroes are so *largely* in the majority are arming (*every man*) with Winchester sixteen shooting rifles. The *best & most formidable* arm ever used. And if our *"New England"* Gov *forces* us into another war (should he escape with his *life*) the Republicanism or *Radicalism* will be for ever "a dead letter" in this state, unenforced by the US Army. . . .

The Vicksb[ur]g troubles are only the beginning of troubles thro out the entire state and I might say *states*. Which in my opinion will only end by the government (US) taking charge of Sambo and *colonizing* him (the sooner the better). . . .

Source: Folder 39, box 2, Albert A. Batchelor Papers, Special Collections, Hill Memorial Library, Louisiana State University.

CALLS FOR A BLACK DEFENSE FORCE

Black leaders emerged in the midst of the crisis of Reconstruction. One of the most famous, T. Thomas Fortune, argued that blacks must arm themselves and fight back. Fortune gave this speech before a New York audience gathered to commemorate the abolitionist leader Charles Sumner. According to one newspaper account of the speech, Fortune "was a gentleman of tall and erect form, sharp features, long bushy hair, and wears gold spectacles." Fortune delivered his speech "in a steady voice, and the salient points were emphasized with sufficient force to add good effect to the words."[3] Fortune made several salient points, most notably in condemning the Supreme Court for denying that the Constitution protected the civil rights of all Americans. In the absence of protection from the government, Fortune called on ordinary black men to rise up and defend themselves.

3. *New York Globe*, January 10, 1884.

Timothy Thomas Fortune's Speech Calling for Self-Defense, 1884

. . . The black men of this republic have a herculean labor to perform. They need not look to others, to men and to parties, to perform it for them. The South has already wrenched from us the freedom and power of the ballot, and the doors of courts of law have been slammed in our faces. Star chamber justice has been instituted throughout the South, and mob and ruffianly outlaws execute the decrees of the star chamber. The criminal is denied the protection of the law; the innocent have no immunity from violent taking off; the laborer is defrauded of his honest wage; and our women are reduced to indignities which would arouse the vengeance of a savage. The South is now under the influence of a reign of terror. The usual processes of the law are suspended and individual license and hatred are the standards by which black men must measure the volume of their security of life and property. It is a sad picture that we are called upon to contemplate, not without parallel, indeed, in the history of mankind, but utterly without parallel in the history of our country. . . .

Unless I have watched the signs of the times erroneously, unless I have read history as I would read a romance, there will be a reaction in the South. Oppression forges the fetters of its own enslavement, lawlessness breeds its own deadly antidote. Oppression breeds rebellion and rebellion produces revolution. "Large oaks from little acorns grow."

The State denies us protection, and the National Government says it has no jurisdiction, so that the black citizens of the South are absolutely without the pale of the law. What shall they do? Where shall they turn for succor or protection? What champion have they on the wave of politics . . . to present their grievances and urge with matchless zeal and eloquence that impartial justice shall be done?

. . . I have the courage here to-night . . . to declare the Supreme Court to be at fault, and to appeal from its arbiter dictum, . . . I care not to what that appeal leads. If it leads to another such conflict as the one which gibbetted treason at Appomattox, let it come. Better that tons of treasure and millions of lives were sacrificed on the field of battle than that the infamous principle should be established that there was one citizen of this grand republic who had not equal and inalienable rights with each and every one of his fellow-citizens. That the just laws incorporated in the Constitution of our country shall have full and ample vindication; that lawlessness may be throttled at Danville, Virginia, and in Copiah county Mississippi, I appeal to the honest sentiment of the country; I appeal to the courage and manhood and intelligence of the race, and I trust that I shall not appeal in vain. We ask for no special favor; we ask for no law reared upon subterfuge or chicanery; we ask for no particular immunity on account of race, we ask simply for justice; we demand justice, pure and simple, and though it be delayed a quarter of a century, *justice we will have*! Let our pulpits thunder against oppression; let our newspapers, be as diligent in defense of the people as the newspapers of the enemy, and let us by individual effort and in convention keep alive these questions until within our ample domains there shall not remain one citizen who cannot flee, with assurance of absolute protection, the feet of the God-dess of Liberty, the beautiful embodiment of our greatness, our magnanity and our justice. Let us agitate! *agitate*! AGITATE! until the protest shall awake the nation from its indifference, and pave the way to the incarnation of the grand sentiment evolved out of the fires of the French revolution: "Liberty! Fraternity! Equality!"

Source: *New York Globe, January 10, 1884.*

THE CARROLLTON MASSACRE

In her autobiography, Ida B. Wells writes that before 1892 she believed lynchings resulted from public anger inspired by the lynching victim's terrible crime. Mobs, she thought, were probably justified in killing frightful criminals. A massacre of innocents was a different story. In 1886, Wells reacted with shock and revulsion to reports that a mob of whites had gunned down thirteen African Americans in Carrollton, Carroll County, Mississippi. The white mob killed twelve of the men for no reason other than that they stood in the vicinity of its intended victim. Wells first read about this affair in the white Memphis newspapers, and her horror at the massacre reflected whites' reporting. White papers found the massacre offensive, all the more so for having taken place in a court-house, in the midst of legal proceedings. The Memphis Appeal *called the killings a "horror" and "revolting."[4] When black ministers called the killings "a case of wanton, cold-blooded butchery," the* Appeal *did not disagree.[5]*

Nonetheless, some whites found the killings, even of innocents attending a trial, ex-cusable. In 1886, James K. Vardaman had not yet made himself famous as a Mississippi demagogue. His analysis of the massacre, published in the Memphis Avalanche, *blamed the black population of Carrollton for provoking the murders.*

James K. Vardaman Justifies the Carrollton Tragedy, 1886

James K. Vardaman, Esq., a most reputable attorney and trustworthy citi-zen of Greenwood, Miss., is in the city, direct from home via Carrollton, the

---

4. *Memphis Appeal,* March 19 and 27, 1886.
5. *Memphis Appeal,* March 19, 1886.

scene of the deplorable tragedy which fell with such startling emphasis upon the country last Wednesday the 17th inst.

Mr. Vardaman has resided at his present home and also at Carrollton, a neighboring town, for a number of years past . . . and is thoroughly acquainted and identified with the people who are most concerned in the terrible difficulty which has made their name and locality known throughout the country. . . . Mr. Vardaman favors the Avalanche with a plain, unvarnished statement which bears upon its face sufficient evidence of truth. . . .

The recent collision, Mr. Vardaman says, was not the result of any wanton and reckless spirit. Several weeks ago, Mr. Robert Moore of Greenwood, passing through Carrollton on his way home, got into a difficulty with the negro, Ed Brown, and received unusually rough treatment. Soon after Hon. James M. Liddell, a former member of the Mississippi legislature (a citizen of Greenwood), a quiet, peaceable young gentleman and more popular with the colored people than perhaps any democrat in the county, met Brown in Carrollton and reproached him for his treatment of his young friend, Mr. Moore. Brown responded with an insulting oath and epithet and received a blow from Mr. Liddell's fist. He thought that would be the end of it, and passed on into the hotel and was at supper when some of his friends sought him with the warning that Ed Brown, Charley Brown and four or five other negroes had armed themselves and were awaiting him on the street. Mr. Liddell left the table—this was about the hour of sunset—and going out found the report correct.

Approaching the negroes, he asked what they were doing, or what they meant by assembling and making such threats.

"It is none of your God d——d business," replied the ring-leader Ed Brown, and with this Mr. Liddell struck him on the cheek with his naked hand.

Thereupon, the negroes, who sure enough had armed themselves for the assault, opened a regular fusillade on Liddell, who, with his pistol, returned the fire, slightly wounding two of the crowd, himself receiving a couple of serious shots, one in the elbow and another through the thigh. While Mr. Liddell lay bed-ridden of his wounds the negroes were put under bonds for trial at the next (April) term of the circuit court.

Blood had been shed on both sides, and white and black for miles around became more or less involved.

There were a number of circumstances not connected with the Liddell-Brown difficulty which served to stir the blood of the white citizens of Carroll. The imposition on Bob Moore was one. A short time before that, Mrs. Caldwell, a most lovable lady and widow of the late pastor of the Presbyterian Church at Carrollton, had rented a house to the Brown negroes, who had been delinquent in paying the rent and offensive when solicited to do so.

Mrs. Caldwell finally instructed the mayor of the town (who is ex officio a justice of the peace) to institute legal process against her tenant if, when urged again to settle, they refused. When informed by the mayor, Mr. Elam, of his purpose, the tenants informed him that they had guns and pistols on the premises and that they would "shoot the first G——d d——d white man" who put his foot on the place to enforce collection of the rent. This threat went abroad far and near, and by no means served to mollify the growing enmity between the races.

A number of this gang of negroes have long been known to carry arms and to elbow white persons off the pavements till most the ladies of Carrollton not only feared to walk the streets at night and on Saturdays, but even to remain at home unless some male friend were in company. After the shooting of Mr. Liddell, which followed the Browns' defiance of the mayor, crimination and recrimination, threats and counter threats passed back and forth till the best and oldest citizens of Carrollton predicted the very catastrophe just as it happened. . . .

Thus one exciting and exasperating event trod fast upon the other's heels, until, hearing that 18 or 20 negroes would appear armed at Liddell's preliminary trial, 40 or 50 of his friends banded together with weapons ready and brought the long-tormenting difficulty to a quick and final issue. None, Mr. Vardaman says, could more regret the bloody event than the people of Carroll, young and old, of all classes and conditions. And yet the best men among them feel that, terrible as the issue was, the necessity to meet it by short, sharp and decisive action was imperative. They knew that this gang of desperate negroes had been guilty months and years, even, of regular encroachment, of most offensive and impudent self-assertion, and felt that the safety of their wives and children depended on crushing at once and for all a spirit which boded nothing but evil. . . .

Source: *Memphis Avalanche*, March 23, 1886.

LYNCHING

In 1892, Ida B. Wells was the young editor of an African American Memphis newspaper, Free Speech. *When a Memphis mob lynched three black businessmen, Wells charged that they were the victims of a conspiracy by white businessmen intent on destroying their competition in the black community. Wells's courageous stand earned the enmity of the white leadership of Memphis, and a white mob destroyed the offices and print shop of* Free Speech. *Wells fled the city before the death threats against her were realized. After a series of successful lecture trips around the North and in England, Wells settled in Chicago, where she began writing books against the continuing practice of racist lynch-*

*ing in the United States. In 1909, Wells joined with W. E. B. DuBois in founding the
National Association for the Advancement of Colored People (NAACP), which made its
primary goal public awareness of white southern savagery.*

Ida B. Wells Documents the Violence against Black Americans, 1895

The first excuse given to the civilized world for the murder of unoffending Negroes was the necessity of the white man to repress and stamp out alleged "race riots." For years immediately succeeding the war there was an appalling slaughter of colored people, and the wires usually conveyed to
northern people and the world the intelligence, first, that an insurrection was
being planned by Negroes, which, a few hours later, would prove to have
been vigorously resisted by white men, and controlled with a resulting loss of
several killed and wounded. It was always a remarkable feature in these insurrections and riots that only Negroes were killed during the rioting, and that
all the white men escaped unharmed.

From 1865 to 1872, hundreds of colored men and women were mercilessly
murdered and the almost invariable reason assigned was that they met their
death by being alleged participants in an insurrection or riot. But this story
at last wore itself out. No insurrection ever materialized; no Negro rioter was
ever apprehended and proven guilty, and no dynamite ever recorded the black
man's protest against oppression and wrong. It was too much to ask
thoughtful people to believe this transparent story, and the southern white
people at last made up their minds that some other excuse must be had.

Then came the second excuse, which had its birth during the turbulent
times of reconstruction. By an amendment to the Constitution the Negro was
given the right of franchise, and, theoretically at least, his ballot became his
invaluable emblem of citizenship. In a government "of the people, for the
people, and by the people," the Negro's vote became an important factor in
all matters of state and national politics. But this did not last long. The
southern white man would not consider that the Negro had any right which
a white man was bound to respect, and the idea of a republican form of government in the southern states grew into general contempt. It was maintained that "This is a white man's government," and regardless of numbers
the white man should rule. "No Negro domination" became the new legend
on the sanguinary banner of the sunny South, and under it rode the Ku Klux
Klan, the Regulators, and the lawless mobs, which for any cause chose to
murder one man or a dozen as suited their purpose best. It was a long, gory
campaign; the blood chills and the heart almost loses faith in Christianity

when one thinks of Yazoo, Hamburg, Edgefield, Copiah, and the countless massacres of defenseless Negroes, whose only crime was the attempt to exercise their right to vote. . . .

The white man's victory soon became complete by fraud, violence, intimidation and murder. The franchise vouchsafed to the Negro grew to be a "barren ideality," and regardless of numbers, the colored people found themselves voiceless in the councils of those whose duty it was to rule. With no longer the fear of "Negro Domination" before their eyes, the white man's second excuse became valueless. With the Southern governments all subverted and the Negro actually eliminated from all participation in state and national elections, there could be no longer an excuse for killing Negroes to prevent "Negro Domination."

Brutality still continued; Negroes were whipped, scourged, exiled, shot and hung whenever and wherever it pleased the white man so to treat them, and as the civilized world with increasing persistency held the white people of the South to account for its outlawry, the murderers invented the third excuse—that Negroes had to be killed to avenge their assaults upon women. There could be framed no possible excuse more harmful to the Negro and more unanswerable if true in its sufficiency for the white man. . . .

A word as to the charge itself. In considering the third reason assigned by the Southern white people for the butchery of blacks, the question must be asked, what the white man means when he charges the black man with rape. Does he mean the crime which the statutes of the civilized states describe as such? Not by any means. With the Southern white man, any mesalliance existing between a white woman and a colored man is a sufficient foundation for the charge of rape. The Southern white man says that it is impossible for a voluntary alliance to exist between a white woman and a colored man, and therefore, the fact of an alliance is a proof of force. In numerous instances where colored men have . . . been lynched on the charge of rape, it was positively known at the time of lynching, and indisputably proven after the victim's death, that the relationship sustained between the man and woman was voluntary and clandestine, and that in no court of law could even the charge of assault have been successfully maintained. . . .

TORTURED AND BURNED IN TEXAS.

Never in the history of civilization has any Christian people stooped to such shocking brutality and indescribable barbarism as that which characterized the people of Paris, Texas, and adjacent communities on the 1st of February, 1893. The cause of this awful outbreak of human passion was the murder of a four year old child, daughter of a man named Vance. This man, Vance, had been a police officer in Paris for years, and was known to be a man of bad temper, overbearing manner and given to harshly treating the prisoners under his care....

In the same town lived a Negro, named Henry Smith, a well known character, a kind of roustabout, who was generally considered a harmless, weak-minded fellow, not capable of doing any important work, but sufficiently able to do chores and odd jobs around the houses of the white people who cared to employ him. A few days before the final tragedy, this man, Smith, was accused of murdering Myrtle Vance. The crime of murder was of itself bad enough, and to prove that against Smith would have been amply sufficient in Texas to have committed him to the gallows, but the finding of the child so exasperated the father and his friends, that they at once shamefully exaggerated the facts and declared that the babe had been ruthlessly assaulted and then killed. The truth was bad enough, but the white people of the community made it a point to exaggerate every detail of the awful affair, and to inflame the public mind so that nothing less than immediate and violent death would satisfy the populace. As a matter of fact, the child was not brutally assaulted as the world has been told in excuse for the awful barbarism of that day. Persons who saw the child after its death, have stated, under the most solemn pledge to truth, that there was no evidence of such an assault as was published at that time, only a slight abrasion and discoloration was noticeable and that mostly about the neck. In spite of this fact, so eminent a man as Bishop Haygood deliberately and, it must also appear, maliciously falsified the fact by stating that the child was torn limb from limb, or to quote his own words, "First outraged with demoniacal cruelty and then taken by her heels and torn asunder in the mad wantonness of gorilla ferocity."

Nothing is farther from the truth than that statement. It is a cold blooded, deliberate, brutal falsehood which this Christian (?) Bishop uses to bolster up the infamous plea that the people of Paris were driven to insanity by learning that the little child had been viciously assaulted, choked to death, and then torn to pieces by a demon in human form. It was a brutal murder, but no more brutal than hundreds of murders which occur in this country, and which have been equalled every year in fiendishness and brutality, and for which the death penalty is prescribed by law and inflicted only after the person has been legally adjudged guilty of the crime. Those who knew Smith, believe that Vance had at some time given him cause to seek revenge and that this fearful crime was the outgrowth of his attempt to avenge himself of some real or fancied wrong. That the murderer was known as an imbecile, had no effect whatever upon the people who thirsted for his blood. They determined to make an example of him and proceeded to carry out their purpose with unspeakably greater ferocity than that which characterized the half crazy object of their revenge.

For a day or so after the child was found in the woods, Smith remained in the vicinity as if nothing had happened, and when finally becoming aware that he was suspected, he made an attempt to escape. He was apprehended, however, not far from the scene of his crime and the news flashed across the country that the white Christian people of Paris, Texas and the communities thereabout had deliberately determined to lay aside all forms of law and inaugurate an entirely new form of punishment for the murder. They absolutely refused to make any inquiry as to the sanity or insanity of their prisoner, but set the day and hour when in the presence of assembled thousands they put their helpless victim to the stake, tortured him, and then burned him to death for the delectation and satisfaction of Christian people.

Lest it might be charged that any description of the deeds of that day are exaggerated, a white man's description which was published in the white journals of this country is used. The New York Sun of February 2d, 1893, contains an account, from which we make the following excerpt:

PARIS, Tex., Feb. 1, 1893.—Henry Smith, the negro ravisher of 4 year-old Myrtle Vance, has expiated in part his awful crime by death at the stake. Ever since the perpetration of his awful crime this city and the entire surrounding country has been in a wild frenzy of excitement. When the news came last night that he had been captured at Hope, Ark., . . . the city was wild with joy over the apprehension of the brute. Hundreds of people poured into the city from the adjoining country and the word passed from lip to lip that the punishment of the fiend should fit the crime—that death by fire was the penalty Smith should pay for the most atrocious murder and terrible outrage in Texas history. Curious and sympathizing alike, they came on train and wagons, on horse, and on foot to see if the frail mind of a man could think of a way to sufficiently punish the perpetrator of so terrible a crime. Whisky shops were closed, unruly mobs were dispersed, schools were dismissed by a proclamation from the mayor, and everything was done in a business-like manner. . . .

About 2 o'clock Friday a mass meeting was called at the courthouse and captains appointed to search for the child. She was found mangled beyond recognition, covered with leaves and brush as above mentioned. As soon as it was learned upon the recovery of the body that the crime was so atrocious the whole town turned out in the chase. The railroads put up bulletins offering free transportation to all who would join in the search. Posses went in every direction, and not a stone was left unturned. Smith was tracked to . . . his old home in . . . Clow, . . . about twenty miles north of Hope. Upon being questioned the fiend denied everything, but upon being stripped for examination his undergarments were seen to be spattered with blood and a part of his shirt was torn off. He was kept under heavy guard at Hope last night, and later on confessed the crime.

This morning he was brought through Texarkana, where 5,000 people awaited the train. . . . At that place speeches were made by prominent Paris citizens, who asked that the prisoner be not molested by Texarkana people, but that the guard be allowed to deliver him up to the outraged and indignant citizens of Paris. Along the road the train gathered strength from the various towns, the people crowded upon the platforms and tops of coaches anxious to see the lynching and the negro who was soon to be delivered to an infuriated mob.

Arriving here at 12 o'clock the train was met by a surging mass of humanity 10,000 strong. The negro was placed upon a carnival float in mockery of a king upon his throne, and, followed by an immense crowd, was escorted through the city so that all might see the most inhuman monster known in current history. The line of march was up Main street to the square, around the square down Clarksville street to Church street, thence to the open prairies about 300 yards from the Texas & Pacific depot. Here Smith was placed upon a scaffold, six feet square and ten feet high, securely bound, within the view of all beholders. Here the victim was tortured for fifty minutes by red-hot iron brands thrust against his quivering body. Commencing at the feet the brands were placed against him inch by inch until they were thrust against the face. Then, being apparently dead, kerosene was poured upon him, cottonseed hulls placed beneath him and set on fire. In less time than it takes to relate it, the tortured man was wafted beyond the grave to another fire, hotter and more terrible than the one just experienced.

Curiosity seekers have carried away already all that was left of the memorable event, even to pieces of charcoal. . . . The father is prostrated with grief and the mother now lies at death's door, but she has lived to see the slayer of her innocent babe suffer the most horrible death that could be conceived.

Words to describe the awful torture inflicted upon Smith cannot be found. The Negro, for a long time after starting on the journey to Paris, did not realize his plight. At last when he was told that he must die by slow torture he begged for protection. His agony was awful. He pleaded and writhed in bodily and mental pain. Scarcely had the train reached Paris than this torture commenced. His clothes were torn off piecemeal and scattered in the crowd, people catching the shreds and putting them away as mementos. The child's father, her brother, and two uncles then gathered about the Negro as he lay fastened to the torture platform and thrust hot irons into his quivering flesh. It was horrible—the man dying by slow torture in the midst of smoke from his own burning flesh. Every groan from the fiend, every contortion of his body was cheered by the thickly packed crowd of 10,000 persons. The mass of beings 600 yards in diameter, the scaffold being the center. After burning the feet and legs, the hot irons—plenty of fresh ones being at hand— were rolled up and down Smith's stomach, back, and arms. Then the eyes were burned out and irons were thrust down his throat.

The men of the Vance family having wreaked vengeance, the crowd piled all kinds of combustible stuff around the scaffold, poured oil on it and set it afire. The Negro rolled and tossed out of the mass, only to be pushed back by the people nearest him. He tossed out again, and was roped and pulled back. Hundreds of people turned away, but the vast crowd still looked calmly on. People were here from every part of this section. They came from Dallas, Fort Worth, Sherman, Denison, Bonham, Texarkana, Fort Smith, Ark., and a party of fifteen came from Hempstead county, Arkansas, where he was captured. Every train that came in was loaded to its utmost capacity, and there were demands at many points for special trains to bring the people here to see the unparalleled punishment for an unparalleled crime.

Source: Ida B. Wells, *A Red Record* (Chicago: Ida B. Wells, 1895), 8–11, 25–29.

WILMINGTON RACE RIOTS

Whites "redeemed" Wilmington, North Carolina, in 1898, wresting political control from black politicians. After taking over the local political structure, whites took to the streets. One riot leader, Colonel Alfred M. Waddell, was proud of his actions and wrote a memoir chronicling his participation in the riot that was published in the national magazine Collier's. *After this wave of violence, fifteen hundred blacks fled the city; whites confiscated their property.*

Colonel Alfred M. Waddell Justifies a Race Riot, 1898

My active connection with what has been termed the Revolutionary Government commenced when the Campaign Committee called upon me to make a speech stating my views; and I would like to say, in this connection, that some of the daily press representatives who have given an account of my speech selected two paragraphs for quotation, sent them out to the country, and the people at large necessarily formed an erroneous opinion of what I said, from those two paragraphs standing alone. They came at the conclusion that I was a violent revolutionist.

I said in my speech:

"If there should be a race conflict here (which God forbid!), the first men who should be held to strict accountability are the white leaders, who would be chiefly reasonable, and the work should begin at the top of the list. I scorn to leave any doubt as to whom I mean by that phrase. I mean the Governor of this State, who is the engineer of all the deviltry and meanness."

That is one part of the speech. I also said:

"We will not live under these intolerable conditions. No society can stand it. We intend to change it, if we have to choke the current of the Cape Fear River with carcasses."

That is the other paragraph which some of the press representatives took out. All the rest of the speech, which was chiefly a statement of facts, was omitted. Those paragraphs, disconnected from the text, were sent out as my speech.

When the crisis came, there was a universal demand that I should take charge. Last week, at the mass meeting, they made me chairman by acclamation, and also chairman of the Citizens' Committee of Twenty-five.

Demand was made for the negroes to reply to our ultimatum to them, and their reply was delayed or sent astray (whether purposely or not, I do not know), and that caused all the trouble. The people came to me. Although two other men were in command, they demanded that I should lead them.

I took my Winchester rifle, assumed my position at the head of the procession, and marched to the "Record" office. We designed merely to destroy the press. I took a couple of men to the door, when our demand to open was not answered, and burst it in. Not I personally, for I have not the strength, but those with me did it.

We wrecked the house. I believe that the fire which occurred was purely accidental; it certainly was unintentional on our part. I saw smoke issuing from the top story. Some one said the house was afire. I could not believe it. There were a number of kerosene oil lamps hanging round. They were thrown down and smashed, and the kerosene ran over the floor. It is possible that some fellow set it afire with a match. Immediately there were shouts when the fire occurred.

"Stop that fire! Put it out! This won't do at all!"

I at once had the fire alarm bell rung. We saved the wooden buildings next to the "Record" office, and soon had the fire out.

I then marched the column back through the streets down to the armory, lined them up, and stood on the stoop and made a speech to them. I said:

"Now you have performed the duty which you called on me to lead you to perform. Now let us go quietly to our homes, and about our business, and obey the law, unless we are forced, in self-defence, to do otherwise." I came home. In about an hour, or less time, the trouble commenced over in the

other end of town, by the negroes starting to come over here. I was not there
at the time. I was here in this part of town. But we began immediately to
turn out and prepare. And right here I want to say this about my part: I
never dreamed the time would come when I would lead a mob. But I want to
say, too, a United States Army officer, a prominent man, was here, and saw
the whole performance. He said:

"I never witnessed anything like this before. It is the most orderly performance I ever witnessed!"

Then they got seven of the negro leaders, brought them downtown, and
put them in jail. I had been elected mayor by that time. It was certainly the
strangest performance in American history, though we literally followed the
law. . . . There has not been a single illegal act committed in the change of
government. Simply, the old board went out, and the new board came in—
strictly according to law. In regard to those men who had been brought to
the jail a crowd said that they intended to destroy them; that they were the
leaders, and that they were going to take the men out of the jail.

I ordered a force of military around the jail. I said to the people:

"My position has been radically changed. I am now a sworn officer of the
law. That jail and those people must have protection."

I went out and appealed to the people in different parts of the town.
They realized the situation and told me I was right, and that they would
stand by me.

I stayed up the whole night myself, and the forces stayed up all night,
and we saved those wretched creatures' lives.

I waited until next morning at nine o'clock, and then I made the troops
form a hollow square in front of the jail. We placed the scoundrels in the
midst of the square and marched them to the railroad station. I bought and
gave them tickets to Richmond, and told them to go and to never show up
again. That bunch were all negroes. Then they had taken other fellows that
they sent out, and had them somewhere protected. They took them under
guard to another train—there were three whites in that party—and sent them
off also.

Rumors fly here and there that the negroes are arming. There is no truth
in that. They are utterly cowed and crushed, and are not going to interfere
with anybody.

I have sent messengers of both races out into the surrounding woods,
where, it is said, fugitives are in hiding, begging the people to come back to
their homes, and to rest assured they will be protected in their persons and
property. A great many have come in, and I expect more will come to-night.

The negroes here have always professed to have faith in me. When I made
the speech in the Opera House they were astounded. One of the leaders said:

"My God! when so conservative man as Colonel Waddell talks about filling the river with dead niggers, *I* want to get out of town!"

Since this trouble many negroes have come to me and said they are glad I
have taken charge. I said:

"Never a hair of your heads will be harmed. I will dispense justice to you
as I would to the first man in the community. I will try to discharge my duty
honestly and impartially." . . .

As to the government we have established, it is a perfectly legal one. The
law, passed by the Republican Legislature itself, has been complied with.
There was no intimidation used in the establishment of the present city government. The old government had become satisfied of their inefficiency and
utterly helpless imbecility, and believed if they did not resign they would be
run out of town. Therefore they came forward, after consulting with men of
our city, and they said each one of them wanted to resign—anxious to do so.
They wanted to get rid of the responsibility. If our people would organize,
they would be glad to resign and let us take the responsibility.

It was not a matter of coercion; the old city government simply realized it
was not able to continue in control and wished to be released from the
weight of responsibility. A change was imperatively necessary. Men were
needed who could and would cope with existing conditions.

In order to accomplish this legally a meeting was held, and the old
Board of Aldermen resigned by wards. One alderman would resign; that
would make a vacancy; and then the mayor (who has escaped from here)
would ask if there were any nominations for the vacancy; and one of his
own men would nominate a man he knew we wanted for the ward, and so
on, in succession, through each ward in town. We really didn't have anything
to do with it. They asked us whom we wanted. Successively they resigned,
and our men were elected. The room was as quiet as a room in a private
house.

It became necessary to elect a mayor. Under the law which they made the
mayor could be elected either from their own body or outside. They elected
me mayor. We took the city and went right to work. There is not a flaw in
the legality of the government. It was the result of revolution, but the forms
of law were strictly complied with in every respect.

The ultimate outcome, of course, I do not know. There is no probability
of further violence. I cannot more graphically or briefly express my opinion
on that point than by repeating what I said to the Board of Aldermen when
we were arranging for the police. I said: "Gentlemen, I will patrol this city
with six women, so quiet and peaceful and orderly is it. It is like Sunday all
the time."

But we went on and wanted to put matters beyond the possibility of a doubt. They have appointed a police force three times as large as I wanted it to be, so that everybody may feel perfectly confident and safe.

It is a fact that a large force of soldiers and naval reserves, armed with rifles, bayonets and revolvers, patrol the streets in squads. I never called on the Governor for any troops myself, but was glad that the commanding officer of the State Guard here notified him of the situation. I am using the State troops to cooperate with the police force, but there is no danger. It is simply to make the women and timid people feel safe that they will not be turned out or maltreated.

I believe the negroes are as much rejoiced as the white people that order has been evolved out of chaos.

They have seen my proclamation and they feel secure, and they are rejoiced over it.

Source: Alfred M. Waddell, "The Story of the Wilmington, N.C., Race Riots," *Collier's Weekly* 22 (November 26, 1898): 4–5.

WHITE OPPOSITION TO MOB VIOLENCE

Not all whites favored mob violence. Historians have criticized moderate whites for weaseling on the question of lynching: they denounced the practice but found ways to excuse, forgive, or, alternatively, actively promote particular killings. One exception was the conservative Vicksburg, Mississippi, journalist John G. Cashman. Cashman, a former Confederate soldier, refused to countenance mob law. He was no racial egalitarian and did not hesitate to describe accused African Americans as "brutes" and "fiends." Nonetheless, his devotion to law led him to launch an editorial campaign against lynching. Ironically, historians have regularly used one of his 1904 newspaper stories, a particularly horrific description of a lynching near Doddsville excerpted here, to suggest that white southern newspapers relished gory stories as a form of pornography. The following articles appeared in Cashman's Vicksburg Evening Post.

John Gordon Cashman Warns of the Danger of Lawlessness, 1902, 1904

EDITORIAL, JULY 25, 1902
Lawlessness begets lawlessness. One lynching by a gang of men will do more to demoralize the law and to arouse and rally the lawless element than the individual acts of a greater number of lawless men. It is, therefore, necessary to the protection of our institutions, to the maintenance of our system of laws, that public sentiment shall always be behind the law and its sure support.

EDITORIAL, SEPTEMBER 30, 1902

The details of the lynching of the negro brute and murderer at Corinth, Mississippi, last Sunday afternoon, read like a chapter of some occurrence in the "dark ages." It was a piece of savagery.

The burning of the wretched criminal at the stake, and the preliminaries for the horrible deed, were carried out with the deliberateness of a legal execution; and the lynching was as spectacular, and as well advertised, as any tragedy of gladiators in ancient Rome.

There seems to have been no State or county official at Corinth, with the courage to attempt to uphold the law. And the only effort of citizens, so far as we can learn, was an appeal to have the negro hanged by the mob instead of burned. All proposed, however, to violate the law and trample upon the Courts.

There is no safety outside of the law, and lynchings are wrong and indefensible from every standpoint.

It will be conceded by every one that the negro deserved no sympathy. But he was in jail, in the custody of the law, and should have been dealt with and punished by the law.

The people who took part in burning the negro at the stake and arranging for it as a grand spectacular show, undoubtedly did more moral harm to themselves and their community than they did physical harm to the negro criminal. . . .

NEWS STORY, FEBRUARY 13, 1904

A citizen from the Doddsville neighborhood, who witnessed the burning of the Holberts, last Sunday was in the city this morning and told of some new horrors connected with the terrible event that have not yet been printed. He said the affair was probably the most terrible one of its kind in history. When the two negroes were captured they were tied to trees and while the funeral pyres were being prepared they were forced to suffer the most fiendish tortures. The blacks were forced to hold out their hands while one finger at a time was chopped off. The fingers were distributed as souvenirs. The ears of the murderers were cut off. Holbert was severely beaten, his skull was fractured, and one of his eyes knocked out with a stick, hung by a shred from the socket. Neither the man nor woman begged for mercy, nor made a groan or plea. When the executioners came forward to lop off fingers Holbert extended his hand without being asked. The most excruciating form of punishment, consisted in the use of a large corkscrew in the hands of some of the mob. This instrument was bored into the flesh of the man and the woman, in the arms, legs and body, and then pulled out, the spirals tearing out big pieces of raw, quivering flesh, every time it was withdrawn. Even this devilish

torture did not make the poor brutes cry out. When finally they were thrown
on the fire and allowed to be burned to death, this came as a relief to the
maimed and suffering victims.

Source: *Vicksburg Evening Post*, July 25, September 30, 1902, February 13, 1904.

THE TULSA RACE RIOTS

*In 1997 the Oklahoma legislature, urged on by Representative Don Ross of Tulsa, orga-
nized the Oklahoma Commission to Study the Tulsa Race Riot of 1921. The commission's
investigators found that at the end of May 1921, black and white Tulsans clashed outside
the Tulsa County courthouse, where authorities had jailed Dick Rowland for attempted
rape of a white woman. Angry whites crowded around the courthouse, attracting armed
blacks determined to foil a lynching. Violence erupted, and rampaging whites invaded
Greenwood, the black district in segregated Tulsa, burning 1,256 homes and killing an
unknown number of victims.*

*The commission filed its final report in 2001, which included a reminiscence by Don
Ross. Ross's recollections suggest how this, one of the worst race riots in American history,
could have been forgotten for so long. In another section of the commission's report,
Danney Goble of the University of Oklahoma urged the state to pay reparations for the
death and destruction whites visited on black Tulsa eighty years before. To date,
Oklahoma legislators have refused to act on the commission's recommendation. The Florida legislature did order reparations to survivors of a similar (if smaller) riot in the town
of Rosewood.*

The Oklahoma Commission to Study the
Tulsa Race Riot of 1921 Seeks Reparations, 2001

State Representative Don Ross
    . . . I first learn[ed] about the riot when I was about 15 from Booker T.
Washington High School teacher and riot survivor W. D. Williams. In his
slow, laboring voice Mr. W. D. as he was fondly known, said on the evening
of May 31, 1921, his school graduation, and prom were canceled. Dick Rowland, who had dropped out of high school a few years before to become rich
in the lucrative trade of shining shoes, was in jail, accused of raping a white
woman Sarah Page, "on a public elevator in broad daylight." After Rowland
was arrested, angry white vigilantes gathered at the courthouse intent on
lynching the shine boy. Armed blacks integrated the mob to protect him.
There was a scuffle between a black and a white man, a shot rang out. The
crowd scattered. It was about 10:00 a.m. A race riot had broken out. He said

blacks defended their community for awhile, "but then the airplanes came dropping bombs. All of the black community was burned to the ground and 300 people died."

More annoyed than bored, I leaped from my chair and spoke: "Greenwood was never burned. Ain't no 300 people dead. We're too old for fairy tales." Calling a teacher a liar was a capital offense Mr. W. D. snorted with a twist that framed his face with anger. He ignored my obstinacy and returned to his hyperbole. He finished his tale and dismissed the class. The next day he asked me to remain after class, and passed over a photo album with picture and post cards of Mount Zion Baptist Church on fire, the Dreamland Theater in shambles, whites with guns standing over dead bodies, blacks being marched to concentration camps with white mobs jeering, trucks loaded with caskets, and a yellowing newspaper article accounting block after block of destruction—"30, 75 even 300 dead." Everything was just as he had described it. I was to learn later that Rowland was assigned a lawyer who was a prominent member of the Ku Klux Klan. "What you think, fat mouth?" Mr. W. D. asked his astonished student. . . .

"I teach U.S. History and those decisions that brought us to the riot," Seymour Williams my high school history professor said to me 45 years ago. He and W. D. Williams (no relation) for many years tutored me on their experience and prodded others of their generation to tell me the story. "The riot isn't known much by young teachers. Many were born after the riot and it was banned by book publishers, as much as U.S. history about blacks and slavery. I could teach a course on just what has been left out of history." Why the silence in our community? The old man then introduced this student to his assessment. "Blacks lost everything. They were afraid it could happen again and there was no way to tell the story. The two Negro newspapers were bombed. With the unkept promises, they were too busy just trying to make it." He added, "There were a lot of big shot rednecks at that courthouse who ran the city and still do. Sinclair Oil Company owned one of the airplanes used to drop fire bombs on people and buildings." Polite white people want to excuse what happen[ed] as being caused by trouble-making blacks and white trash ruffians. "Nope," he said, noting that blacks did not like to talk about the riot. "The killers were still running loose and they're wearing blue suits as well as Klan sheets." . . .

[Danney Goble:]

. . . [U]nderstand that the Tulsa race riot was the worst event in that city's history—an event without equal and without excuse. Understand, too, that it was the worst explosion of violence in this state's history—an episode late to be acknowledged and still to be repaired. But understand also that it was

part of a message usually announced not violently at all, but calmly and quietly and deliberately.

Who sent the message? Not one person but many acting as one. Not a
"mob;" it took forms too calculated and rational for that word. Not "society;"
that word is only a mask to conceal responsibility within a fog of impreci-
sion. Not "whites," because this never spoke for all whites; sometimes it
spoke for only a few. Not "America," because the federal government was, at
best, indifferent to its black citizens and, at worst, oblivious of them. Fifty
years or so after the Civil War, Uncle Sam was too complacent to crusade for
black rights and too callous to care. Let the states handle that—states like
Oklahoma.

Except that it really was not "Oklahoma" either. At least, it was not all of
Oklahoma. It was just one Oklahoma, one Oklahoma that is distinguishable
from another Oklahoma partly by purpose. This Oklahoma had the purpose
of keeping the other Oklahoma in its place, and that place was subordinate.
That, after all, was the object of suffrage requirements and segregation laws.
No less was it the intent behind riots and lynchings, too. One Oklahoma was
putting the other Oklahoma in its place.

One Oklahoma also had the power to effect its purpose, and that power
had no need to rely on occasional explosions of rage. Simple violence is, after
all, the weapon of simple people, people with access to no other instruments
of power at all. This Oklahoma had access to power more subtle, more regular, and more formal than that. Indeed, its ready access to such forms of
power partially defined that Oklahoma.

No, that Oklahoma is not the same as government, used here as a rhetor-
ical trick to make one accountable for the acts of the other. Government was
never the essence of that Oklahoma. Government was, however, always its potential instrument. Having access to government, however employed, if employed at all—just having it—defined this Oklahoma and was the essence of
its power.

The acts recounted here reveal that power in one form or another, often
several. The Tulsa race riot is one example, but only an example and only
one. Put alongside it earlier, less publicized pogroms—for that is what they
were—in at least ten other Oklahoma towns. Include the systematic disfran-
chisement of the black electorate through constitutional amendment in 1910,
reaffirmed through state statute in 1916. Add to that the constitution's segregation of Oklahoma's public schools, the First Legislature's segregation of its
public transportation, local segregation of Oklahoma neighborhoods through
municipal ordinances in Tulsa and elsewhere, even the statewide segregation
of public telephones by order of the corporation commission. Do not forget
to include the lynchings of twenty-three African-Americans in twelve

Oklahoma towns during the ten years leading to 1921. Stand back and look at those deeds now.

In some government participated in the deed.

In some government performed the deed.

In none did government prevent the deed.

In none did government punish the deed.

And that, in the end, is what this inquiry and what these recommendations are all about. Make no mistake about it: There are members of this commission who are convinced that there is a compelling argument in law to order that present governments make monetary payment for past governments' unlawful acts. . . .

This is a moral argument. . . . It gets down to this: The 1921 riot is, at once, a representative historical example and a unique historical event. It has many parallels in the pattern of past events, but it has no equal for its violence and completeness. It symbolizes so much endured by so many for so long. It does it, however, in one way that no other can: in the living flesh and blood of some who did endure it.

These paradoxes hold answers to questions often asked: Why does the state of Oklahoma or the city of Tulsa owe anything to anybody? Why should any individual tolerate now spending one cent of one tax dollar over what happened so long ago?

The answer is that these are not even the questions. This is not about individuals at all—not any more than the race riot or anything like it was about individuals.

This is about Oklahoma—or, rather, it is about two Oklahomas. It must be about that because that is what the Tulsa race riot was all about, too. That riot proclaimed that there were two Oklahomas; that one claimed the right to push down, push out, and push under the other; and that it had the power to do that.

That is what the Tulsa race riot has been all about for so long afterwards, why it has lingered not as a past event but lived as a present entity. It kept on saying that there remained two Oklahomas; that one claimed the right to be dismissive of, ignorant of, and oblivious to the other; and that it had the power to do that.

That is why the Tulsa race riot can be about something else. It can be about making two Oklahomas one—but only if we understand that this is what reparation is all about. Because the riot is both symbolic and singular, reparations become both singular and symbolic, too. Compelled not legally by courts but extended freely by choice, they say that individual acts of reparation will stand as symbols that fully acknowledge and finally discharge a collective responsibility.

Because we must face it: There is no way but by government to represent the collective, and there is no way but by reparations to make real the responsibility.

Source: *Tulsa Race Riot: A Report by the Oklahoma Commission to Study the Tulsa Race Riot of 1921* (February 28, 2001), iv–v, vii, 19–20.

FURTHER READINGS

On Reconstruction-era violence, see Eric Foner, *Reconstruction: America's Unfinished Revolution, 1863–1877* (New York: Harper and Row, 1988); Lou Falkner Willliams, *The Great South Carolina Ku Klux Klan Trials, 1871–1872* (Athens: University of Georgia Press, 1996); Christopher Waldrep, *Roots of Disorder: Race and Criminal Justice in the American South, 1817–80* (Urbana: University of Illinois Press, 1998).

On southern race relations after the end of Reconstruction, see Glenda Elizabeth Gilmore, *Gender and Jim Crow: Women and the Politics of White Supremacy in North Carolina, 1896–1920* (Chapel Hill: University of North Carolina Press, 1996); Leon F. Litwack, *Trouble in Mind: Black Southerners in the Age of Jim Crow* (New York: Knopf, 1998); Stephen Kantrowitz, *Ben Tillman and the Reconstruction of White Supremacy* (Chapel Hill: University of North Carolina Press, 2000); Edward L. Ayers, *Vengeance and Justice: Crime and Punishment in the Nineteenth-Century American South* (New York: Oxford University Press, 1984).

Recently, there has been a flood of books on lynching. Many of the new books study a particular lynching; see, for instance, Stephen J. Whitfield, *A Death in the Delta: The Lynching of Emmett Till* (New York: Free Press, 1988); Dennis B. Downey and Raymond M. Hyser, *No Crooked Death: Coatesville, Pennsylvania, and the Lynching of Zachariah Walker* (Urbana: University of Illinois Press, 1991); Harry Farrell, *Swift Justice: Murder and Vengeance in a California Town* (New York: St. Martin's Press, 1993); Richard B. McCaslin, *Tainted Breeze: The Great Hanging at Gainesville, Texas, 1862* (Baton Rouge: Louisiana State University Press, 1994); Dominic J. Capeci Jr., *The Lynching of Cleo Wright* (Lexington: University Press of Kentucky, 1998); Ben Green, *Before His Time: The Untold Story of Harry T. Moore, America's First Civil Rights Martyr* (New York: Free Press, 1999); Steve Oney, *And the Dead Shall Rise: The Murder of Mary Phagan and the Lynching of Leo Frank* (New York: Pantheon, 2003); Laura Wexler, *Fire in the Canebreak: The Last Mass Lynching in America* (New York: Scribner's, 2003).

These case studies build on the work of recognized classics in the field such as Leonard Dinnerstein, *The Leo Frank Case* (New York: Columbia University Press, 1968); James R. McGovern, *Anatomy of a Lynching: The Killing of Claude Neal* (Baton Rouge: Louisiana State University Press, 1982); Howard Smead, *Blood*

Justice: The Lynching of Mark Charles Parker (New York: Oxford University Press, 1986). These authors had, in their turn, followed the lead of the case study work of several NAACP investigators, most famously Walter White, *Rope and Faggot: A Biography of Judge Lynch* (New York: Knopf, 1929). Arthur F. Raper also collected a series of case studies in *The Tragedy of Lynching* (Chapel Hill: University of North Carolina Press, 1933). The pioneer of the case study approach is Ida B. Wells. Her writings are collected in several sources, but see Jacqueline Jones Royster, ed., *Southern Horrors and Other Writings: The Anti-lynching Campaign of Ida B. Wells, 1892–1900* (Boston: Bedford, 1997). Although Wells died in 1931, her autobiography did not reach print until 1970: Alfred M. Duster, ed., *Crusade for Justice: The Autobiography of Ida B. Wells* (Chicago: University of Chicago Press, 1970). Two recent biographies are Linda O. McMurry, *To Keep the Waters Troubled: The Life of Ida B. Wells* (New York: Oxford University Press, 1998); and Patricia A. Schechter, *Ida B. Wells-Barnett and American Reform, 1880–1930* (Chapel Hill: University of North Carolina Press, 2001).

Several books offer broader surveys of lynching. See W. Fitzhugh Brundage, *Lynching in the New South: Georgia and Virginia, 1880–1930* (Urbana: University of Illinois Press, 1993); Stewart E. Tolnay and E. M. Beck, *A Festival of Violence: An Analysis of Southern Lynchings, 1882–1930* (Urbana: University of Illinois Press, 1995); Philip Dray, *At the Hands of Persons Unknown: The Lynching of Black America* (New York: Random House, 2002). James Allen et al., *Without Sanctuary: Lynching Photography in America* (Santa Fe, NM: Twin Palms, 2000), dwarfs all the textual surveys in terms of influence and impact on the general public.

Like the case studies, these surveys follow a well-traveled path. However, there are only two academic histories of lynching from the Revolution to the present: James Elbert Cutler, *Lynch-Law: An Investigation into the History of Lynching in the United States* (1905); and Christopher Waldrep, *The Many Faces of Judge Lynch: Extralegal Violence and Punishment in America* (New York: Palgrave Macmillan, 2002).

Several books have been published on the Tulsa Race Riot. See Scott Ellsworth, *Death in a Promised Land: The Tulsa Race Riot of 1921* (Baton Rouge: Louisiana State University Press, 1982); Tim Madigan, *The Burning: Massacre, Destruction, and the Tulsa Race Riot of 1921* (New York: St. Martin's Press, 2001); James S. Hirsch, *Riot and Remembrance: The Tulsa Race War and Its Legacy* (Boston: Houghton Mifflin, 2002).

SEVEN

THE WILD WEST IN MYTH
AND REALITY

T he "Wild West" dominates most people's understanding of American violence. Many writers have linked the violent nature of American society directly to the frontier experience in the West, though they tend to isolate that heritage in the last half of the nineteenth century. Some historians have called this perception into question, arguing that the frontier West was more about farming, mining, and building communities than about gunplay. Scholars differ on the actual number of homicides in the West but generally agree that the rate was no higher on average than in the contemporary urban East and probably lower than in the South. As a leading historian of western law enforcement, Frank Prassel, observed, western settlers "probably enjoyed greater security in both person and property than did his contemporary in the urban centers of the East."[1] Recently, historians have also attempted to move our collective vision of the West beyond the chronological confines of the fifty years after the California gold rush. And yet, despite the growing evidence arguing against a peculiarly violent West, the perception of the Wild West remains popular in American culture.

The image of the gunfight, the walk-down on the town's main street, appears permanently embedded in the public consciousness. The walk-down was largely an invention of Owen Wister, from the climactic scene in his 1902 best seller, *The Virginian*. While it is a staple of Western movies through the twentieth century, historians are hard put to find an actual example of such a confrontation. The typical western shooting came from ambush or from behind, or bushwhacking, as it was known in the West.

---

1. Frank R. Prassel, *The Western Peace Officer: A Legacy of Law and Order* (Norman: University of Oklahoma Press, 1972).

As Patricia Limerick has pointed out, the very concept of the "West" is the product of conquest, and thus of violence.[2] Indians conquered the lands of other tribes while European and American armies moved against native peoples. Those armies continued to enforce central authority after conquest as well, moving against rebellious subjects whether white or Indian. For instance, Spanish soldiers crushed several insurrections in Texas between 1811 and 1821, killing hundreds of people as the Spanish-Mexican population of Texas declined by 50 percent before the region became part of the new Republic of Mexico.

Mexico in its turn found it necessary to move against Texas as a consequence of its liberal immigration policy, which allowed settlers from the United States to move freely across the Mexican border. The Texas rebellion of 1836 included an exchange of slaughters: Santa Ana ordered the execution of the prisoners taken at the Alamo in San Antonio, and of three hundred more after the Battle of Goliad; Sam Houston allowed his troops to kill hundreds of Mexicans after the Battle of San Jacinto. In contrast, California and New Mexico fell in the war between the United States and Mexico in the years 1846 to 1848 with little loss of life. It is thus difficult to generalize about the pattern of conquest even within a brief period.

The discovery of gold in California in 1848 drew thousands of men to the West. If ever there was a formula for personal violence born of chaos, the gold rush was it. Most of these young men came alone, drank heavily, and were determined to make money as quickly as possible in a region that lacked legal agencies and traditional community structures. There were incidents of violence, but on the whole the miners displayed an astounding respect for America's legal customs. Generals Persifor F. Smith and Bennett Riley toured the area separately to determine if military forces were needed to maintain order; both thought not, observing that towns lacking a single permanent building had already elected a mayor and sheriffs. Travelers observed that goods were left lying around busy streets undisturbed, doors (and tents) bore no locks, and miners would mark mining claims with personal possessions, confident that these goods, and their claim, would be respected by others.

Historians of the Overland Trail have found a similar respect for legal norms. John Phillip Reid's important books on the subject provide compelling evidence that the overland migrants brought with them customs of both personal and social behavior that ameliorated violence.

There were certainly acts of violence in the West. While each violent event had its unique circumstances, historians have identified a few persistent influences: race, alcohol, social status, gender, and guns. Beyond a doubt, racism

2. Patricia Nelson Limerick, *The Legacy of Conquest: The Unbroken Past of the American West* (New York: Norton, 1987).

caused a great deal of violence and warped the legal system of all the western states, as it did in the South. Alcohol fit prominently in most murder cases as a spur to violence, while those of a lower social status were most likely to be victims of violence and convicted if their cases went to trial. Men tended to be both the murderers and the victims of at least 90 percent of all homicides. And, in the words of Clare V. McKanna, "guns were an invitation to violence."[3] Contemporaries perceived and feared the growing gun culture of the West and attempted to limit its impact through legislation.

The image of western violence is of individual confrontations. The reality was very different, most violence tending to be collective in nature. Many studies of violence emphasize the need for some sort of collective context in order to break down the individual's barriers against the commission of violence, even among trained troops. For instance, in the midst of the Bear River Massacre of 1863, as ranks of soldiers fired on a Shoshoni village, a young boy ordered by his mother to lie still and pretend to be dead, then raised his head and looked straight into the eyes of a soldier who had a gun pointing at him. "The soldier stared at the boy and the boy at the soldier. The second time the soldier raised his rifle the little boy knew his time to die was near. The soldier then lowered his gun and a moment later raised it again. For some reason he could not complete his task. He took his rifle down and walked away."[4] Seeing one's victim eye to eye could preclude violence for many people.

Nonetheless, the individualistic perception of the West dominates popular culture. As Richard White wrote, the irony of the individualistic image is that "the American West, more than any other section of the United States, is a creation not so much of individual or local efforts, but of federal efforts. More than any other region, the West has been historically a dependency of the federal government."[5] The government dominated the use of violent force in the West. The army conquered the West and stationed troops along the Overland Trail, oversaw the removal of the Cherokee and other eastern Indians to Oklahoma on the Trail of Tears, and suppressed strikes. In conjunction with federal marshals, the army established legal order in the West and secured the conquered territory for its new settlers.

The Western myth emphasizes Indian attacks on wagon trains, and such attacks did occur. Prior to the Civil War there were two major attacks along the Overland Trail. In 1854 the Shoshone attacked the Ward party, killing nine-

---

3. Clare V. McKanna Jr., *Race and Homicide in Nineteenth-Century California* (Reno: University of Nevada Press, 2002), 85.

4. Memoir of Mae T. Parry, in Brigham D. Madsen, *The Shoshoni Frontier and the Bear River Massacre* (Salt Lake City: University of Utah Press, 1985), 235.

5. Richard White, *"It's Your Misfortune and None of My Own": A History of the American West* (Norman: University of Oklahoma Press, 1991), 57.

teen migrants, and in 1860 they killed twenty-nine members of the Otter–Van Orman wagon train. But the deadliest attack on white civilians in western history was the Mountain Meadows Massacre of 1857 in which a Mormon gang and their Piute allies killed an estimated one hundred immigrants.[6]

Far more common and deadly were white massacres of Indians. The majority of these slaughters occurred during the most violent period in American history, the years of the Civil War and Reconstruction. The bloodiest massacre of Indians was probably that at Bear River in Idaho in 1863, in which volunteer troops from California under the command of Colonel Patrick Connor surrounded a Shoshoni village and killed between 200 and 255 Indians, about one-third of them women and children. Twenty-three soldiers died as a result of this action. The army was not always successful, though, suffering some humiliating defeats at the hands of the Plains Indians. In the 1850s Sioux-led forces fought the army to a standstill, slaughtering Lieutenant John L. Grattan and his thirty men in 1854 and forcing the United States to abandon much of the Overland Trail for several years during the Civil War.[7]

With the end of the Civil War the federal government was no longer content to negotiate agreements with Indians as sovereign peoples and acted with notable brutality. In 1869 President U. S. Grant announced his "peace policy," which declared any Indians found off the reservation "hostiles." The ensuing wars against the Plains Indians brought out the worst in both sides. Indian and white combatants refused to acknowledge civilian status, killing indiscriminately; among the Indians, the old, women, and children probably suffered more deaths than did the warriors. According to government sources, the Plains Indians killed 919 U.S. soldiers between 1865 and 1898. More than a third of this total fell at the Fetterman Massacre in 1866, at which seventy-nine soldiers died, and the Little Bighorn in 1876, with its 258 deaths (plus 10 civilians). At the same time, many Indians fought with the U.S. Army, while several traditional animosities persisted. For instance, in 1873 the Sioux killed between 70 and 100 Pawnee at Massacre Canyon.[8]

Occasionally, white civilians slaughtered groups of Indians. The victims of

6. Scholars disagree on the precise number killed in many of these actions. Ward Massacre Site, Idaho State Historical Society; Carl Schlicke, "Massacre on the Oregon Trail in the Year 1860: A Tale of Horror, Cannibalism & Three Remarkable Children," *Columbia Magazine* 1 (1987): 33-43; Juanita Brooks, *The Mountain Meadow Massacre* (Norman: University of Oklahoma Press, 1991).

7. Howard R. Lamar, ed., *The New Encyclopedia of the American West* (New Haven, CT: Yale University Press, 1998), 1045; Harold Schindler, "The Bear River Massacre: New Historical Evidence," *Utah Historical Quarterly* 67 (1999): 300-308; Stephen E. Ambrose, *Crazy Horse and Custer: The Parallel Lives of Two American Warriors* (New York: Meridian, 1975), 61-65.

8. Dee Brown, *The Fetterman Massacre: An American Saga* (London, 1972); Ambrose, *Crazy Horse and Custer*; Massacre Canyon Battlefield and Woodland Site, Nebraska State Historical Society.

these attacks were usually peaceful people, so as to avoid the possibility that their victims might actually fight back. In northern California in 1860, a group of ranchers on the Humboldt Bay killed 185 peaceful Wiyots in response to some cattle thefts by a different Indian tribe. More commonly, state militia or the U.S. Army conducted such massacres. For example, in 1864 the Colorado militia under Colonel John Chivington fired on the sleeping Cheyenne village at Sand Creek with howitzers, despite the fact that Sand Creek was officially under the protection of the U.S. Army. Chivington's men spent several hours raping, murdering, and sexually mutilating the survivors, mostly women and children. The militia killed some 200 Indians and started a war with the Cheyenne, displaying body parts to cheering Denver crowds. The army condemned the massacre but four years later committed its own against a reservation village supposedly under government protection at the Washita in Oklahoma. Colonel George A. Custer's Seventh Cavalry killed Black Kettle, an ally of the whites, and 100 other Indians. In 1871 the Tucson Committee of Public Safety attacked the Apache village at Camp Grant, Arizona, killing 108 Apaches, only eight of whom were adult males, selling 29 of the surviving children into slavery, despite the Thirteenth Amendment of the Constitution. The most notorious massacre came at Wounded Knee in 1890. While attempting to disarm a group of Sioux, members of the Seventh Cavalry opened fire, shooting down the fleeing Indians regardless of age or gender. The Sioux fought back, killing 25 soldiers but suffering 150 dead and 50 wounded; 44 of the dead were women, 18 children.[9]

Murderous violence was directed at other ethnic groups in the West, especially the Chinese and those of Mexican descent. White mobs killed nineteen Chinese in Los Angeles in 1871; twenty-eight Chinese in Rock Springs, Wyoming, in 1885; lynched five more in Pierce, Idaho, that same year; and ten more in Log Cabin Bar, Oregon, in 1887. Organized mobs drove the Chinese out of Tacoma and Seattle in 1885, their violence so disrupting the state that the governor required federal troops to restore order.[10] Hispanics suffered most at the hands of white mobs in Texas, often getting caught in the cross fire between competing white groups as in the San Sabra County War of 1893 to 1898 and the

9. Albert L. Hurtado, *Indian Survival on the California Frontier* (New Haven, CT: Yale University Press, 1988), 122; Duane P. Schultz, *Month of the Freezing Moon: The Sand Creek Massacre, November 1864* (New York: St. Martin's Press, 1991); Ambrose, *Crazy Horse and Custer*, 313–24; Odie B. Faulk, *The Geronimo Campaign* (New York: Oxford University Press, 1969), 12–13; Robert M. Utley, *The Last Days of the Sioux Nation* (New Haven, CT: Yale University Press, 1963); Dee Brown, *Bury My Heart at Wounded Knee: An Indian History of the American West* (New York: Holt, Rinehart & Winston, 1973).

10. Lamar, ed., *The New Encyclopedia of the American West*, 204–5; Craig Storti, *Incident at Bitter Creek: The Story of the Rock Springs Chinese Massacre* (Ames: Iowa State University Press, 1991); Shih-Shan Henry Tsai, *The Chinese Experience in America* (Bloomington: Indiana University Press, 1986), 67–72.

Sutton-Taylor feud, which lasted from the Civil War into the 1890s. This latter conflict was notable for the participation of the psychopath John Wesley Hardin, who sided with the racist Taylor faction and killed twenty men between 1868 and 1878, a record for a western gunman.[11]

Despite the clearly racist roots of these actions, vigilantism retains an almost romantic aura. In 1887 Hubert Howe Bancroft distinguished "mob violence or lynch-law" from vigilante committees, a distinction that proved both popular and enduring. Bancroft conceded that lynch mobs closely resembled vigilante mobs but insisted they differed in principle: "One aims to assist a weak and entrammelled [sic] government, whose officers cannot or will not execute the law; the other breaks the law for evil purpose."[12] In 1971 Richard Maxwell Brown disputed Bancroft on his nomenclature, writing that he would not distinguish "lynch law" from "vigilantism," and deliberately used the terms interchangeably.[13] Brown, though, agreed with Bancroft on the larger point: there were "good" or "socially constructive" mobs just as there were also "bad" or "socially destructive" mobs. By 1975, Brown had decided his good mobs should no longer carry the lynching label. Lynch mobs, being "spontaneous" and "ephemeral," differed from the more "systematic" vigilante movements.[14]

Both Bancroft and Brown used class to distinguish the "good" from the "bad." Brown wrote that "respectable leading men" filled the ranks of vigilante movements with "the help of the middle level farmers."[15] The foremost challenger to Bancroft and Brown's class argument is Joel Williamson, who framed violence through a lens of racism. Williamson raised questions about academics' "persisting class interpretation" that lynching somehow "ran contrary to the wishes of the elite." Williamson condemned class analysis as "dangerous" and cautioned that "upper-class Southern whites can be physically violent if they want to be."[16] Williamson wrote about southern racial violence, but class distinctions have problems in the West, too. Most recent scholarship finds western legal systems respecting the technical rules of evidence and justice with surprising fairness. Many vigilantes objected specifically to this adherence to the rule of law as dangerously respectful of the rights of the accused, while other

11. Lamar, ed., The New Encyclopedia of the American West, 468–69; C. L. Sonnichsen, I'll Die Before I'll Run: The Story of the Great Feuds of Texas (New York, 1951).

12. Hubert Howe Bancroft, Popular Tribunals (San Francisco: History Company, 1887), 1:11–12.

13. Richard Maxwell Brown, "Legal and Behavioral Perspectives on American Vigilantism," in Donald Fleming and Bernard Bailyn, eds., Perspectives in American History 5 (1971): 100n5.

14. Richard Maxwell Brown, Strain of Violence (New York: Oxford University Press, 1975), 21.

15. Richard Maxwell Brown, "The American Vigilante Tradition," in Hugh Graham and Ted Robert Gurr, eds., Violence in American Historical and Comparative Perspectives (Washington, DC: Government Printing Office, 1969), 1:143.

16. Joel Williamson, The Crucible of Race: Black-White Relations in the American South since Emancipation (New York: Oxford University Press, 1984), 291–95.

vigilante actions served as covers for political or economic conflicts. For instance, in a California mining camp in the 1850s, a vigilante group arrested a Mexican charged with stealing two donkeys and a horse. When the jury found the defendant innocent, armed men locked the jury members in a small room and ordered them to reconsider. When they finally agreed to find the defendant guilty, the leader of the vigilantes shouted, "Correct! . . . We hung him an hour ago." That night the donkeys and horse were discovered peacefully resting under a nearby tree; they had never been stolen, just forgotten.[17]

In the last quarter of the nineteenth century the wealthiest western landowners sought to concentrate their holdings and power, using force when necessary. Their opponents were farmers and agricultural workers, the former often settled on federal land claims, the latter generally hoping to establish themselves on smallholdings. The western elite did not hesitate to hire gunmen and Pinkerton agents, foster vigilante groups, and call upon marshals and the army to support their efforts to win control of the West.

In addition to New Mexico's famous Lincoln County War of 1878-81, there were similar violent encounters in Texas, Wyoming, Montana, Nevada, Arizona, and California. Most of these wars ended with the triumph of the large landowners. An exception was the Johnson County War of 1892. Several powerful Wyoming cattlemen organized a vigilante movement, calling themselves "Regulators" in a link to an American tradition of extralegal action. They identified their victims as "rustlers" and drove a large number of small farmers and their families off of their holdings. After the vigilantes killed two "rustlers," they were confronted by a posse of local citizens. The Regulators were saved only by the intervention of the army, and there the Johnson County War came to an end. But it is worth noting that the pro-vigilante Republicans lost the state elections later that year, indicating a lack of popular support for these violations of legal procedures.

One of the most dramatic of these western conflicts came in the Mussel Slough area of California. The Southern Pacific Railroad claimed land already settled by dozens of farm families and called on the courts to expel the farmers as trespassers. In 1879 federal judge Lorenzo Sawyer, who just happened to be a close friend of the Southern Pacific's Leland Stanford, found in favor of the railroad. A confrontation between the two sides the next year led to the bloodiest civilian gunfight in western history, leaving seven men dead—five settlers and two of the railroad's agents. The professional gunman Walter J. Crow, who died in the encounter, took more lives in this single shootout, three, than did any other known gunfighter on a single day.

17. W. Eugene Hollon, *Frontier Violence: Another Look* (New York: Oxford University Press, 1974), 66-67.

Such shootouts were exceptional. Far more common were industrial actions. The owners of mines and businesses proved perfectly willing to employ hired thugs against workers. Strikes led to lethal violence at Coeur d'Alene in 1892, Leadville in 1894, Telluride in 1901, Cripple Creek in 1903–4, Wheatland in 1913, Ludlow in 1914, Everett in 1916, Butte in 1917, Centralia in 1919, and Los Angeles in 1920. As elsewhere in the United States, industrialists called upon the militia and U.S. Army to enforce their will. Some businesses, such as Wells Fargo and Southern Pacific, even had their own police forces. Workers often responded to management's violence in kind.

As this partial list indicates, western violence did not come to an end with the dawn of the twentieth century. The main difference between the massacres at Wounded Knee in 1892 and Ludlow in 1913 was that the former was of Indians, the latter of workers. In both instances government-sanctioned troops opened fire with Hotchkiss guns (a predecessor of the machine gun) on un-armed people. Vigilante mobs also continued to appear, though more rarely and generally with a "patriotic" orientation. Thus American Legion mobs went after political radicals throughout the West in the first "red scare" following World War I, and U.S. servicemen in Los Angeles attacked non-Anglos they saw as "shirking" their military duty in the Zoot Suit Riot of 1943.

Race persisted as a factor in many western riots in the twentieth century. Most famous were the Watts Riot of August 1965, which marked the beginning of a wave of inner-city disturbances in the 1960s, and the peculiar "Rodney King Riot" of 1992, which claimed fifty-three lives. This latter riot appeared the spon-taneous expression of frustration over an all-white jury finding several police officers innocent of beating a black driver named Rodney King—a beating caught on video. African Americans in Los Angeles took to the streets, beating whites and Koreans, and destroying an estimated billion dollars in property in the second deadliest riot in American history. For a few days in the late twen-tieth century, the popular perception of a chaotically violent West existed in reality on the streets of Los Angeles.

DOCUMENTS

THE MEXICAN WAR

The conquest of the western half of North America by the United States was the product of war, first against Mexico and then against the Indians. What we now know as the Southwest was originally the northern third of the Republic of Mexico. Mexico initially sought to increase the population of its northeasternmost province of Texas by inviting citizens of the United States to settle these lands. Stephen F. Austin led hundreds of his fellow Americans into Texas in the 1820s with the full support of the Mexican government, which even offered cheap land as an inducement. But the new arrivals seemed to always want more land and more authority, and they also wanted to bring their slaves into a nation that had outlawed slavery. By 1834 there were twenty thousand U.S.-born inhabitants in Texas, two thousand of whom were slaves.

In 1836, with an eye toward annexation by the United States, the Americans in Texas proclaimed Texas an independent nation. Mexican forces commanded by General Antonio López de Santa Anna overran the garrison at the small San Antonio Catholic church called the Alamo, killing all two hundred defenders, including former U.S. congressman Davy Crockett. At the battle of San Jacinto a month later, in April, Texans under the leadership of Samuel Houston defeated the Mexicans, captured Santa Anna, and forced him to sign a peace treaty recognizing Texan independence. The Texans quickly petitioned the United States for statehood.

These events to the west fired a passion for expansion among some Americans, and deep skepticism from others. The latter, not wanting either a war with Mexico or a huge new area for the expansion of slavery, successfully blocked Texas statehood for eight years. But in 1844 Congress admitted Texas into the Union by joint resolution. Supporters of Texas proclaimed that its entry into the union was but a part of a larger divine plan for the United States. In 1845 John O'Sullivan declared it "the fulfillment of our manifest destiny to overspread the continent allotted by Providence for the free development of our yearly multiplying millions."[18] Manifest Destiny became the code for American conquest of the West. Mexico stood in the way of that expansion, requiring the federal government to act to fulfill God's plan for the nation.

In May 1846 President James K. Polk met these ambitions by declaring war on Mexico, using a border skirmish as his pretext. Polk's declaration of war stated, "The cup of forbearance has been exhausted," and charged Mexico with invading the United States.[19] The war met serious and sustained opposition from thousands of Americans, especially in the North. Leading Americans saw the war as part of a conspiracy to extend slavery, while others, including Representative Abraham Lincoln, opposed the war as an act of immoral aggression. The Massachusetts legislature spoke for thousands of northerners when it voted that the war was an immoral and unconstitutional war of conquest, intended to increase the power of the slave states. American military victories overwhelmed these objections, as the U.S. Army repeatedly defeated the Mexicans and marched into the Mexican capital in triumph. In the peace treaty, the United States gained the northern third of Mexico, disappointing many advocates of Manifest Destiny who wanted it all.

18. John O'Sullivan, "Annexation," *United States Magazine and Democratic Review* 17 (July–August 1845): 5–10.
19. *Journal of the House of Representatives of the United States: Being the First Session of the Twenty-ninth Congress* (Washington, D.C.: Ritchie & Heiss, 1845–46), 788.

American historians long treated the Mexican War as a glorious victory in the heroic tale of westward expansion by which the United States "rounded out her continental area."[20] One textbook titled its section on the war's causes, "Warlike Measures of the Mexican Government." Those measures were "an attempt to float a new government loan," calling a special session of Congress, and strengthening "the fortifications at Vera Cruz and along the northern frontier."[21] In contrast, President Polk aimed to expand the United States "by pacific methods, if possible," pursuing a policy of "patient diplomacy," which led Mexico to treat the United States with contempt.[22] Maps of the war were often labeled "Mexican Cessions" and "Territorial Adjustments."[23] Even leading historians referred to the Mexicans as "greasers" and "excitable Mexicans."[24] There were other interpretations.

In 1850 an amazing book was published in New York. Led by Ramon Alcaraz, the editors of several Mexican newspapers collaborated on a history of the conflict, giving a rare view into the loser's vision of Manifest Destiny. From the Mexican standpoint, their republic was invaded and dismembered by their aggressive northern neighbor. Many U.S. veterans of the war shared this perspective, including Ulysses S. Grant, who in his memoirs labeled the Mexican War "the most unjust [war] ever waged by a stronger against a weaker nation."[25] For these Mexican editors, aggressive expansion appeared as the heart of American character, and they found no signs of divinity in Manifest Destiny. American expansion was the result and cause of a great deal of violence. Or, as the poet James Russell Lowell put it:

They jest want this Californy
    So 's to lug new slave-states in
To abuse ye, an' to scorn ye,
    An' to plunder ye like sin.[26]

A Group of Mexican Editors Blame U.S. Aggression for an Unnecessary War, 1850

To explain then in a few words the true origin of the war, it is sufficient to say that the insatiable ambition of the United States, favored by our weak-

20. Samuel Eliot Morison and Henry Steele Commager, *The Growth of the American Republic*, 2 vols., 4th ed. (New York: Oxford University Press, 1960), 1:597.

21. Asa Earl Martin, *History of the United States*, 2 vols. (Boston: Ginn and Co., 1928), 1:483.

22. Homer C. Hockett and Arthur M. Schlesinger, *Land of the Free* (New York: Macmillan, 1944), 260–62.

23. Hockett and Schlesinger, *Land of the Free*, 261; Morison and Commager, *Growth of the American Republic*, 1:618.

24. Morison and Commager, *Growth of the American Republic*, 1:588, 596.

25. Ulysses S. Grant, *Personal Memoirs of U.S. Grant*, 2 vols. (New York: C. L. Webster, 1885–86), 1:53.

26. James Russell Lowell, *The Poetical Works of James Russell Lowell*, vol. 2, *The Biglow Papers* (Boston: J. R. Osgood, 1876), 65–66.

ness, caused it. But this assertion, however veracious and well founded, requires the confirmation which we will present, along with some former transactions, to the whole world. This evidence will leave no doubt of the
correctness of our impressions. . . .

. . . The object which we aim at is to show that the United States intended to obtain this territory at any price; and to accomplish it, introduced
there her citizens, taking care to increase the population. Whereby, already in
the year 1829, they counted 20,000 inhabitants in [Texas] where formerly they
only had 3,000. Their minds were prepared gradually to embrace the first opportunity that might offer to strike the blow. . . .

The Republic could not remain indifferent to the cry of a rebellion raised
within her borders. It endeavored to have order restored in the department in
a state of revolt, trying in the first place the conciliatory method of agreement. It proposed to the colonies new advantages, and franchises; among
others, that of being exempt for another period of ten years from paying
taxes. When it was seen only that every peaceable proposition was discarded,
it was decided to declare war, and subject, by actual force, those who were
not willing to hear any other argument than the roar of the cannon. The
army marched upon Texas; General Santa Anna placed himself at its head;
and the campaign opened under the most favorable circumstances.

The Texans, on their side, prepared to make a vigorous resistance. To sustain it they counted on effectual aid from the United States, which gave protection to them,—covert, indeed, but still decided and constant. Supplies for
the war, arms, men, and whatever was requisite, left the most populous cities
of the Union to assist the cause of the Texans, while it protested that it observed the most strict neutrality. . . .

[T]he Mexican army obtained triumphs constantly until the battle of San
Jacinto. In that a defeat was suffered which no one anticipated. Unfortunately
for us, acts of cruelty were perpetrated in this campaign not deserving extenuation. . . . But the national censure which fell on their authors proved that
they had been viewed with disgust. The responsibility ought to be borne exclusively by those who committed them. Other acts of clemency and humanity frequently repeated in this war and afterwards, exonerate us from the
charge which has been made of barbarity and wickedness. . . .

The question of justice then only remained, and no doubt was entertained that forthwith we ought to declare war against the neighboring Republic. This was not done nevertheless, from the urgent reasons of the incal-
culable evils which would flow from an open contest with a powerful nation.
We were disposed to let the cloud blow over; and even subsequently, when
new causes of complaint were frequently received. Among these may be stated
as the principal, the unwarrantable affair of the taking of Monterey in California, by Commodore Jones, which was passed over so as not to interrupt

the peace subsisting. Moreover, the means were sought for to give to the United States the guarantees and indemnities which they had in turn demanded. . . .

On the 12th April, 1844, the President of the United States made a treaty with Texas relative to the incorporation of that country into the Union. This treaty was not ratified by the Senate; the usurpation remained for the present suspended, which was soon, however, effected in a new way. But the step which had been taken in this business was sufficient to do Mexico a new wrong. There might have been noticed at this period some preparations that indicated a sincere wish to carry on the war with Texas, which had for some time past been nothing more in the mouths of our Governors than an excuse for extortion on our unhappy people. The American Minister, Mr. Shannon, whether from his really believing the war was positively to be undertaken, or because a pretext was sought to compel Mexico to declare hostilities against the United States, and to make us appear as aggressors, transmitted an official note. In it he made known in the name of his government, that its policy had always been directed to the incorporation of Texas into the American Union, and the invasion which was proposed by Mexico against that Department would now be deemed an offence to the United States.

In this celebrated communication, which will disgrace for ever the diplomatist who subscribed it, a protest was entered against a war with Texas, while the project of annexation was pending. . . .

At this time, more properly than before, it would have been exact justice to have immediately made war on a power that so rashly appropriated what by every title belonged to us. . . .

. . . [But there was a revolution and the new government] acted upon the principle, in the firm belief that the Department of Texas had from the year 1830 been lost for ever; from which it was madness to suppose that our victorious eagles could be borne to the other side of the Sabine. They therefore decided on negotiation, and war on no account. . . .

While the United States seemed to be animated by a sincere desire not to break the peace, their acts of hostility manifested very evidently what were their true intentions. Their ships infested our coasts; their troops continued advancing upon our territory, situated at places which under no aspect could be disputed. Thus violence and insult were united: thus at the very time they usurped part of our territory, they offered to us the hand of treachery, to have soon the audacity to say that our obstinacy and arrogance were the real causes of the war.

To explain the occupation of the Mexican territory by the troops of General Taylor, the strange idea occurred to the United States that the limits of Texas extended to the Rio Bravo del Norte. This opinion was predicated upon two distinct principles: one, that the Congress of Texas had so declared it in December, in 1836; and another, that the river mentioned had been the natural line of Louisiana. To state these reasons is equivalent at once to deciding the matter; for no one could defend such palpable absurdities. The first, which this government prizing its intelligence and civilization, supported with refined malice, would have been ridiculous in the mouth of a child. Whom could it convince that the declaration of the Texas Congress bore a legal title for the acquisition of the lands which it appropriated to itself with so little hesitation? If such a principle were recognized, we ought to be very grateful to these gentlemen senators who had the kindness to be satisfied with so little. Why not declare the limits of the rebel state extended to San Luis, to the capital, to our frontier with Guatemala?

. . . [T]his same province, and afterwards State of Texas, never had extended its territory to the Rio Bravo, being only to the Nueces, in which always had been established the boundary. Lastly, a large part of the territory situated on the other side of the Bravo, belonged, without dispute or doubt, to other states of the Republic—to New Mexico, Tamaulipas, Coahuila, and Chihuahua.

Then, after so many and such plain proceedings, is there one impartial man who would not consider the forcible occupation of our territory by the North American arms a shameful usurpation? Then further, this power desired to carry to the extreme the sneer and the jest. When the question had resolved itself into one of force which is the *ultima ratio* of nations as well as of kings, when it had spread desolation and despair in our populations, when many of our citizens had perished in the contest, the bloody hand of our treacherous neighbors was turned to present the olive of peace. . . . [T]hey ordered a commissioner with the army, which invaded us from the east, to cause it to be understood that peace would be made when our opposition ceased. Whom did they hope to deceive with such false appearances? Does not the series of acts which we have mentioned speak louder than this hypocritical language? By that test then, as a question of justice, no one who examines it in good faith can deny our indisputable rights. Among the citizens themselves, of the nation which has made war on us, there have been many who defended the cause of the Mexican Republic. These impartial defenders have not been obscure men, but men of the highest distinction. Mexico has counted on the assistance, ineffectual, unfortunately, but generous and illustrious, of a Clay, an Adams, a Webster, a Gallatin; that is to say, on the noblest men, the most appreciated for their virtues, for their talents, and for their services. Their conduct deserves our thanks, and the authors of this work have a true pleasure in paying, in this place, the sincere homage of their gratitude.

Such are the events that abandoned us to a calamitous war. . . . From the acts referred to, it has been demonstrated to the very senses, that the real and effective cause of this war that afflicted us was the spirit of aggrandizement of the United States of the North, availing itself of its power to conquer us. Impartial history will some day illustrate for ever the conduct observed by this Republic against all laws, divine and human, in an age that is called one of light, and which is, notwithstanding, the same as the former—one of *force and violence.*

Source: Albert C. Ramsey, ed., *The Other Side: or Notes for the History of the War between Mexico and the United States* (New York, 1850), 2, 18–26, 30–32.

THE LITTLE BIGHORN MASSACRE

George Armstrong Custer was no stranger to massacres. In 1868 he led his troops in destroying a Cheyenne village on the Washita, as noted earlier, abandoning part of his command in his hurry to get away before the Indians could counter-attack. Custer's Seventh Cavalry was responsible for enforcing President U. S. Grant's "peace policy," which sought to keep all Indians on their reservations so that the white settlement of the West could proceed unhindered. Custer's superior officers, Generals Philip Sheridan and William Tecumseh Sherman, both explicitly framed this effort in terms of "exterminating" the Indians.

In 1874 rumors of gold in the Black Hills led Custer to organize an expedition onto land belonging by treaty to the Sioux and Cheyenne. With the discovery of gold, the federal government determined that the Black Hills were no longer Indian lands, and it ordered the Sioux and Cheyenne to leave an area they held to be sacred. Most Indians ignored these instructions and moved to join Sitting Bull at the Little Bighorn River in Montana.

On orders of the government, General Alfred Terry moved against Sitting Bull. Colonel Custer commanded one of the two columns converging on the Sioux and Cheyenne. Custer's orders were to wait for a conjunction of his troops with those of General Terry, but Custer apparently hoped for a quick victory such as that on the Washita. On June 25, 1876, Custer left behind his artillery and led the Seventh Cavalry on a rapid march to the Little Bighorn, right into the largest concentration of Indian warriors known to history, 1,500 men under the brilliant leadership of Crazy Horse. As he neared the Indian camp, Custer divided his force, sending some 80 men under Major Marcus Reno to attack the village along the river while he swung around the other side. Crazy Horse outmaneuvered Custer, sweeping down on the Seventh Cavalry from the high ground. In the worst single defeat suffered by the American army in the Indian wars, Custer and all 225 men who followed him into battle lost their lives. Curiously, the press moved to transform Custer into a martyr, and he received a hero's burial at West Point, where he had finished last in his class.

News of the massacre on the Little Bighorn reached the east on July 4, 1876, the centennial of the Declaration of Independence. Initial stories, such as this one from the Chicago Tribune, *found little to praise in Custer's reckless action, but it did call for greater ruthlessness in the war against the Indians. The following account of the battle is by Two Moon, a Cheyenne war chief. He told his version of the battle, many details of which are verifiably accurate, through a Cheyenne interpreter to the prominent novelist Hamlin Garland in 1898.*

In the months following the battle at the Little Bighorn, the U.S. Army moved relentlessly against the Plains Indians, corralling them onto bleak reservations. By the time Crazy Horse surrendered the remnants of his band in May 1877, the resistance of the American Indians had been effectively crushed. There would be one last effort by the Sioux to escape their confinement thirteen years later, which would be crushed with even greater brutality.

The *Chicago Tribune* Reports Custer's Defeat, 1876

Since the murder of Gen. CANBY by the Modocs the country has not been more startled than it was by the announcement that Gen. CUSTER and five companies of his regiment, the Seventh Cavalry, had been massacred by the Sioux Indians in a ravine on the Little Horn River, a tributary to the Big Horn, which in turn empties into the Yellowstone, the Indians outnumbering our troops ten to one.

Gen. CUSTER had personal and soldierly traits which commended him to the people. He was an officer who did not know the word fear, and, as is often the case with soldiers of this stamp, he was reckless, hasty, and impulsive, preferring to make a dare-devil rush and take risks rather than to move slower and with more of certainty. He was a brave, brilliant soldier, handsome and dashing, with all the attributes to make him beloved of women and admired of men; but these qualities, however admirable they may be, should not blind our eyes to the fact that it was his own madcap haste, rashness, and love of fame that cost him his own life, and cost the service the loss of many brave officers and gallant men.

From the reports which have come to hand, it appears that, after assigning Maj. RENO with seven companies to attack the lower part of the Indian camp, and stationing three companies in reserve, Gen. CUSTER placed himself at the head of five companies—about 300 men—and dashed into a nest of three or four thousand Sioux warriors, the same men who under Sitting Bull

recently defeated Gen. [George] CROOK on Rosebud Creek. They drew him
into an ambuscaded ravine just as they did CROOK's troopers, only the results
were more disastrous. In the latter case it was a defeat with small loss; in this
instance, three hundred troops were instantly surrounded by 3,000 Indians,
and the fatal ravine became a slaughter-pen from which but few escaped.
Nearly the whole 300 went to a death as instant as if an earthquake had swallowed them.

No account seems to have been taken of numbers, of the leadership of
the Sioux, of their past record of courage and military skill. No account was
even taken of the fact that Gen. GIBBON was coming to the Little Horn with
reinforcements, only a day's march behind, although Gen. CUSTER was aware
of it. He preferred to make a reckless dash and take the consequences, in the
hope of making a personal victory and adding the glory of another charge to
the long list which he has so successfully headed, rather than to wait for a
sufficiently powerful force to make the fight successful, and share the glory
with others. He took the risk and he lost, and all that Gen. GIBBON could
accomplish when he arrived the next day was to come to the relief of the
remnant of the regiment under Maj. RENO, which for twenty-four hours had
been hotly pressed by the victorious Indians.

There are two important lessons to be learned from this massacre, which
has not been equaled in our Indian wars since the BRADDOCK defeat. The first
is the folly of underestimating the strength and fighting qualities of the Indians. Gen. CUSTER acted upon the old theory that one well-armed white man is
a match for half-a-dozen Indians,—a theory derived from exceptional cases,
like FORSYTHE's gallant defense. During the present spring and summer the
Sioux have shown themselves not only brave and enduring in battle, and capable of fierce resistance, but possessed of military skill of a very creditable
character. At the battle of Rosebud Creek SITTING BULL showed himself the
equal of the great Indian fighter, CROOK, in the disposition and handling of
his forces. It teaches the lesson that, if the Indians are to be conquered, they
must be treated as a formidable foe.

Second, under the operations of the Quaker policy, the Government has
been supplying these very Indians with arms and ammunition to carry on the
war, and, while they are on the war-path, is feeding their wives and children
on the reservations with parental fondness. These Indians are provided with
the very best long-range rifles, which they have bought of traders with the
annuities furnished them by the Government. They are amply supplied from
the same sources with horses and ammunition, and they are using their material against small white forces with terribly disastrous effect. Their success
will inspire them with new hope and courage, and will rally the Indians from
all points, thus making a long and expensive war, unless measures are taken

to stamp them out at once. It is time to quit the Sunday school policy, and let Sheridan recruit regiments of Western pioneer hunters and scouts, and exterminate every Indian who will not remain upon the reservations. The best use to make of an Indian who will not stay upon a reservation is to kill him. It is time that the dawdling, maudlin, peace-policy was abandoned. The Indian can never be subdued by Quakers, and it is certain that he will never be subdued by such madcap charges as that made by Custer. He must be treated as a cunning, courageous, and desperate foe, who must be met with something like equal forces, and with a strategy and boldness equal to his own.

Source: *Chicago Tribune*, July 7, 1876.

Hamin Garland Records the Cheyenne Two Moon's Version of the Battle, 1876

That spring [1876] I was camped on Powder River with fifty lodges of my people—Cheyennes. . . . One morning soldiers charged my camp. They were in command of Three Fingers [Colonel McKenzie]. We were surprised and scattered, leaving our ponies. The soldiers ran all our horses off. That night the soldiers slept, leaving the horses [to] one side; so we crept up and stole them back again, and then we went away.

We traveled far, and one day we met a big camp of Sioux at Charcoal Butte. We camped with the Sioux, and had a good time, plenty grass, plenty game, good water. Crazy Horse was head chief of the camp. Sitting Bull was camped a little ways below, on the Little Missouri River.

Crazy Horse said to me, "I'm glad you are come. We are going to fight the white man again."

The camp was already full of wounded men, women, and children.

I said to Crazy Horse, "All right. I am ready to fight. I have fought already. My people have been killed, my horses stolen; I am satisfied to fight." . . .

I believed at that time the Great Spirits had made Sioux, put them there—he drew a circle to the right—and white men and Cheyennes here—indicating two places to the left—expecting them to fight. The Great Spirits I thought liked to see the fight; it was to them all the same like playing. So I thought then about fighting. . . .

About May, when the grass was tall and the horses strong, we broke camp and started across the country to the mouth of the Tongue River. Then Sitting Bull and Crazy Horse and all went up the Rosebud. There we had a big fight with General Crook, and whipped him. Many soldiers were killed—few Indians. It was a great fight, much smoke and dust.

From there we all went over the divide, and camped in the valley of Little Horn. Everybody thought, "Now we are out of the white man's country. He can live there, we will live here." After a few days, one morning when I was in camp north of Sitting Bull, a Sioux messenger rode up and said, "Let everybody paint up, cook, and get ready for a big dance."

Cheyennes then went to work to cook, cut up tobacco, and get ready. We all thought to dance all day. We were very glad to think we were far away from the white man.

I went to water my horses at the creek, and washed them off with cool water, then took a swim myself. I came back to the camp afoot. When I got near my lodge, I looked up the Little Horn towards Sitting Bull's camp. I saw a great dust rising. It looked like a whirlwind. Soon Sioux horsemen came rushing into camp shouting: "Soldiers come! Plenty white soldiers."

I ran into my lodge, and said to my brother-in-law, "Get your horses; the white man is coming. Everybody run for horses."

Outside, far up the valley, I heard a battle cry, *Hay-ay, hay-ay!* I heard shooting, too, this way [clapping his hands very fast]. I couldn't see any Indians. . . . After I had caught my horse, a Sioux warrior came again and said, "Many soldiers are coming."

Then he said to the women, "Get out of the way, we are going to have hard fight."

I said, "All right, I am ready."

I got on my horse, and rode out into my camp. I called out to people all running about: "I am Two Moon, your chief. Don't run away. Stay here and fight. You must stay and fight the white soldiers. I shall stay even if I am to be killed."

I rode swiftly toward Sitting Bull's camp. There I saw the white soldiers fighting in a line [Reno's men]. Indians covered the flat. They began to drive the soldiers all mixed up—Sioux, then soldiers, then more Sioux, and all shooting. The air was full of smoke and dust. I saw the soldiers fall back and drop into the river-bed like buffalo fleeing. They had no time to look for a crossing. The Sioux chased them up the hill, where they met more soldiers in wagons, and then messengers came saying more soldiers were going to kill the women, and the Sioux turned back. Chief Gall was there fighting, Crazy Horse also.

I then rode toward my camp, and stopped squaws from carrying off lodges. While I was sitting on my horse I saw flags come up over the hill to the east like that [he raised his finger-tips]. Then the soldiers rose all at once, all on horses, like this [he put his fingers behind each other to indicate that Custer appeared marching in columns of fours]. They formed into three bunches [squadrons] with a little ways between. Then a bugle sounded, and they all got off [their] horses. . . .

Then the Sioux rode up the ridge on all sides, riding very fast. The Cheyennes went up the left way. Then the shooting was quick, quick. Pop—pop—pop very fast. Some of the soldiers were down on their knees, some standing. Officers all in front. The smoke was like a great cloud, and everywhere the Sioux went the dust rose like smoke. We circled all round him—swirling like water round a stone. We shoot, we ride fast, we shoot again. Soldiers drop, and horses fall on them. Soldiers in line drop, but one man rides up and down the line—all the time shouting. He rode a sorrel horse with white face and white fore-legs. I don't know who he was. He was a brave man.

Indians keep swirling round and round, and the soldiers killed only a few. Many soldiers fell. At last all horses killed but five. Once in a while some man would break out and run toward the river, but he would fall. At last about a hundred men and five horsemen stood on the hill all bunched together. All along the bugler kept blowing his commands. He was very brave too. Then a chief was killed. I hear it was Long Hair [Custer], I don't know; and then the five horsemen and the bunch of men, may be so[me] forty, started toward the river. The man on the sorrel horse led them, shouting all the time. He wore a buckskin shirt, and had long black hair and mustache. He fought hard with a big knife. His men were all covered with white dust. I couldn't tell whether they were officers or not. One man all alone ran far down toward the river, then round up over the hill. I thought he was going to escape, but a Sioux fired and hit him in the head. He was the last man. He wore braid on his arms [sergeant].

All the soldiers were now killed, and the bodies were stripped. After that no one could tell which were officers. The bodies were left where they fell. We had no dance that night. We were sorrowful. . . . There were thirty-nine Sioux and seven Cheyennes killed, and about a hundred wounded.

Source: Hamlin Garland, "General Custer's Last Fights as Seen by Two Moon," *McClure's Magazine* II (September 1898): 444–48.

BILLY THE KID

Born Henry McCarty, Billy the Kid was one of the most famous killers in American history. Many legends grew up around his short life, the first biographies appearing within weeks of his death. The reality was less dramatic than the legends but was very much a nineteenth-century tale. Born in New York City in 1859 of Irish immigrant parents, Henry McCarty moved with his family to Indiana when he was three. After his father died, McCarty's mother married again, and the family moved first to Kansas and then to New Mexico. His first arrest came shortly after his mother's death in 1874, for stealing clothes. Escaping from jail, McCarty fled to Arizona, where in 1877 he shot a blacksmith during a fistfight. The Kid, as he was now known, was arrested and again escaped from jail, fleeing this time to Mesilla, New Mexico, where he took the pseudonym of William H. Bonney.

McCarty, or Bonney, or the Kid, arrived in New Mexico just in time to gain employment as a hired gun for both sides in the Lincoln County War. The violence began in 1878 as a contest between two factions competing for economic and political advantage, and access to government contracts. On one side stood John Chisum and a host of allies, mostly ambitious ranchers; on the other side were Lawrence G. Murphy and a number of rich and powerful associates. The Kid started working for Murphy, but after he befriended John Tunstall, an ally of Chisum, he switched sides. Tunstall, a young Englishman who came to the West in search of adventure, was murdered by a posse led by Sheriff William S. Morton on February 18, 1878. With local law enforcement mostly on Murphy's side, the Chisum faction organized a vigilance committee, taking the traditional name of Regulators. Prominent among these men proclaiming that they simply sought to establish order was Billy the Kid, who was now working for Alexander McSween. Another Chisum adherent, constable Dick Brewer, wanted to try the murderers of Tunstall, while the Regulators felt otherwise, as is related here in Pat F. Garrett's memoir.

When New Mexico's governor Lew Wallace called on the U.S. Army for aid, the soldiers acted in the interest of the Murphy faction and played a role in McSween's murder. But the conflict did not end there, as many criminals rushed to the area to take advantage of this lawlessness created in part by the government. Billy the Kid was part of the ambush that shot Sheriff William Brady on Lincoln's main street, while constable Brewer was shot down by followers of Murphy. Brady's replacement as sheriff, Pat Garrett, pursued the Kid relentlessly, finally catching him in 1881. The Kid was tried and convicted of the murder of Sheriff Brady, but he escaped yet again, killing two deputies in the process. Garret caught up with Billy the Kid on July 14, 1881. The Lincoln County War ended shortly afterward when the Murphy faction decided it was more cost-effective to share business opportunities with Chisum and some other large ranchers.

Many western criminals took on mythic proportions. Like Jesse James, Billy the Kid quickly changed in the popular imagination from a ruthless killer into an amiable Robin Hood, a friend of the poor and champion of the underdog. Over the ensuing century he would be portrayed sympathetically in novels, plays, and films and on television as a misunderstood young man just trying to do the right thing. While Pat Garrett liked the Kid and offered a largely sympathetic portrait of a courageous youth, he did not hesitate to describe him as a cruel killer responsible for the cold-blooded murder of at least six men, three of them officers of the law.

Pat Garrett's Version of the Lincoln County War, 1877

"The Lincoln County War," in which the Kid was now about to take a part, had been brewing since the summer of 1876, and commenced in earnest in the spring of 1877. It continued for nearly two years, and the robberies and murders consequent thereon would fill a volume. The majority of these outrages were not committed by the principals or participants in the war proper, but the unsettled state of the country caused by these disturbances called the lawless element, horse and cattle-thieves, footpads, murderers, escaped convicts, and outlaws from all the frontier states and territories; Lincoln and surrounding counties offered a rich and comparatively safe field for their nefarious operations. . . .

The principals in this difficulty were, on one side, John S. Chisum, called "The Cattle King of New Mexico," with Alex A. McSween and John H. Tunstall as important allies. On the other side were the firm of Murphy & Dolan, merchants at Lincoln, the county seat, and extensive cattle-owners, backed by nearly every small cattle-owner in the Pecos Valley. This latter faction was supported by Hon. T. B. Catron, United States attorney for the Territory, a resident and eminent lawyer of Santa Fé, and a considerable cattle-owner in the Valley.

John S. Chisum's herds ranged up and down the Rio Pecos, from Fort Sumner way below the line of Texas, a distance of over two hundred miles, and were estimated to number from 40,000 to 80,000 head of full-blood, graded, and Texas cattle. A. A. McSween was a successful lawyer at Lincoln, retained by Chisum, besides having other pecuniary interests with him. John H. Tunstall was an Englishman, who only came to this country in 1876. He had ample means at his command, and formed a co-partnership with McSween at Lincoln, the firm erecting two fine buildings and establishing a mercantile house and the "Lincoln County Bank," there. Tunstall was a liberal, public-spirited citizen, and seemed destined to become a valuable acquisition to the reliable business men of our country. He, also, in partnership with McSween, had invested considerably in cattle.

This bloody war originated about as follows: The smaller cattle-owners in Pecos Valley charged Chisum with monopolizing, as a right, all this vast range of grazing country—that his great avalanche of hoofs and horns engulfed and swept away their smaller herds, without hope of recovery or compensation—that the big serpent of this modern Moses, swallowed up the lesser serpents of these magicians. They maintained that at each "round-up" Chisum's vast herd carried with them hundreds of head of cattle belonging to others.

On Chisum's part he claimed that these smaller proprietors had combined together to round-up and drive away from the range—selling them at various military posts and elsewhere throughout the country—cattle which were his property and bearing his mark and brand under the system of reprisals. Collisions between the herders in the employ of the opposing factions were of frequent occurrence, and, as above stated, in the winter and spring of 1877 the war commenced in earnest. Robbery, murder, and bloody encounters ceased to excite either horror or wonder.

Under this state of affairs it was not so requisite that the employes of these stockmen should be experienced *vaqueros* as that they should possess courage and the will to fight the battles of their employers, even to the death. The reckless daring, unerring marksmanship, and unrivalled horsemanship of the Kid rendered his services a priceless acquisition to the ranks of the faction which could secure them. As related, he was enlisted by McDaniels, Morton, and Baker, who were adherents to the Murphy-Dolan cause. . . .

The Kid was not satisfied. Whether conscientious scruples oppressed his mind, whether he pined for a more exciting existence, or whether policy dictated his resolve, he determined to desert his employers, his companions, and the cause in which he was engaged and in which he had wrought yeoman's service. He met John H. Tunstall, a leading factor of the opposition. Whether the Kid sought this interview, or Tunstall sought him, or befell by chance is not known. At all events, our hero expressed to Tunstall his regret for the course he had pursued against him and offered him his future services. Tunstall immediately put him under wages and sent him to the Rio Feliz, where he had a herd of cattle.

The Kid rode back to camp and boldly announced to his whilom [some time] confederates that he was about to forsake them, and that when they should meet again, [that blood would spill].

Dark and lowering glances gleamed out from beneath contracted brows at this communication, and the Kid half-dreaded and half-hoped a bloody ending to the interview. Angry expostulation, eager argument, and impassioned entreaty all failed to shake his purpose. Perhaps the presence and intervention of his old and tried friend Jesse Evans stayed the threatened explosion. Argued Jesse: "Boys, we have slept, drank, feasted, starved, and fought cheek by jowl with the Kid; he has trusted himself alone amongst us, coming like a man to notify us of his intention; he didn't sneak off like a cur, and leave us to find out, when we heard the crack of his Winchester, that he was fighting against us. Let him go. Our time will come. We shall meet him again, perhaps in fair fight." Then, under his breath:—"and he'll make some of you brave fellows squeak." Silently and sullenly the party acquiesced, except Frank Baker, who insinuated in a surly tone that now was the time for the fight to come off.

"Yes, you d——d cowardly dog!" replied the Kid; "right now, when you are nine to one; but don't take me to be fast asleep because I look sleepy. Come you, Baker, as you are stinking for a fight; you never killed a man you did not shoot in the back; come and fight a man that's looking at you."

Red lightnings flashed from the Kid's eyes as he glared on cowering Baker, who answered not a word. With this banter on his lips, our hero slowly wheeled his horse and rode leisurely away, casting one long regretful glance at Jesse, with whom he was loth to part. . . .

In the month of February, 1878, William S. Morton (said to have had authority as deputy sheriff), with a posse of men composed of cow boys from the Rio Pecos, started out to attach some horses which Tunstall and McSween claimed. Tunstall was on the ground with some of his employes. On the approach of Morton and his party, Tunstall's men all deserted him—ran away. Morton afterwards claimed that Tunstall fired on him and his posse; at all events, Morton and party fired on Tunstall, killing both him and his horse. One Tom Hill, who was afterwards killed whilst robbing a sheep outfit, rode up as Tunstall was lying on his face, gasping, placed his rifle to the back of his head, fired, and scattered his brains over the ground.

. . . Before night the Kid was apprised of his friend's death. His rage was fearful. Breathing vengeance, he quitted his herd, mounted his horse, and from that day to the hour of his death his track was blazed with rapine and blood. . . .

The Kid rode to Lincoln and sought McSween. Here he learned that R. M. Bruer [Brewer] had been sworn in as special constable, was armed with a warrant, and was about to start, with a posse, to arrest the murderers of Tunstall. The Kid joined this party, and they proceeded to the Rio Pecos.

On the 6th day of March, Bruer and his posse "jumped up" a party of five men. . . . They fled and the officer's party pursued. They separated, and the Kid, recognizing Morton and Baker, . . . took their trail and was followed by his companions. For fully five miles the desperate flight and pursuit was prolonged. The Kid's Winchester belched fire continually, and his followers were not idle; but distance and the motion of running horses disconcerted their aim, and the fugitives were unharmed. Suddenly, however, their horses stumbled, reeled, and fell, almost at the same instant . . . the prisoners were disarmed and taken to Chisum's ranch. . . . On the 9th day of March, 1878, the officer, with posse and prisoners, left Chisum's for Lincoln. . . .

The Kid . . . cursed Bruer, in no measured terms for giving a pledge of safety to the prisoners, but said, as it had been given, there was no way but to keep their word.

He further expressed his intention to kill them both. . . . [Frank] McNab . . . rode up to McClosky [who had pledged to protect the prisoners,] . . . placed his revolver to McClosky's head and said: "You are the son-of-a-bitch that's got to die before harm can come to these fellows, are you?" and fired as he spoke. McClosky rolled from his horse a corpse. The terrified, unarmed prisoners fled as fast as their sorry horses could carry them, pursued by the whole party and a shower of harmless lead. . . . [The Kid] shouted to them to halt. They held their course, with bullets whistling around them. A few bounds of the infuriated gray carried him to the front of the pursuers—twice only, his revolver spoke, and a life sped at each report. Thus died McClosky, and thus perished Morton and Baker. . . . They left the bodies where they fell. They were buried by some Mexican sheep-herders.

[The Kid is captured by Garrett, but escapes after killing two deputies. Garrett goes in pursuit with two deputies, finding him at the house of Peter Maxwell in the town of Fort Sumner. Garret enters Maxwell's room near midnight, leaving the deputies on the porch.] I walked to the head of the bed and sat down on it, beside him, near the pillow. I asked him as to the whereabouts of the Kid. He said that the Kid had certainly been about, but he did not know whether he had left or not. At that moment a man sprang quickly into the door, looking back, and called twice in Spanish, "Who comes there?" [He had seen the deputies.] No one replied and he came on in. He was bareheaded. From his step I could perceive he was either barefooted or in his stocking-feet, and held a revolver in his right hand and a butcher knife in his left.

He came directly towards me. Before he reached the bed, I whispered: "Who is it, Pete?" but received no reply for a moment. . . . The intruder came close to me, leaned both hands on the bed, his right hand almost touching my knee, and asked, in a low tone:—"Who are they Pete?"—at the same instant Maxwell whispered to me. "That's him!" Simultaneously the Kid must have seen, or felt, the presence of a third person at the head of the bed. He raised quickly his pistol, a self-cocker, within a foot of my breast. Retreating rapidly across the room he cried: "Quien es? Quien es?" . . . All this occurred in a moment. Quickly as possible I drew my revolver and fired, threw my body aside, and fired again. The second shot was useless; the Kid fell dead. He never spoke. A struggle or two, a little strangling sound as he gasped for breath, and the Kid was with his many victims.

Source: Pat F. Garrett, *An Authentic Life of Billy the Kid: The Noted Desperado of the Southwest* (Santa Fe: New Mexican Printing Co., 1882), 22–23, 41–49, 126–29.

POPULAR TRIBUNALS

The American West has long been a subject of fascination for many people. The most popular novelist in Germany in the twentieth century was Karl May, who wrote highly imaginative adventure stories set in the western United States, even though he had never been to North America. In the Czech Republic in the twenty-first century, enthusiasts wear fanciful western clothes and go on treks in the Czech woods. Americans themselves have often fallen to the western mystique, the Western film having taken on iconic qualities. Even scholars can find themselves enamored by an imagined Wild West. Though born in Ohio, Hubert Howe Bancroft pursued his obsession with the West through thirty-nine volumes chronicling its history.

Bancroft often came to the defense of the vigilantes. In the popular imagination, vigilantes tend to be good citizens joining together to try and hang horse thieves and murderers, though with the occasional error. In the Florence, Idaho, cemetery there is a simple epitaph on one tombstone, "Hung by mistake."[27] Many contemporaries felt that vigilantism violated the rule of law and was often the cover for criminal conduct—as ex emplified by Billy the Kid leading a group of Regulators. For Bancroft, vigilantes were not members of a lynch mob but part of the "popular tribunals" establishing law where none existed in the people's name. To that degree, Bancroft saw them as democratic instruments, not to be confused with the "mobocracy," crowds lost to passionate violence without observable purpose. The primary goal of the vigilantes, according to Bancroft, was to put an end to violence. Since, in Bancroft's view, settlement preceded law, American expansion required vigilantism to establish order; legal institutions would follow upon these more informal methods. It is appropriate that Bancroft's last book, The New Pacific, *published in 1898, called for further western expansion by the United States. But now the West was to extend into the Pacific, seizing ever more lands for an American empire.*

Hubert Howe Bancroft Defends Vigilance Committees, 1887

What then has the popular tribunal here become? What is a vigilance committee, and what mobocracy? The terms vigilance committee, mob-law, lynch-law, are not, as many suppose, synonymous. In some respects they are diametrically opposed in principle and in purpose. The vigilance committee is not a mob; it is to a mob as revolution is to rebellion, the name being somewhat according to its strength. Neither is a tumultuous rabble a vigilance committee. Indeed, prominent among its other functions is that of holding brute force and vulgar sentiment in wholesome fear. The vigilance committee will itself break the law, but it does not allow others to do so. It has the highest respect for law, and would be friendly with the law, notwithstanding the law is sometimes disposed to be ill-natured; yet it has a higher respect for itself than for ill-administered law. Often it has assisted officers of the law in catching offenders, and has even gone so far as to hand insignifi-

27. Hollon, *Frontier Violence*, 92.

cant and filthy criminals over to courts of justice for trial rather than soil its
fingers with them

The doctrine of Vigilance, if I may so call the idea or principle embodied
in the term vigilance committee, is that the people, or a majority of them,
possess the right, nay, that it is their bounden duty, to hold perpetual vigil in
all matters relating to their governance, to guard their laws with circumspec-
tion, and sleeplessly to watch their servants chosen to execute them. Yet more
is implied. Possessing this right, and acknowledging the obligation, it is their
further right and duty, whenever they see misbehavior on the part of their
servants, whenever they see the laws which they have made trampled upon,
distorted, or prostituted, to rise in their sovereign privilege and remove such
unfaithful servants, lawfully if possible, arbitrarily if necessary. The law must
govern, absolutely, eternally, say the men of vigilance. Suffer inconvenience,
injustice if need be, rather than attempt illegal reform.

Every right-minded man recognizes the necessity of good conduct in human associations, to secure which experience teaches that rule is essential. In
a free republican form of government every citizen contributes to the making
of the laws, and is interested in seeing them executed and obeyed. The good
citizen, above all others, insists that the law of the land shall be regarded.
But to have law, statutes must be enacted by the people; governments must
be administered by representatives of the people; officials, to be officials,
must be chosen by the people. Law is the voice of the people. Now it is not
the voice of the people that vigilance would disregard, but the voice of corrupt officials and bad men. Law is the will of the community as a whole; it is
therefore omnipotent. When law is not omnipotent, it is nothing. This is
why, when law fails—that is to say, when a power rises in society antagonistic
at once to statutory law and to the will of the people—the people must crush
the enemy of their law or be crushed by it. A true vigilance committee is this
expression of power on the part of the people in the absence or impotence of
law. Omnipotence in rule being necessary, and law failing to be omnipotent,
the element here denominated vigilance becomes omnipotent, not as a
usurper, but as a friend in an emergency. Vigilance recognizes fully the supremacy of law, flies to its rescue when beaten down by its natural enemy,
crime, and lifts its up, that it may always be supreme; and if the law must be
broken to save the state, then it breaks it soberly, conscientiously, and under
the formulas of law, not in a feeling of revenge, or in a manner usual to the
disorderly rabble.

Surely vigilance has no desire to hamper legislation, to interfere with the
machinery of courts, to meddle in politics, to alter or overthrow the constitution, or to usurp supreme authority. Its issue is with the mal-administration
of government, rather than with government itself. Its object is to assist the

law, to see the law righteously executed, to prevent perversion of the law, to defeat prostitution of the law, and not to subvert or debase the law. And to accomplish its purpose, it claims the right to resort to unlawful means, if necessary. Therefore it is easy to see that the vigilance principle does not spring from disrespect for law. Wherever law has been properly executed there never yet was a vigilance committee. The existence of a vigilance organization is *a priori* proof of the absence of good government. No well-balanced, impartial mind will condemn the existence of a vigilance committee in the absence of properly executed law; no right-thinking man will for a moment countenance a vigilance organization, could such a thing be, in the presence of good laws, well executed.

Thus defined, the principle of vigilance takes its place above formulated law, which is its creature, and is directly antagonistic to the mobile spirit which springs from passion and contemptuously regards all law save the law of revenge. While claiming the full right of revolution, it does not choose to use it, because it is satisfied with the existing forms of government. I do not like the term *imperium in imperio*, so often applied to it. Vigilance is the guardian of the government, rather than a government within a government. This, then, is vigilance; the exercise informally of their rightful power by a people wholly in sympathy with existing forms of law. It is the same inexorable necessity of nature which civilization formulates in statutes, codes, and constitutions under the terms law and government, but acting unrestrictedly, absolute will being its only rule. The right is claimed by virtue of sovereignty alone. Under nature man is his own master. As God cannot make a being superior to himself, so society cannot establish rules for its convenience which the central power or majority of the people have not the right at any time or in any manner they see fit to disregard or annul. . . .

. . . A mob composed of a majority of the people . . . is not a mob. I say, a majority of the respectable, intelligent, order-loving, and law-making portion of the people is not the *mobile vulgus*, or movable common people, by which name from time immemorial a disorderly crowd convened for riotous purpose has been known, Nor did I ever hear of a riotous majority of any people claiming the right to overthrow their own laws for evil purpose, and wage illegal warfare against themselves and to their own destruction. Mobs are not composed of individuals calmly associating for the purpose of self-sacrifice for the benefit of the community, but rather for those who would sacrifice the community for self. Government under the banners of liberty and progress is as strong as the people constituting it, and never by any possibility can it be stronger until the people go back to their ancient superstition. The government of the United States, in its fundamental principles, Mr. Wyse calls weak, because founded on the vacillating will of the people. This is fallacy. Only the strong and intelligent can live together under a so-called weak government. In becoming strong and intelligent, men invariably emancipate themselves from the tyrannies of form. . . .

Source: Hubert Howe Bancroft, *Popular Tribunals* (San Francisco: History Co., 1887), 1:8–11, 14–15.

THE VIRGINIAN

Owen Wister was an unlikely champion of the American cowboy. Born in Philadelphia, the son of a prominent physician and grandson of the famous actress Fanny Kemble, Wister went to school in Switzerland and England and graduated from Harvard in 1882. He then studied music in Paris for two years before moving to New York to become a banker. Like his friend and classmate Theodore Roosevelt, Wister went to the West for his health in the 1880s and then returned to study law at Harvard, opening his practice in Philadelphia. Along the way, Wister wrote a number of short stories set in the West, as well as a few romances.

Encouraged by Roosevelt, Wister published what would become the most famous novel of the Wild West. Though written in 1902, after the end of the frontier period, The Virginian *constructed the image of the violent West that would last at least a century. For Wister, violence was a constant presence in the West, lurking beneath the surface of all activities, even a card game. As a social Darwinist, Wister did not find this violence without its uses, keeping the West individualist, masculine, pure, and heroic. Wister laced* The Virginian *with patriotic speeches and Darwinist arguments that made clear the role of the West in preserving American values. Theodore Roosevelt, to whom the book was dedicated, praised* The Virginian *as an American epic in the mode of Virgil or Homer.*

The details of this American epic will be all too familiar to any fan of the Western. The Virginian, *like most Westerns, is set sometime in the early 1880s. Wister's hero was a quiet, mysterious cowboy known only as "the Virginian" who worked on a Wyoming cattle ranch. He falls in love with the local schoolteacher, Molly Wood, but finds it difficult to express his emotions, seemingly preferring the company of his horse. He has regular confrontations with the evil Trampas, who lures the Virginian's best friend, Steve, into a life of crime. Reluctantly the Virginian presides over Steve's lynching, which is justified by the judge as necessary because the law is so unreliable. The book moves relentlessly toward the final encounter between Trampas and the Virginian. This shootout is Wister's most significant invention, becoming the standard climax of Western stories and films through the twentieth century. Though not necessarily connected with reality,* The Virginian *set the popular image of the Wild West in stone, complicating considerably the historian's task.*

Owen Wister Creates the Standard Image
of the Wild West, 1902

And again my eyes sought the prisoners. Certainly there were only two. One was chewing tobacco, and talking now and then to his guard as if nothing were the matter. The other sat dull in silence, not moving his eyes; but his face worked, and I noticed how he continually moistened his dry lips. As I looked at these doomed prisoners, whose fate I was invited to sleep through to-morrow morning, the one who was chewing quietly nodded to me.

"You don't remember me?" he said.

It was Steve! Steve of Medicine Bow! The pleasant Steve of my first evening in the West. Some change of beard had delayed my instant recognition of his face. Here he sat sentenced to die. A shock, chill and painful, deprived me of speech.

He had no such weak feelings. "Have yu' been to Medicine Bow lately?" he inquired. "That's getting to be quite a while ago."

I assented. I should have liked to say something natural and kind, but words stuck against my will. . . .

. . . In a little while I saw light suddenly through my closed eyelids, and then darkness shut again abruptly upon them. They had swung in a lantern and found me by mistake. I was the only one they did not wish to rouse. Moving and quiet talking set up around me, and they began to go out of the stable. At the gleams of new daylight which they let in my thoughts went to the clump of cottonwoods, and I lay still with hands and feet growing steadily cold. Now it was going to happen. I wondered how they would do it; . . . would one have to wait and see the other go through with it first?

. . . The Virginian I never heard speak. But I heard the voice of Steve; he discussed with his captors the sundry points of his capture. . . .

"So Trampas escaped too, did he?" said the prisoner.

"Yes, Steve, Trampas escaped—this time; and Shorty with him—this time. . . ."

"I reckon if every one's ready we'll start." It was the Virginian's voice once more, and different from the rest. I heard them rise at his bidding, and I put the blanket over my head. I felt their tread as they walked out, passing my stall. The straw that was half under me and half out in the stable was stirred as by something heavy dragged or half lifted along over it. "Look out, you're hurting Ed's arm," one said to another, as the steps with tangled sounds passed slowly out. I heard another among those who followed say, "Poor Ed couldn't swallow his coffee." Outside they began getting on their horses; and next their hoofs grew distant, until all was silence round the stable except the dull, even falling of the rain. . . .

[A few days later the narrator is riding with the Virginian.]

... "You never did this before," I said.

"No. I never had it to do." He was riding beside me, looking down at his saddle-horn.

"I do not think I should ever be able," I pursued.

Defiance sounded in his answer. "I would do it again this morning."

"Oh, I don't mean that. It's all right here. There's no other way."

"I would do it all over again the same this morning. Just the same."

... A third time his hand brushed his forehead, and I ventured some sympathy.

"I'm afraid your head aches."

"I don't want to keep seeing Steve," he muttered.

"Steve! I was astounded. Why he—why all I saw of him was splendid. Since it had to be. It was—"

... "Well, he took dying as naturally as he took living. Like a man should. Like I hope to." Again he looked at the pictures in his mind. "No play-acting nor last words. He just told good-by to the boys as we led his horse under the limb—you needn't to look so dainty," he broke off. "You ain't going to get any more shocking particulars."

... He had stretched out his hand to point, but it fell, and his utterance stopped, and he jerked his horse to a stand.

My nerves sprang like a wire at his suddenness, and I looked where he was looking. There were the cottonwoods, close in front of us. As we had travelled and talked we had forgotten them. Now they were looming within a hundred yards; and our trail lay straight through them.

"Let's go around them," said the Virginian.

When we had come back from our circuit into the trail he continued: "... [A] man goes through with his responsibilities. . . . I would do it all over again," he began. "The whole thing just the same. He knowed the customs of the country, and he played the game. No call to blame me for the customs of the country. You leave other folks' cattle alone, or you take the consequences, and it was all known to Steve from the start. . . . He knew well enough the only thing that would have let him off would have been a regular jury. For the thieves have got hold of the juries in Johnson County. I would do it all over, just the same."

... We followed the backward trail in among the pines, and came after a time upon [Shorty and Trampas's] camp. And then I understood the mistake that Shorty had made. He had returned after his failure, and had told that other man of the presence of new horses. He should have kept this a secret; for haste had to be made at once, and two cannot get away quickly upon one horse. But it was poor Shorty's last blunder. He lay there by their extinct fire, with his wistful, lost-dog face upward, and his thick yellow hair unparted as it had always been. The murder had been done from behind. We closed the eyes.

"There was no natural harm in him," said the Virginian. "But you must do a thing well in this country."

[Judge Henry, the Virginian's employer, learns of the lynching and goes to talk with Molly Wood, the Virginian's fiancé.]

. . . Judge Henry . . . had been a federal judge; he had been an upright judge; he had met the responsibilities of his difficult office not only with learning, which is desirable, but also with courage and common sense besides, and these are essential. He had been a stanch servant of the law. And now he was invited to defend that which, at first sight, nay, even at second and third sight, must always seem a defiance of the law more injurious than crime itself. . . .

"I sent him myself on that business," the Judge reflected uncomfortably. "I am partly responsible for the lynching. . . ."

"Judge Henry," said Molly Wood, also coming straight to the point, "have you come to tell me that you think well of lynching?"

He met her. "Of burning Southern negroes in public, no. Of hanging Wyoming cattle thieves in private, yes. You perceive there's a difference, don't you?"

"Not in principle," said the girl, dry and short.

"Oh—dear—me!" slowly exclaimed the Judge. "I am sorry that you cannot see that, because I think that I can. And I think that you have just as much sense as I have." The Judge made himself very grave and very good-humored at the same time. The poor girl was strung to a high pitch, and spoke harshly in spite of herself.

"What is the difference in principle?" she demanded.

". . . I consider the burning a proof that the South is semi-barbarous, and the hanging a proof that Wyoming is determined to become civilized. We do not torture our criminals when we lynch them. We do not invite spectators to enjoy their death agony. We put no such hideous disgrace upon the United States. We execute our criminals by the swiftest means, and in the quietest way. Do you think the principle is the same?"

Molly had listened to him with attention. ". . . Both defy law and order."

"Ah, but do they both? Now we're getting near the principle."

"Why, yes. Ordinary citizens take the law in their own hands."

". . . Out of whose hands do they take the law?"

"The court's."

"What made the courts?"

"I don't understand."

"How did there come to be any courts?"

"The Constitution."

"How did there come to be any Constitution? Who made it?"

"The delegates, I suppose."

"Who made the delegates?"

"I suppose they were elected, or appointed, or something.

"And who elected them?"

"Of course the people elected them."

"Call them the ordinary citizens," said the Judge. "I like your term. They are where the law comes from, you see. For they chose the delegates who made the Constitution that provided for the courts. There's your machinery. These are the hands into which ordinary citizens have put the law. So you see, at best, when they lynch they only take back what they once gave. Now we'll take your two cases that you say are the same in principle. I think that they are not. For in the South they take a negro from jail where he was waiting to be duly hung. The South has never claimed that the law would let him go. But in Wyoming the law has been letting our cattle-thieves go for two years. We are in a very bad way, and we are trying to make that way a little better until civilization can reach us. At present we lie beyond its pale. The courts, or rather the juries, into whose hands we have put the law, are not dealing the law. . . . And so when your ordinary citizen sees this, and sees that he has placed justice in a dead hand, he must take justice back into his own hands where it was once at the beginning of all things. Call this primitive, if you will. But so far from being a *defiance* of the law, it is an *assertion* of it— the fundamental assertion of self-governing men, upon whom our whole social fabric is based. . . ."

Source: Owen Wister, *The Virginian* (New York: Macmillan, 1902), 380, 383–84, 387–88, 391–95, 410, 420, 429–36.

WOUNDED KNEE

Originally it was called the Battle of Wounded Knee. The U.S. Army claimed that it had acted in self-defense, awarding commendations to its men, including the Medal of Honor to one soldier who continued to shoot fleeing Indians even after he had burned his hand on an overheated Hotchkiss gun. James Mooney of the Bureau of Ethnology appeared a few days later to interview the survivors. The bureau had sent Mooney west to observe the Ghost Dance, a religious revival among the Plains Indians that many in Washington saw as a threat. The nativist spiritualism of the Ghost Dance convinced many people, especially among the Sioux, to leave their reservations and seek salvation in the old ways. The efforts of the army to return the Sioux to their reservation led to the tragedy now known as the Massacre of Wounded Knee. Mooney returned to the area in 1896 to measure the impact of these events, publishing his report on the Ghost Dance and Wounded Knee that year.

James Mooney Documents the Ghost Dance Religion and Its Consequence, 1890

On the morning of December 29, 1890, preparations were made to disarm the Indians preparatory to taking them to the agency and thence to the railroad. . . .

Shortly after 8 oclock in the morning the warriors were ordered to come out from the tipis and deliver their arms. They came forward and seated themselves on the ground in front of the troops. They were then ordered to go by themselves into their tipis and bring out and surrender their guns. The first twenty went and returned in a short time with only two guns. It seemed evident that they were unwilling to give them up, and after consultation of the officers part of the soldiers were ordered up to within ten yards of the group of warriors, while another detachment of troops was ordered to search the tipis. After a thorough hunt these last returned with about forty rifles, most of which, however, were old and of little value. The search had consumed considerable time and created a good deal of excitement among the women and children, as the soldiers found it necessary in the process to overturn the beds and other furniture of the tipis and in some instances drove out the inmates. All this had its effect on their husbands and brothers, already wrought up to a high nervous tension and not knowing what might come next. While the soldiers had been looking for the guns Yellow Bird, a medicine-man, had been walking about among the warriors, blowing on an eagle-bone whistle, and urging them to resistance, telling them that the soldiers would become weak and powerless, and that the bullets would be unavailing against the sacred "ghost shirts," which nearly every one of the Indians wore. As he spoke in the Sioux language, the officers did not at once realize the dangerous drift of his talk, and the climax came too quickly for them to interfere. It is said one of the searchers now attempted to raise the blanket of a warrior. Suddenly Yellow Bird stooped down and threw a handful of dust into the air, when, as if this were the signal, a young Indian, said to have been Black Fox from Cheyenne river, drew a rifle from under his blanket and fired at the soldiers, who instantly replied with a volley directly into the crowd of warriors and so near that their guns were almost touching. From the number of sticks set up by the Indians to mark where the dead fell, as seen by the author a year later, this one volley must have killed nearly half the warriors. . . . The survivors sprang to their feet, throwing their blankets from their shoulders as they rose, and for a few minutes there was a terrible hand to hand struggle, where every man's thought was to kill. Although many of the warriors had no guns, nearly all had revolvers and knives in their belts under their blankets, together with some of the murderous war-clubs still carried by the Sioux. The very lack of guns made the fight more bloody, as it brought the combatants to closer quarters.

At the first volley the Hotchkiss guns trained on the camp opened fire and sent a storm of shells and bullets among the women and children, who had gathered in front of the tipis to watch the unusual spectacle of military display. The guns poured in 2-pound explosive shells at the rate of nearly fifty per minute, mowing down everything alive. The terrible effect may be judged from the fact that one woman survivor, Blue Whirlwind, with whom the author conversed, received fourteen wounds, while each of her two little boys was also wounded by her side. In a few minutes 200 Indian men, women, and children, with 60 soldiers, were lying dead and wounded on the ground,[28] the tipis had been torn down by the shells and some of them were burning above the helpless wounded, and the surviving handful of Indians were flying in wild panic to the shelter of the ravine, pursued by hundreds of maddened soldiers and followed up by a raking fire from the Hotchkiss guns, which had been moved into position to sweep the ravine.

There can be no question that the pursuit was simply a massacre, where fleeing women, with infants in their arms, were shot down after resistance had ceased and when almost every warrior was stretched dead or dying on the ground. . . .

This is no reflection on the humanity of the officer in charge. On the contrary, Colonel Forsyth had taken measures to guard against such an oc-currence by separating the women and children, as already stated, and had also endeavored to make the sick chief, Big Foot, as comfortable as possible. . . . Strict orders had also been issued to the troops that women and children were not to be hurt. The butchery was the work of infuriated soldiers whose comrades had just been shot down without cause or warning. In justice to a brave regiment it must be said that a number of the men were new recruits . . . who had never before been under fire, were not yet imbued with military discipline, and were probably unable in the confusion to distinguish between men and women by their dress. . . .

[These Sioux accounts of events leading up to and at Wounded Knee are

---

28. At least 153 Indians, including 44 women and 18 children, were killed on the spot. It is estimated that another 20 to 30 died of their wounds. Twenty-five soldiers were killed, many by their comrades.

from a meeting with the commissioner of Indian affairs in Washington, D.C., in February 1891.]

   ... TURNING HAWK, Pine Ridge [29].... A certain falsehood [the Ghost Dance] came to our agency from the west which had the effect of a fire upon the Indians, and when this certain fire came upon our people those who had farsightedness and could see into the matter made up their minds to stand up against it and fight it. The reason we took this hostile attitude to this fire was because we believed that ... the people in authority did not like this thing and we were quietly told that we must give up or have nothing to do with this certain movement. Though this is the advice from our good friends in the east, there were, of course, many silly young men who were longing to become identified with the movement, although they knew that there was nothing absolutely bad, nor did they know there was anything absolutely good, in connection with the movement.

   In the course of time we heard that the soldiers were moving toward the scene of trouble. After awhile some of the soldiers finally reached our place and we heard that a number of them also reached our friends at Rosebud.[30] Of course, when a large body of soldiers is moving toward a certain direction they inspire a more or less amount of awe, and it is natural that the women and children who see this large moving mass are made afraid of it and be put in a condition to make them run away.... [W]hile the soldiers were there, there was constantly a great deal of false rumor flying back and forth. The special rumor I have in mind is the threat that the soldiers had come there to disarm the Indians entirely and to take away all their horses from them. That was the oft-repeated story.

   So constantly repeated was this story that our friends from Rosebud, instead of going to Pine Ridge, the place of their destination, veered off and went to some other direction toward the "Bad Lands." We did not know definitely how many, but understood there were 300 lodges of them, about 1,700 people....

   Well, the people after veering off in this way, many of [us] who believe in peace and order at our agency, were very anxious that some influence should be brought upon these people.... So we sent out peace commissioners [including Turning Hawk] to the people who were thus running away from their agency.

   I understood at the time that they were simply going away from fear because of so many soldiers. So constant was the word of these good men from

29. Turning Hawk was one of the leaders of the Oglalas (a Sioux tribe) at Pine Ridge, a reservation in South Dakota.
30. The main Sioux reservation in South Dakota.

Pine Ridge agency that finally they succeeded in getting away half of the party from Rosebud, from the place where they took refuge, and finally were brought to the agency at Pine Ridge. . . .

The remnant of the party from Rosebud not taken to the agency finally reached the wilds of the Bad Lands. Seeing that we had succeeded so well, once more we sent to the same party in the Bad Lands and succeeded in bringing these very Indians out of the depths of the Bad Lands and were being brought toward the agency. When we were about a day's journey from our agency we heard that a certain party of Indians (Big Foot's band) from the Cheyenne River agency was coming toward Pine Ridge in flight.

CAPTAIN SWORD.[31] . . . There were a number of Ogalallas, old men and several school boys, coming back with that very same party, and one of the very seriously wounded boys was a member of the Ogalalla boarding school at Pine Ridge agency. He was not on the warpath, but was simply returning home to his agency and to his school after a summer visit to relatives on the Cheyenne river.

TURNING HAWK. When we heard that these people were coming toward our agency we also heard this. These people were coming toward Pine Ridge agency, and when they were almost on the agency they were met by the soldiers and surrounded and finally taken to the Wounded Knee creek, and there at a given time their guns were demanded. When they had delivered them up, the men were separated from their families, from their tipis, and taken to a certain spot. When the guns were thus taken and the men thus separated, there was a crazy man, a young man of very bad influence and in fact a nobody, among that bunch of Indians fired his gun, and of course the firing of a gun must have been the breaking of a military rule of some sort, because immediately the soldiers returned fire and indiscriminate killing followed.

SPOTTED HORSE. This man shot an officer in the army; the first shot killed this officer. I was a voluntary scout at that encounter and I saw exactly what was done, and that was what I noticed; that the first shot killed an officer. As soon as this shot was fired the Indians immediately began drawing their knives, and they were exhorted from all sides to desist, but this was not obeyed. Consequently the firing began immediately on the part of the soldiers.

TURNING HAWK.[32] All the men who were in a bunch were killed right there, and those who escaped that first fire got into the ravine, and as they went along up the ravine for a long distance they were pursued on both sides by the soldiers and shot down, as the dead bodies showed afterwards. The

31. George Sword, captain of the Pine Ridge Indian Police.
32. A Sioux opponent of the Ghost Dance.

women were standing off at a different place from where the men were stationed, and when the firing began, those of the men who escaped the first onslaught went in one direction up the ravine, and then the women, who were bunched together at another place, went entirely in a different direction through an open field, and the women fared the same fate as the men who went up the deep ravine.

AMERICAN HORSE.[33] The men were separated, as has already been said, from the women, and they were surrounded by the soldiers. Then came next the village of the Indians and that was entirely surrounded by the soldiers also. When the firing began, of course the people who were standing immediately around the young man who fired the first shot were killed right together, and then they turned their guns, Hotchkiss guns, etc., upon the women who were in the lodges standing there under a flag of truce, and of course as soon as they were fired upon they fled, the men fleeing in one direction and the women running in two different directions. So that there were three general directions in which they took flight.

There was a women with an infant in her arms who was killed as she almost touched the flag of truce, and the women and children of course were strewn all along the circular village until they were dispatched. Right near the flag of truce a mother was shot down with her infant; the child not knowing that its mother was dead was still nursing, and that especially was a very sad sight. The women as they were fleeing with their babes were killed together, shot right through, and the women who were very heavy with child were also killed. All the Indians fled in these three directions, and after most all of them had been killed a cry was made that all those who were not killed or wounded should come forth and they would be safe. Little boys who were not wounded came out of their places of refuge, and as soon as they came in sight a number of soldiers surrounded them and butchered them there.

Of course we all feel very sad about this affair. I stood very loyal to the government all through those troublesome days, and believing so much in the government and being so loyal to it, my disappointment was very strong, and I have come to Washington with a very great blame on my heart. Of course it would have been all right if only the men were killed; we would feel almost grateful for it. But the fact of the killing of the women, and more especially the killing of the young boys and girls who are to go to make up the future strength of the Indian people, is the saddest part of the whole affair and we feel it very sorely.

Source: James Mooney, *The Ghost-Dance Religion and Wounded Knee* (Washington, DC: Government Printing Office, 1896), 868–70, 884–86.

33. Oglala opponent of the Ghost Dance at Pine Ridge.

FURTHER READINGS

On the military conflict in the West, see Stanley Vestal, *Warpath and Council Fire: The Plains Indians' Struggle for Survival in War and in Diplomacy, 1851–1891* (New York: Random House, 1948); Robert M. Utley, *The Last Days of the Sioux Nation* (New Haven, CT: Yale University Press, 1963); Utley, *Frontier Regulars: The United States Army and the Indian, 1866–1891* (New York: Macmillan, 1974); Stephen E. Ambrose, *Crazy Horse and Custer: The Parallel Lives of Two American Warriors* (Garden City, NY: Doubleday, 1975); Albert L. Hurtado, *Indian Survival on the California Frontier* (New Haven, CT: Yale University Press, 1988); Duane P. Schultz, *Month of the Freezing Moon: The Sand Creek Massacre* (New York: St. Martin's Press, 1990); David Roberts, *Once They Moved Like the Wind: Cochise, Geronimo, and the Apache Wars* (New York: Simon and Schuster, 1993).

On the Overland Trail, see John Mack Faragher, *Women and Men on the Overland Trail* (New Haven, CT: Yale University Press, 1979); John Phillip Reid, *Law for the Elephant: Property and Social Behavior on the Overland Trail* (San Marino, CA: Huntington Library, 1997); Reid, *Policing the Elephant: Crime, Punishment, and Social Behavior on the Overland Trail* (San Marino, CA: The Huntington Library, 1997).

On western vigilantism and range, wars, see Harry S. Drago, *The Great Range Wars: Violence on the Grasslands* (Lincoln: University of Nebraska Press, 1970); Richard Maxwell Brown, *Strain of Violence: Historical Studies of American Violence and Vigilantism* (New York: Oxford University Press, 1975); Robert M. Utley, *Billy the Kid: A Short and Violent Life* (Lincoln: University of Nebraska Press, 1989); Richard Maxwell Brown, *No Duty to Retreat: Violence and Values in American History and Society* (New York: Oxford University Press, 1991).

For studies of the realities of the western mythology, see Robert R. Dykstra, *The Cattle Towns* (New York: Knopf, 1968); W. Eugene Hollon, *Frontier Violence: Another Look* (New York: Oxford University Press, 1974); Patricia Nelson Limerick, *The Legacy of Conquest: The Unbroken Past of the American West* (New York: Norton, 1987); Frank R. Prassel, *The Great American Outlaw: A Legacy of Fact and Fiction* (Norman: University of Oklahoma Press, 1993). For the ambitious, there are few more thorough and compelling works than Richard Slotkin's triology: *Regeneration through Violence: The Mythology of the American Frontier, 1600–1860* (Middletown, CT: Wesleyan University Press, 1973); *The Fatal Environment: The Myth of the Frontier in the Age of Industrialization, 1800–1890* (New York: Atheneum, 1985); *Gunfighter Nation: The Myth of the Frontier in Twentieth-Century America* (New York: Atheneum, 1992).

EIGHT

THE INDUSTRIALIZATION
OF VIOLENCE

In the immediate aftermath of the Civil War, homicide rates appear to have declined. Though scholars continue to dispute this point, many agree with Roger Lane that American society "grew less free-swinging and more sober, regimented, and introspective." As a result, Lane argues, the murder rate went down while suicides increased.[1] Eric Monkkonen explains the postwar decline in murder as resulting from control efforts inevitably triggered by worrisome peaks in the homicide rate. Except in the South, which became ever more violent,[2] personal violence crested about 1864, leading to new and effective institutional efforts to control crime.[3]

At the same time individual murders declined, Americans demonstrated an enhanced willingness to use violence to settle their disputes. After all, Henry Adams wrote, here was a generation that "had just helped waste five or ten thousand million dollars and a million lives, more or less, to enforce unity and uniformity on people who objected to it."[4] As Adams suggested, the Civil War lent legitimacy to the use of institutional violence. Coercion, not political persuasion or compromise, had preserved the Union and ended the blight of slavery. Why should it not be used to resolve other conflicts? Southern white racists

---

1. Roger Lane, *Murder in America: A History* (Columbus: Ohio State University Press, 1997), 183–91, quotation on p. 186. Elsewhere, Lane identified "a brief surge" in homicide rates immediately after the Civil War, but he argued that the overall trend in the succeeding decades was "unmistakably down." Roger Lane, "Murder in America: A Historian's Perspective," in Michael Tonry, ed., *Crime and Justice: An Annual Review of Research* 25 (1999): 201.
2. See, for instance, George C. Rable, *But There Was No Peace: The Role of Violence in the Politics of Reconstruction* (Athens: University of Georgia Press, 1984).
3. Eric Monkkonen, *Murder in New York City* (Berkeley: University of California Press, 2001), 20–25.
4. Henry Adams, *The Education of Henry Adams* (New York: Vintage, 1954), 211–12.

had demonstrated the utility of violence in reestablishing white rule and denying nearly all civil rights to black Americans during the last years of Reconstruction, and they continued to use the most brutal methods to keep African
Americans in line for the next eighty years. Out West, large ranchers had found
violence effective in expanding their holdings and extending their control of
political institutions. But one of the more dramatic changes in American life
came in the large industrial conflicts in the United States in the half century
following the end of the Civil War. Neither labor nor management hesitated to
use deadly force in their battles, with the state usually intervening on the side
of management. These conflicts often bordered on explicit class warfare.

Changes in public attitudes toward violence in the aftermath of the Civil
War did not exist in isolation from other events. Among many significant al-
terations in the nation was a shift from a rural agricultural base to an urban
industrial economy. The nation grew from fifty million people in 1880 to
seventy-six million in 1900, with the cities leading that expansion. While several
million Americans moved from the countryside into the cities, many millions
more came from abroad. The managerial class and government officials treated
these immigrants as less worthy of the rights of citizenship. Even lead poisoning
on the job was attributed to the foreign born: "The Americans know how to
take care of themselves," an article in a trade journal reported. "They wash their
hands and faces . . . [while] the immigrants from Eastern Europe do not unless
someone stands over them and makes them do it."[5]

It was an age when nearly every issue, from sports to religion to politics,
was colored by economic inequalities. As the gap between the rich and poor
increased, there was a rising tide of protest against the system of industrial
capital that many critics charged was being imposed on the country. The socialist labor leader Eugene V. Debs thought large-scale capitalism violated American traditions, while the economist Henry George warned that the trend was
toward a polarized society where a few very wealthy men controlled the levers
of power and a repressed majority of poor workers lived on the verge of star-
vation and mass violence. Labor unrest in these years demonstrated that workers who found no sympathy for their plight in legislatures and courtrooms
were capable of acts of violence that could threaten social stability. The nation's
elite struggled to keep a cap on these calls for reform, using force to maintain
order. As a consequence, the late nineteenth century appeared to many contemporaries a time of accelerating class conflict.

American workers did not accept social inequality passively, launching more
strikes than in any other industrial country in the late nineteenth century.
Historians estimate that there were twenty-three thousand strikes in the United

5. Arno Dosch, "Our Expensive Cheap Labor," *World's Work* 26 (1913): 699.

States between 1875 and 1900, involving 6.5 million workers. The vast majority of these labor actions were peaceful, with most violence being confined to attacks on property—such as the breaking of windows. But on a few significant occasions workers turned to physical violence, driven, they usually claimed, by frustration with a political system that was heavily biased against them.

Aggravating employees' grievances was a factory system that dehumanized workers, killing tens of thousands every year by ignoring the sorts of safety standards that were becoming common in Europe. Most workers toiled for ten to twelve hours a day, six days a week, for less than subsistence wages, according to federal government reports. Management tended to blame the workers for their injuries. As one trade journal reported, "Carelessness, thoughtlessness and lack of knowledge all conspire to cause him [the worker] injury."[6] Employers did not hesitate to cast aside injured workers or those who demanded more pay, replacing them with immigrants and children.

To combat this harsh system, thousands of workers came together in 1876 to form the Noble Order of the Knights of Labor, America's first national labor union. The union opened membership to all workers, including women and African Americans and excluding only the "parasitic," such as gamblers and lawyers. The Knights of Labor had some unusually progressive ideals, such as an insistence on "equal pay for equal work" for women workers. But their primary goals were the eight-hour day, "the adopting of measures providing for the health and safety of those engaged in mining, manufacturing, or building pursuits," and the elimination of child labor.[7] By the mid-1880s, the Knights of Labor had seven hundred thousand members, nearly one-tenth of whom were African American. The Knights of Labor disavowed violence, though their membership became involved in a number of violent labor actions. Most labor violence was not planned but came in response to actions by management. In a society that seemed to give little value to manual labor or dignity to workers, the Knights of Labor, who were supplanted by the American Federation of Labor in the 1890s, aimed to enhance workers' self-respect.

On the opposite extreme was William Graham Sumner, one of the founders of sociology and the leading proponent of social Darwinism. Sumner had complete faith in laissez-faire policies, dismissing every effort at reform as romantic nonsense out of touch with reality. Labor unions sought nothing less than "bloodshed and destruction." "If they cannot make everybody else as well off as themselves," Sumner predicted, everybody would "be brought down to the same misery as others." Social Darwinists followed Sumner in believing that

---

6. Fred D. Lange, "Safety and Accident Prevention," *Industrial Management* 61 (1921): 257, quoted in David Rosner and Gerald Markowitz, eds., *Dying for Work: Workers' Safety and Health in Twentieth-Century America* (Bloomington: Indiana University Press, 1987), xv.

7. T. V. Powderly, *Thirty Years of Labor, 1859 to 1889* (Columbus, Ohio, 1890), 239–46.

society benefited from inequality, as it drove people to strive harder, which in turn generated social advancement. Movements for equality were counterproductive, for "every effort to realize equality necessitates a sacrifice of liberty." Sumner held that "poverty is the best policy." The poor deserve to be poor, and "Every man and woman in society has one big duty. That is, to take care of his or her own self." But it was not clear why, then, individual workers should not organize and even use violence in order to attain their ends.[8]

Most employers seem to have shared Sumner's attitudes. One manufacturer told Samuel Gompers, "I regard my employees as I do a machine, to be used to my advantage, and when they are old and of no further use I cast them into the street." A woolen maker in New England did not hesitate to state that if workers wanted higher wages, they should all be "starved" to the point that "they will go to work at just what you can afford to pay." Workers, in Jay Gould's famous "axiom," were just another "commodity . . . governed absolutely by the law of supply and demand."[9] Such attitudes fed a willingness to use violence against employees, while encouraging workers to feel that they had few alternatives.

Employers had the entire apparatus of the state at their disposal. The courts consistently issued injunctions against strikes as "unfair restraints on trade," jailing labor leaders who violated their orders and upholding the right of employers to use force when required to keep their businesses open. Not only were local police generally supportive of big business in any labor dispute, but industry also employed private police agencies, most notably the Pinkertons. These forces could range from a small guard of three or four agents to the three hundred private police employed by management during the strike at Kehley Run, Pennsylvania, in 1887. These police generally had no legal standing but were almost never prosecuted for the use of lethal force.

If the police, public and private, proved insufficient, the industrialists could call upon the state militia. By the late nineteenth century the militia, usually known as the National Guard by that time, was a middle-class or even elite organization. Its membership routinely sided with management in any confrontation with labor, protecting strikebreakers, guarding factories, and keeping strikers in thrall. The militia's willingness to use force was notorious. In 1891, one militia commander, addressing his fellow officers in Washington, D.C., said that they need feel no hesitation in "eradicating" members of a mob since 85 percent of them were "roughs, tramps, thieves, convicts, and anarchists." He went on to predict ever more trouble with workers and radicals because of the

---

8. William Graham Sumner, *What Social Classes Owe to Each Other* (New York, 1903), 8–15, 20–24, 113, 119–20.

9. Henry David, *The History of the Haymarket Affair: A Study in the American Social-Revolutionary and Labor Movements* (New York: Farrar and Rinehart, 1936).

arrival of "hundreds for thousands of the most criminal and ignorant classes of Europe."[10]

Such attitudes convinced many labor leaders that workers needed to arm themselves for protection against the state's police forces. Workers organized gun clubs, often along ethnic as well as class lines. For instance, in the Chicago area there were the German Jaeger Verein, the Bohemian Sharpshooters, and the Irish Labor Guards. In 1879 the Illinois legislature banned all such unofficial militias, an action upheld by the Illinois and the U.S. Supreme Courts. After the state militia opened fire on strikers in Lemont, Illinois, on May 4, 1885, killing two, this call for taking up arms intensified. On May 7, 1885, the *Chicago Tribune* quoted Lucy Parsons: "Let every dirty, lousy tramp arm himself with a revolver or knife, and lay in wait on the steps of the palaces of the rich and stab or shoot the owners as they come out. Let us kill them without mercy, and let it be a war of extermination."[11] A German workers' newspaper argued, "Each workingman ought to have been armed long ago. Daggers and revolvers are easily to be gotten. Hand grenades are cheaply . . . produced; explosives, too, can be obtained."[12] Even a moderate labor leader such as Terence Powderly reportedly said, "I am anxious that each of our lodges should be provided with powder and shot, bullets and Winchester rifles, when we intend to strike. If you strike, the troops are called out to put you down. You cannot fight with bare hands. You must consider the matter very seriously, and if we anticipate strikes, we must prepare to strike and use arms against the forces brought against us."[13] Even if Powderly did not use exactly these words, members of the elite thought he did and felt real cause for concern, if not fear.

Despite these attitudes, violence between management and labor was not inevitable. Initially a few industrialists shared Andrew Carnegie's view that unions could prove useful. In the prosperous 1880s, Carnegie found that the craft unions helped to keep wages for skilled workers constant nationwide, which meant that his competitors could not hope to undercut his labor costs. But by 1892 Carnegie dominated the steel industry in the United States and no longer needed the unions. Carnegie moved first against the unions at his mills in Homestead, Pennsylvania, refusing to sign a new contract. Being a sensitive man, Carnegie did not want to witness the hardships his policy produced, so he sailed to Scotland, leaving Henry Clay Frick responsible for crushing the union. Frick, expecting violence, turned the Homestead mill into a fortress,

---

10. *The National Guard in Service: A Course of Lectures for the Instruction of the Officers of the District of Columbia National Guard* (Washington, DC, 1891), 311, 307–9.

11. Paul Avrich, *The Haymarket Tragedy* (Princeton, NJ: Princeton University Press, 1984), 91.

12. *Arbeiter-Zeitung*, March 23, 1885.

13. Quoted in Henry Mayers Hyndman, *The Chicago Riots and the Class War in the United States* (London, 1886), 3.

surrounding it with barbed wire and hiring more than three hundred Pinkerton agents. He then locked out the union members. The union declared a strike and laid siege to the Homestead mill.

When Frick brought two barges of additional Pinkerton agents up the Monongahela River, workers camped along the river tried to keep them from coming ashore. Both sides opened fire, killing ten workers and three Pinkertons, one of whom had his eye put out by a woman armed with an umbrella. Though the agents were heavily armed with 300 revolvers and 250 Winchester rifles, they were greatly outnumbered and surrendered.[14] The workers took over the plant, electing a council to run the operation.

With the Pinkertons defeated, Frick turned to the governor of Pennsylvania for militia. For ninety-five days, eight thousand state militia occupied Homestead, costing the state more than $1 million and evoking widespread popular support for the union. But when an anarchist shot but did not kill Frick, public support for the union collapsed. Carnegie and Frick destroyed the steelworkers' union, which would not revive for nearly a half century. Carnegie seized the opportunity to cut wages and increase the working day to twelve hours. Though the labor unions had superior numbers, they stood little chance for success so long as the corporations had the state and its troops on their side.

At the same time that the Homestead Strike was putting an end to the steelworkers' movement, the United States was entering its worst depression to that date. The panic of 1893, as it was called, saw unemployment climb to an estimated one-fifth of the total workforce. As conditions worsened and Democratic president Grover Cleveland refused to act in any way to help those who lost their jobs or land, many unemployed and underpaid workers turned to radical political movements.

While fifteen thousand businesses and six hundred banks went bankrupt, some leading corporations prospered through the depression. For instance, Carnegie's profits increased tenfold in the eight years after his state-supported victory at Homestead. Even though George Pullman, maker of railroad cars, used the depression as justification for cutting his workers' wages by one-quarter, his company made large profits during the depression and paid sizable dividends to its stockholders. Thousands of his workers responded by joining the new American Railway Union (ARU) founded by Eugene V. Debs. Knowing that Debs hoped to avoid any immediate labor action because the union had not had a chance to build up a strike fund, Pullman acted to provoke a strike, firing the union's leaders and locking out his workers, as Frick had done at Homestead. Debs called for arbitration, but Pullman refused, forcing the union

14. U.S. Congress, Committee on the Judiciary, *Employment of Pinkerton Detectives*, 52d Cong., 2nd sess., House Report 2447, serial 3142 (Washington, DC, 1873), ix.

to declare a strike that included a national boycott of the Pullman Company, its members refusing to handle any train pulling Pullman cars.

Railroad management had its union as well, the General Managers Association (GMA), which fired all union members in the nation's railroads and hired strikebreakers, bringing the national rail network to a complete stop. The GMA circulated false stories of labor violence, which conservative newspapers published. Even though Debs was an adherent of nonviolent action, the GMA convinced the Democratic attorney general of the United States, Richard Olney—coincidentally an attorney for the railroads—to call out the U.S. Army to settle the strike.

While the U.S. Constitution grants Congress the power to "suppress insurrections" (Article 1, Section 8), it also states that the federal government can send troops into a state only "on application of the legislature, or of the executive" (Article 4, Section 4). But Illinois governor John Altgeld refused to either use the militia against the workers or call for federal assistance. Attorney General Olney circumvented the law by convincing President Cleveland that the strike interfered with the federal mails, which moved by train. On July 4, 1894, eight thousand federal troops arrived in Chicago to "restore order." In the ensuing violence, twenty-five workers were shot, many buildings seriously damaged, and the headquarters of the ARU ransacked. Federal courts then ignored the First Amendment in ordering Debs to not speak in public, declared boycotts illegal, and prohibited any further strike action by the ARU. When Debs exercised what he thought to be his right to free speech, the court sentenced him to jail, a punishment upheld by the U.S. Supreme Court. With the full force of the state against them, the union collapsed, and the railroads fired sixteen thousand union members. This demonstration of the power of major corporations to control the federal government convinced thousands of American workers that their own government would not hesitate to use force to crush their aspirations. Upon his release from jail, Debs organized the Socialist Party. Many other frustrated workers turned to even more radical groups, including those that advocated the use of violence. Some of these adherents of violence attempted to alter social relations through assassination, most famously Leon Czolgosz, the assassin of President William McKinley. But there were several other assassinations and attempted murders by anarchists and revolutionaries through the 1890s and the first two decades of the twentieth century, such as the murder of Idaho's former governor Frank Steunenberg, described in this chapter.

While violence associated with industrialization lessened during the Progressive Era, it did not vanish. One of the most fervent antiunion voices in the United States at that time was Harrison Gray Otis, the publisher of the *Los Angeles Times*. In addition to speaking out against unions, Otis was ruthless in his relations with the paper's workers. On October 1, 1910, dynamite destroyed a wall of the Times Building, collapsing the second floor and trapping dozens of workers inside. At least twenty workers were killed in the blast and ensuing fire. Several labor organizers were arrested for the bombing, most notably John J. McNamara, the treasurer of the International Union of Bridge and Structural Iron Workers, and his brother James. Samuel Gompers, president of the American Federation of Labor, saw the arrests as an attack on the effort to organize unions and hired the most famous lawyer in America, Clarence Darrow, to defend the McNamaras. To the shock of workers throughout the country, Darrow became convinced that the brothers were guilty and persuaded them to so plead. James McNamara received a life sentence; John was sentenced to fifteen years in prison. Organized labor suffered a serious blow from the trial, which seemed to show that union supporters were willing to kill workers to attain their end. An equivalent blow against the public perception of the industrialists came in 1914 with the Ludlow Massacre, described in this chapter, which aroused public antipathy toward management's use of force to suppress strikes. Union workers would continue to beat strikebreakers while company guards and the police beat up union organizers throughout the twentieth century. But the use of lethal force by either side became ever more illegitimate in the eyes not just of the general public but also of the workers and managers themselves.

Other forms of violence are associated with industrialization. Guards opening fire on workers and union members beating nonunion workers were intentional acts of violence. Far more deadly were the unintentional but avoidable industrial accidents. There were no safety standards in nineteenth-century America; it was entirely up to the employer to decide if safety features would be installed in the workplace. And since there was no profit to be garnered by such efforts, it is little wonder that walkways high above the factory floor or hovering over vats of molten steel did not have safety rails.

Nor was the employer in the least responsible for any worker injured on the job. The worker who had an arm torn off by a machine or who could no longer breathe properly because of years of inhaling coal dust was simply fired. The courts consistently upheld the employer's right to remove an injured employee who would lessen the company's profits. The courts reasoned that a worker understood "an assumption of risk" by taking employment. After all, no worker was compelled to hold a particular job. The worker "bargained" away his safety for his income with a full understanding of the risks involved. As Justice Lemuel Shaw wrote, "In legal presumption, the compensation is adjusted accordingly."[15] The legal logic reached the point that a worker ordered to labor in violation of state laws was himself responsible for any accident that ensued.

15. Farwell v. Boston & Worcester Railroad, 45 Mass. 49 (1842).

The employer remained above liability, for, as the New York Court of Appeals unanimously declared in 1873, "We must have factories, machinery, dams, canals and railroads. They are demanded by the manifold wants of mankind, and lay at the basis of all our civilization."[16] Such perceptions by the courts guaranteed that the greatest form of violence against individuals in the United States would not only persist but be seen as normal.

DOCUMENTS

THE STRIKE OF 1877

A significant landmark came in the year 1877, with the first use of federal troops in peacetime to suppress a strike. Starting in West Virginia, a strike against the railroads spread across the country, immobilizing the nation's railways. The unorganized and spontaneous nature of this strike demonstrated convincingly the deep grievances of the workers. Lacking organization, different strikers had different goals, often determined by the railroad for which they worked. Safety was a primary issue for many workers, as more than four thousand workers a year died in accidents involving the coupling and decoupling of trains alone—fatalities that mostly could have been avoided had the railroads adopted the safety features required by the European nations. In addition, most workers had seen their wages cut by as much as a quarter in the previous two years, despite the fact that their employers continued to pay dividends to stockholders. Within a few weeks, a hundred thousand railroad workers were out on strike.

The employers immediately called on the state governments for aid in their struggle with the workers. Most states obliged by sending the militia to protect strikebreakers and keep the workers out of the rail yards. But several militia companies refused to cooperate. When the commander of the Reading, Pennsylvania, militia ordered his men to fire on striking workers, the militia unanimously refused to shoot their fellow citizens. The governor of Pennsylvania learned from this encounter to send militia from different cities to put down strikes. The middle-class Philadelphia militia seemed to actually welcome the opportunity to fire on striking workers in Pittsburgh, killing twenty people. But what no one expected is that the workers would fight back. The militia were chased out of town, the railroad yards destroyed, and most of the tracks in the area torn up. Pittsburgh suffered forty deaths and $2 million in property damage.

A sense of terror gripped much of the country's leadership, a real fear that the United States was teetering on the brink of chaos. Many newspapers charged that the strikes were part of a communist conspiracy, while President Rutherford B. Hayes called the

16. Losee v. Buchanan et al., 51 N.Y. 476, 484 (1873).

railroad strikes an "insurrection."¹⁷ The railroads called on the governors of nine states to demand federal troops to put down this "domestic insurrection." President Hayes obliged by sending the U.S. Army to see that the trains ran on time, protecting trains and rail yards, and imposing martial law on cities like Pittsburgh. The first national strike was crushed by this demonstration of federal force.

A total of one hundred people had been killed during this strike. When it was over, management fired hundreds of workers and blacklisted them from further employment with any railroad. Even Allan Pinkerton, whose detective agency provided the spies and enforcers who so effectively undermined the efforts of workers to organize unions throughout the late nineteenth century, felt "a close sympathy" for the strikers, who had suffered many wrongs and been much ignored, though he felt that strikes had no place in the United States. Others were far less sympathetic, some newspaper editors calling for the vote to be taken from workers. Even Christian magazines called for violence against the workers. An editorial in the Congregationalist Independent *of New York stated, "If the club of the policeman knocking out the brains of the rioter will answer, then well and good; but if it does not promptly meet the exigency, then bullets and bayonets, canister and grape" are called for.¹⁸ Public figures from the liberal editor of the* Nation, *Edwin L. Godkin, to the conservative secretary of war, felt that the U.S. Army should be used as a national police force to suppress strikes that threatened to disrupt the country's security.¹⁹ Allan Pinkerton clearly preferred that the suppression of strikes remain privatized, a position with which Congress remained sympathetic.*

Allan Pinkerton on Putting Down the Great Strike of 1877

I must confess to a close sympathy with workingmen of all classes. For quite a portion of my life I have been a laborer, while all my life I have been a workingman. I believe I can truly appreciate the struggles and trials of the intelligent laborer, and well understand the rigorous barriers that often hem him in. I also believe it cruelly unjust for any body of men, or portion of society, to hold him and his little world of labor and sacrifice and few pleasures so thoroughly at arm's length, as though it were an unclean thing to touch or to consider. To this miserable and too frequent custom it is most certain that we are indebted for a measure of the turbulent viciousness of what are termed the laboring classes.

---

17. R. B. Hayes, Proclamation, July 18, 1877, Proclamation, July 21, 1877. Proclamation, July 23, 1877, all in James D. Richardson, ed., *A Compilation of the Messages and Papers of the Presidents* (Washington: U.S. Government Printing Office, 1898) 7: 447-49.
18. Robert V. Bruce, *1877: Year of Violence* (Indianapolis: Bobbs. Merrill, 1959), 313.
19. "The Rioters and the Regular Army," *Nation* 25 (August 9, 1877): 85-86.

But, on the other hand, I would as rigorously hold the workingman to his duty. With the numberless opportunities for the bettering of one's condition, which, in these times, every country, and particularly this country, affords, there is no excuse for other than a straightforward, honest, and honorable course on the part of any man, capitalist or laborer. No man who is able to labor at all, is unable, by persistent honesty and persistent frugality, to, in time, secure a fair competence and a fair measure of life's amenities and pleasures. . . .

A good deal has been written and said regarding the causes of our great strike of '77. To my mind they seem clear and distinct. For years, and without any particular attention on the part of the press or the public, animated by the vicious dictation of the International Society [Communists], all manner of labor unions and leagues have been forming. No manufacturing town, nor any city, has escaped this baleful influence. Though many of these organizations have professed opposition to communistic principles, their pernicious influence has unconsciously become powerful among them. . . . For years we have been recovering from the extravagances of the war period. Labor has gradually, but surely, been becoming cheaper, and its demand less. Workingmen have not economized in the proportion that economy became necessary. Want and penury followed. Workingmen consequently have become discontented and embittered. They have been taught steadily, as their needs increased, that they were being enslaved and robbed, and that all that was necessary for bettering their condition was a general uprising against capital. So that when, under the leadership of designing men, that great class of railroad employees—than whom no body of workingmen in America were ever better compensated—began their strike, nearly every other class caught the infection, and by these dangerous communistic leaders were made to believe that the proper time for action had come. . . .

THE TROUBLES AT PITTSBURG. . . .

After ascertaining that such action was of extreme necessity, in June, '77, the Pennsylvania Railroad Company announced a reduction of ten per cent. upon the wages of all officers and employees receiving more than one dollar a day, the same to take effect on and after the first of July following. This order and the subsequent introduction of what is known as the "double-headers," or freight trains composed of a larger number of cars than the single train, and drawn by two engines, which economized labor, and consequently displaced a few employees, constituted the "grievances" which resulted in the reorganization of the Trainmen's Union, and eventually the strike and its terribly disastrous results.

No sooner had these measures for economy in the company's manage-

ment gone into effect, than the class, and only the class—these utterly worthless employees—referred to, began their secret meetings and their seditious efforts. But it is an established fact that the great body of employees accepted
the reduction with good grace; and the charge made against Col. Scott and
other officers of the road, that they were inaccessible and treated all employees with cruel indifference, however respectfully they might offer a petition or
remonstrance, is found to be false when it is known that a joint committee
from the Brotherhood of Locomotive Engineers and Brotherhood of Locomotive Firemen, in June, and just subsequent to the proposed reduction, waited
upon Col. Scott and were most courteously received by that gentleman, who
took the trouble to explain the most minute details of the company's business. He fully demonstrated not only the justice of, but the extreme necessity
for, the reduction; which so impressed the committee that they gave in writing an unqualified indorsement to this imperative policy, and pledged, also in
writing, for themselves and the important classes which they represented, a
most hearty cooperation and loyalty.

In fact, more than three-fourths of the employees of the road, and immeasurably the most deserving, capable, and valuable class of its employees,
had received the reduction in an appreciative and manly way; and the management had every reason to believe that the most harmonious relations still
existed. But all this time factious and unruly elements were plotting schemes
of revenge. They had not the candor to utter a manly protest or approach the
president of the company which gave them and their families the means of
support, in a respectful and decorous manner; but, traitorous to their own
and their employer's interests, they drank in the accursed communistic spirit
of the times, and drew together a desperate body of men with *professed* principles of reciprocal help and brotherhood ministrations, but really for riot and
revenge.... [This] pernicious order ... soon extended to the Baltimore and
Ohio Railroad, with the results that have been previously mentioned. From
Pittsburg it pushed its slimy length back over the Fort Wayne road towards
Chicago; it crept along the sinuous windings of the Allegheny Valley; and to
the East it trailed over the grand mountains and beautiful valleys along the
Pennsylvania road, spreading everywhere the seeds of disaffection and riot....

At noon of Thursday, July 19th, the unexpected blow was struck; and, il-
lustrative of the powerlessness of our State laws and imbecile inefficiency of
local authorities, a handful of men, who might have been subdued by a determined corporal's guard, were permitted to precipitate what led to the most
deplorable riots in history. Freight conductor Ryan's train was nearly ready
for starting out. The "crew" had been assigned and the engineers were only
waiting for the signal to unloose their iron steeds, when, after a short conference among the brakemen, the conductor was informed that they would not

go out with the train. He, as was his duty, promptly passed the dreaded word to the dispatcher. Two yard crews of brakemen were then asked to take the train, but the intimidation had begun, and they refused. They were very properly discharged, but very improperly permitted to remain and help swell the rapidly-increasing crowd of strikers, for now the strike had begun.

So swiftly did this striking fever run through the worst element of the trainmen lingering about, that scarcely an hour had elapsed before a crowd of fully five hundred employees had gathered, and all efforts at starting trains proved ineffectual. The first brute force used by the strikers was near Twenty-eighth Street, about one o'clock in the afternoon, when D. M. Watt, Superintendent Pitcairn's chief clerk, ordered an employee to descend from a shifting engine and change the switch so as to permit of the passage of a freight train. The employee refused, fearing he would be killed. Thereupon Mr. Watt sprang from the engine, and as he attempted to change the switch, the entire crowd rushed upon him, some of the leaders shouting in an extremely heroic way: "Boys, we'll die right here!" "Bread or blood!" and the like. One brute, a yardman named Thomas McCall, struck Mr. Watt a terrific blow, felling him to the earth. This action dismayed the strikers somewhat, and enabled the inefficient police to arrest a few of the most harmless, as usual. But the crowd soon rallied, and, with increased numbers, moved up and down the tracks, beating and stoning loyal employees from their work, and reenacting that old and savage labor tragedy which, for the last century, has cursed both continents. In the meantime, notices signed by the "President" of the Trainmen's Union had been posted along the line from the Union Depot to East Liberty, a distance of nearly six miles, calling on all the members of that organization to meet at Phoenix Hall, on Eleventh Street, at seven o'clock in the evening; and around these, excited groups were constantly gathering to discuss the all-absorbing topic, while hundreds of others, comprising the more daring of the men, carrying all before them like a storm, moved out to East Liberty stock-yards, compelling the train and yard men there to join with them.

Quick work was now made, and a sudden end put to all order and authority. Trains were run upon side-tracks and left there. Then matters on the main tracks were taken in hand, and all trains east or west were stopped. Those coming from the east were allowed to proceed into the city after the situation had been explained and their crews so thoroughly threatened and otherwise frightened that they sacredly promised to "go out," or join the strikers, as soon as Pittsburg proper had been reached, which under the circumstances they invariably did. It was necessary that some of the stock-trains be pulled up to the sidings to be unloaded; but the strikers would in no instance permit of the use of the company's engines, that work being done only by engines from the Pan Handle road, and though no detention was suf-

fered by passenger trains. Thus the work went on for the day, and the numberless tracks and sidings grew black with closely-packed cars, which were
destined, many of them, never to be put to use again.

At night a strong guard of strikers patroled the tracks, and complete possession had been taken of the Western Division of the road, while at Phoenix
Hall, on Eleventh Street, there were gathered four times the number that
could gain admission. . . .

This meeting was unusually orderly and quiet. But it was the ominous
quiet that surely tells of the coming storm. The result of the meeting was the
following ultimatum to the company:

First—We, the undersigned committee, appointed by the Western Division
of the Pennsylvania Railroad Company, do hereby demand from said company through its proper officers, the wages as per department of engineers,
firemen, conductors, and brakemen received prior to June 1, 1877.

Second—That each and every employee who has been dismissed for taking
part in the present strike or meetings held prior to or during said strike be
restored to their position, as held prior to the strike.

Third—That the classification of each of said departments be abolished
now and forever, and that hereafter engineers and conductors receive the
same wages as received by engineers and conductors of the highest class prior
to June 1, 1877.

Fourth—That the running of double trains be abolished, except coal trains.

Fifth—That each and every engine, whether road or shifting, shall have its
own fireman.

At nine o'clock the same evening the strikers at the outer depot decided
to stop the arrival of Pan Handle trains. One was heard coming thundering
along, when fully five hundred men quickly formed on either side and across
the track, but as it approached they discovered that it was an express train,
and it was allowed to pass, amid jeers and yells. A half hour later another
train was heard, and the line was formed again, as promptly and solidly as
with a battalion of soldiers. It was really an interesting sight—almost a study
for a picture. Nearly every man had unconsciously assumed an attitude of defiance, and they stood there like grim and silent statues. But the moment it
was made certain that the coming train was of freight, a deafening yell went
up from the crowd, which was answered by signal shrieks from the engine
like a series of shrill echoes screamed back from some bold mountain side.
In vain did the engineer excitedly sound the whistle and ring the bell. The
strikers stood there like a wall. It was of no avail. The train slackened, and
finally came to a halt after about fifty of the men had boarded it. Then they
climbed upon the engine and tender in every conceivable spot where a foot-
hold could be secured, brandishing clubs and shaking their fists at the poor

fellows in the cab, while the engineer, utterly nonplussed and aghast, stammered out: "Why, boys, God knows this's the first I've seen of all this!" With this the Pan Handle road became helpless with the other lines. This event and another fruitless though determined attempt to move trains, which occurred within the city at ten o'clock, and the weak efforts of Sheriff Fife to disperse the strikers at Twenty-eighth Street, closed the exciting day. But I cannot pass the latter subject without referring to the criminal weakness of the officers in and for the city of Pittsburg and the County of Allegheny. Right here were lost the opportunities to prevent the Pittsburg riot. . . .

All Sheriff Fife did . . . was to go to Twenty-eighth Street and solemnly order the strikers to disperse. No one could blame these rough fellows for laughing and jeering at him. Almost any other person would have considered so impotent an action really laughable. But he "remained on the ground until nearly three o'clock in the morning!" as the dispatches told the public. It would have been pleasanter for him to have remained in bed, and quite as serviceable. While "remaining on the ground" he forwarded a message to Governor Hartranft, explaining how he had strenuously labored to put down the riot; that he had not the "means at command;" and urging the Governor to exercise his authority in calling out the militia to suppress the lawlessness. . . .

Everything being in readiness, the order for the advance was given, and by columns of four, like veterans on drill, the retreat was begun. . . .

The crowd increased and increased. . . . The same thieves and thugs, loafers and garroters, tramps and communists—not all of them, but very many of them—were there, and began to gain upon the soldiers, as well as swiftly increase in numbers; while the same oaths, and threats, and jeers began to be heard. It was the same fiendish crowd, and they had come together like a swift breath of pestilence to do over and over again their same fiendish work.

Suddenly a little puff of smoke shot out from a second-story window, followed by a ringing report and a quick cry from a soldier who had been struck, but not dangerously wounded.

Back along the column came the officers, exhorting the men to be patient and not return the fire.

The speed of the troops increased. The energy of the mob redoubled. The pistol-shot from the window seemed almost a signal, for instantly afterwards, from along the crowd's front, several more shots were fired, and but a few minutes more had elapsed, until from behind every lamppost, over every hydrant-head, and from out every door and window, shot the flame, shot the smoke, the flame and the bullets.

Soldiers fell; and now their comrades returned the fire, while, as in every other instance, the disorganized, howling mob received far the worst punishment. Some of the wounded soldiers would escape with their lives through the devices, and at the personal risk, of humane people along the street who gave them help and shelter. Others, not so fortunate, were heartlessly murdered when too helpless for defense.

On and on the soldiers fled, for now the street had become a defile of death. Soon a street-car was overtaken, the horses unhitched, and dozens of strong men gathered behind and pushed it on up the track, while armed members of the mob, accompanied by armed policemen, entered the car and fired upon the troops through the windows. Many hand-to-hand conflicts took place, in which the troops, as a rule, were beaten back in greater precipitancy upon the column, adding fresh impetus of flight to the panic-stricken soldiers and fresh vigor and fury to the mob.

In this way the rout went on—the crowd behind receiving additions at every-cross-street, court, and alley, the soldiers harder pressed and in a more desperate, pitiable condition.

At last the [Federal] Arsenal came in view. . . .

Reaching the Arsenal, General Brinton halted his fainting, half-starved troops, and begged of Major Buffington, the commandant, for their admission, protection, and for food.

But the red tape that seems to be wound tightly around the throats of all governments, republican as well as monarchical, shut the strong gates in the faces of these men who had been sent into danger by the highest authority of the State and had simply done their duty.

The continued retreat from this, the most disgraceful of scenes during the Pittsburg riot, was simply one grand rush for some place of safety.

Each soldier ran on his own account, but they all kept a general direction, the mob, having spent its fury, falling back, and in time returning to the city with shouts of victory, not forgetting to cheer the generous and gallant United States troops at the Arsenal for their brave rebuff of the hunted and dismayed militia.

The latter made no halt until the shady grounds at Claremont—nearly twelve miles away—were reached, when the Philadelphians sank upon the ground, nearly famished, and utterly exhausted, where they slept the rest of the day and away into the night. . . .

THE END AT PITTSBURG. . . .

. . . Within five days from the breaking out of the riot, Governor Hartranft, who arrived from the West on Tuesday evening, had brought together nearly six thousand troops. . . . For a week the city of Pittsburg resembled a military post during the early days of the war. . . .

The strike really ended Sunday, July 29th, when the first freight train, af-

ter the abandonment of work by the trainmen, was moved. . . . As soon as this
train had been successfully started, others soon followed; and all day long the
tracks, from the ruins of the Union Depot away out to East Liberty, presented a most animated appearance, and away into the night the long-delayed
trains were being made up and despatched.

So ended the strike at Pittsburg. What had seemed a revolution resulted
in a most imbecile fiasco. All the striking trainmen on roads centering at this
city, as soon as the first train began moving, made a precipitate rush for their
old places, and as much excitement was developed through the fear of losing
them as had been shown during the first days of the strike in defying the
roads and trampling upon all authority.

Source: Allan Pinkerton, *Strikers, Communists, Tramps and Detectives* (New York, 1878), 15, 23–
24, 216–24, 254, 257–60, 282–83.

THE HAYMARKET TRIALS

In 1889 Michael J. Schaack published Anarchy and Anarchists, *a combination memoir
of his experiences as a Chicago police captain and history of anarchism. In 1886 Schaack
had been responsible for investigating the notorious Haymarket bombing. On May 4,
1886, anarchist speakers delivered inflammatory speeches to a crowd of two thousand
Chicagoans gathered to protest police violence against striking workers. The peaceful
meeting had mostly ended, leaving only a few hundred stragglers, when 170 police officers
arrived. The police demanded that the remaining protesters disperse, but before they could,
a bomb exploded, killing a Chicago police officer. The police responded with gunfire, killing
some of their own men as well as civilians. Seven officers died as a result of wounds
received that day.*

*In the days that followed, Chicago police rounded up scores of radicals. A grand jury
indicted ten of them for the bombing. Eight went to trial, though no witness could testify
that any had thrown the fatal bomb. State's Attorney Julius Grinnell claimed that the
protesters' speeches had caused the bombing. In other times and in different circumstances
defense attorneys would have easily brushed aside such a specious argument. In 1886,
though, labor strife, anarchist rhetoric, and dynamite violence had combined to create an
overheated, almost hysterical environment. The jury swiftly convicted all eight. Judge
Joseph Gary sentenced seven to death. Governor Richard Oglesby commuted two of the
sentences to life in prison. One convicted man committed suicide. The remaining four,
Albert Parsons, August Spies, George Engel, and Adolph Fischer, perished on the gallows.*

*Michael Schaack's memoir tells how he organized a "red squad" of police officers
operating outside the normal bureaucracy and, often, outside the law, to gather information on "reds," or Communists. The excerpt here begins at the police station nearest
the Haymarket bombing just minutes after the explosion. Schaack's account presents*

violence as spectacle and implicitly calls on his readership to become a "public" energized to strike down its enemies. The late nineteenth century also launches the era of the detective, and Schaack presents himself as America's premier sleuth, an operative of the middle class uncovering public enemies. Schaack shamelessly quotes Grinnell as calling him "one of the greatest detectives in America." The Chicago police never solved the crime.

Michael J. Schaack Remembers "the Red Terror" in Chicago, 1886

The scene at the Desplaines Street Station was one which would appal [*sic*] the stoutest heart. Every available place in the building was utilized, and one could scarcely move about the various rooms without fear of accidentally touching a wound or jarring a fractured limb. In many instances mangled Anarchists were placed side by side with injured officers. The floors literally ran with blood dripping and flowing from the lacerated bodies of the victims of the riot. The air was filled with moans from the dying and groans of anguish from the wounded. As the news had spread throughout the city of the terrible slaughter, wives, daughters, relatives and friends of officers as well as of Anarchists, who had failed to report at home or to send tidings of their whereabouts, hastened to the station and sought admission. Being refused, these set up wailing and lamentations about the doors of the station, and the doleful sounds made the situation all the more sorrowful within.

Everything in the power of man was done to alleviate the suffering and to make the patients as comfortable as possible. Drs. Murphy, Lee and Henrotin, department physicians, were energetically at work, and, with every appliance possible, administered comparative relief and ease from the excruciating pains of the suffering. The more seriously wounded, when possible, were taken to the Cook County Hospital. Throughout the night following the riot, the early morning and the day succeeding, the utmost care was given the patients, and throughout the city for days and weeks the one inquiry, the one great sympathy, was with reference to the wounded officers and their condition. The whole heart of the city was centered in their recovery. Everywhere the living as well as the dead heroes were accorded the highest praise. The culprits who had sought to subvert law and order in murder and pillage were execrated on all hands. For days and weeks, the city never for a moment relaxed its interest. . . .

It is impossible to say how many of the Anarchists were killed or wounded. As soon as they were in a condition to be moved, those in the Desplaines Street Station were turned over to their relatives and friends. The Anarchists have never attempted to give a correct list, or even an approximate estimate, of the men wounded or killed on their side. The number, however, was largely in excess of that on the side of the police. After the moment's bewilderment, the officers dashed on the enemy and fired round after round. Being good marksmen, they fired to kill, and many revolutionists must have gone home, either assisted by comrades or unassisted, with wounds that resulted fatally or maimed them for life. . . . It is known that many secret funerals were held from Anarchist localities in the dead hour of night. For many months previous to the Haymarket explosion, the Anarchists had descanted loudly on the destructive potency of dynamite. One bomb, they maintained, was equivalent to a regiment of militia. A little dynamite, properly put up, could be carried in a vest pocket and used to destroy a large body of police. They probably reasoned that if it was known that many more of their number had fallen than on the side of the police, it would not only tend to diminish the faith of their adherents in the real virtues of dynamite, but would prove that the police were more than able to cope with the Social Revolution. . . . The public is not, therefore, likely ever to know how many of their number suffered. . . .

About January, 1887, one of my privates [a private detective] informed me that there was a place on Clybourn Avenue where the Anarchists were accustomed to hold private meetings. He said that he could not get in as yet, and I told him to pick up some one whom he could work handily. He must first form the man's acquaintance, and then hang around the saloons in the neighborhood and read the *Arbeiter-Zeitung*. I gave him one of John Most's books and made him wear a red necktie. I advised him also to get about half drunk, sing the Marseillaise and curse the police. By so doing, I told him, it would not be long before he would find a partner. . . .

For the first couple of weeks, the newly formed friends of this detective would not take him to any of their meetings. I advised him not to make inquiries. As soon as they thought him all right, they would speak themselves. Within three weeks some one took him to a meeting and vouched for him as being true to their cause. At the first meeting he attended he saw that he was as intelligent as any one of them, and so he delivered a short speech. That captured them, and they pronounced him a good man. They asked him to call again at their next meeting, and he promised that he would be on hand. . . . I . . . told him that at the next meeting he should ascertain the size of the room and notice whatever furniture might be there and where it was standing. This he did. He made a small diagram. I then detailed a man to take a position in the basement at several meetings. . . . I sent for Officer Schuettler. He responded promptly, and I told him what I wanted done. He said that he was ready to carry out my instructions. I told him to go and buy a one-inch auger, and next procure a funnel with the large end the circumference of a saucer, and a pipe about four inches long. After an hour's absence he returned with the desired articles. I handed him several keys with which to open the door, showed him the plat, and told him where to bore a hole. I also told him to secure a cork and plug up the hole after he was through. . . . A few days subsequently the officer reported back, and his face was wreathed in smiles.

"You must have had success," I said.

"Yes, everything worked like a charm."

He handed me a good report and remarked that it contained the most important part of the business done by the meeting. He suggested that he ought to have some one with him so that he could secure all the details. For the next meeting I sent another officer with him, and this man had a dark lantern. Schuettler would listen, and as he whispered the words and sentiments of the speakers, the other officer, with the aid of the light from his lantern, would commit them to paper. The next morning I received a full report of all the transactions.

This sort of work was kept up for several months, and during all this time I was kept pretty well informed of the secret movements of the old North Side groups. At the beginning of all their meetings the speakers would declare their wish to see Judge Gary, Mr. Grinnell, all the officers working on the case and myself hung. They generally closed with a promise to kill all capitalists and blow up all the newspaper buildings. . . .

Source: Michael J. Schaack, *Anarchy and Anarchists: A History of the Red Terror and the Social Revolution in America and Europe* (Chicago: F. J. Schulte, 1889), 149, 155, 210–12.

CLASS WAR IN COEUR D'ALENE

Labor unions and strikes are usually associated with an urban environment, but some of the most violent clashes between labor and management occurred in the West, most particularly in the mining industry. For instance, in 1891, the Mine Owners Protective Association of Coeur d'Alene, Idaho, announced that all wages would be cut by a quarter. The miners' union, the Western Federation of Miners, refused to accept this new contract. Management locked out the workers, declared that their companies would never hire a union member, and brought in nonunion laborers and armed guards supplied by the Pinkerton detective agency. Workers and guards confronted each other for nearly a year, until July 1892, when a Pinkerton agent shot and killed a union member. Workers retaliated by blowing up the guards' barracks, killing one and wounding a score more. The union then drove the nonunion workers out of town, killing several and injuring scores in the process, as described here by the Spokane Weekly Review. *After two days of near civil war in Coeur d'Alene, the governor of Idaho declared a state of emergency and sent in the National Guard. The Guard rounded up union members and put them in mass detention centers, where they were held without charges. But the union refused to give in, and at the end of 1892 the mine owners made a deal with the union for a new contract, one that management violated a few years later.*

The *Spokane Weekly Review* Reports on the Violence in Coeur d'Alene, 1892

WAR BREAKS OUT IN THE COEUR D'ALENE

Wallace, Idaho, July 11—This has been the most exciting day in the history of Coeur d'Alene. The hitherto peaceful canyons of these mountains have echoed with the sharp and deadly report of the rifle, and the cliffs of Canyon Creek have reverberated with the detonations of bomb and dynamite used in the destruction of valuable property.

The long-dreaded conflict between the forces of the strikers and the non-union men who have taken their places has come at last. As a result five men are known to be dead and 16 are already in the hospital; the Frisco mill on Canyon Creek is in ruins; the Gem mine has surrendered to the strikers, the arms of its employees have been captured, and the employers themselves have been ordered out of the country. Flushed with the success of these victories the turbulent element among the strikers are preparing to move upon other strongholds of the non-union men and will probably show their hand at Wardner tomorrow.

About 6 o'clock this morning a non-union miner from the Gem mine . . . was fired upon at a point near the Frisco mine. He ran back to the Gem mine and afterward died of his wound.

This shot seemed to be the signal for the non-union forces, who quickly gathered in considerable numbers and marched upon the mine, a lively firing being kept up by both sides. The attacking forces, however, were too strong for the besieged forces, and to avoid further bloodshed the mine was surrendered, the arms given up and the non-union men were marched down the canyon and sent out of the district.

In the meantime a similar attack was made upon the property of the Helena and San Francisco company at the same place, and with a like result. The men in the mine and mill surrendered, and the besiegers then went up the hill and sent down a lot of dynamite on the tramway, expecting it to explode and wreck the mill. They did this in revenge for the severe manner in which Mr. Esler has spoken of their cause and themselves, but the first attempt failed. They then shot a bomb down the iron water flume, and when it struck the bottom there was a tremendous explosion that wrecked the mill and destroyed $125,000 worth of property.

After this a sort of truce was held and hostilities were suspended. The arms of the non-union men were stacked and placed in charge of one man, from each side, but they were afterward taken by the strikers, the mine owners claiming in violation of the agreement.

The dead, wounded, and prisoners were then placed aboard a special train and taken down to Wallace, and Canyon Creek is now in complete control of the strikers, and no one is permitted to invade the district. . . .

The arms belonging to the Frisco and Gem mines were placed in charge of Captain Human and J. S. Ears, but members of the union held them up and took the arms away.

There are no scabs on Canyon creek and the miners' union are masters of the situation. A few hundred of the union men are now in Wallace, and some of them are armed. It is thought that there are a few bodies still in the wreck of the Frisco mill. . . .

W. W. Wood, a refugee from the fury of the union strikers, arrived in the city last evening. . . . Wood . . . was one of the 90 men at work at the Frisco mill when the strikers besieged it. It was his lot to share in the terrible explosion there when the union men attempted to sacrifice the lives of every one in the building. . . .

"I went up to the Coeur d'Alene country about a week ago. I was out of work and needy, and was glad to get hold of anything I could. . . . They hired me and sent me to the Frisco mill to do shoveling work. The first indication I had of approaching trouble was on Sunday night, when two boxes of arms were received at the mill for distribution among the scabs, as the union men are pleased to call us. . . . I awoke just about dawn on Monday morning and looked out. The first thing I saw was about 50 armed men on the hills around us. . . . For the first time I really felt scared, but what could I do? I was there, and I proposed to stay there with the boys.

"The men around us drew nearer; then commenced a fusilade of shot like a hailstorm. There must have been 50 shots fired before any of us returned a shot. This I'll swear to. The shot continued to pour in upon us through the roof and through the windows. . . .

"After a while some of the union men withdrew. . . . They fixed up a car with giant powder and started it down the grade toward the mill. . . . I tell you there were some awful thoughts gliding through our minds at that moment, as the roar of the explosion reached our ears and shook the building. The most of us took to the bottom of the mill in search of places of temporary safety; we didn't know what was coming and expected that every minute would be our last. Hardly had we partially recovered from the first explosion,

when crash went the buildings over our heads—flat to the ground as if lev-
eled by an earthquake. I scarcely realized myself alive for a moment. The
strikers had floated giant powder down the spout that leads to the flume.
Just as soon as it struck the water wheel it went off.

"We all rushed to the new building that was standing beside the mill and
was untouched. . . . When we reached there we hung out a flag of truce and
they stopped firing. Then they ran us down to the miners' union hall at Gem
and kept us there until the Gem had surrendered. Then we were shipped to
Wallace in boxcars and sent home from there by the mine-owners. . . ."

The blackest feature of the direful conflict in the Coeur d'Alene was the
tragedy enacted at the Old Mission on the Coeur d'Alene River. . . . After driving many of the fugitive non-union men into the canyon and the river the
desperate and impassioned strikers followed them up and shot them down
like deer. Among those shot down was Foreman Monaghan of the Gem mine,
who was coming out with his family. The family was spared, but Monaghan
was run into the bush and shot through the back. He was picked up yesterday morning and taken back to the mines. It is thought he will die. . . . The
non-union men had been entirely disarmed and were at the mercy of their
pursuers. The boat that came down the lake yesterday picked up 20 more of
the fugitives who had taken to the river and bush. They tell tales of frightful
cruelty. Some of them were beaten with revolvers and many were robbed of
all their valuables.

When it became known Tuesday night that many of the non-union men
had been driven into the wilderness, Mr. Lane Gilliam was dispatched to
Coeur d'Alene City by Messrs. Campbell & Finch, with directions to purchase
supplies and go out into Fourth of July canyon to meet the fugitives. Yesterday a telephone message was received from him at Wolf Lodge, saying that it
was reported that 12 bodies had been found already, and that the bloodthirsty
strikers were following up the fugitives and shooting them wherever they
could be found. Mr. Gilliam asked for further directions, but Mr. Campbell
answered that he was on the ground and should use his own discretion. It is
reported last night that he had returned to Coeur d'Alene City. . . .

Wallace, Idaho, July 12 . . . The men from the Gem and Frisco mines were
paid off today and they have nearly all left. The saloons were closed nearly all
day, and the town has been very quiet. A special [train] has left for Saltese,
supposed to go after the troops. This afternoon the union men from Burke
and Gem went home and then came back. There is a rumor that an armed
body of men are on the hills east of town, supposed to be watching for the
troops. The funeral of the men killed on Monday will take place Wednesday.
Two of the wounded men died at the hospital last night.

Sheriff Cunningham made a show of authority today. He started out to raise a posse of 300 citizens, and subpenaed many people supposed to be in sympathy with the mine-owners, but the citizens failed to respond, whereupon the sheriff very valiantly went all alone to Wardner, where of course he could do nothing.

Source: *Spokane Weekly Review,* July 14, 1892.

THE ASSASSINATION OF FRANK STEUNENBERG

In 1896, Idaho's labor unions joined with other reformers to elect Frank Steunenberg governor. But in 1899, when the Mine Owners Protective Association of Coeur d'Alenes broke its contract with the workers, Steunenberg sent state troops to crush his former supporters in the Western Federation of Miners (WFM). Six years later, Steunenberg was assassinated, and many immediately suspected revenge by the WFM. The assassin, Harry Orchard, was caught and confessed, but he denied union involvement until the famous Pinkerton agent James McParland, who had helped break the Molly Maguires in Pennsylvania, offered a deal to save Orchard from the gallows. Orchard confessed to a whole series of murders carried out on union orders, identifying the leadership of the WFM as the instigators of the Steunenberg assassination. Pinkerton agents kidnapped three of these officials, including the union's president, and brought them to Idaho to stand trial for murder. Defended brilliantly by Clarence Darrow, all three were set free. Orchard, who died in prison in 1954, can only be relied on for the following description of the actual murder.

Harry Orchard on Making a Bomb, 1905

. . . Friday, I went to Nampa and thought I might get a chance to put the bomb under Governor Steunenberg's seat, if I found him on the train, as the train usually stops fifteen to twenty minutes at Nampa. I had taken the powder out of the wooden box, and packed it in a little, light, sheet-iron box with a lock on, and I had a hole cut in the top of this and a little clock on one side. Both this and the bottle of acid were set in plaster-Paris on the other side of the hole from the clock with a wire from the key which winds the alarm to the cork in the bottle. The giant-caps were put in the powder underneath this hole, and all I had to do was to wind up the alarm and set it and, when it went off, it would wind up the fine wire on the key, and pull out the cork, and spill the acid on the caps. I had this fitted in a little grip and was going to set it, grip and all, under his seat in the coach, if I got a chance. I went through the train when it arrived at Nampa, but did not see

Mr. Steunenberg, and the train was crowded, so I would not have had any chance, anyway. I saw Mr. Steunenberg get off the train at Caldwell, but missed him on the train.

I saw him again around Caldwell Saturday afternoon. I was playing cards in the saloon at the Saratoga, and came out in the hotel lobby at just dusk, and Mr. Steunenberg was sitting there talking. I went over to the post-office and came right back, and he was still there. I went up to my room and took this bomb out of my grip and wrapped it up in a newspaper and put it under my arm and went down-stairs, and Mr. Steunenberg was still there. I hurried as fast as I could up to his residence, and laid this bomb close to the gate-post, and tied a cord into a screw-eye in the cork and around a picket of the gate, so when the gate was opened, it would jerk the cork out of the bottle and let the acid run out and set off the bomb. This was set in such a way, that if he did not open the gate wide enough to pull it out he would strike the cord with his feet, as he went to pass in. I pulled some snow over the bomb after laying the paper over it, and hurried back as fast as I could.

I met Mr. Steunenberg about two and a half blocks from his residence. I then ran as fast as I could, to get back to the hotel if possible before he got to the gate. I was about a block and a half from the hotel on the foot-bridge when the explosion of the bomb occurred, and I hurried to the hotel as fast as I could. I went into the bar-room, and the bartender was alone, and asked me to help him tie up a little package, and I did, and then went on up to my room, intending to come right down to dinner, as nearly every one was in at dinner. . . .

Now, I cannot tell what came across me. I had some plaster-Paris and some chloride of potash and some sugar in my room, also some little bottles, and screw-eyes, and an electric flashlight, and I knew there might be some little crumbs of dynamite scattered around on the floor. I intended to clean the carpet, and throw this stuff that might look suspicious all away, and I had plenty of time. . . .

I was sitting in the saloon of the hotel in the afternoon and a stranger asked me to take a little walk, and pretended to be acquainted with me. I afterward learned this was Sheriff Brown, of Baker City, Ore. I told him he was mistaken, and he told me that they suspected me of having something to do with the assassination, and he said he told them that he thought he knew me. I told him I would go and see the sheriff at once, which I did and asked him if he wanted to see me, and he asked me if I was going away, and I told him I was not at the present, and he said we would have a talk after a while. I went over to the hotel and sat down and in a few minutes the sheriff came over and said he would have to arrest me. I told him all right, and he went off and came back in a few minutes, and told me the governor had ordered him to take charge of my things that were in my room, and he said he would parole me and I was not to leave town or the hotel. I have forgotten which.

Then I thought what a fool I had been to leave all those things in the room, when I had all kinds of chances to take them out, and had even let them get away with my gun. I would have made an attempt to get away that night, but I knew they were watching me, and again if I had succeeded in getting away from the hotel, it was bitter cold and the ground was covered with snow, and therefore I made no attempt to get away. I knew that they had organized a committee to investigate, and thought they might take me before this committee, and ask me to explain what I had such stuff for, and I was thinking how I would answer them if they did.

But they said nothing to me until the next day—Monday—about four o'clock, when the deputy sheriff asked me to go over to the district attorney's office, and when I went over there they said they would have to search me. This is the time I would have used my gun had I had it. They searched me and the sheriff read the warrant to me, and they said they wanted me to go to Boisé with them. We went over to the depot and waited a while, and then they took me up to the county jail at Caldwell.

Source: Harry Orchard, *The Confessions and Autobiography of Harry Orchard* (New York, 1907), 216–23.

THE LUDLOW MASSACRE

Management routinely relied on troops, public and private, to defeat strikes. The most notorious instance of the excess use of force by these soldiers came in Ludlow, Colorado, in 1914. The United Mine Workers, representing the vast majority of the mine workers in the region, appealed to the federal government in mid-1913 for aid in opening a discussion with the mine operators, promising to adhere to the results of arbitration. But the mine owners refused to even speak with the union's representatives. In September 1913 the workers went on strike, demanding the enforcement of state laws, especially those covering worker safety. Management immediately assembled a private army to protect the mines and defeat the strikers. On October 7, some of these "special deputies" fired on the workers' tent colony, killing a miner. Colorado's governor Elias Ammons sent in the state militia to maintain order. But as the following report of the United States Commission on Industrial Relations reveals, tensions increased as the militia acted on behalf of the mine owners. By the time President Woodrow Wilson sent in federal troops to restore order on April 29, 1914, more than seventy people had been killed, many of them children. On December 30, 1914, the workers admitted defeat and abandoned the strike.

Ludlow remained a symbol of the brutality of management toward striking workers and of the willingness of the state to commit acts of violence at the behest of the wealthy.

The United States Commission on Industrial Relations Charges the Colorado National Guard with Inciting Violence, 1913

Active in the management of the companies' armed guards were agents and officials of the notorious Baldwin–Felts Detective Agency of West Virginia. This agency already had a record for ruthless and brutal treatment of strikers, acquired during the coal strike in West Virginia. It was employed by the Colorado Fuel & Iron Company to aid in recruiting guards, to install and operate machine guns at the principal mines, and generally to supervise and assist the work of protecting the properties and suppressing the strike. Under direction of A. C. Felts and Detectives Belk and Belcher of this agency, an armored automobile was built at the shops of the Colorado Fuel & Iron Company at Pueblo. This car, christened "The Death Special," was mounted with a machine gun and used first by company guards and later by militia officers. . . .

On Oct. 7, 1913, there was an exchange of shots between a party of detectives and company agents and a party of strikers from the Ludlow tent colony. An attack by mine guards was made on the Ludlow tent colony Oct. 9, and one miner was killed. Following this attack, the Policy Committee of the Union sent a letter to the operators deploring the killing at Ludlow and asking their assistance and cooperation to prevent any similar occurrences in the future. No reply was received.

On Oct. 17 a party of mine guards rode to the Forbes tent colony in an armored automobile and opened fire on the colony with a machine gun. One man was killed and a boy was shot nine times through the leg. A few days later mine guards fired on strikers in the streets of Walsenburg and killed three union men. . . .

While the strikers and mine guards were waging guerrilla warfare on October 26 and 27, Governor Ammons of Denver was making a last effort to bring about a settlement. When his efforts failed he issued orders to Adjutant General Chase, calling out the militia and ordering General Chase to occupy the strike district. . . . On the following day the State troops took the field. The units sent into the field included cavalry, infantry and artillery. . . .

Good reason existed for a distrustful and suspicious attitude toward the State troops on the part of the strikers. Lieutenant Linderfelt had come to the strike zone as a representative of General Chase, . . . and instead of acting impartially had taken command of a detail of mine guards and deputies engaged in escorting strikebreakers from the Ludlow station to the mines. General Chase himself, nine years before, had commanded the State troops at Cripple Creek during the strike of metalliferous miners, and had been active in arresting strikers in large numbers and imprisoning them in the notorious "bull pens." Senator Patterson testified before this Commission that he was convinced at the time, and still believes, that the Mine Owners' Association, through its committee, really directed the operation of the troops. . . .

In spite of occasional acts of violence the strike zone remained comparatively quiet so long as Governor Ammons' orders against the use of troops to escort imported strikebreakers remained in effect. The Governor's policy in this respect had been vigorously opposed by the operators, and immediately after the calling out of the troops they began a campaign to coerce the Governor into withdrawing his original orders and directing the troops to act as escorts for imported strikebreakers. . . .

Governor Ammons himself testified that he rescinded his order to the militia, prohibiting the importation of strikebreakers, after all efforts to obtain a settlement had failed, . . . but believed it was justifiable in the effort to bring about a settlement. The change was effected by the issuance of general order No. 17 by General Chase from military headquarters in Trinidad on November 28. . . .

Mother Jones, a general organizer for the United Mine Workers, more than eighty years of age, arrived in Trinidad from El Paso on the morning of January 4, 1914. On her arrival she was met by militiamen and a few hours later deported to Denver. She returned on January 12th, was again arrested and taken to San Rafael Hospital, where she was held incommunicado for nine weeks. She was then sent to Denver and there released. A few days later, in March, she boarded a sleeper for Trinidad. She was awakened at Walsenburg before daylight and taken off the train by militiamen. They took her to an insanitary and rat-infested cell in the basement of the jail. She was kept there for twenty-six days and was then released, just before the Supreme Court was expected to act on a writ of habeas corpus. Mother Jones and attorneys for the strikers charged that she was released in order to prevent an opportunity by the Supreme Court to pass on the Moyer decision, by which the military authorities justified her imprisonment. Governor Ammons justified the arrest and imprisonment of Mother Jones on the ground that her speeches incited violence. She had been given to understand at all times during her imprisonment that she would be released if she would promise to leave the district and remain away. Mother Jones refused to make such a promise, claiming a constitutional right to stay in Trinidad. . . .

Lieutenant Linderfelt who was the actual, although not the nominal, commanding officer was the object of an intenser hatred from the strikers than any other man in the field. They had complained against him during the hearings of the Congressional Committee and there had been bad blood between him and Louis Tikas, leader of the Greek strikers in the Tent Colony. . . . Linderfelt had an intense hatred for the strikers and especially for the Greeks and southern Europeans who predominated in the Tent Colony at Ludlow. In spite of all this he seems to have been considered a particularly valuable officer for the work that the State had in hand. . . .

Thus, by April 20th the Colorado National Guard no longer offered even a pretense of fairness or impartiality, and its units in the field had degenerated into a force of professional gunmen and adventurers who were economically dependent on and subservient to the will of the coal operators. This force was dominated by an officer whose intense hatred for the strikers had been demonstrated, and who did not lack the courage and the belligerent spirit required to provoke hostilities. . . .

On April 20th militiamen destroyed the Ludlow Tent Colony, killing five men and one boy with rifle and machine gun fire and firing the tents with a torch.

Eleven children and two women of the colony who had taken refuge in a hole under one of the tents were burned to death or suffocated after the tents had been fired. During the firing of the tents, the militiamen became an uncontrolled mob and looted the tents of everything that appealed to their fancy or cupidity.

Hundreds of women and children were driven terror stricken into the hills or to shelter at near-by ranch houses. Others huddled for twelve hours in pits underneath their tents or in other places of shelter, while bullets from rifles and machine guns whistled overhead and kept them in constant terror.

The militiamen lost one man. He was shot through the neck early in the attack.

Three of the strikers killed at Ludlow were shot while under the guard of armed militiamen who had taken them prisoners. They included Louis Tikas, a leader of the Greek strikers, a man of high intelligence who had done his utmost that morning to maintain peace and prevent the attack and who had remained in or near the tent colony throughout the day to look after the women and children. Tikas was first seriously or mortally wounded by a blow on the head from the stock of a Springfield rifle in the hands of Lieutenant K. E. Linderfelt of the Colorado National Guard, and then shot three times in the back by militiamen and mine guards. . . .

Having burned and looted the tent colony and killed or driven off its inhabitants, the militiamen on the following day maintained a close watch in all directions and fired at all persons who showed themselves on the roads or nearby fields and hillsides. . . .

By Wednesday, April 22, two days after the Ludlow killings, armed and enraged strikers were in possession of the field from Rouse, twelve miles south of Walsenburg, to Hastings and Delagua, southwest of Ludlow. Within this territory of eighteen miles north and south by four or five miles east and west were situated many mines manned by superintendents, foremen, mine guards and strikebreakers. Inflamed by what they considered the wanton slaughter of their women, children and comrades, the miners attacked mine after mine, driving off or killing the guards and setting fire to the buildings. . . .

On Wednesday morning, or late in the preceding night, a party of about 200 armed strikers left the strikers' military colony near Trinidad and marched over the hills to Forbes, a mining camp which lies at the bottom of a canyon surrounded by steep hills. Most of the party were Greeks. Earlier in the strike, before the visit of the Congressional Committee, the strikers' tent colony at Forbes, situated on ground leased by them, had been twice destroyed by militiamen and mine guards, and on one occasion it had been swept by machine gun fire and a striker killed. . . . Bent on revenge for this earlier attack and for the killings at Ludlow, the strikers took up positions on the hills surrounding the mine buildings, and at daybreak poured a deadly fire into the camp. Nine mine guards and strikebreakers were shot to death and one striker was killed. The strikers fired the mine buildings, including a barn in which were thirty mules, and then withdrew to their camp near Trinidad.

Twenty-four hours later the federal troops arrived and all fighting ceased. . . .

In Denver every newspaper in the city denounced the militia for what was termed "the Ludlow massacre," and the reports of every newspaper showed varying degrees of sympathy with the strikers. . . .

It seems of vast importance that it should be understood how nearly the situation in Colorado approached a condition of absolute prostration of government and of actual revolution. This is apparent not so much in the record of battles and skirmishes fought and lives lost, as in the evidences given above of the state of public feeling. It was apparent in the frankness with which strike leaders admitted that they were gathering and distributing arms, in the open admissions made by many strikers that they or others whom they named had taken part in one or other of the various attacks, and in the refusal of the District Attorney of Las Animas County to take official notice of the killings which followed Ludlow, that the rules of "civilized warfare" formed the only criterion for public criticism of acts on either side during this period.

Enlightened public sentiment existing in Denver and other Colorado communities found itself helpless of effective expression. That expression, of course, should have come through the State. This leads to the direct causes of the failure of government and of all the horrors that resulted from it. Their consideration is vitally important because there is no guarantee that the same cause may not operate again in Colorado or other States, and that some day they may produce a situation far more serious even than that under discussion.

The State of Colorado through its military arm was rendered helpless to maintain law and order because that military arm had acted, not as an agent of the commonwealth, but as an agent of one of the parties in interest, as an agent, that is, of the coal operators, as against the strikers.

Source: George P. West, *United States Commission on Industrial Relations: Report on the Colorado Strike* (Washington, DC, 1915), 102–4, 107, 109, 111, 115, 122, 124–25, 126–27, 131, 133, 135–37.

THE HAWK'S NEST TUNNEL

In 1930 Union Carbide began work in West Virginia on a three-mile-long tunnel to divert water to a hydroelectric plant that in turn provided power to the company's petrochemical plant. Thousands of workers, most of them African Americans from the South, came to work on the Hawk's Nest tunnel.

The workers carved the tunnel from a mountain consisting mostly of pure silica. As early as 1915 doctors had identified the inhalation of silica dust as the cause of the deadly lung disease silicosis. The silica dust slowly suffocated the sufferer by coating the lungs and making it impossible to breathe. The management of Union Carbide knew of this disease and its causes, and always wore protective masks whenever entering the tunnel. But they saved money by not supplying their workers with masks; nor did they supply machines that would wet the tunnel face, which reduced the danger of silicosis. The workers were never informed of the dangers they faced, and when they began complaining of an inability to breathe, company doctors told them they had colds or pneumonia and prescribed worthless sugar pills. Ordinarily it took at least ten years to contract a case of silicosis; at Hawk's Nest the working conditions were so horrific that workers began dying after only one year. An employee who became too sick to work was fired and evicted from company housing.

By 1935 the death rate had risen to such levels as to attract wide public attention. The United Mine Workers demanded a congressional hearing, which was chaired by Indiana Democrat Glenn Griswold but guided by New York Republican Vito Marcantonio, a champion of workers' rights. The details seemed to many to be a tale from a foreign nation, such as the mass grave in which 169 workers were thrown "with cornstalks as their gravestones and with no other means of identification." Equally shocking was the Union Carbide manager who admitted, "I knew they was going to kill these niggers within 5 years, but I didn't know it was going to kill them so quick." Despite the hearings, some one to two thousand workers died without receiving any but the most minimal medical care, and Congress ignored the committee's recommendations.[20]

Hawk's Nest was just the most dramatic industrial tragedy in American history. Major corporations have occasionally acted to suppress knowledge of workplace-related diseases. For instance, the dangers of asbestos were first observed in the early twentieth century, with the Prudential Insurance Company receiving warnings from its medical statistician in 1918 that it should not offer coverage to individuals who worked with asbestos. Other insurance companies reached similar conclusions over the next few years, with their medical staffs observing a direct relation between asbestos and fibrosis of the lungs. Despite many studies conducted in the 1920s and 1930s, the Journal of the American Medical Association *did not publish an article on the problem until 1944, at that time stating that asbestos was a well-known cause of lung disease. Manufacturers of asbestos continued to fund studies that denied any danger from asbestos into the 1960s, assuring workers that no precautions were required.*[21]

The federal government took few steps to relieve the more harmful side effects of industrialism until 1970. In that year, Congress passed the Occupational Safety and Health Act creating the Occupational Safety and Health Administration (OSHA), with the power to investigate working conditions and order changes. And still the United States retained the highest fatality rate among the industrialized nations, with some ten thousand workplace deaths a year in the 1980s and another seventy thousand workers disabled on the job annually.[22]

Philippa Allen, Arthur Peyton, Rush Dew Holt, and John W. Finch Testify before the House of Representatives on America's Worst Industrial Disaster, 1936

STATEMENT OF PHILIPPA ALLEN [A SOCIAL WORKER WITH THE JACOB RIIS SETTLEMENT IN NEW YORK]

When we said we would like to talk to some of the men who had worked in the tunnel, Mr. Gibson called to a colored man who was passing, "Come here, George, and tell these ladies your story." And George Houston, a hard–

---

20. Martin Cherniack, *The Hawk's Nest Incident: America's Worst Industrial Disaster* (New Haven, CT: Yale University Press, 1986), 106–7.

21. Sheldon Rampton and John Stauber, *Trust Us, We're Experts!* (New York: Taucher/Putnam, 2001), 84–87.

22. William Serrin, "The Wages of Work," *Nation* 252, no. 3 (January 28, 1991): 80.

muscled, strongly built man of 23, came up to us walking very slowly and breathing with effort. He is in what the doctors call "the third stage" of silicosis, which means that he has not much longer to live. There were dark rings under his red-rimmed eyes, and when he climbs stairs, "It gets me to breathing so hard I have to lay down," he said. George worked only 48 weeks toting water, shoveling muck, or operating a drill in no. 1 heading of the Gauley Junction–Hawk's Nest tunnel, yet in that short time he breathed so much silica dust in the badly ventilated heading that the disease is rapidly destroying his lungs. . . .

They made the men work whether [they] wanted to do so or not. If the men were sick they made them work. They had a shack rouster named Mc-Cloud, who carried a gun. He was a deputy sheriff licensed by Fayette County, the license having been given on recommendation of the New Kanawha Power Co., and every morning he went up to the shacks and made the men to go work. McCloud threatened to jail men who would not work. When George's partner in the drill had his head cut off by falling rock, George did not want to go back into the tunnel, therefore, Deputy Sheriff McCloud arrested him. . . .

The majority of the men working on the tunnel, who died when the work was first started, were colored men. Perhaps because negroes catch lung diseases more easily than white men do. Mrs. Jones, who lives at Gauley River, told us that, "They buried them like they were burying hogs, putting two or three of them in a hole. . . ."

The story of the treatment of the colored men on the job at the tunnel is the same old one of discrimination against them as a race. Look at how much they were docked each week for the company doctor, 75 cents, which was 25 cents more than the white workers paid. They paid 75 cents weekly for the services of a doctor who never came to see them. "I sent in a call for the doctor for 4 weeks and he never came," George Houston said, "and I was still paying for him." . . .

Behind that record other facts stand.

First, the New Kanawha Power Co., Union Carbide & Carbon subsidiary, had geologists who had made test bores and who knew that the tunnel was to go through pure silica and then they enlarged the tunnel of project no. 2 from 32 to 46 feet at the location of the richest silica deposit. This was to enable them to take out more valuable silica rock, which was loaded on cars at the tunnel mouth and shipped on the C. & O. tracks down to Alloy, W. Va., plant of the Electro Metallurgical Co., where it was stored in the yard. It was so pure that it was used without refining. Knowing that this was pure silica, these contractors, with 30 years' experience, must have known that there was danger of silicosis for every man who worked in that tunnel. As

Attorney Bock of Townsend, Bock & Moore, Charleston, pointed out at the Donald Shay trial in Fayetteville, "the engineers of the New Kanawha Power Co. used masks when they went daily in the heading gathering samples of rock."

Second, the men did not know of the danger they were being sent into, because E. J. Perkins, superintendent of Rinehart & Dennis, did not post notices of the danger as required by law, so that the workers did not voluntarily assume the risk. Many of the workers came from agricultural communities in the South where the disease was unknown. They were not experienced tunnel men or hardrock miners who would have known. Their testimony is universal that it was not until the "ambulance was clanging day and night to the Coal Valley Hospital" that they realized there must be something wrong. Then, there were various diagnoses, one doctor finally hitting upon the word "tunnelitis." When the men realized the danger, it was too late. . . .

Again, the amount of dust could have been cut down by the use of wet drilling throughout. This was one of the most hotly fought points of difference at the Donald Shay trial, the executives testifying that there was wet drilling and the men who did the drilling testifying that most of it was dry drilling. Charley Jones told me of the men warning the foreman when the State inspectors came so that the dry drilling could be stopped. He did not realize then what was going on before his eyes: That it was going to destroy the lives of his three sons and his own health—the men were just "trying to keep the bosses in the clear," as he explained it to me. Here again is a disputed point where the final deadly results seem to arbitrate the differences in testimony. Only one man who worked in the tunnel, a foreman, testified for the company at the Shay trial—and he was racked with the silicosis cough as he testified.

As to the most important point in the neglected protection of the health of the men there was no difference of opinion. Clearly the men were not furnished respirators or masks. The men say that some of the engineers wore masks when they came into the tunnel, and one told me that he bought himself a mask when he saw the head men wearing them. But the 2,000 men who went into that silica tunnel in all ignorance of what it meant to them in the future were given no masks of any kind. There is absolutely no debate on that question. . . .

In summary, the men did not and could not have known of the danger they underwent. The company did know the danger they were sending these men to face. They deliberately failed to furnish sufficient protection. The results have been devastating in their deadliness. . . .

STATEMENT OF ARTHUR PEYTON [AN ENGINEER]

MR. PEYTON. . . . The contractor for whom I worked, the New Kanawha Power Co., furnished us with respirators, but the men who were working with Rinehart & Dennis were not furnished with respirators. The men who work for Rinehart & Dennis were not afforded any precautionary measures.

MR. RANDOLPH. Did you have any conversation with any engineer representing the contracting firm of Rinehart & Dennis about conditions in the tunnel?

MR. PEYTON. Yes; I have talked to the foremen.

MR. RANDOLPH. Did any foreman admit to you that conditions in the tunnel were bad?

MR. PEYTON. Yes. They just laughed about it, though.

MR. RANDOLPH. They did not take any measures to correct the conditions?

MR. PEYTON. They did not. . . .

MR. MARCANTONIO. What was the practice by the contractor when the mine inspectors were coming to the job?

MR. PEYTON. . . . [S]omebody would be kept watching in the tunnel to see when the inspectors came in. When the inspectors would come in the one . . . watching would inform the foremen and then the process of operation would be changed temporarily while the inspectors were in the mines. For instance, if the men were doing dry drilling at the time the inspectors came, they would stop gradually and go to wet drilling, and also they would get the gasoline motors out of the heading. . . . I have been in there several times when the inspectors came into the tunnel, and I have seen the men stop the dry drilling while the inspectors were there. . . .

MR. RANDOLPH. Did you or anybody else report that violation of mining laws to the Bureau of Mines?

MR. PEYTON. Yes; they received letters about using these motors in the place where they should not use them.

MR. RANDOLPH. Do you yourself feel that the Bureau of Mines of the State of West Virginia was negligent also?

MR. PEYTON. I do. . . .

STATEMENT OF HON. RUSH DEW HOLT, A SENATOR OF THE UNITED STATES FOR THE STATE OF WEST VIRGINIA

. . . [S]ilicosis was not a compensable disease, but in the 1933 session of our State legislature Senator Fleming introduced a bill to make it compensable, and the bill passed the Senate. The bill was referred to the house of delegates, . . . [where it] was defeated on a point of order that it did not have a properly constituted group. The bill was reintroduced in 1935 and finally passed on March 8, 1935. Before that time there was no compensation for these men so far as the workmen's compensation law of our State was concerned. These men only had the right to sue in court. I find that when they first took the cases up the company was not particularly interested in the passage of the silicosis bill, and it actually fought it, but when the supreme court of our State decided that the men had a right to sue I find that in the next session of the legislature the delegates from that section who had gone against making silicosis compensable turned and were then willing to make it compensable in order to protect the company.

. . . This statement is by a man who worked there as a foreman and who knows what he is talking about. Writing under the caption of Money Versus Human Life, this man said:

> On March 16, 1930, the Hawks Nest, W. Va., power project for the New Kanawha Power Co., was started by Rinehart & Dennis Co., Charlottesville, W. Va. . . . After the rock was tested the report showed better than 90 percent silica (glass). . . . No precaution was taken to protect human life after the contractors knew [what] they were working in.
>
> In most every shift some of the workmen had to come out of the tunnel, some in very bad condition, and at times the Coal Valley Hospital, Montgomery, W. Va., was nearly filled with whites and blacks from this tunnel job. Respirators were never used in camp no. 1 or camp no. 2. Respirators were used at camp no. 3 only, and Mr. Blank called the writer and told him it was wasting the company's money to try to use respirators. Many deaths occurred on this job, from superintendents down to the common laborers. . . .
>
> I have some other letters that I think will prove of interest to the committee, and I shall quote briefly from them. This letter is dated December 12, 1935. . . .
>
> At one point Mr. Blank and his friend had to leave the boardwalk laid between the railroad tracks in order to circumvent a pile of rock lying on the floor. Mr. Blank estimated this to be about a 2-ton drop from the ceiling, and his friend Mr. Blank told him it was a recent fall not yet cleared up. . . .
>
> Another quotation reads: Well, what about those poor fellows who die on the job? Do you not check up on your crews and discover some of the men missing?
>
> The answer was:

No; when we find out they are not there, we do not bother much. We know there are always plenty more. . . . ["]

STATEMENT OF HON. JOHN W. FINCH, DIRECTOR OF THE BUREAU OF MINES

MR. GRISWOLD. In the early part of your statement you said, as I remember, that the Bureau of Mines had recommended wetting in these dust cases.

MR. FINCH. Yes.

MR. GRISWOLD. Just what authority has the Bureau of Mines to enforce its recommendations?

MR. FINCH. Its organic act does not enable the Bureau of Mines to enforce anything. . . .

MR. GRISWOLD. But if some particular mine or other operation willfully saw fit to disobey your recommendations, there was nothing in law by which you could enforce those recommendations?

MR. FINCH. No. It is purely an educational process. We try to give the matter all the publicity we can.

MR. GRISWOLD. No matter how essential the Bureau of Mines might find certain operations in mining or how essential it might find certain things to protect the health, there is no way the Bureau could enforce its recommendation along that line?

MR. FINCH. No; but we can induce them to do it.

MR. GRISWOLD. In what manner can you induce them to do it?

MR. FINCH. By making them ashamed of themselves.

MR. GRISWOLD. Some people do not get ashamed of themselves.

Source: *Investigation Relating to Health Conditions of Workers Employed in the Construction and Maintenance of Public Utilities*, Hearings before a Subcommittee of the Committee on Labor, House of Representatives, 74th Cong., 2nd sess., on H.J. Res. 449 (Washington, DC: Government Printing Office, 1936), 2, 7–8, 20–21, 53–55, 121–23, 135.

FURTHER READINGS

The subject of industrial accidents has been seldom explored. See Martin Cherniack, *The Hawk's Nest Incident: America's Worst Industrial Disaster* (New Haven, CT: Yale University Press, 1986); David Rosner and Gerald Markowitz, eds., *Dying for Work: Workers' Safety and Health in Twentieth-Century America* (Bloomington: Indiana University Press, 1987); Sheldon Rampton and John Stauber, *Trust Us, We're Experts!* (New York: Taucher/Putnam, 2001); Bill Minutaglio, *City on Fire: The Forgotten Disaster That Devastated a Town and Ignited a Landmark Legal Battle* (New York: HarperCollins, 2003).

In contrast, the labor disputes are much studied by historians. See, for instance, Henry David, *The History of the Haymarket Affair: A Study in the American Social-Revolutionary and Labor Movements* (New York: Farrar and Rinehart, 1936); Paul Avrich, *The Haymarket Tragedy* (Princeton, NJ: Princeton University Press, 1984); Michael Frisch and Daniel Walkowitz, eds., *Working-Class America: Essays on Labor, Community, and American Society* (Urbana: University of Illinois Press, 1983); Paul Gilje, *The Road to Mobocracy: Popular Disorder in New York City, 1763–1834* (Chapel Hill: University of North Carolina Press, 1987); Steven Hahn and Jonathan Prude, eds., *The Countryside in the Age of Capitalist Transformation* (Chapel Hill: University of North Carolina Press, 1985); Bruce Laurie, *Artisans into Workers: Labor in Nineteenth-Century America* (New York: Hill and Wang 1989); Melvyn Dubofsky, *We Shall Be All: A History of the Industrial Workers of the World* (Urbana: University of Illinois Press, 1988); Philip Foner, *The Great Labor Uprising of 1877* (New York: Monad Press, 1977); David Montgomery, *Beyond Equality: Labor and the Radical Republicans, 1862–1872* (New York: Knopf, 1967), and *The Fall of the House of Labor: The Workplace, the State, and American Labor Activism* (New York: Cambridge University Press 1987); Nick Salvatore, *Eugene Debs: Citizen and Socialist* (Urbana: University of Illinois Press, 1982); Jeffory A. Clymer, *America's Culture of Terrorism: Violence, Capitalism, and the Written Word* (Chapel Hill: University of North Carolina Press, 2003); Christopher Waldrep, *Night Riders: Defending Community in the Black Patch, 1890–1915* (Durham: Duke University Press, 1993).

NINE

VIOLENCE AS A MEANS OF CRIME CONTROL

Y ou can't be a varsity letterman when you deal with these barfbags,"
Joseph Wambaugh has Bumper Morgan, his fictional police officer, declare in *The Blue Knight*. Police officers who follow the letter of the law
probably become "a captain, or Chief of Police or something," Wambaugh's
Blue Knight says contemptuously, "but you can bet there'd always have to be
guys like me out on the street . . . keeping the assholes from taking over the
city."[1] Wambaugh depicts police officers as good shepherds, protecting the
sheep from the wolves, but often using wolfish tactics to do so. Standing as a
blue line between law and lawlessness, the police occupy an ambiguous position
in American life. Charged by society with protecting citizens' lives and property,
police sometimes act in vigilante-like fashion. It can seem more important to
catch and punish the violently evil than to scrupulously obey the law themselves. The first police, city night watchmen or slave patrollers, prowled the
streets, more interested in quickly whipping miscreants than administering due
process. In 1838 and 1844, Boston and New York City organized their police
departments, at a time when many Americans saw urban rioting as a dangerous
and frightening threat to order and expected their new military-like police to
beat back discordant lower classes.

Politics, not professionalism, ruled the first police departments. Politicians
called "bosses" ran the big cities, maintaining power by the favors they bestowed
and the crime they chose to tolerate or squelch. Officers won their jobs through
their political connections. They received no special training and only reluctantly agreed to wear blue uniforms—reluctant because nonuniformed officers
could more easily take a break in a saloon while on duty. Like the political

1. Joseph Wambaugh, *The Blue Knight* (Boston: Little, Brown, 1972), 68–69.

machines they represented, police departments provided a wide variety of services to their neighborhoods, acting as welfare agencies and offering housing for the homeless. And, also like the machines, police departments were often corrupt. Many times they simply "licensed" criminal activities by taking bribes from brothels and gambling organizations. Recognized as agents for their local political machines rather than neutral enforcers of law, police officers received little respect from the citizens they encountered.

In the twentieth century, cities inaugurated civil service reform, requiring that officers be selected according to testable standards. American federalism meant that every locality could pursue policing in its own way. Some cities began training programs. Education became more important as policing became more technical, with the introduction of fingerprinting and other "scientific" efforts at crime fighting. Some cities began setting up police academies. As education required more professional policing, reformers attacked the corruption so characteristic of late nineteenth-century urban government. Often these reformers organized "crime commissions" to dramatize the need for change, investigating police misconduct and scandal. Some of these crime commissions produced sensational revelations about the realities of big-city policing. In 1929, problems with enforcing the national prohibition law prompted President Herbert Hoover to appoint George Wickersham, a former attorney general, to investigate crime and corrupt policing. The National Commission on Law Observance and Enforcement, or the Wickersham Commission, published fourteen volumes, including a report exposing how the police used the "third degree" to beat confessions from suspects.

Despite efforts to improve law enforcement, Americans continued to harbor ambivalent feelings about the police. Revelations of shocking police misconduct genuinely alarmed many, but the specter of crime raging out of control frightened many more. In 1903, a Supreme Court justice urged that appeals be eliminated in serious criminal cases so as to make the criminal justice system work more efficiently. Justice David Brewer's suggestion came amid a wave of similar proposals. At the turn of the century, many saw the citizenry as a powder keg of barely repressed righteous indignation. If the police and the courts did not effectively move against evil, then the citizenry would, acting outside the law. Brutal treatment of suspects by police remained a problem through the entire twentieth century.

At the same time Brewer and others urged harsher treatment of criminals, some of the victims of this "more efficient policing" protested. To its critics, harsh policing seemed like class or ethnic warfare. In some places, the police were seen as nothing more than shock troops for the capitalist elite. Police departments broke strikes and put down labor unrest, protected the replacement workers hired by employers to destroy the unions, and, increasingly, abused ethnic minorities, especially the supposedly criminally inclined Italians. After 1890, with the assassination of David Hennessey, the New Orleans superintendent of police, many Americans associated immigrants with crime. Sicilians had a particularly bad reputation for settling disputes according to a violent code of honor. Some alleged that America imported its modern crime problem from Sicily, in the form of a centrally controlled Mafia. In the 1930s, New Deal rhetoric promoted this notion of an ethnic conspiracy as a way of expanding the crime-fighting power of the national government.

Vigorous policing sometimes had the ironic effect of actually promoting crime and violence. From the beginning of the twentieth century, an important part of the government's picture of a national criminal syndicate involved narcotics. In the nineteenth century, the typical narcotics abuser was a middle-class housewife, addicted to morphine or opium prescribed by her doctor. In the first years of the twentieth century, federal authorities made consumption of addictive drugs such as opium and morphine illegal, harassing those doctors willing to prescribe such medications. Driving drug consumption underground had the effect of creating a drug culture of violent young men.

By the end of the twentieth century, the minority groups often targeted by the police rebelled. Segregated or all-white police departments regularly brutalized minority groups, as when Los Angeles police officers beat seven jailed Mexican Americans with gloved fists and wet towels. This 1951 incident, which came to be known as "Bloody Christmas," was only the worst of many such acts of mistreatment. In 1965, frustrated African Americans in Los Angeles attacked police cars during the Watts Riot; thirty-four people died in six days of rioting. The Los Angeles police prepared for future riots by purchasing armored personnel carriers, vowing to nip disorder in the bud.

The Watts Riot boosted the political career of Ronald Reagan, ushering in a more conservative political culture. This political shift meant more attention to "law-and-order" issues and the harsher treatment of criminals. Nonetheless, Los Angeles remained a volatile ethnic environment. In 1992, when a jury acquitted officers after they had been videotaped beating a black suspect, rioting again erupted in Los Angeles. The problems of 1965, including police brutality, remained in 1992. One explanation for the acquittal of O. J. Simpson, a black man tried before a predominantly black jury, was the frustration blacks felt toward the police and police abuse.

The tension between an American insistence on personal liberty and a fear of disorder continues to place police officers in an ambiguous position. Americans want the police to prevent crime as well as respond to it, yet they seemingly resent any police interference with their actions, even to being pulled over for a traffic ticket. These attitudes are reflected in popular films and television shows, where the police are pictured as both heroic and corrupt. They do the dirty work of society, sometimes frustrated by legal restrictions on their efforts to fight crime. Sometimes, too eager to punish extralegally those they "know" are guilty, they still abuse minorities. The "war on terror" following the attacks of September 11, 2001, have reminded the public of the tension between unrestrained police techniques and personal liberty, while events at Guantanamo and Abu Ghraib demonstrate the ease with which interrogation can become torture.

DOCUMENTS

THE PROBLEM WITH DUE PROCESS

Son of a missionary, David J. Brewer served on the Supreme Court from 1889 until his death in 1910. Though known as a stalwart defender of individual liberty, he thought lynching could best be controlled by making the punishment of criminals swift and certain, unhampered by legal "technicalities." Toward that goal, he advocated an end to appeals in criminal cases. Few lawyers endorsed this idea, but Brewer spoke for many who sought swift justice unencumbered by an overly strict regard for defendants' due process rights. Certainly most whites agreed with Brewer when he declared that "men would disgrace their manhood" if they did not seek to act when women are raped. Brewer's endorsement of the San Francisco vigilante movement signals his real attitude toward criminals, one shared by many of his fellow Americans.

Justice David J. Brewer Downplays the Importance of Due Process, 1903

What can be done to stay this epidemic of lynching? One thing is the establishment of a greater confidence in the summary and certain punishment of the criminal. Men are afraid of the law's delays and the uncertainty of its results. Not that they doubt the integrity of the judges, but they know that the law abounds with technical rules, and that appellate courts will often reverse a judgment of conviction for a disregard of such rules, notwithstanding a full belief in the guilt of the accused. If all were certain that the guilty ones would be promptly tried and punished, the inducement to lynch would be largely taken away. In an address which I delivered before the American Bar Association at Detroit some years since, I advocated doing away with appeals in criminal cases. It did not meet the favor of the association, but I still believe in its wisdom. For nearly a hundred years there was no appeal from the judgment of conviction of criminal cases in . . . which, two judges sitting, a difference of opinion on a question of law was certified to the Supreme Court. In England the rule has been that there was no appeal in criminal cases, although a question of doubt might be reserved by the presiding judge for the consideration of his brethren. Hon. E. J. Phelps, who was minister to England during Mr. Cleveland's first administration, once told me that while he was there only two cases were so reserved. Does any one doubt that justice was fully administered by the English courts?

Opponents of this suggestion fall back on the ancient maxim that "It is better that ninety-nine guilty men escape than that one innocent man be punished." Maxims, like other things, are good in their times and places, but, like other things, may often be overworked. When criminal trials were conducted as they were in England a century and a half ago—defendant without counsel, trial with little publicity, and the press an unknown factor—that maxim was good enough; but today, when a prisoner is guaranteed counsel, when trials are viewed by throngs of spectators, and the press makes public every detail, it seems well to as often consider President Grant's direction, "Let no guilty man escape."

Further, laws have been passed requiring an immediate convening of courts and giving priority of hearing to certain civil cases deemed of public moment. Why may not direction be given to the presiding judge of the proper court, when such an atrocious crime has been committed as those giving rise to lynchings, to immediately convene that court and put the accused at once on trial? If this were done and no appeal were allowed, would not the community be more confident that full punishment would be promptly meted out? If it be said that under the haste of such a trial some innocent men might be punished, a sufficient reply would seem to be that justice will be more likely done than when a mob takes the law into its own hands. If it were deemed necessary to guard against even a possibility of injustice, the statute might require that the testimony be taken down by a stenographer and at once presented to the Supreme Court, and if, in its judgment, not that some technical rules of law have been disregarded, but that an innocent man has been convicted, authorize it to stay the execution and grant a new trial.

It is said in extenuation of lynching in case of rape that it is an additional cruelty to the unfortunate victim to compel her to go upon the witness stand and in the presence of a mixed audience tell the story of her wrongs, especially when she may be subject to cross-examination by over-zealous counsel. I do not belittle this matter, but it must be remembered that often the unfortunate victim never lives to tell the story of her wrongs; that if she does survive she must tell it to some, and the whole community knows the fact. Even in the court-room any high-minded judge will stay counsel from any unnecessary cross-examination; and finally, if any lawyer should attempt it the community may treat him as an outcast. I can but think that if the community felt that the criminal would certainly receive the punishment he deserves, and receive it soon, the eagerness for lynching would disappear, and mobs, whose gatherings too often mean not merely the destruction of jails and other property, but also the loss of innocent lives, would greatly diminish in number.

One thing is certain—the tendency of lynching is to undermine respect for the law, and unless it be checked we need not be astonished if it be resorted to for all kinds of offenses, and oftentimes innocent men suffer for wrongs committed by others.

Source: David J. Brewer, "Plain Words on the Crime of Lynching," *Leslie's Weekly* 97 (August 20, 1903): 182.

THE PROBLEM OF CLASS

The 1920s, famous as a time of wild parties and fads, was also a decade of notable intolerance. The special target of law enforcement and popular culture were radicals and immigrants. Two Italian radicals, Nicola Sacco and Bartolomeo Vanzetti, stood as symbolic victims of oppressive state power. Sacco, a shoemaker, and Vanzetti, a fishmonger, were accused of killing a paymaster and his guard on April 15, 1920, during a robbery of a South Braintree, Massachusetts, shoe factory. Their trial before Judge Webster Thayer involved a great number of irregularities, including the defendants' poor English which led them into incriminating statements and the judge's oft-stated certainty that the two defendants were guilty. When a convicted murderer confessed to the crime, but Sacco and Vanzetti still could not get a new trial, their fate became an international cause, with thousands of liberals and radicals, from Felix Frankfurter to Eugene Debs, joining in the effort to free the two men. In 1927 Judge Thayer oversaw the hearing that reconsidered and confirmed his verdict in the first trial. In their broken English, Sacco and Vanzetti condemned the court for its corruption of justice. The two men were executed in the electric chair on August 23, 1927.

The Final Statements of Nicola Sacco and Bartolomeo Vanzetti to the Court Sentencing Them to Death, 1927

Dedham, Massachusetts, Saturday, April 9, 1927. . . .

Clerk WORTHINGTON. Nicola Sacco, have you anything to say why sentence of death should not be passed upon you?

STATEMENT BY NICOLA SACCO

Yes, sir. I am not an orator. It is not very familiar with me the English language. . . .

I never know, never heard, even read in history anything so cruel as this Court. After seven years prosecuting they still consider us guilty. And these gentle people here are arrayed with us in this court today.

I know the sentence will be between two class, the oppressed class and the rich class, and there will be always collision between one and the other. We fraternize the people with the books, with the literature. You persecute the people, tyrannize over them and kill them. We try the education of people always. You try to put a path between us and some other nationality that hates each other. That is why I am here today on this bench, for having been the oppressed class. Well, you are the oppressor.

You know it, Judge Thayer,—you know all my life, you know why I have been here, and after seven years that you have been persecuting me and my poor wife, and you still today sentence us to death. I would like to tell all my life, but what is the use? . . . You forget all the population that has been with us for seven years, to sympathize and give us all their energy and all their kindness. You do not care for them. . . .

STATEMENT BY BARTOLOMEO VANZETTI

Yes. What I say is that I am innocent. . . . That I am not only innocent . . . but in all my life I have never stole and I have never killed and I have never spilled blood. That is what I want to say. And it is not all. Not only am I innocent of these . . . crimes, not only in all my life I have never stole, never killed, never spilled blood, but I have struggled all my life, since I began to reason, to eliminate crime from the earth.

. . . I have refused myself the commodity or glory of life, the pride of life of a good position, because in my consideration it is not right to exploit man. I have refused to go in business because I understand that business is a speculation on profit upon certain people that must depend upon the business man, and I do not consider that that is right and therefore I refuse to do that.

. . . [T]he flower of mankind of Europe, the better writers, the greatest thinkers of Europe, have pleaded in our favor. The scientists, the greatest scientists, the greatest statesmen of Europe, have pleaded in our favor. The people of foreign nations have pleaded in our favor.

Is it possible that only a few on the jury, only two or three men, who would condemn their mother for worldly honor and for earthly fortune; is it possible that they are right against what the world, the whole world has say it is wrong and that I know that it is wrong? . . . You see it is seven years that we are in jail. What we have suffered during these seven years no human tongue can say, and yet you see me before you, not trembling, you see me looking you in your eyes straight, not blushing, not changing color, not ashamed or in fear.

. . . We have proved that there could not have been another Judge on the face of the earth more prejudiced and more cruel than you have been against us. We have proven that. Still they refuse the new trial. We know, and you know in your heart, that you have been against us from the very beginning, before you see us. Before you see us you already know that we were radicals, that we were underdogs, that we were the enemy of the institution that you can believe in good faith in their goodness—I don't want to condemn that—and that it was easy on the time of the first trial to get a verdict of guiltiness.

We know that you have spoke yourself and have spoke your hostility against us, and your despisement against us with friends of yours on the train, at the University Club of Boston, on the Golf Club of Worcester, Massachusetts.[2]

. . . You know that my life, my private and public life in Plymouth, and wherever I have been, was so exemplary that one of the worst fears of our prosecutor [Frederick Gunn] Katzmann was to introduce proof of our life and of our conduct. He has taken it off with all his might and he has succeeded. . . .

We were tried during a time that has now passed into history. I mean by that, a time when there was a hysteria of resentment and hate against the people of our principles, against the foreigner, against slackers, and it seems to me—rather, I am positive of it, that both you and Mr. Katzmann has done all what it were in your power in order to work out, in order to agitate still more the passion of the juror, the prejudice of the juror, against us. . . .

Now, this, it seems, has nothing to do with us directly. It seems to be a thing by incident on the stand between the other thing that is the essence here. But the jury were hating us because we were against the war, and the jury don't know that it makes any difference between a man that is against the war because he believes that the war is unjust, because he hate no country, because he is a cosmopolitan, and a man that is against the war because he is in favor of the other country that fights against the country in which he is, and therefore a spy, and he commits any crime in the country in which

2. Vanzetti refers here to a number of incidents in which Thayer made clear his bias against the defendants, speaking of them in the most derogatory terms to other members of his private club.

he is in behalf of the other country in order to serve the other country. We are not men of that kind. Katzmann know very well that. Katzmann know that we were against the war because we did not believe in the purpose for which they say that the war was done. . . . We believe more now than ever that the war was wrong, and we are against war more now than ever, and I am glad to be on the doomed scaffold if I can say to mankind, "Look out; you are in a catacomb of the flower of mankind. For what? All that they say to you, all that they have promised to you—it was a lie, it was an illusion, it was a cheat, it was a fraud, it was a crime. They promised you liberty. Where is liberty? They promised you prosperity. Where is prosperity? . . .

In the best of my recollection and of my good faith, during the trial Katzmann has told to the jury that a certain Coacci has brought in Italy the money that, according to the State theory, I and Sacco have stole in Braintree. We never steal that money. But Katzmann, when he told that to the jury, he know already that that was not true. He know already that . . . the Federal policeman has taken away the trunks from the very boarding where he was, and bring the trunks over here and look them over and found not a single money.

Now, I call that murder, to tell to the jury that a friend or comrade or a relative or acquaintance of the charged man, of the indicted man, has carried the money to Italy, when he knows it is not true. I can call that nothing else but a murder, a plain murder.

. . . The jury don't know nothing about us. They have never seen us. The only thing that they know is the bad things that the newspaper have say when we were arrested and the bad story that the newspaper have say on the Plymouth trial. . . .

This is what I say: I would not wish to a dog or to a snake, to the most low and misfortunate creature of the earth—I would not wish to any of them what I have had to suffer for things that I am not guilty of. But my conviction is that I have suffered for things that I am guilty of. I am suffering because I am a radical and indeed I am a radical; I have suffered because I was an Italian, and indeed I am an Italian; I have suffered more for my family and for my beloved than for myself; but I am so convinced to be right that if you could execute me two times, and if I could be reborn two other times, I would live again to do what I have done already.

I have finished. Thank you.

THE COURT . . . . First the Court pronounces sentence upon Nicola Sacco. It is considered and ordered by the Court that you, Nicola Sacco, suffer the punishment of death by the passage of a current of electricity through your body within the week beginning on Sunday, the tenth day of July, in the year of our Lord, one thousand, nine hundred and twenty-seven. This is the sentence of the law.

It is considered and ordered by the Court that you, Bartolomeo Vanzetti. . . .

MR. SACCO. You know I am innocent. . . . You condemn two innocent men.

THE COURT. —by the passage of a current of electricity through your body within the week beginning on Sunday, the tenth day of July, in the year of our Lord, one thousand nine hundred and twenty-seven. This is the sentence of the law.

We will now take a recess.

Source: *Commonwealth v. Nicola Sacco and Bartolomeo Vanzetti* (1927), 4895–902, 4904–5.

THE PROBLEM WITH THE POLICE

In the 1930s, a series of exposés revealed violent police treatment of prisoners. Police abuse of suspects was not a recent development, nor would the national revelation of the problem by the Wickersham Commission end such transgressions of the law by the police. New York police captain "Clubber" Williams (three hundred formal complaints as of 1887) famously declared that he had more law on his nightstick than in all the law books. "Respectable" people tolerated officers like "Clubber" because they kept the "dangerous" classes at bay. The problem remained in 1966, when the Supreme Court ruled that police must advise arrested persons of their constitutional right to remain silent. Police quickly routinized the required warning, and studies have shown that suspects confess at the same rate as before 1966. The Supreme Court had little impact on so-called street justice. Well after the Court's decision, one New York City police officer remembered learning that "any suspect who assaulted a police officer in any way was never supposed to be able to walk into the station house on his own." Officers bringing in prisoners uninjured with such charges were admonished by fellow officers and superiors. It was an unwritten rule that officers were supposed to beat suspects who led them on a chase.[3] Periodically, though, scandals would erupt, prompted by revelations like the Wickersham Commission's investigation of the "third degree."[4] The Wickersham Commission sent investigators to the fifteen largest U.S. cities and found the third degree flourishing in ten of them. The commission did not doubt police departments in smaller towns also used violence in

---

3. Lieutenant Arthur Doyle, "From the Inside Looking Out," in Jill Nelson, ed., *Police Brutality: An Anthology* (New York: Norton, 2000), 173–74.

4. For the Wickersham Commission report, see Zechariah Chafee, *The Third Degree* (Washington, DC: Government Printing Office, 1931); and Chafee, *The Mooney-Billings Report: Suppressed by the Wickersham Commission.* (New York: Gotham House, 1932).

extracting confessions. This excerpt, from the Wickersham Commission's report, details police violence in Chicago.

The Wickersham Commission Documents Police Brutality, 1931

A consideration of the evidence and of the reported cases leaves no doubt that, despite these statutes, the third degree is thoroughly at home in Chicago. This opinion is corroborated by interviews with a large number of persons, including leading members of the bar and experienced newspaper men; by many writers; and by the Illinois Crime Survey (1929), especially the statements therein by a former State's attorney.

One of the best informed persons on Chicago practices tells us that it was an exception when a suspect was not subjected to personal violence.

At the time of the Leopold-Loeb case, when an innocent school-teacher was arrested and beaten until he falsely confessed, public attention was focused upon the third degree. An order was issued against it by Captain Stege, who was in charge of the detective bureau under Commissioner Russell. Well-informed persons, however, state that this order had little permanent effect.

Violence against suspects still exists, although it is said to be diminishing. Some informants believe that this diminution is partly due to apprehension of retaliation: there are said to have been instances in the past where, after brutality was used, the victim's friends or gang have found out which policemen were responsible and taken revenge.

The belief is expressed by competent observers that corruption and influence protect certain suspects; that fear of reprisal protects others, and that this protection due to fear of reprisals is increasing. Violence is regarded as general and prevailing in cases outside of the protected groups of suspects.

The methods described as in use in Chicago include the application of rubber hose to the back or the pit of the stomach, kicks in the shins, beating the shins with a club, blows struck with a telephone book on the side of the victim's head. The Chicago telephone book is a heavy one and a swinging blow with it may stun a man without leaving a mark. (The use of this practice is described by a responsible eyewitness of more than one occurrence.) Other methods stated to be used are suspending a prisoner upside down by handcuffs or manacles and the administration of tear gas.

Formerly there was a room at police headquarters known as the "goldfish room," where suspects were taken "to see the goldfish"; that is, to be beaten. The main weapon was the rubber hose. . . .

The frequent participation of prosecuting attorneys in the third-degree sessions is stated by several informants. Indeed a distinction is drawn between the type of third degree in which beatings are used by the police in daily practice upon ordinary kinds of suspects and the more severe and exceptional type of third degree employed by the State attorney's investigators in the solution of outstanding crimes.

Illegal detention and detention *incommunicado* are said to be common. The police are slow about bringing prisoners into court or even booking them. As far as the records show, men are usually produced in court not later than 48 hours after the entry of the arrest; but in fact, the true date of the arrest is often not entered on the police blotter. An advance period of kidnapping "prior to arrest" makes the records wholly untrustworthy. Men are frequently not booked at all and there is no record of their being in custody. "Losing" men for days at a time is common. This absence of record blocks attorneys when they go to the police demanding to see their clients. The professional criminals usually have their attorneys on the watch in advance of arrest, but persons who do not make such arrangements often have difficulty in getting in touch with attorneys.

The arrests are at times without any legal basis, as in a recent drive after a gang outbreak in which 2,000 persons were rounded up. They were crowded into cells so closely that it was impossible to sit down even on the floor. After varying periods of confinement they were released. Such a drive is a gesture on the part of the police to satisfy newspaper demands for spectacular action. Numerous complaints of brutal arrests have been reported in the press; but in accordance with our practice we regard them as significant only in mass, not in individual instances. (The present Police Commissioner, Alcock, has recently issued a drastic order directing the police to exercise greater care in making arrests.)

... The first number of the Journal of Scientific Crime Detection was published ... in January, 1930, and the journal already has a considerable circulation. The directors suggested to the Chicago police department that they try out the "lie detector," but a leading official said, "Here's the best lie detector," and extended his clenched fist. The presence in Chicago of this laboratory, with its many scientific facilities, ought in time to stimulate the local prosecuting attorneys and detectives to place an increasing reliance on the investigation of outside evidence of crimes instead of the extortion of confessions by brutal methods.

The foregoing conclusions of the field investigation as to the existence of the third degree in Chicago may be supplemented from the accounts of police practices in that city, as described in opinions of the Supreme Court of Illinois.

In the ... cases to be discussed the third-degree allegations were proved to the satisfaction of the Supreme Court.

The "goldfish" room, already mentioned, appears in Judge Dunn's account of the uncontradicted testimony of two men arrested in 1921 for causing an explosion in a laundry building.

Sweeney testified that he was arrested on Thursday, May 19, at 1:30 or 2 o'clock, and kept at Brighton Park station until about noon the next day, at which time he was taken to Chief Fitzmorris's office in the city hall and kept there about an hour. He was then taken to the State attorney's office and questioned for three or four hours by Smith, Wharton, and Chief Hughes, of the detective bureau. He remained in the State attorney's office until early Saturday morning, when he was taken to a cell and remained there about 16 or 20 minutes, and then taken across the street to the central station, by three officers. He was kept there about 15 or 20 minutes, and was then taken to Chief Hughes's office. The three officers said, as they took him across the street, that they would show him the "goldfish." They showed him the "goldfish," which was a beating. They dragged him around by his hair and started beating him with a rubber hose. He said that Chief Hughes beat him, and two or three other officers whom he did not know by name; that Egan (a police sergeant) was there at the time and used his fist; that he could recognize the other two officers and had seen one of them in the courtroom since the trial started that is, one besides Egan. He said that they told him at the time that he would either make a statement and come clean and tell everything he knew, and plenty besides, or be found out in some prairie. Wharton and Smith were not there at the time, but Chief Hughes told him he would be found out on the prairie. He was then taken downstairs to a cell for about three-quarters of an hour and then back to Hughes' office and again beaten. The police officers kept telling him to make a statement, and then he was dragged downstairs to a cell again for an hour or an hour and a half and was then taken upstairs and beaten again. From the time he was taken from the Brighton Park station he did not get any sleep, and he was given one sandwich to eat at the State attorney's office and had a cup of coffee. After this final beating he made the statement which was admitted in evidence as his confession. The only contradiction of his testimony was Egan's statement, which has been mentioned—that he did not see any ill-treatment or abuse during the time he was present.

Bartlett testified that he was arrested about 1 o'clock Wednesday afternoon and taken to the Hudson Avenue station until Friday afternoon, when he was taken to the office of the chief of police for about two hours. He was then taken to the State's attorney's office, where he was kept until about 2 o'clock in the morning, and during that time questioned by Smith, Wharton, and Hughes. He was then taken to the central station and kept there about two hours, and then taken to Hughes' office. Hughes, O'Connor, Gasperik, and others were there: They were hitting him. He did not talk. Saturday he was questioned 10 or 15 times. There was more violence on Sunday morning, when he was brought up the last time. He did not remember making any statement. While at Hudson Avenue he got a sandwich now and then. On Friday he got one sandwich at the State's attorney's office, but he got nothing to eat Saturday and no sleep Saturday night. . . .

In 1920 Vinci, charged with murder, was detained *incommunicado* and questioned during the greater part of three days and four nights by the State's attorney, two of his assistants, his secretary, and several police officers. The conviction was reversed. Judge Thompson said:

He (defendant) was thereupon arrested and brought to the State's attorney's office, where he was held as a "suspect under interrogation." The arrest occurred at his home about 6.30 o'clock Wednesday evening, February 22. He arrived at the State's attorney's office about 7 o'clock and was there questioned about the Enright case until after midnight. About 1 o'clock Thursday morning he was taken to the West Chicago police station and there locked up under the direction of the State's attorney as a "suspect under interrogation." Thursday he was brought back to the State's attorney's office and there questioned regarding the Enright murder during the day and until after midnight Thursday night. About 1 o'clock Friday morning he was taken to the Fiftieth Street police station and turned over to the turnkey to be held as a "suspect under interrogation." Friday he was brought back again to the State's attorney's office and there questioned during the day and until after midnight Friday night, when he was returned to the Fiftieth Street police station. Saturday night he was brought back to the State's attorney's office for further interrogation regarding the Enright murder. Up to this time he had persisted in his denial of any knowledge of the murder. No warrant had been issued for his arrest and he had not been taken before a magistrate for examination. No one was permitted to communicate with him except by permission of the State's attorney's office, and he was purposely confined in different outlying stations so that he could not get in touch with people from the outside. The interrogation of plaintiff in error continued throughout the day Saturday until past midnight Saturday night. Shortly after midnight plaintiff in error, in answer to questions of the State's attorney, admitted that he drove the car from which Enright was shot and that Cosmano was the man who fired the shots. * * *

The plaintiff in error was questioned during the greater part of three days and four nights by the State's attorney, two of his assistants, his private secretary, and several police officers. While we do not believe any physical force was used nor that direct threats or promises were made, there can be no doubt at all that the repeated questioning by these officers, like the constant dropping of water upon a rock, finally wore through Vinci's mental resolution of silence. Admittedly his refusal at first to answer incriminating questions gave evidence of a desire to make no statement. The examination was persisted in by turns until plaintiff in error finally yielded to the importunities of his questioners and gave answers which they sought. It seems clear to us that the accused became convinced that he was bound to make a statement to secure relief from the continuous questioning of those having him in charge, and under the circumstances we do not see how a confession thus obtained can be said to be voluntary.

In a robbery examination in 1924 the uncontradicted testimony of the prisoner, Berardi, showed prolonged questioning and beating. Nobody identified the robber, and the confession was the basis of the conviction. Judge Duncan, in reversing the conviction, described the treatment of the prisoner:

He further testified to his arrest and imprisonment in the police station by the police officers and to their questioning him day after day for three or four days, and that he continually, through all this questioning to the last, denied any and all connection with the robbery or knowledge of it. He also testified that Officer Carroll, after they had questioned him for considerable time, brought a strap into the room where he was confined and beat him with the strap, and that another policeman whom he did not know questioned him about the robbery and kicked him on the shin; that his mother and father were allowed to see him at the police station, and that he showed them his body, which was then black and blue from the beatings given him by the officers.

The two policemen who testified to his confession themselves admit that the statements that they say he made to them as a confession were in part untrue.

Source: National Commission on Law Observance and Enforcement, *Report on Lawlessness in Law Enforcement* (Washington, DC: Government Printing Office, 1931), 123–34.

THE PROBLEM OF ORGANIZED CRIME

In the wake of World War II, murder rates declined, but citizens' fears of crime soared. Organized crime seemed especially threatening.[5] American criminals had long been "organized"; gangs menaced western settlers and nineteenth-century cities before anyone heard the word "mafia." A small minority of late nineteenth-century European immigrants and their offspring formed street gangs. By the end of World War I, the Irish dominated politics, the police, and crime in the largest cities. Prohibition provided new opportunities, and the Cosa Nostra (the thing, or our business) became the most powerful crime syndicate in American history.

In the 1930s, rival Italian crime groups fought each other in the Castellammarese War. Violent street battles began in New York but quickly reached Chicago. Charles Luciano survived and built the modern Mafia, allowing only those of Italian descent entry as "made men." A national commission presided over autonomous crime families. Organized crime gangs sold drugs and hustled prostitutes, but they also infiltrated legitimate business operations and occasionally acted as enforcers for political machines, further blurring the line between legal and illegal activities.[6]

President Harry S Truman attributed the new fears over crime to wartime dislocation and insisted the solution lay in the home and in church. Local authorities, he accurately pointed out, had responsibility for fighting crime. Many thought Truman ducked responsibility; they wanted national action, not empty exhortations. In the absence of effective presidential leadership, members of Congress maneuvered for advantage. Senator Joseph R. McCarthy toyed with the idea of launching an investigation of crime before deciding to go after communists instead. Tennessee Democrat Estes Kefauver rather than McCarthy led the Senate's inquiry. The ambitious Kefauver hoped to use his hearings as a springboard for national office, and he did run for president in 1952 and 1956.

Kefauver predicated his investigation on the theory that some national criminal authority, or syndicate, controlled gambling, narcotics, and vice. This view had been promoted since the 1930s by the Federal Bureau of Narcotics, which cooperated with Kefauver and his investigators, supplying them with witnesses like agent Claude Follmer.

In his testimony, Follmer argued that drug abuse in America flowed from organized crime controlled by the Italian-based mafia. Moreover, blame for a host of violent acts could be traced to narcotics peddlers. The government did not attribute either violence or drug abuse to any social context; instead, a secret conspiracy of evil men pulled the strings. According to this scenario, it was the task of men like Agent Follmer and Senator Kefauver to pull back the curtain of secrecy, revealing the inner working of the cabal. With this accomplished, crime would disappear as a national problem.

5. Roger Lane, *Murder in America: A History* (Columbus: Ohio State University Press, 1997), 249–51; Eric Monkkonen, *Murder in New York City* (Berkeley: University of California Press, 2001), 18–19.
6. Robert J. Kelly, *The Upperworld and the Underworld* (New York: Kluwer, 1999).

Testimony of Claude A. Follmer
before a Congressional Committee, 1950

TESTIMONY OF CLAUDE A. FOLLMER, UNITED STATES NARCOTIC AGENT, TREASURY
DEPARTMENT, KANSAS CITY, MO.

... For many years Kansas City has been the scene of violence, bloodshed, and terror, in connection with the traffic in illicit narcotic drugs, involving for the most part persons of similar origin banded together in a secret society known as the Mafia. One of the most vivid examples of this organized interstate criminal enterprise is shown in the events and circumstances of the case known in the files of the Federal Narcotic Bureau as SE–202: Carl Carramusa, Joseph De Luca et al. ...

Surveillance of Carramusa prior to his arrest indicated he had access to a large quantity of drugs, and by elimination the agents eventually located his cache, an ingeniously devised secret panel in the wall of an apartment. The wholesale value of heroin then seized was in excess of $40,000. When "cut" and delivered to the addict consumer, these drugs would yield approximately one-quarter of a million dollars. Samuel and Fellipo Pernice, occupants of the residence, where the drugs were concealed, were then arrested.

On April 1, 1942, new indictments were returned charging Joseph De Luca, Nicolo Impostato, Paul Antinori, Joseph Antinori, Charles Bengimina, Louis Ventola, Patsy Ventola, Charles Taibi, Samuel Pernice, Fellipo Pernice, and Carl Carramusa all with conspiracy to violate the Federal narcotic laws.

The story behind these indictments began in 1929 when narcotic officers learned a man known only as Nicoline, later identified as Impostato, arrived in Kansas City from Chicago and became the strong-arm man for John Lazia, underworld czar. Lazia was later assassinated.

In New York City in 1937 narcotic agents arrested Nicola Gentile in connection with a Nation-wide narcotic syndicate involving 88 persons throughout the United States and Europe. Gentile was found to be a traveling delegate for the Mafia, and an address book in his possession was a veritable Who's Who of Mafia narcotic traffickers. The names of Impostato and other members of the Kansas City syndicate were duly listed. Gentile later jumped a heavy bond and fled to his native Sicily, where he is now an intimate of the notorious Lucky Luciano.

Shortly after his arrival in Kansas City, Impostato, according to reliable information, became second in command under Joseph De Luca, who was then in charge of the narcotic branch of the Mafia organization, which included James Balestrere, Pete and Joe Di Giovanni, Tony Gizzi, James De Simone, Jack Ancona, Joe Oliver, Angelo Nigro, Mike Lascoula, Lonnie Affronti, and a Kansas City attorney of Sicilian origin. All of these persons were members of the Mafia or Black Hand, and were financed in the narcotic traffic as a group by the Mafia. This Mafia subsidiary placed the illicit drug traffic on a businesslike basis and hired a legal adviser, supervisor, general manager, traveling representative, a bookkeeper, and an extensive retail sales force. They soon developed contacts with major sources of narcotic drugs at various ports and in a short while were supplying not only the Kansas City area but addicts in the States of Texas, Oklahoma, Iowa, Nebraska, Arkansas, Kansas, and Illinois.

At St. Louis, Mo., a branch office of this organization operated under the direction of John Vitale, who was in turn under the domination of Thomas Buffa and Tony Lopiparo, chiefs of the St. Louis Mafia.

In 1942 it was determined one of the sources of supply for the Kansas City group was a Mafia organization in Tampa, Fla., who in turn received smuggled drugs from Marseilles, France, via Havana, Cuba. The traveling representative who brought the drugs to Kansas City was James De Simone. It was also indicated that Sebastino Nani, one-time Brooklyn Mafia hoodlum now established in California, had furnished several large shipments of drugs to the Kansas City syndicate from New York.

At Tampa, Paul and Joseph Antinori were the principal dealers, succeeding their father, Ignatious Antinori, who had been murdered over a narcotic deal a few years before. They obtained their drugs from a Cuban politician and internationally known narcotic smuggler.

As a result of all these investigations, on December 18, 1942, new indictments charging 155 counts of narcotic-law violations were returned against the following 14 persons: Joseph De Luca, Nicolo Impostato, James De Simone, Paul Antinori, Joseph Antinori, Carl Carramusa, Charles Taibi, Thomas Buffa, Tony Lopiparo, Fellipo Pernice, Samuel Pernice, Louis Ventola, Patsy Ventola, and Charles Bengimina. Sentences were imposed as follows:

Nicolo Impostato, 2 years; Charles Taibi, 1 day in jail; Fellipo Pernice, 4 years probation; Samuel Pernice, dismissed to enter Army; Carl Carramusa, 4 years, later reduced and probated; Joseph De Luca, 3 years ; James De Simone, 6 years; Paul Antinori, 5 years; Joseph Antinori, 5 years.

Pending indictments against Bengimina, Louis and Patsy Ventoia, previously sentenced on the original indictment, were dismissed. Thomas Buffa and Tony Lopipara were dismissed due to lack of evidence. Buffa testified for the Government in a collateral matter involving perjury on the part of the paramour of De Luca. She was convicted. Upon Buffa's return to St. Louis an attempt was made to assassinate him, and he fled to California. In 1946, at Lodi, Calif., he was slain by shotgun blasts.

The successful culmination of this investigation resulted through the active cooperation of Carl Carramusa, who openly testified for the Government at the trial of these men. Carramusa went into hiding, changed his name, and began a new life with his wife and family in Chicago. Three years later in June 1945, at Chicago, Carramusa's head was blown off by a shotgun just as his family was about to join him in his automobile en route to a wedding anniversary party.

It is interesting to note that the modus operandi of the Carramusa killers was almost identical with that used in the murder 5 years later of Wolf Riman at Kansas City.

In addition to the murders of Carramusa, Ignatious Antinori, and Tom Buffa, some of the other murders relating to this case in recent years are those of Nick De John, a Chicago narcotic peddler, at San Francisco, in which Sebastino Nani is still a primary suspect, and the recent murder at Tampa, Fla., of James Lumia, Antinori associate and suspect in the Carramusa killing.

Carramusa's own brother had been murdered by the Mafia in 1919 at the age of 11, and it may have been this circumstance that persuaded Carramusa to become a Government witness many years thereafter, even though he knew better than anyone the inherent danger. . . .

The murderer of the Carramusa child was caught red-handed by outraged bystanders and was almost beaten to death before being arrested by the police. He was identified as Paul Cantanzaro; but he was never convicted, as the host of witnesses were methodically terrorized. Even the police detective who arrested Cantanzaro, Louis Olivero, was himself later murdered [in Kansas City] by the Mafia. . . .

Cantanzaro has been employed ever since as night watchman for the Di Giovanni wholesale liquor firm. At the trial of De Luca et. al., Cantanzaro was called back to active service and sat in the front row of the courtroom while Carl Carramusa testified. With subtle threatening gestures he attempted to intimidate the witness until it was found necessary to eject him from the courtroom.

. . . As I understand it, the Mafia is a secret organization which has no written rules or regulations, and it is made up of a national head in Palermo.

THE CHAIRMAN. You mean an international head.
MR. FOLLMER. An international head in Palermo, and a national head in the various countries of the world that have any sizable Sicilian population.

According to the information there are two distinct classes in the Mafia, the inner circle and the outer circle. The inner circle consists of persons who either through the fact that they occupy a high position or had high standing before they were members, or the fact that they have performed some special feat of merit for the organization, make up that group, and the outer circle are lesser lights, sort of do the rough work and do the bidding of the men in the inner circle.

THE CHAIRMAN. Mr. Follmer, at that point, I think we should make it clear that you do not mean that any Sicilian is a member. It is a very small percentage of the Sicilian population of this country.

MR. FOLLMER. That is right. It is my understanding that the membership of the organization is very limited.

THE CHAIRMAN. And, of course, we know there are a lot of good citizens who are of Sicilian origin, so it is a very limited number of the people of Sicilian origin.

MR.. FOLLMER. It is a very small minority.

SENATOR WILEY. What is the purpose or objective of the Mafia, as you understand it? It is a secret society?

MR. FOLLMER. According to historical records, it was originally founded for the purpose of dealing with the oppression of the rich and of the crooked politicians and law–enforcement officers in Sicily.

Source: Hearings before the Special Committee to Investigate Organized Crime in Interstate Commerce 81st Cong., 2nd sess., pt. 4, Missouri Y4.C86/2: C86/pt.4, 81–84, 91.

THE PROBLEM OF RACE

On August 12, 1965, the complacency of white Americans was shattered by a violent outburst of frustration and anger in Los Angeles. Many whites thought that the successes of the civil rights movement, exemplified by the recent passage of the Civil Rights Act, would lead to a lessening of racial animosity. Most leaders were therefore completely unprepared for the riots that broke out not in the South but in the West, in liberal California. What had been largely ignored was the long-simmering anger of urban African Americans over their poverty, mistreatment by largely white police forces, and confinement to ghettos. On August 12, 1965, amid repeated tales of police brutality, some of them accurate, a crowd began stoning police cars and the cars of passing whites. There followed six days of burning, looting, and shooting, culminating in thirty-four deaths, more than a thousand injuries, the destruction of hundreds of buildings, and nearly four thousand arrests. The following account was complied by the California Governor's Commission on the Los Angeles Riots, chaired by John McCone, with Warren Christopher serving as vice-chairman and primary author of the report. Though the commission felt that a small number of criminals bore responsibility for the riots, they estimated that at least ten thousand people took part in the uprising. McCone and his commission largely ignored questions about the Los Angeles Police Department (LAPD), viewing all police actions in the most sympathetic light. Instead, the commission focused on the "sickness in the center of our cities." The commission argued that future rioting could only be prevented through vast new social programs.

The California Governor's Commission Looks for the Causes of the Watts Riot of 1965

The rioting in Los Angeles in the late, hot summer of 1965 took six days to run its full grievous course. In hindsight, the tinder-igniting incident is seen to have been the arrest of a drunken Negro youth about whose danger-ous driving another Negro had complained to the Caucasian motorcycle offi-cer who made the arrest. The arrest occurred under rather ordinary circum-stances, near but not in the district known as Watts, at seven o'clock on the evening of 11 August, a Wednesday. The crisis ended in the afternoon of 17 August, a Tuesday, on Governor Brown's order to lift the curfew which had been imposed the Saturday before in an extensive area just south of the heart of the City.

In the ugliest interval, which lasted from Thursday through Saturday, per-haps as many as 10,000 Negroes took to the streets in marauding bands. They looted stores, set fires, beat up white passersby whom they hauled from stopped cars, many of which were turned upside down and burned, ex-changed shots with law enforcement officers, and stoned and shot at firemen. The rioters seemed to have been caught up in an insensate rage of destruc-tion. By Friday, the disorder spread to adjoining areas, and ultimately . . . an area covering 46.5 square miles had to be controlled with the aid of military authority before public order was restored.

The entire Negro population of Los Angeles County, about two thirds of whom live in this area, numbers more than 650,000. Observers estimate that only about two per cent were involved in the disorder. Nevertheless, this vio-lent fraction, however minor, has given the face of community relations in Los Angeles a sinister cast.

When the spasm passed, thirty-four persons were dead, and the wounded and hurt numbered 1,032 more. Property damage was about $40,000,000. Ar-rested for one crime or another were 3,952 persons, women as well as men, including over 500 youths under eighteen. The lawlessness in this one seg-ment of the metropolitan area had terrified the entire county and its 6,000,000 citizens.

SOWING THE WIND

In the summer of 1964, Negro communities in seven eastern cities were stricken by riots. Although in each situation there were unique contributing circumstances not existing elsewhere, the fundamental causes were largely the same:

- Not enough jobs to go around, and within this scarcity not enough by a wide margin of a character which the untrained Negro could fill.

- Not enough schooling designed to meet the special needs of the disadvantaged Negro child, whose environment from infancy onward places him under a serious handicap.

- A resentment, even hatred, of the police, as the symbol of authority.

These riots were each a symptom of a sickness in the center of our cities. In almost every major city, Negroes pressing ever more densely into the central city and occupying areas from which Caucasians have moved in their flight to the suburbs have developed an isolated existence with a feeling of separation from the community as a whole. Many have moved to the city only in the last generation and are totally unprepared to meet the conditions of modern city life. At the core of the cities where they cluster, law and order have only tenuous hold; the conditions of life itself are often marginal; idleness leads to despair and finally, mass violence supplies a momentary relief from the malaise.

WHY LOS ANGELES?

In Los Angeles, before the summer's explosion, there was a tendency to believe, and with some reason, that the problems which caused the trouble elsewhere were not acute in this community. A "statistical portrait" drawn in 1964 by the Urban League which rated American cities in terms of ten basic aspects of Negro life—such as housing, employment, income—ranked Los Angeles first among the sixty-eight cities that were examined. ("There is no question about it, this is the best city in the world," a young Negro leader told us with respect to housing for Negroes.)

While the Negro districts of Los Angeles are not urban gems, neither are they slums. Watts, for example, is a community consisting mostly of one- and two-story houses, a third of which are owned by the occupants. In the riot area, most streets are wide and usually quite clean; there are trees, parks, and playgrounds. A Negro in Los Angeles has long been able to sit where he wants in a bus or a movie house, to shop where he wishes, to vote, and to use public facilities without discrimination. The opportunity to succeed is probably unequaled in any other major American city.

Yet the riot did happen here, and there are special circumstances here which explain in part why it did. Perhaps the people of Los Angeles should have seen trouble gathering under the surface calm. In the last quarter century, the Negro population here has exploded. While the County's population has trebled, the Negro population has increased almost tenfold from 75,000 in 1940 to 650,000 in 1965. Much of the increase came through migration from Southern states and many arrived with the anticipation that this dynamic city would somehow spell the end of life's endless problems. To those who have come with high hopes and great expectations and see the success of others so close at hand, failure brings a special measure of frustration and disillusionment. Moreover, the fundamental problems, which are the same here as in the cities which were racked by the 1964 riots, are intensified by what may well be the least adequate network of public transportation in any major city in America.

Looking back, we can also see that there was a series of aggravating events in the twelve months prior to the riots.

- Publicity given to the glowing promise of the Federal poverty program was paralleled by reports of controversy and bickering over the mechanism to handle the program here in Los Angeles, and when the projects did arrive, they did not live up to their press notices.

- Throughout the nation, unpunished violence and disobedience to law were widely reported, and almost daily there were exhortations, here and elsewhere, to take the most extreme and even illegal remedies to right a variety of wrongs, real and supposed.

- In addition, many Negroes here felt and were encouraged to feel that they had been affronted by the passage of Proposition 14—an initiative measure passed by two-thirds of the voters in November 1964 which repealed the Rumford Fair Housing Act and unless modified by the voters or invalidated by the courts will bar any attempt by state or local governments to enact similar laws.

When the rioting came to Los Angeles, it was not a race riot in the usual sense. What happened was an explosion—a formless, quite senseless, all but hopeless violent protest—engaged in by a few but bringing great distress to all.

Nor was the rioting exclusively a projection of the Negro problem. It is part of an American problem which involves Negroes but which equally concerns other disadvantaged groups. In this report, our major conclusions and recommendations regarding the Negro problem in Los Angeles apply with equal force to the Mexican-Americans, a community which is almost equal in size to the Negro community and whose circumstances are similarly disadvantageous and demand equally urgent treatment. That the Mexican-American community did not riot is to its credit; it should not be to its disadvantage.

THE DULL DEVASTATING SPIRAL OF FAILURE

In examining the sickness in the center of our city, what has depressed and stunned us most is the dull, devastating spiral of failure that awaits the average disadvantaged child in the urban core. His home life all too often fails to give him the incentive and the elementary experience with words and ideas which prepares most children for school. Unprepared and unready, he may not learn to read and write at all; and because he shares his problem with 30 or more in the same classroom, even the efforts of the most dedicated teachers are unavailing. Age, not achievement, passes him on to higher grades, but in most cases he is unable to cope with courses in the upper grades because they demand basic skills which he does not possess. ("Try," a teacher said to us, "to teach history to a child who cannot read.")

Frustrated and disillusioned, the child becomes a discipline problem. Often he leaves school, sometimes before the end of junior high school. (About two-thirds of those who enter the three high schools in the center of the curfew area do not graduate.) He slips into the ranks of the permanent jobless, illiterate and untrained, unemployed and unemployable. All the talk about the millions which the government is spending to aid him raise his expectations but the benefits seldom reach him.

Reflecting this spiral of failure, unemployment in the disadvantaged areas runs two to three times the county average, and the employment available is too often intermittent. A family whose breadwinner is chronically out of work is almost invariably a disintegrating family. Crime rates soar and welfare rolls increase, even faster than the population.

This spiral of failure has a most damaging side effect. Because of the low standard of achievement in the schools in the urban core and adjacent areas, parents of the better students from advantaged backgrounds remove them from these schools, either by changing the location of the family home or by sending the children to private school. In turn, the average achievement level of the schools in the disadvantaged area sinks lower and lower. The evidence is that this chain reaction is one of the principal factors in maintaining de facto school segregation in the urban core and producing it in the adjacent areas where the Negro population is expanding. From our study, we are persuaded that there is a reasonable possibility that raising the achievement levels of the disadvantaged Negro child will materially lessen the tendency towards de facto segregation in education, and that this might possibly also make a substantial contribution to ending all de facto segregation. . . .

Source: Governor's Commission on the Los Angeles Riots, *Transcripts, Depositions, Consultants' Reports, and Selected Documents* (Sacramento: State of California, 1966), 1:1–6.

The Independent Commission on the Los Angeles Police Department Looks for the Causes of the Los Angeles Riot of 1992

In 1992, more rioting erupted in Los Angeles after a jury acquitted officers who had been videotaped beating Rodney King. The Rodney King affair began when King led police officers on a high-speed chase through the streets of Los Angeles. When King finally stopped his car, a crowd of officers beat him unmercifully, administering fifty-six baton blows and numerous kicks. The officers did not know that their sirens had awakened a neighbor armed with a video camera. When Rodney King's brother complained to the police about Rodney's treatment, officers brushed him off. The photographer, George Holliday, took his video to television station KTLA, which showed it to shocked senior police officials before broadcasting it.

In the resulting public uproar, Mayor Tom Bradley asked Warren Christopher to head a new commission, this time charged with investigating the LAPD. Rather than depend on the police for information, as had McCone, Christopher did his own investigating. What he found stunned some commissioners. One black police officer told interviewers he feared his fellow officers would harass him going home at night. The department placed poorly trained officers on patrol, leaving them ill equipped to deal with resistant offenders. The commission also found computer communications typed by officers from their patrol cars on a high-tech messaging system, messages that included crude sexual and racial references. One officer wrote that he wanted to drive through a black neighborhood with a flamethrower, indicating, "We could have a barbecue." Another said, "They found something that does the work of 5 women—1 man."[7] In the end, while McCone's report blamed that rioting on social conditions in Watts, Christopher's report focused on LAPD mismanagement and misconduct. Christopher wanted the police chief, Daryl Gates, to resign.

After Christopher's commission handed in its report charging systemic racism in the LAPD, California charged four of the officers videotaped beating King with assault. It was widely assumed in Los Angeles and across the nation that the trial would be a formality, followed by quick guilty verdicts. The videotape showing the officers behaving with shocking violence seemed to make the prosecution's case ironclad. Nonetheless, in a decision that stunned the judge and even the defense attorneys, the jury acquitted all four officers. Most observers attributed the verdict to a successful change-of-venue motion by defense attorneys, which took the trial to the mostly white neighborhood of Simi Valley, populated with police and their sympathizers. Jurors also saw the entire videotape, including the part KTLA had cut that showed Rodney King charging the police officers. Their verdict baffled many and led to bloody rioting. In five days, 54 people died, more

---

7. Lou Cannon, *Official Negligence: How Rodney King and the Riots Changed Los Angeles and the LAPD* (New York: Times Books, 1997), 137.

than in the 1965 Watts riot, more, in fact, than in any American riot since 1863. Four times more structures were destroyed in 1992 than in 1965. An excerpt from the Christopher report follows.

Rarely has the work of an amateur photographer so captured the nation's attention as did the dramatic and disturbing scene recorded by George Holliday's video camera in the early morning of March 3, 1991—the morning Rodney G. King, a 25-year-old African-American, was beaten by three uniformed officers of the Los Angeles Police Department while a sergeant and a large group of LAPD, California Highway Patrol, and Los Angeles Unified School District officers stood by. The Holliday tape showed the officers clubbing King with 56 baton strokes and kicking him in the head and body. Within days, television stations across the country broadcast and rebroadcast the tape, provoking a public outcry against police abuse. . . .

California Highway Patrol Officers Melanie Singer and Timothy Singer first observed King's white Hyundai at approximately 12:40 A.M. on Sunday morning, March 3, 1991, in the Pacoima area of the northeastern San Fernando Valley in Los Angeles. King's vehicle was approaching from the rear of the CHP vehicle at a high speed as the Singers drove westbound on the Interstate 210 freeway. King was driving, accompanied by two passengers, both of whom were also African-Americans. King passed the patrol car and then slowed. The CHP unit left the freeway and immediately reentered to pace King's vehicle, which had resumed traveling at a high speed. . . .

When King first stepped out of the car, Koon said he "felt threatened, but felt enough confidence in his officers to take care of the situation." Koon described King as big and muscular. (The arrest report lists King as 6'3" tall, weighing 225 pounds.) He said he believed King was "disoriented and unbalanced" and under the influence of PCP.

After he left the car, King was ordered to lie flat on the ground. According to Koon and Powell, King responded by getting down on all fours, slapping the ground, and refusing to lie down. Powell said he tried to force King to the ground, but King rose up and almost knocked him off his feet. . . .

Koon ordered the officers to "stand clear." King was still on the ground. Koon fired the Taser electric stun gun once, and then again. Koon subsequently reported that King did not respond to either firing. Powell's arrest report states that the Taser "temporarily halt[ed] deft's [King's] attack," and Solano stated that the Taser appeared to affect King at first because the suspect shook and yelled for almost five seconds. . . .

As George Holliday's videotape begins, King is on the ground. He rose and moved toward Powell. Solano termed it a "lunge," and said it was in the direction of Koon. It is not possible to tell from the videotape if King's movement is intended as an attack or simply an effort to get away. Taser wires can be seen coming from King's body.

As King moved forward, Powell struck King with his baton. The blow hit King's head, and he went down immediately. Powell hit King several additional times with his baton. The videotape shows Briseno moving in to try to stop Powell from swinging, and Powell then backing up, Koon reportedly yelled "that's enough." King then rose to his knees; Powell and Wind continued to hit King with their batons, while he was on the ground. King was struck again and again.

Koon acknowledged that he ordered the baton blows, directing Powell and Wind to hit King with "power strokes." According to Koon, Powell and Wind used "bursts of power strokes, then backed off."

Notwithstanding the repeated "power strokes" with the batons, the tape shows that King apparently continued to try to get up. Koon ordered the officers to "hit his joints, hit his wrists, hit his elbows, hit his knees, hit his ankles." Powell said he tried to strike King only in the arms and legs.

Finally, after 56 baton blows and six kicks, five or six officers swarmed in and placed King in both handcuffs and cordcuffs restraining his arms and legs. King was dragged on his stomach to the side of the road to await arrival of a rescue ambulance. . . .

Source: *Report of the Independent Commission on the Los Angeles Police Department* (Los Angeles: The Commission, 1991), 3–7.

THE DEATH PENALTY

The world's first electrical execution took place on August 6, 1890. William Kemmler, convicted of killing his wife, has the dubious honor of being the first prisoner executed by electrocution. Though an indigent, Kemmler had the benefit of prestigious counsel, including a former member of Congress. Kemmler's lawyers argued that electrical execution constituted an unconstitutional, cruel, and unusual punishment. Thomas Edison testified in support of this method of execution, describing his experiments on animals. Edison recommended using the alternating current employed by his bitter rival, George Westinghouse, insisting that it would most effectively kill a person, which his direct current would not. Edison clearly hoped to plant the idea in the public mind that alternating current kills. One Edison supporter even proposed using Westinghouse's name as a verb for the new mode of execution. If this had caught on, prisoners would be said to have been "Westinghoused."[8] As it developed, either means worked just fine.

8. Stuart Banner, *The Death Penalty: An American History* (Cambridge, MA: Harvard University Press, 2002), 177–96.

The Supreme Court did not think electrocution cruel or unusual. New York strapped Kemmler into its new chair, and the doomed man assured onlookers that he was going to "a good place." A state officer threw the switch, and Kemmler stiffened and then relaxed. A doctor pronounced Kemmler dead, but as he loosened the straps, someone yelled, "Great God! He is alive!" Everyone present could hear him breathing. When technicians sent a new jolt of electricity through Kemmler's body, the capillaries in his face burst and he appeared to sweat blood. The smell of scorched flesh and burning hair offended spectators. New York had discarded hanging in favor of electrocution in hopes of a more humane death penalty. "I would rather see ten hangings than one such execution as this," one witness said.[9]

Nonetheless, New York continued with electrocution. Other states followed, and by 1950, Alabama, Florida, Georgia, the District of Columbia, Illinois, New Mexico, Connecticut, South Dakota, Louisiana, Mississippi, West Virginia, and the United States government had all switched to electrical executions. The western states and the South generally preferred gas, while Utah and Nevada allowed shooting. Before 1878, Utah allowed prisoners to choose beheading if they preferred that over hanging or shooting.[10]

The debate over capital punishment goes back to at least the mid–eighteenth century, when those committed to the Enlightenment questioned the morality and utility of putting criminals to death. At that time, though, the death penalty was applied to a wide variety of crimes, from theft to treason. When the American Revolution tore American law away from its English common-law roots, there were more than four hundred capital crimes on the books in Great Britain. Over the next seventy years the more progressive state governments slowly removed more crimes from the list of capital offenses, until by the 1850s most northern and western states reserved death for homicide. But few people questioned capital punishment as a legitimate extension of state power for purposes of controlling crime. Chief Justice Melville Fuller's 1890 decision upholding the constitutionality of the death penalty appeared definitive.

The Supreme Court Considers the Electrocution of Convicted Criminals, *In re Kemmler*, 1890

MR. CHIEF JUSTICE FULLER delivered the opinion of the court:

... [C]ounsel for the petitioner offered to prove that the infliction of death by the application of electricity as directed "is a cruel and unusual punishment, within the meaning of the constitution, and that it cannot, therefore, be lawfully inflicted, and to establish the facts upon which the court can pass as to the character of the penalty. The attorney general objected to the taking of testimony as to the constitutionality of this law, on

9. Banner, *Death Penalty*, 186.
10. Banner, *Death Penalty*, 189, 203.

the ground that the court has no authority to take such proof. The objection was thereupon overruled, and the attorney general excepted." A voluminous mass of evidence was then taken as to the effect of electricity as an agent of death, and upon that evidence it was argued that the punishment in that form was cruel and unusual, within the inhibition of the constitutions of the United States and of the State of New York, and that therefore the act in question was unconstitutional. The county judge observed that the "constitution of the United States and that of the state of New York, in language almost identical, provide against cruel and inhuman punishment, but it may be remarked, in passing, that with the former we have no present concern, as the prohibition therein contained has no reference to punishments inflicted in state courts for crimes against the state, but is addressed solely to the national government, and operates as a restriction on its power." He held that the presumption of constitutionality had not been overcome by the prisoner, because he had not "made it appear, by proofs or otherwise, beyond doubt, that the statute of 1888 in regard to the infliction of the death penalty provides a cruel and unusual, and therefore unconstitutional, punishment, and that a force of electricity sufficient to kill any human subject with celerity and certainty, when scientifically applied, cannot be generated." He therefore made an order dismissing the writ of *habeas corpus*. . . .

It appears that the first step which led to the enactment of the law was a statement contained in the annual message of the governor of the state of New York, transmitted to the legislature January 6, 1885, as follows: "The present mode of executing criminals by hanging has come down to us from the dark ages, and it may well be questioned whether the science of the present day cannot provide a means for taking the life of such as are condemned to die in a less barbarous manner. I commend this suggestion to the consideration of the legislature." The legislature accordingly appointed a commission to investigate and report "the most humane and practical method known to modern science of carrying into effect the sentence of death in capital cases." This commission reported in favor of execution by electricity, and accompanied their report by a bill which was enacted and became chapter 489 of the Laws of 1888. Page 778. Among other changes, section 505 of the Code of Criminal Procedure of New York was amended so as to read as follows: "Sec. 505. The punishment of death must, in every case, be inflicted by causing to pass through the body of the convict a current of electricity of sufficient intensity to cause death, and the application of such current must be continued until such convict is dead." Various other amendments were made, not necessary to be considered here. . . .

The enactment of this statute was, in itself, within the legitimate sphere of the legislative power of the state, and in the observance of those general rules prescribed by our systems of jurisprudence; and the legislature of the state of New York determined that it did not inflict cruel and unusual punishment, and its courts have sustained that determination. We cannot perceive that the State has thereby abridged the privileges or immunities of the petitioner, or deprived him of due process of law.

In order to reverse the judgment of the highest court of the state of New York, we should be compelled to hold that it had committed an error so gross as to amount in law to a denial by the state of due process of law to one accused of crime, or of some right secured to him by the constitution of the United States. We have no hesitation in saying that this we cannot do upon the record before us. The application for a writ of error is Denied.

Source: 136 U.S. 436 (1890).

Following World War II, an increasing number of Americans opposed the death penalty as inappropriate for a modern, democratic nation. There were far too many instances of its misuse by the courts; too often the poor and ethnic minorities were sentenced to death without adequate counsel or for crimes that drew lesser punishments when committed by prosperous whites. In addition to this inconsistency of application, many critics charged that there was no evidence that executions deterred other criminals. At the very least, would not a proper deterrence require public executions? Further undermining the logic of the death penalty was the occasional instance of a condemned man being proved innocent, after it was too late to matter.

In 1972 the Supreme Court took these and other criticisms into account in effectively shutting down the death penalty in America. The high court declared capital punishment a cruel and unusual punishment as currently practiced, though only two justices thought the death penalty inherently unconstitutional. Unable to reach a consensus, each justice filed an individual decision in Furman v. Georgia, *an abbreviated version of which follows.*

Death penalty abolitionists celebrated, and even President Richard Nixon told a news conference that executions seemed cruel, though, he insisted, necessary. But polls indicated wide popular support for the death penalty, though whites liked it more than nonwhites. Confident of public support, state legislators rewrote capital punishment laws to get around the Supreme Court's limitations, most particularly by striving to make application of the death penalty more predictable and less random and therefore constitutional. Supporters of the death penalty insisted that not only did it act as a deterrent but that society also had a responsibility to extract retribution from those who had committed murder. At the very least the victims of homicide deserved this equity.

In 1976, in another Georgia case, Gregg v. Georgia, *the Supreme Court found the new wave of death penalty laws constitutional. Utah's Gary Gilmore became the first*

*person executed in the United States after the Supreme Court ended its brief moratorium.
State legislatures rushed the death penalty back onto the books in thirty-eight states.*

*The controversy did not end there. In the 1990s most state governments sought to
make the death penalty more "humane" through lethal injection. Those favoring the use
of chemicals as a means to terminate a condemned criminal argued that it "is a rapid,
pleasant way of producing unconsciousness" followed by death.[11] By the end of the decade,
thirty-seven states used lethal injection, while Nebraska stayed with electrocution.*

*But research into the chemicals employed indicated that they might produce a slow,
agonizing death. Most lethal injections consist of three chemicals: a short-acting barbitu-
rate that produces a brief anesthesia; pancuronium bromide, which paralyzes the muscles
but not the nerves; and potassium chloride, which stops the heart and causes excruciating
pain. Though those viewing the execution do not realize it, the injected prisoner is probably conscious and in great pain during the several minutes it takes the drugs to end his
or her life. Interestingly, in 2000, the American Veterinary Medical Association condemned the use of pancuronium bromide in the euthanasia of animals as unnecessarily
cruel. In 2003, a Tennessee Chancery Court judge felt that the same standard should be
applied to humans as to pets. Judge Ellen Hobbs Lyle wrote that lethal injection "gives
a false impression of serenity to viewers, making punishment by death more palatable
and acceptable to society."[12]*

*Further complicating the debate over the death penalty was the increased use of DNA
tests in the early twenty-first century. In 2001 and 2002, DNA tests led to the freeing of
more than a dozen men sitting on death row. Convinced that each case required more
careful review, George Ryan, the Republican governor of Illinois, declared a moratorium
on the death penalty. Outraged, his own party repudiated him, and Ryan, who also faced
corruption charges, did not run for reelection. One of his last acts as governor was to
commute the sentence of every prisoner on death row to a life sentence. But Governor
Ryan was the exception. Despite evidence of the cruelty of the primary method of execution and the unfortunate occurrences of the state putting innocent people to death,
most state governments and the majority of American voters remained content with both
the death penalty and lethal injection.*

The Supreme Court Considers the Death Penalty in *Furman v. Georgia*, 1972

PER CURIAM.

. . . The Court holds that the imposition and carrying out of the death
penalty in these cases constitute cruel and unusual punishment in violation

---

11. Dr. Stanley Deutsch, who developed the chemical protocol used in most states, quoted in
Adam Liptak, "Critics Say Execution Drug May Hide Suffering," *New York Times*, October
7, 2003.

12. Liptak, "Critics Say Execution Drug May Hide Suffering."

of the Eighth and Fourteenth Amendments. The judgment in each case is therefore reversed insofar as it leaves undisturbed the death sentence imposed, and the cases are remanded for further proceedings.

So ordered.

MR. JUSTICE DOUGLAS, MR. JUSTICE BRENNAN, MR. JUSTICE STEWART, MR. JUSTICE WHITE, and JR. JUSTICE MARSHALL have filed separate opinions in support of the judgments. THE CHIEF JUSTICE, MR. JUSTICE BLACKMUN, MR. JUSTICE POWELL, and MR. JUSTICE REHNQUIST have filed separate dissenting opinions.

MR. JUSTICE BRENNAN, concurring.

. . . Death is truly an awesome punishment. The calculated killing of a human being by the State involves, by its very nature, a denial of the executed person's humanity. The contrast with the plight of a person punished by imprisonment is evident. An individual in prison does not lose "the right to have rights." A prisoner retains, for example, the constitutional rights to the free exercise of religion, to be free of cruel and unusual punishments, and to treatment as a "person" for purposes of due process of law and the equal protection of the laws. A prisoner remains a member of the human family. Moreover, he retains the right of access to the courts. His punishment is not irrevocable. Apart from the common charge, grounded upon the recognition of human fallibility, that the punishment of death must inevitably be inflicted upon innocent men, we know that death has been the lot of men whose convictions were unconstitutionally secured in view of later, retroactively applied, holdings of this Court. The punishment itself may have been unconstitutionally inflicted . . . yet the finality of death precludes relief. An executed person has indeed "lost the right to have rights." As one 19th century proponent of punishing criminals by death declared, "When a man is hung, there is an end of our relations with him. His execution is a way of saying, 'You are not fit for this world, take your chance elsewhere.' "

In comparison to all other punishments today, then, the deliberate extinguishment of human life by the State is uniquely degrading to human dignity. I would not hesitate to hold, on that ground alone, that death is today a "cruel and unusual" punishment, were it not that death is a punishment of longstanding usage and acceptance in this country. I therefore turn to the second principle—that the State may not arbitrarily inflict an unusually severe punishment.

The outstanding characteristic of our present practice of punishing criminals by death is the infrequency with which we resort to it. The evidence is conclusive that death is not the ordinary punishment for any crime.

There has been a steady decline in the infliction of this punishment in every decade since the 1930's, the earliest period for which accurate statistics are available. In the 1930's, executions averaged 167 per year; in the 1940's, the average was 128; in the 1950's, it was 72; and in the years 1960–1962, it was 48. There have been a total of 46 executions since then, 36 of them in 1963–1964. Yet our population and the number of capital crimes committed have increased greatly over the past four decades. The contemporary rarity of the infliction of this punishment is thus the end result of a long-continued decline. That rarity is plainly revealed by an examination of the years 1961–1970, the last 10-year period for which statistics are available. During that time, an average of 106 death sentences was imposed each year. Not nearly that number, however, could be carried out, for many were precluded by commutations to life or a term of years, transfers to mental institutions because of insanity, resentences to life or a term of years, grants of new trials and orders for resentencing, dismissals of indictments and reversals of convictions, and deaths by suicide and natural causes. On January 1, 1961, the death row population was 219; on December 31, 1970, it was 608; during that span, there were 135 executions. Consequently, had the 389 additions to death row also been executed, the annual average would have been 52. In short, the country might, at most, have executed one criminal each week. In fact, of course, far fewer were executed. Even before the moratorium on executions began in 1967, executions totaled only 42 in 1961 and 47 in 1962, an average of less than one per week; the number dwindled to 21 in 1963, to 15 in 1964, and to seven in 1965; in 1966, there was one execution, and in 1967, there were two.

When a country of over 200 million people inflicts an unusually severe punishment no more than 50 times a year, the inference is strong that the punishment is not being regularly and fairly applied. To dispel it would indeed require a clear showing of nonarbitrary infliction.

Although there are no exact figures available, we know that thousands of murders and rapes are committed annually in States where death is an authorized punishment for those crimes. However the rate of infliction is characterized—as "freakishly" or "spectacularly" rare, or simply as rare—it would take the purest sophistry to deny that death is inflicted in only a minute fraction of these cases. How much rarer, after all, could the infliction of death be?

When the punishment of death is inflicted in a trivial number of the cases in which it is legally available, the conclusion is virtually inescapable that it is being inflicted arbitrarily. Indeed, it smacks of little more than a lottery system. The States claim, however, that this rarity is evidence not of arbitrariness, but of informed selectivity: Death is inflicted, they say, only in "extreme" cases. . . .

Thus, although "the death penalty has been employed throughout our history," . . . in fact the history of this punishment is one of successive restriction. What was once a common punishment has become, in the context of a continuing moral debate, increasingly rare. The evolution of this punishment evidences, not that it is an inevitable part of the American scene, but that it has proved progressively more troublesome to the national conscience. The result of this movement is our current system of administering the punishment, under which death sentences are rarely imposed and death is even more rarely inflicted. It is, of course, "We, the People" who are responsible for the rarity both of the imposition and the carrying out of this punishment. Juries, "express[ing] the conscience of the community on the ultimate question of life or death," . . . have been able to bring themselves to vote for death in a mere 100 or so cases among the thousands tried each year where the punishment is available. Governors, elected by and acting for us, have regularly commuted a substantial number of those sentences. And it is our society that insists upon due process of law to the end that no person will be unjustly put to death, thus ensuring that many more of those sentences will not be carried out. In sum, we have made death a rare punishment today.

The progressive decline in, and the current rarity of, the infliction of death demonstrate that our society seriously questions the appropriateness of this punishment today. . . . The objective indicator of society's view of an unusually severe punishment is what society does with it, and today society will inflict death upon only a small sample of the eligible criminals. Rejection could hardly be more complete without becoming absolute. At the very least, I must conclude that contemporary society views this punishment with substantial doubt. . . .

Death is an unusually severe and degrading punishment; there is a strong probability that it is inflicted arbitrarily; its rejection by contemporary society is virtually total; and there is no reason to believe that it serves any penal purpose more effectively than the less severe punishment of imprisonment. The function of these principles is to enable a court to determine whether a punishment comports with human dignity. Death, quite simply, does not.

I concur in the judgments of the Court.

MR. JUSTICE STEWART, concurring.

. . . I cannot agree that retribution is a constitutionally impermissible ingredient in the imposition of punishment. The instinct for retribution is part of the nature of man, and channeling that instinct in the administration of criminal justice serves an important purpose in promoting the stability of a society governed by law. When people begin to believe that organized society is unwilling or unable to impose upon criminal offenders the punishment they "deserve," then there are sown the seeds of anarchy—of self-help, vigilante justice, and lynch law.

The constitutionality of capital punishment in the abstract is not, however, before us in these cases. For the Georgia and Texas Legislatures have not provided that the death penalty shall be imposed upon all those who are found guilty of forcible rape. And the Georgia Legislature has not ordained that death shall be the automatic punishment for murder. In a word, neither State has made a legislative determination that forcible rape and murder can be deterred only by imposing the penalty of death upon all who perpetrate those offenses. As Mr. Justice White so tellingly puts it, the "legislative will is not frustrated if the penalty is never imposed."

Instead, the death sentences now before us are the product of a legal system that brings them, I believe, within the very core of the Eighth Amendment's guarantee against cruel and unusual punishments, a guarantee applicable against the States through the Fourteenth Amendment. In the first place, it is clear that these sentences are "cruel" in the sense that they excessively go beyond, not in degree but in kind, the punishments that the state legislatures have determined to be necessary. In the second place, it is equally clear that these sentences are "unusual" in the sense that the penalty of death is infrequently imposed for murder, and that its imposition for rape is extraordinarily rare. But I do not rest my conclusion upon these two propositions alone.

These death sentences are cruel and unusual in the same way that being struck by lightning is cruel and unusual. For, of all the people convicted of rapes and murders in 1967 and 1968, many just as reprehensible as these, the petitioners are among a capriciously selected random handful upon whom the sentence of death has in fact been imposed. My concurring Brothers have demonstrated that, if any basis can be discerned for the selection of these few to be sentenced to die, it is the constitutionally impermissible basis of race. But racial discrimination has not been proved, and I put it to one side. I simply conclude that the Eighth and Fourteenth Amendments cannot tolerate the infliction of a sentence of death under legal systems that permit this unique penalty to be so wantonly and so freakishly imposed.

For these reasons I concur in the judgments of the Court.

Source: 408 U.S. 238 (1972).

FURTHER READINGS

The history of policing in the United States is surprisingly thin, though there are a number of first-rate books on the subject. See Roger Lane, *Policing the City, Boston, 1822–1885* (Cambridge, MA: Harvard University Press, 1967); Robert M. Fogelson, *Big-City Police* (Cambridge, MA: Harvard University Press, 1977); Eric H. Monkkonen, *Police in Urban America, 1860–1920* (Cambridge: Cambridge University Press, 1981); Lawrence M. Friedman, *Crime and Punishment in American*

History (New York: Basic Books, 1993); Dennis Rousey, *Policing the Southern City: New Orleans, 1805–1889* (Baton Rouge: Louisiana State University Press, 1996); Sanford H. Kadish, "Fifty Years of Criminal Law: An Opinionated Review," *Columbia Law Review* 87 (July 1999): 943–982. For an interesting comparative study, see Wilbur R. Miller, *Cops and Bobbies: Police Authority in New York and London, 1830–1870* (Chicago: University of Chicago Press, 1977). Few works deal specifically with police abuse of authority. See, however, Jill Nelson, ed., *Police Brutality: An Anthology* (New York: Norton, 2000).

On the social aspects of policing in America, see David Courtwright, *Dark Paradise: Opiate Addiction in America before 1940* (Cambridge, MA: Harvard University Press, 1982); Lou Cannon, *Official Negligence: How Rodney King and the Riots Changed Los Angeles and the LAPD* (New York: Times Book, 1997); Janis Appier, *Policing Women: The Sexual Politics of Law Enforcement and the LAPD* (Philadelphia: Temple University Press, 1998); Edward J. Escobar, *Race, Police, and the Making of a Political Identity: Mexican Americans and the Los Angeles Police Department, 1900–1945* (Berkeley: University of California Press, 1999).

Organized crime has generated a rich and often exaggerated scholarship. Among the most thoroughly researched works are Donald R. Cressey, *Theft of a Nation: The Structure and Operations of Organized Crime in America* (New York: Harper and Row, 1969); William Howard Moore, *The Kefauver Committee and the Politics of Crime, 1950–1952* (Columbia: University of Missouri Press, 1974); Alan Block and William Chambliss, *Organizing Crime* (New York: Elsevier, 1981); Stephen Fox, *Blood and Power: Organized Crime in Twentieth-century America* (New York: Morrow, 1989); Robert J. Kelly, *The Upperworld and the Underworld* (New York: Kluwer, 1999).

The death penalty has generated an extensive literature, including many studies of individual executions such as Norman Mailer's *Executioner's Song* (Boston: Little, Brown, 1979) on the Gilmore case. For a general study of the issue, see Stuart Banner, *The Death Penalty: An American History* (Cambridge, MA: Harvard University Press, 2002). For more specific studies, see Victor L. Streib, *Death Penalty for Juveniles* (Bloomington: Indiana University Press, 1987); Louis P. Masur, *Rites of Execution: Capital Punishment and the Transformation of American Culture, 1776–1865* (New York: Oxford University Press, 1989); William S. McFeely, *Proximity to Death* (New York: Norton, 2000); Marlin Shipman, *"The Penalty Is Death": U.S. Newspaper Coverage of Women's Executions* (Columbia: University of Missouri Press, 2002); Michael A. Foley, *Arbitrary and Capricious: The Supreme Court, the Constitution, and the Death Penalty* (Westport, CT: Praeger, 2003).

TEN

CIVIL RIGHTS

A frican Americans emerged from the Civil War and Reconstruction knowing that the balance of power between the states and the federal government was no mere academic question. Their lives depended on the willingness of Washington to "interfere" in matters traditionally left to the states. Before the Civil War, the states had looked after citizens' rights and controlled crime with no thought that federal authorities might have any role to play. In the Civil War and its aftermath it seemed for a moment that the federal government might take over some of those responsibilities, protecting the lives and the rights of freed slaves from their former owners. Congress passed laws against discrimination and vigilantism. For African Americans it was a choice between state authorities, the same people who had maintained slavery, and the federal government that had fostered emancipation and now offered to guard their rights. Put simply, when the Union army came to town, slavery was over. When the army left, something a lot like slavery resumed.

The Supreme Court dashed whatever hopes African Americans held for long-term federal protection. When the Supreme Court ruled in 1883 that "when a man has emerged from slavery . . . there must be some stage in the progress of his elevation when he . . . ceases to be the special favorite of the laws," it left the job of protecting African Americans' rights and lives to the states.[1] A wave of racial violence followed, with whites burning, torturing, brutalizing, and hanging black Americans, confident the federal government would do nothing.

Civil rights in the twentieth century is a chronicle of a long struggle to persuade the federal government to protect the lives of its citizens, to realize the promise of the Civil War. The most important right blacks sought was the

---

1. Civil Rights Cases, 109 U.S. 3 (1883).

right to stay alive. In the first decades of the twentieth century, the National Association for the Advancement of Colored People (NAACP) lobbied Congress for a law against lynching. White southerners refused to accept federal protection of even this most basic right. Southern congressmen rallied against this effort, successfully beating it back every time, often with lengthy filibusters.

The 1932 election of Franklin D. Roosevelt promised a season of reform, reviving hope that Congress might finally pass an antilynching law. At the end of 1933 Walter White, the NAACP's executive secretary, recruited Senators Edward Costigan and Robert Wagner to cosponsor a bill punishing communities that tolerated mob rule. White mobilized popular support, but his most important lobbying occurred at the White House. Winning Roosevelt's approval was vital as the president could energize the congressional leadership and demand action from Congress. White made his case directly to Roosevelt, but the president explained that he could not jeopardize his New Deal program by actively supporting a measure his southern congressional allies so vehemently opposed. FDR told journalists he opposed lynching and favored Costigan and Wagner's objectives but did little more.

White's friendly relations with the Roosevelt administration did him little good. It is one of the great ironies of the civil rights struggle that proponents of civil rights legislation could always count on their enemies for help. In 1934, Florida lynchers immeasurably boosted White's cause by kidnapping and hanging Claude Neal, forcing him to eat his own genitalia. The NAACP publicized this grisly episode. Many congressmen found Neal's death, and the way his killers had tortured him, strong support for a federal law against lynching. Even without a law, White hoped that federal authorities might act. Since Neal's killers kidnapped their victim before torturing and hanging him, White thought the federal government might investigate the crime as a kidnapping rather than a lynching, yet even that strategy failed.

World War II, and Roosevelt's choice of Frank Murphy as a successor to Homer Cummings as attorney general, sparked a genuine federal effort to punish lynchers. Murphy created a civil rights unit within the Justice Department just a month after he took office in 1939. Murphy's appointment did nothing for a federal antilynching law in Congress, but his Justice Department prosecutors sincerely tried to reinvigorate old laws in a new war on mob violence. Murphy tried to shift power over one kind of crime from the states to the federal government.

In 1944 Murphy's efforts yielded results: a Georgia jury convicted Sheriff M. Claude Screws and two other men of violating the civil rights of Robert Hall. Hall had been beaten to death, a murder Georgia refused to investigate. This murder by a violently racist sheriff was exactly the sort of crime Costigan and Wagner had wanted to cover with their failed antilynching law. Since white southerners defeated the Costigan-Wagner measure, the Justice Department relied on a Reconstruction-era law that forbade violations of civil rights "under color of law." Government prosecutors said that the world war and the need to present a more positive image abroad meant that neighborhood "lynching bees" now had international consequences. Unfortunately, the Supreme Court remained entirely unmoved by such rhetoric. It not only overturned the convictions but set standards of proof so high as to make it more difficult to win convictions in future cases. In Mississippi in 1955, two white men murdered a young black man named Emmett Till. A state jury quickly acquitted the pair, and the federal government played no role in the prosecution. The Department of Justice took no action even when the two killers confessed their crime on the pages of *Look* magazine.

The same year Emmett Till died, African Americans in Montgomery, Alabama, decided to boycott city buses until drivers showed greater courtesy and the bus company hired black drivers. Boycott organizers elected a charismatic young minister named Martin Luther King as their leader. As a student King had become enamored of Reinhold Niebuhr's vision of nonviolent protest as a strategic tool for oppressed people. Niebuhr presented Gandhi's protest strategy as a combination of religion and politics in a way that King found appealing. King's nonviolence became a centerpiece of the American civil rights movement.

Just as King and his followers came to embrace nonviolence, white southern racists doggedly persisted in their violence. But in the postwar environment, whites' spectacular violence worked to fire national and international indignation. Reports of some new sensational act of violence revolted Americans who otherwise might have been sympathetic toward racism.

Reformers exploited white southerners' violent tendencies as a way of forcing the federal government to become more involved. The goal of the civil rights movement, at its most basic, was to shift power away from the states and into the hands of federal officials. James Farmer, head of the Congress of Racial Equality, organized parties of activists, Freedom Riders, to desegregate interstate bus travel. Farmer notified federal authorities, calling on them for protection. Failing that, he hoped widespread reporting of the violence he expected his Freedom Riders to encounter would move northerners away from their racial indifference. In 1964 a coalition of reform organizations sent college students into Mississippi ostensibly to teach black citizens to read and write so they could register to vote. In fact, the organizers of Freedom Summer expected white southern racists to brutalize some of the college students. Julian Bond supervised public relations, photographing each college student and taking note of their hometown newspapers and radio and television stations. The idea was to publicize every attack, every brutality.

The racists played their part to tragic extremes. In Neshoba County, Mississippi, the local sheriff's office conspired with members of the Ku Klux Klan to murder three of the civil rights workers. Michael Schwerner, Andrew Goodman, and James Chaney died in rural Mississippi, murdered and buried under an earthen dam. Agents of the Federal Bureau of Investigation uncovered the bodies and gathered evidence against eighteen suspects. A jury composed entirely of Mississippi whites convicted seven of the accused men, including Deputy Sheriff Cecil Ray Price. The convictions came in 1967, but in some ways the real drama came a year earlier when the Supreme Court ruled that state officers and civilians consorting with state officers could be convicted in federal court of civil rights crimes. The federal government finally asserted itself as ultimately responsible for the rights and lives of American citizens.

DOCUMENTS

A LAW AGAINST LYNCHING

Walter White's difficulties with Roosevelt's attorney general, Homer Cummings, document the NAACP's inability to extract serious support from the administration for an anti-lynching bill in Congress. In his memorandum recounting his meeting with Cummings, White, the NAACP's executive secretary, refers to himself as "the Secretary." White's best ally in the Roosevelt administration was Eleanor Roosevelt, the president's wife. Congress never passed a law against lynching, but in 2005 the senate apologized for this failure, expressing its regrets to the descendants of lynching victims.

Walter White Meets with Attorney General Homer Cummings, 1936

MEMORANDUM OF CONFERENCE OF THE SECRETARY WITH THE ATTORNEY GENERAL, JANUARY 16, 1936

At the beginning of the interview the Attorney General seemed slightly as though his mind was not upon the interview. Although the Secretary had written the Attorney General that he wished to talk with him at the request of the President, the Attorney General asked the Secretary his name and address, which he wrote on a pad, and some five or six minutes later interrupted the Secretary to ask, "And who do you say you represent?"

The Secretary told Mr. Cummings of the President's suggestion of a bill authorizing the Department of Justice to investigate the improper interference with the courts and due process. He told Mr. Cummings of the Association's doubts, the chief of which was that this would not specifically reach lynchings and that either a hostile or indifferent Department of Justice would unquestionably find means of not investigating lynchings under the law if passed; and (2) that the chief weapon against lynching is the financial penalty against the county as provided in the Costigan-Wagner Bill, which financial penalty is not included in the bill as suggested by the President.

At the conclusion of his statement the Attorney General asked the Secretary, somewhat bluntly, "And what do you want me to do about it?" The Secretary replied, "Nothing. I am here only because the President of the United States asked me to talk with you."

After this the Attorney General was considerably more friendly. He expressed doubt as [to] the value of the legislation, saying that its effect would be only a moral one, and that the Department of Justice would be unable to enforce it unless Congress appropriated more money for additional investigators through the Department of Justice. At some considerable length he told of the Department's having some 1400 cases awaiting investigation and of the prerequisites for investigators and the training which they had to undergo. As this was not a matter on which the Secretary could do anything and was not wholly pertinent to the discussion, the Secretary expressed his sympathy with the Attorney General but reminded him that this was a problem which he and the President and the Congress would have to work out.

The Secretary asked the Attorney General if he would support an amendment to the Lindbergh Kidnapping Law providing for federal action in the case of persons kidnapped for the purpose of injuring or lynching them. The Attorney General said he would enforce the law if it was passed but would not commit himself as to whether he would actually support such an amendment. . . .

The Attorney General read at great length from the *World Almanac*'s figures on the number of lynchings since 1889, stating that opponents of federal anti-lynching legislation had used the argument to him (which the Secretary gained the impression the Attorney General agreed with) that lynchings were decreasing and would soon die out. The Secretary pointed out that during recent years lynchings were increasing rather than decreasing and that the growing lawlessness in the country, coupled with the economic depression and the growth of Fascist tendencies, made it well within the range of possibility that there might be still further increase in lynchings not only of Negroes but of white people as well. . . .

The Secretary gained the impression that the Attorney General is neither hostile nor favorable to federal legislation against lynching but that instead he is indifferent and not particularly interested in lynching at all. . . .

The Secretary left the interview with the distinct impression that the Attorney General is not particularly interested in the Negro, nor is he hostile; that despite his somewhat frequent assertions that the Department was run on a basis of efficiency and not politics, politics was not an inconsiderable factor in his thinking; that the Attorney General is not a man of great strength of character or ability.

Source: Papers of the NAACP Part I, special correspondence. Microfilm: University Publications of America, reel 26.

Walter White Appeals to Eleanor Roosevelt, 1936

Walter White to Mrs. Eleanor Roosevelt, February 28, 1936
Dear Mrs. Roosevelt:

I tried to reach you by telephone while in Washington this week but was unable to do so because of your absence from the city. I was told at the White House that you were to be away for the week. As the matter which I wished to discuss with you is so pressing and grave, I am writing you instead of waiting until I can discuss it with you personally.

I am very much disturbed by some of the things I learned at Washington this week. I well realize that in an election year controversial issues are uncomfortable for members of the Congress, especially those who are to stand for reelection. But there seems to be timidity on the part of a good many people on the matter of lynching or any other issue affecting the Negro to an extraordinary degree, which, added to the hostility of certain southern senators to any form of action against lynching, makes the outlook distinctly discouraging. I don't as a rule pay much attention to rumors, especially in Washington; but several persons told me that an order had gone out this week from the Democratic National Committee advising Democratic senators and congressmen to avoid all controversial issues. This report, naturally, did not add any hope for action on lynching. . . .

On January 2 the President told me that he wished some sort of action by this Congress on lynching. Apparently, there is little hope of getting the Costigan-Wagner Bill up for debate and vote. Attorney General Cummings, with whom I talked again on Wednesday, has made a very careful study of the Supreme Court's decision in the Gooch case (Arthur Gooch vs. United States of America #559), and he is of the opinion that Mr. Justice McReynolds in writing the decision sufficiently stressed possible pecuniary advantage to the kidnapper to make it doubtful that the kidnappers of Claude Neal could be punished under the Lindbergh Kidnapping Law.

Thus we face a situation where there is little likelihood of action on the Costigan-Wagner Bill, no possibility of action by the Department of Justice against the kidnappers of Claude Neal. . . .

I am not making a plea for the N.A.A.C.P. or for myself personally, but here is the plight in which this debacle puts us: . . .

Just a fortnight ago more than a thousand persons paid their own expenses to attend a "National Negro Congress" in Chicago. The N.A.A.C.P. refused to participate in or to endorse this Congress, first, because we were not given sufficient information about its sponsorship, program or purposes, and, second, because there were too many rumors that it was being pushed in some respects by Communists and in others by Republicans. But at this Congress statements were made especially critical of the N.A.A.C.P. to the effect that we had been promising action against lynching and failed to show any results. I do not know yet who the sponsors were of the meeting in Chicago, but the spirit of unrest and revolt which it represented is not in the main an artificially stimulated one but is instead an expression of a widespread dissatisfaction which cannot and should not be ignored.

Investigation since I last saw you has established that there were twenty-five authenticated lynchings during 1935, nineteen of them after the filibuster; there are six additional cases being investigated; there were eleven cases where the mob spirit ran so high that troops with drawn bayonets, machine guns, tear gas bombs and the like were necessary to protect prisoners while they were being tried; and there were fifty-five cases, involving a total of eighty-five persons, where lynchings were narrowly averted by the augmenting of guards, removal of prisoners and the like. Students of the lynching situation like Dr. Arthur Raper of the Interracial Commission and Judge Orville Parks of Georgia declare that an averted lynching of this sort is fundamentally as serious as a consummated lynching, in that it shows the presence of potential lynching. If this point of view be accepted, one will realize how very serious the situation is growing when there were one hundred and twenty-seven cases in a single year of actual or potential lynching. This will amply explain the rapidly growing and very widespread feeling regarding inaction on the Costigan-Wagner Bill. . . . Now that warm weather is coming when people can gather out of doors I look for a resumption of lynchings.

Please forgive me for writing at such length and in such a gloomy vein. But I have returned from Washington more discouraged than I have ever before. I think it is a very serious mistake to assume that it will be safer politically to pass the buck and dodge the issue simply because this is an election year. Such a course may conceivably cost in November far more than will be gained by letting the Costigan-Wagner Bill . . . be strangled to death.

   If you will do so, I would be glad if you would share these facts with the President. Should either you or he wish me to do so, I shall be glad to talk them over with you at your convenience.

Source: Papers of the NAACP Part I, special correspondence. Microfilm: University Publications of America, reel 26.

Victor Rotnem Argues for a Civil Right "Not to Be Lynched," 1943

With the outbreak of World War II, the attitudes White found so intractable in 1936 changed. Historians have recently emphasized the importance of American concerns about world opinion in shaping civil rights policy. These concerns are voiced in this law review article, written by Victor Rotnem, head of the Department of Justice's Civil Rights unit.

   Prior to January 25, 1942, Cleo Wright, a Negro citizen of the State of Missouri and of the United States, had been arrested by the local police offi-cers of Sikeston, Missouri, was being held under arrest in the local jail, and was facing charges of assault and attempted rape under the criminal laws of the State of Missouri. On January 25, 1942, in broad daylight, a mob broke into the jail, seized and removed Cleo Wright, tied his feet to the rear of an automobile, dragged him through the Negro section of the town, and then poured gasoline on his body and burned him to death.

   Within forty-eight hours thereafter, the German and Japanese short wave radio broadcasters featured discussions of the "Sikeston Affair" in all its sor-did details. These broadcasts were relayed to the peoples of the Dutch East Indies and India at a time immediately preceding the fall of Java; and listen-ers were told, in effect:—

   "If the democracies win the War, here is what the colored races may ex-pect of them."

   Thus the lynching at Sikeston, Missouri, became a matter of international importance and a subject of Axis propaganda.

   On February 13, 1942, Assistant Attorney General Wendell Berge requested the Federal Bureau of Investigation to make a full inquiry into the lynching at Sikeston to determine whether there was any basis for prosecution by the federal government of the members of the mob, or other persons concerned. In authorizing the federal investigation, Attorney General Biddle indicated the significance of the incident to war morale, for he stated:—

   "With our country at war to defend our democratic way of life throughout the world a lynching has significance far beyond the community, or even the state, in which it occurs. It becomes a matter of national importance and thus properly the concern of the federal government."

Although it is a matter of national importance, yet, under our system of government, there must be found constitutional power for federal legislation before the federal government can concern itself through federal action; and before an act can be made the basis for federal prosecution, even where there is constitutional power to legislate, applicable federal legislation must in fact exist.

Attorney General Biddle directed that evidence on the lynching at Sikeston be presented to a federal grand jury. The session of the federal grand jury to hear this evidence began in St. Louis on May 13, 1942. On July 30, 1942, the United States Department of Justice made public the grand jury's report. The grand jury returned no indictments but made an advisory report to the United States District Court. This report recommended both state legislative and executive action, but it made no recommendation for a federal statute to make the lynching of a person *in custodia legis* of the state a federal crime. Nor did the grand jury find that a federal crime had been committed.

Describing the lynching as "a shameful outrage," and censuring the Sikeston police for having "failed completely to cope with the situation," the federal grand jury report nevertheless concluded, "with great reluctance," that the facts disclosed did not constitute a federal crime under existing laws. Still, the grand jury report stated:—

"In this instance a brutal criminal was denied *due process*. The next time the mob might lynch a person entirely innocent. But whether the victim be guilty or innocent, the blind passion of a mob cannot be substitute for *due process of law* if orderly government is to survive."

... No disrespect for the conclusions of the federal grand jury is intended. However, the determination of a grand jury that the facts disclosed do not constitute a federal crime under existing laws is not conclusive. A final determination of that question can be had only when an appeal presents to the United States Supreme Court the opportunity to hear and decide the issue. ...

A grand jury is not the final arbiter or even a persuasive voice of what comes within the purview of either the Constitution or the statutes of the United States. . . . it would appear that the grand jury in the Sikeston matter should have overcome its "great reluctance," returned indictments, and left to the final arbiter in our constitutional system, the Supreme Court, the clarification of this important area of the law.

The evil of lynchings exists and doubt as to whether or not federal power now exists to remedy it can only adversely affect our national morale. Hence,

it is highly desirable that whatever doubt that may exist be authoritatively resolved.

Source: Victor W. Rotnem, "The Federal Civil Right 'Not to Be Lynched,' " *Washington University Law Quarterly* 28 (February 1943): 57–59, 73.

Justice Frank Murphy's Notes on the Supreme Court Debate over a Right Not to Be Lynched, 1944

*Although it may be that global concerns animated interest in civil rights, the limits of
this rhetoric became evident when the Justice Department finally managed to win a
conviction of three Georgia lynchers. The Supreme Court showed no concern whatsoever
with America's standing as a global competitor on the world stage.*

*In 1944 the Supreme Court reviewed the convictions of Sheriff M. Claude Screws and
two other Georgia lawmen, guilty of beating a black man to death. Frank Murphy, who
as attorney general had created the Civil Rights Unit, now sat on the Court. There are
no official records of the Supreme Court's conferences; Murphy, though, took sixteen pages
of handwritten notes. His notes are sometimes cryptic, as notes often are, but they capture
the justices' hostility toward the strategy of the federal government's lawyers. In 1944 the
Supreme Court still believed that crime control was a job for the states and not the
federal government. The justices had, since shortly after the Civil War, protected the states'
prerogatives by insisting that the Constitution only forbade state actions—not the activities
of private persons, even if those persons were state employees. The justices also worried
that the 1870 law the government had used to prosecute Screws was too vague in that it
promised to protect citizens' rights, without specifying just what those rights might be.*

CJ [Chief Justice Harlan Fiske Stone] Screws petitioners indicted under section 20 of CC goes back to civil rights time.

Petitioners, local sheriff, police officer & citizen summoned to his aid acting under warrant beat him to death. prisoner was armed. Case was submitted to jury on narrow case whether they used unnecessary force. Jury found
against him.

Does state officer proceeding under state law exceed his authority violate
this section? . . .

2 questions here.

1st is action of state officer in performance of his duties . . . cause in application of state law acts in excess state law.

2 is this statute to[o] vague to authorized its application. . . .

Where he went beyond taking & arresting his prisoner if he intentionally
goes beyond that he exceeds authority & it is state action. . . .

In respect to indefiniteness . . . it is not as vague as Sherman act case. if man intentionally does not act, under color of his office, under authority of his office he denies rights & privileges of 14th Amendment if he does the act. I would affirm.

[Justice Owen] *Roberts* . . . I don't believe 14th [amendment] was meant to justify action under Federal jurisdiction whatever might have been state remedy. The 14th amendment was never intended to reach this. I pass. . . .

[Justice Stanley] *Reed* This was action by state officer. Next statute protects all categories of state law of privileges & immunities arriving from federal law.

This comes under due process & that alone. it is difficult for me to define this as a denial of due process. I would reverse.

[Justice Felix Frankfurter] *FF* If you can indict—you can also bring a civil suit. There would be pressure on state officials—indictment & civil action over every-state official. . . .

The point is the affect upon the whole administration of law within the state government.

I *would* reverse on grounds statute does not apply to this case. . . .

[Justice Robert] *Jackson—* . . . I don't think we can transfer into Federal action things that are not intended to be.

You can't run these things from Washington.

Problems of local justice must be left to their communities.

If we sustain this every time a negro is beaten you are going to have [Frank Murphy] and others jumping on state for action.

And then your local officer will lay down on the job—so will the local judge. They will say let Washington do it. . . .

CJ But when Congress passed this they didn't want to limit.

Jackson I consider the [Reconstruction] period one of the most shameful of our times. . . .

This interpretation belongs to Frank.

It was never used up until that time.

We are going to be misunderstood as favoring a beating.

They didn't contemplate 14th amendment doing anything as here.

CJ I don't believe they contemplated every excess of authority. They had in mind what was happening then—deprivation of negro's suffrage. . . .

[Justice Hugo] *Black* . . . If act means something you can't set it aside because of consequences. Every officer in the union could be indicted for search & seizure, and for assaults on prisoners.

You are deciding guilt of murder—we are talking here right to try every state officer.

(C.J. but here he is doing it under color of his office.)

If Congress had passed law saying any state officer then I would have a different question.

I can't believe involvement of that law was intended to embrace conduct of every state officer in denying due process. . . .

Roberts I am certain 14th Amendment was not meant to punish every petty offender. . . .

Jackson This is anti-lynching bill if government is sustained.

Black We, if we uphold this, are doing what Congress had not intended to do.

Reed I shudder from declaring statute unconstitutional when we go into legislative history it will go bad for us.

Black This statute does violate due process. This man is not to be tried under a statute that should definitely inform him. . . .

Source: Frank Murphy Papers, microfilm roll 129, Bentley Historical Library, Ann Arbor, Michigan.

EMMETT TILL

In 1955 two Mississippi white men, Ray Bryant and J. W. Milam, killed young Emmett Till deep in the Mississippi Delta. They went on trial for murder, and an all-white jury quickly acquitted them. Alabama journalist William Bradford Huie contacted the men's lawyers and arranged to pay for an interview.

Huie paints an ugly picture of two men at the bottom of Mississippi society who admitted to murder yet sought justification by describing Till as defiant and challenging. Huie's version of the killers' story fascinates for opening a window on the thinking of two violent racists.

Even after Huie published his interview in Look, *the federal government took no action. In* Screws v. United States, *the Supreme Court ruled that prosecutors had to prove that those charged with the violation of a citizen's civil rights had it in mind to take away federally protected rights when they acted, a high standard of proof. Though the local sheriff had protected Bryant and Milam, neither of the killers of Emmett Till worked for Mississippi. Despite their confessions, Bryant and Milam both escaped conviction. In 2004 the Department of Justice announced it was finally opening an investigation into Till's death.*

William Bradford Huie Describes "The Shocking Story of Approved Killing in Mississippi," 1956

Milam: "Well, what else could we do? He was hopeless. I'm no bully; I never hurt a nigger in my life. I like niggers—in their place—I know how to work 'em. But I just decided it was time a few people got put on notice. As long as I live and can do anything about it, niggers are gonna stay in their place. Niggers ain't gonna vote where I live. If they did, they'd control the government. They ain't gonna go to school with my kids. And when a nigger even gets close to mentioning sex with a white woman, he's tired o' livin'. I'm likely to kill him. Me and my folks fought for this country, and we've got some rights. I stood there in that shed and listened to that nigger throw that poison at me, and I just made up my mind. 'Chicago boy,' I said, 'I'm tired of 'em sending your kind down here to stir up trouble. Goddamn you, I'm going to make an example of you—just so everybody can know who me and my folks stand.' "

So big Milam decided to act. He needed a weight. He tried to think where he could get an anvil. Then he remembered a gin which had installed new equipment. He had seen two men lifting a discarded fan, a metal fan three feet high and circular, used in ginning cotton.

Bobo wasn't bleeding much. Pistol-whipping bruises more than it cuts. They ordered him back in the truck and headed west again. They passed through Doddsville, went to the Progressive Ginning Company. This gin is 3.4 miles east of Boyle; Boyle is two miles south of Cleveland. The road to this gin turns left off U.S. 61, after you cross the bayou bridge south of Boyle.

Milam: "When we got to that gin, it was daylight, and I was worried for the first time. Somebody might see us and accuse us of stealing the fan."

Bryant and Big Milam stood aside while Bobo loaded the fan. Weight: 74 pounds. The youth still thought they were bluffing.

They drove back to Glendora, then north toward Swan Lake and crossed the "new bridge" over the Tallahatchie. At the east end of this bridge, they turned right, along a dirt road which parallels the river. After about two miles, they crossed the property of L. W. Boyce, passing near his bouse.

About 1.5 miles southeast of the Boyce home is a lonely spot where Big Milam has hunted squirrels. The river bank is steep. The truck stopped 30 yards from the water.

Big Milam ordered Bobo to pick up the fan.

He staggered under its weight . . . carried it to the river bank. They stood silently . . . just hating one another.

Milam: "Take off your clothes."

Slowly, Bobo sat down, pulled off his shoes, his socks. He stood up, unbuttoned his shirt, dropped his pants, his shorts.

He stood there naked.

It was Sunday morning, a little before 7.

Milam: "You still as good as I am?"

Bobo: "Yeah."

Milam: "You've still 'had' white women?"

Bobo: "Yeah."

That big .45 jumped in Big Milam's hand. The youth turned to catch that big, expanding bullet at his right ear. He dropped.

They barb-wired the gin fan to his neck, rolled him into 20 feet of water.

For three hours that morning, there was a fire in Big Milam's back yard: Bobo's crepe-soled shoes were hard to burn.

Seventy-two hours later—eight miles downstream—boys were fishing. They saw feet sticking out of the water. Bobo.

The majority—by no means *all*, but the *majority*—of the white people in Mississippi 1) either approve Big Milam's action or else 2) they don't disapprove enough to risk giving their "enemies" the satisfaction of a conviction.

Source: William Bradford Huie, "The Shocking Story of Approved Killing in Mississippi" *Look* 20 (January 24, 1956): 50.

FREEDOM RIDES

In 1961 James Farmer headed the Congress on Racial Equality (CORE). Farmer organized the Freedom Rides, integrated groups of bus riders traveling across the South. The Supreme Court had already declared segregation unconstitutional, but the southern states persisted in maintaining separate facilities, requiring black riders to sit in the back of the bus and to use "colored" restrooms and waiting areas at bus stops. Farmer, who had a lifelong commitment to Gandhian principles, was a firm adherent of the nonviolent activism favored by civil rights advocates. When Martin Luther King Jr. promoted nonviolence, Farmer said later, "no one asked, 'What are you—some kind of nut or something?' " The majority of those working for civil rights supported nonviolent methods, even though they realized that white racists acted under no such moral constraints. In fact, Farmer expected southern racists to attack the Freedom Riders, attracting the attention of the nation to the continuing plight of African Americans. Farmer himself began the Freedom Ride, leaving only when called to attend his father's funeral.

James Farmer Leads the Freedom Riders, 1961

It was February 1, 1961, my first day at my desk as national director of CORE. Several letters were already before me from blacks in the South, complaining that despite the Irene Morgan Supreme Court decision in 1946 and the Boynton decision in 1960, when they sat on a front seat of an interstate bus or tried to use waiting room facilities other than those consigned to blacks, they were beaten, ejected, or arrested. "What do decisions of the United States Supreme Court mean?" they asked.

Gordon Carey proposed a second Journey of Reconciliation patterned after the first one conducted in 1947, with a small interracial group riding interstate buses through the South with the blacks sitting on front seats and the whites on back seats, refusing to move when ordered. . . .

I thought it a capital idea, a superb answer to the question "What next?" But it would not be called a Journey of Reconciliation. Such a name would be out of touch with the scrappy nonviolent movement that had emerged. The cry, I said, was not for "reconciliation" but for "*freedom.*" It would be called the "Freedom Ride." . . .

The detailed plans for the Freedom Ride evolved quickly. We would recruit from twelve to fourteen persons, call them to Washington, D.C., for a week of intensive training and preparation, and then embark on the Ride. Half would go by Greyhound and half by Trailways. We would leave Washington, D.C., on May 4, 1961, and follow an itinerary that would take us through Virginia, the Carolinas, Georgia, Alabama, and Mississippi. We hoped we would arrive in New Orleans on May 17, the anniversary of the Supreme Court's desegregation decision.

In March, I wrote to the president of the United States, the attorney general, the director of the Federal Bureau of Investigation, the chairman of the Interstate Commerce Commission, and the presidents of the Greyhound and Trailways corporations, informing them of our plans and enclosing copies of our itinerary. This was in line with the Ghandian principles of being open and aboveboard, informing officials—even those unfriendly to the cause—of what we intended to do, how and when. No replies came. . . .

From all sources—my staff, the Freedom Riders themselves, and the press— word came to me of a carnage in Alabama. When the first bus had crossed the Alabama state line, a half dozen young white toughs had boarded with their weapons in sight—pieces of chain, brass knuckles, blackjacks, and pistols. Shortly thereafter, the driver pulled the vehicle off the road and brought it to a stop.

"I ain't movin' this bus another foot," he said, "until the niggers get into the back [of] the bus where they belong."

No one moved.

The thugs then got up and began beating the black Freedom Riders who were seated in the front.

Doctor Bergman and Jim Peck tried to intervene.

"Here, you stop that!" one of them said. "These men haven't done anything to you."

"They have a right to sit where they want to," the other said. "You leave them alone."

Peck was hit with an uppercut that lifted him off the floor and deposited him unconscious in the aisle. Bergman was knocked down and repeatedly kicked in the head. As his wife, who was also on the bus, described it, "They used my husband's head for a football." Dr. Bergman later suffered a cerebral hemorrhage, which put him in a wheelchair permanently. His doctors agree that the stroke was a direct result of the beating he had suffered.

The blacks were then thrown bodily into the back of the bus. The driver moved the blood-splattered vehicle on. One woman passenger, not a Freedom Rider, exclaimed, "Doggone, it looks like there has been a hog killing on this bus!"

At Birmingham, the Freedom Riders entered the terminal to test its facilities in prearranged fashion. Jim Peck, who led the testing, was accosted by a mob of whites, who beat him and left him unconscious, lying in a pool of his own blood. They probably thought him dead. It required fifty-six stitches and prolonged hospitalization to close the cuts on his head. . . .

At Anniston, Alabama, the bus carrying Freedom Riders stopped at the terminal. A mob of angry whites was waiting with lethal weapons in hand. Quite properly deciding that discretion was the better part of valor, the Freedom Riders informed the driver that they were not leaving the bus at Anniston. The driver started his motor, preparing to move on. Members of the mob, with knifes and ice picks, slashed and punctured the tires on the bus. Mingling with that mob were several uniformed policemen, laughing and chatting with its members and not interfering. The bus moved on, but just outside town its tires blew out and it came to a halt. The mob had followed the bus in cars and now surrounded it and held its doors shut. They broke one of the windows and hurled a firebomb into the vehicle. It filled with smoke and burst into flames.

One of the Freedom Riders on that bus was Albert Bigelow, the former navy captain and combat veteran from World War II. Cool and schooled in making decisions under fire, he took charge. No doubt, he saved lives. Bigelow got the emergency door of the bus open and began evacuating its passengers in orderly fashion, deciding that it was better to face the mob outside than certain incineration inside.

One of the policemen who was among the mob then fired his revolver into the air. As if upon signal, the mob pulled away from the bus, allowing the front door to open. Freedom Riders stumbled out, choking and coughing, and fell on the ground, writhing and gasping for air.

Source: James Farmer, *Lay Bare the Heart: An Autobiography of the Civil Rights Movement* (New York: Arbor House, 1985), 195–97, 202–3. Permission granted by estate of Dr. James Farmer, Tami Farmer Gonzalez, executrix.

FBI Informant Gary Thomas Rowe Jr.
Participates in Klan Violence, 1961

In August 1955 an Atlanta auto assembly worker named Eldon Edwards formed the U.S. Klans, Knights of the Ku Klux Klan, Inc. Edwards's group probably attracted about fifty thousand members at most. In some areas, local police collaborated with the new Ku Klux Klan even though Klan members carried out brutal murders and bombings. In Birmingham, Grand Dragon Bobby Shelton emerged as the highest-ranking Alabama officer in Edwards's Klan and even developed contacts with Alabama governor John Patterson. After a feud with Edwards, Shelton formed his own Klan, the Alabama Knights, Knights of the Ku Klux Klan, Inc. The various klans' violence seemed so anarchic and dangerous that even J. Edgar Hoover, director of the virtually all-white FBI and indifferent to the plight of African Americans, made it a priority to infiltrate Klan cells.

One of the informants the Federal Bureau of Investigation recruited in its war with the Ku Klux Klan was an Alabama man named Gary Thomas Rowe Jr. An eighth-grade dropout, Rowe liked to hang out in bars frequented by police officers and often told people he was a policeman or FBI agent. In fact, the FBI first encountered Rowe in such a "cop bar." FBI agents encouraged Rowe to join Shelton's Alabama Knights, which he did in June 1960. Rowe's relationship with the FBI and the KKK documents the peculiar connections that evolved between the government agency and the terrorists. FBI agents warned Rowe not to participate in Klan violence, but when he did, the agents covered it up. He had wormed his way into the confidence of top Klan leaders, making himself too good of a source to be sacrificed on principle.

The Klan vowed to stop the Freedom Rides, described earlier in this chapter. In Birmingham local police allowed Klansmen to beat the riders as they exited their bus. One of the Klansmen at the center of the beatings was Gary Thomas Rowe, the FBI's informant. In 1979 the FBI formed an investigative task force to find out just what had happened between the FBI, the Klan, and Rowe.

The attack on the Freedom Riders at the Trailways bus station in Birmingham on May 14, 1961, is a critical event in Rowe's career as an FBI informant, because the evidence obtained by the Task Force shows that of the hundreds gathered for the CORE bus arrival, Rowe was one of the handful most responsible for the violence at the bus station. The evidence available to Special Agent Kemp within hours of the incident was such that it would have been difficult for him not to have known the full extent of Rowe's involvement. However, there is nothing in FBI files which indicates he brought this information to the attention of Birmingham's Special Agent in Charge or Headquarters.

The incident illustrates the rewards and the dangers of having an aggres-

sive informant like Rowe. Only a month before, he had uncovered a link between the klan and the Birmingham Police Department. On April 17, 1961,
Rowe told Kemp that he had been talking to Robert Shelton, Imperial Wizard of the Alabama Knights of the Ku Klux Klan, and that Shelton had told
him to contact a sergeant Tom Cook of the Birmingham Police Department
to pick up some information Cook had. By coincidence, the same day Sergeant Cook called Special Agent C. B. Stanberry, who handled klan matters
for the Bureau, and inquired if Stanberry knew one Tommy Lowe [*sic*], a
member of the klan. When Stanberry said no, Cook said he intended to talk
to Lowe, but would not do so if he was "one of your boys."

Later that day, Rowe met with Cook at a Birmingham restaurant. Cook
told Rowe that the Imperial Wizard had assured him that "Rowe was 100%,"
and that Cook wanted to use Rowe as a contact to pass information to the
klan. . . .

The Birmingham FBI office knew Sergeant Cook was then in charge of
"racial matters" for the Birmingham Police Department and a close associate
of Public Safety Commissioner Eugene "Bull" Connor. At the time, Connor
was running for re-election, and the Birmingham SAC speculated that:

["]It is possible that Commissioner CONNOR is using Cook to help him
line up votes from klan members by feeding them information which comes
to his attention, not only through their own informants, but also information received from this office, in order to ingratiate himself with members of
the klan. . . . ["]

Word of impending violence against the Freedom Riders came in on May
4 and 5, 1961, when [words deleted] reported to the FBI that the Grand Titan,
Hubert Page, had been making the rounds at klavern meetings with the news
that the Congress of Racial Equality (CORE) was planning to test desegregation on interstate buses in Alabama and that Robert Shelton wanted all
klansmen to stand by to stop them if the police did not. Page had obtained
his information about the CORE plans, Rowe was able to learn, from Sergeant Tom Cook. On May 12, the SAC cautiously advised Police Chief Jamie
Moore of Shelton's threat.

There were other signs that the klan was planning to take action at the
bus stations. Rowe reported that an angry discussion broke out at a December 15, 1960, meeting of Eastview 13 when klansmen learned that nothing had
been done about a sit-in at Birmingham's Greyhound station. Klan officers
apologized and promised to prepare plans for future sit-ins. . . .

On May 12, 1961, Rowe alerted the Bureau that Hubert Page, the Grand
Titan, had visited Eastview 13 the night before and announced he had just
learned that the CORE "Freedom Riders" would arrive in Birmingham on
Sunday, May 14, and that the klan leadership was preparing plans to attack

the passengers when they arrived. After the meeting, Page told Rowe that he learned the date of their arrival from Shelton, who got it from Sergeant Tom Cook. Page said that Bull Connor had promised that, when trouble broke out, Connor would see that fifteen to twenty minutes would elapse before sending in the police. If blacks attempted to enter the depot restaurant, Connor reportedly advised the klansmen to start a fight and blame it on the blacks; and if they attempted to enter the restrooms, to beat them up until it "looked like a bulldog got a hold of them," remove their clothes, allowing the police to arrest them as they emerged naked. Connor advised the klan leadership not to worry if any klansmen were arrested. He would see that the blacks would be found at fault and would insure that any sentences, if meted out to klansmen, would be light.

. . . The first CORE bus left Atlanta as scheduled and traveled westward along U.S. 78 to Anniston, Alabama, sixty miles east of Birmingham, where a mob of Calhoun County klansmen forced it off the road and threw a fire-bomb inside, destroying the entire bus. Somehow, the passengers managed to escape without serious injury. Rowe was not involved in this incident.

The second bus, trailing by two hours, arrived at the Trailways station in downtown Birmingham at about 4:15 P.M. The CORE group disembarked amidst a crowd of regular passengers and walked from the platform to the rear of the station through a corridor toward the "white only" waiting room. A mass of klansmen stood in their way. Someone yelled, "Get that SOB," and a brawl broke out. Men swinging bats and chains jumped two CORE leaders, James Peck and Charles Person, and beat them to the floor. None of the witnesses can remember exactly what happened next in the crowded corridor, but within seconds, newsmen and innocent bystanders, white and black, were attacked indiscriminately. . . . nine persons were sent to the hospital, only two of whom were CORE freedom riders.

One of the injured blacks was George Webb, who had come to the station to pick up his fiance, a passenger on the bus, but not part of the CORE group. He was standing near the rear door of the corridor when four men grabbed him and started to beat him with fists and clubs. Webb doubled over to protect himself about the time a photographer from the *Birmingham Post-Herald*, Tom Langston, pushed open the station's rear door and triggered the shutter on his camera. The following day, the *Post-Herald* carried the photograph across five columns of the front page.

The Bureau obtained a copy of the photograph and used it extensively in their investigation. . . .

In addition to the photograph, there was sufficient evidence from witnesses' statements to reconstruct with some precision the extent of Rowe's violence that day. The photographer, Tom Langston, stated that his camera flash caused the men who were beating up Webb to drop their victim and chase Langston out the building and onto a platform where they smashed his camera and beat him unconscious. Julian "Bud" Gordon, a reporter for the *Birmingham News*, was standing in the parking lot at the rear of the depot and saw them pummeling the photographer. He told the Bureau that the men who got Langston were the same ones who were shown doing the beating in the newspaper picture. . . . Gordon told the Bureau that "the big fellow" who was bending over the victim in the newspaper picture was the one who took his camera, but later restrained the pipe-wielding man from hitting Gordon. [Words deleted]

Meanwhile, Clancy Lake, News Director for Station WAPI, arrived on the scene in a mobile broadcasting unit. He left his car and ran to the rear of the station where he saw several fights in progress, and in particular, a heavy-set white man with a yellow polo shirt stomping on a black man. Lake ran back to his mobile unit and began a live broadcast of the action. Minutes later, the heavy-set, yellow-shirted man and two others approached his car. They smashed his car window, jerked the microphone off the dash, and threw Lake on to the pavement. Then they threw him against a wall and took two swings at him with a blackjack, which missed. Then, Lake watched them as they walked casually up the street toward the police station. Several days later, Rowe admitted he smashed Clancy Lake's window.

At 7:15 P.M., on May 14, Kemp telephoned Rowe's house to find out what had happened. Rowe's wife told Kemp that he had returned home briefly at 5:00 P.M. and left again in the company of three other men. At 12:15 A.M., May 15, Rowe returned Kemp's call and told him that he had just returned from Pinson, Alabama, where a "klan" doctor had put eight stitches in his neck to close a knife wound. . . .

Source: Ralph Hornblower et al., "The FBI, the Department of Justice and Gary Thomas Rowe, Jr." (Task Force Report on Gary Thomas Rowe, Jr., July 1979), 48–52, 55–60.

CONFRONTATION AT OLE MISS

In 1962 James Meredith decided to desegregate the flagship university of Mississippi, located in Oxford and known affectionately throughout the state as "Ole Miss." The governor of Mississippi, Ross Barnett, vowed to resist integration, forcing President John F. Kennedy to dispatch federal marshals to Oxford.

On September 30, 1962, the marshals occupied the University of Mississippi's Lyceum building. Deputy Attorney General Nicholas Katzenbach commanded the detachment of federal officers. Through the night a large mob gathered, hurling epithets and bricks. Snipers fired hunting rifles into the assembled marshals.

The marshals, vastly outnumbered, fought back with tear gas, but soon ran low. As the crowd closed in and gunfire and thrown rocks picked off federal officers, Katzenbach realized he had to call for help from the only source available: the Mississippi National Guard. Since the Guardsmen were white residents of Oxford, the same as members of the mob, he wondered if he could really count on their support. He called the Armory, reaching the commanding officer of the local detachment, Captain Murry "Chooky" Falkner, a nephew of the novelist William Faulkner.

Falkner's men mostly opposed the use of federal power to desegregate their university. But, when confronted with violence, they rallied to the cause. History has made the mob the embodiment of white Mississippi. Yet, as the Guardsmen fixed bayonets and charged into the crowd to do their duty and uphold order, one soldier called out, "Let's go, Mississippi!" At that moment, the Mississippi National Guard saw itself and not the murderously howling mob they fought against as the embodiment of Mississippi. The assertion of national authority was carried out by Mississippi patriots who saw themselves as the true spirit of their state.

The civil rights movement was a struggle over federalism, a weighing of the power of state versus national governments, but it was more than that. It was also a fight over individual consciences and the willingness of ordinary people to identify with a polity and ideals larger than their community. As the great historian David Potter recognized long ago, national loyalty begins at home. Loyalty to nation, to an ideal of rights that can stretch across racial lines, began in neighborhoods.

The Mississippi National Guard Confronts Rioters at the University of Mississippi, 1962

. . . Chooky Falkner was politically conservative and like many of his men and many white Mississippians, he strongly opposed the way the federal government was handling the Meredith case. At their evening meal, Falkner and his troops laughed in disbelief when they heard a report that a large contingent of U.S. Marshals was arriving at the Oxford airport. "Surely the Federal Government would not take this means to cram the issue down our throats," Falkner thought.

By 9:00 P.M., Falkner reported, "I had a troop on my hands eager to join forces to preserve segregation and States' Rights". . . .

When Katzenbach had called in with the order, Falkner replied that his men had only a few hours of riot-control training, but they'd assist as best they could. Katzenbach asked how fast they could get to the Lyceum. Falkner told him they could pull out in ten minutes and get to the campus in fifteen. As the Guardsmen fell into formation, Falkner called his immediate superior, Lieutenant Colonel J. P. Williams, at squadron headquarters in Ripley to confirm the unusual order. "I just got the craziest chain of command," Falkner said, explaining the presidential command that had just managed to bypass the entire U.S. military command structure. "Better do it," Williams noted, "JFK is the commander in chief." Williams then ordered Falkner to leave his aummunition at the Armory, presumably to reduce the risk of civilian blood being spilled.

The Guardsmen didn't realize it yet, but they were being sent into combat with unloaded weapons. The seven-vehicle convoy lined up in administration march formation: Falkner's command Jeep, two more Jeeps, a pair of two-and-a-half-ton trucks, a three-quarter-ton truck stuffed with troops, and a trail jeep carrying his executive officer.

Katzenbach called again at 10:00 P.M. to confirm that the men were ready to mobilize. He wasn't sure they would obey. Falkner replied, "Yes, sir, all men are loaded on the vehicles," except the five-man cook detail, which Falkner ordered to stay behind to guard the Armory. . . . "Are you positive?" the deputy attorney general asked. "Yes, sir," said Falkner. Katzenbach ordered Falkner outside to check that his enlisted men were loaded and would obey the order to come to the Lyceum. Falkner did this, ran back, and reported in the affirmative. . . .

As they barreled west, Falkner reflected on Katzenbach's questioning of his men's loyalty. He mused, "This was a great National Guard unit and the thought never occurred to me that they wouldn't follow." . . .

On July 21, 1861, Chooky Falkner's great-great-grandfather Colonel William C. Falkner, commanding the Second Mississippi Infantry Regiment at Manassas, led a charge toward the Union lines with a stylish feather jammed in his hat. A Confederate general saw him and called out to his troops, "Men, follow yonder knight of the black plume and history will not forget you!"

Tonight, as the National Guard convoy entered the campus of the University of Mississippi, Falkner realized he, too, was about to crash into a wave of full-scale combat. Throngs of people lining the streets began yelling curses and throwing rocks at the Guardsmen.

Corporal Antwine was driving the lead command Jeep into the campus with Captain Falkner in the passenger seat. Ted Lucas Smith, correspondent for the *Memphis Commercial-Appeal*, saw them enter campus: "I clearly remember seeing one boy standing on the opposite curb with a huge piece of concrete raised over his head, ready to throw. The convoy was easing along. It seemed they didn't expect what they suddenly got. The boy with the concrete slab waited until the jeep pulled even with him and he threw with all his might. The concrete smashed into the officer and literally knocked him almost out of the jeep on the driver's side. He saved himself with his uninjured left hand, pulling himself back into the jeep. . . ."

"I could see the mob in the Circle and the Lyceum building," Falkner reported in his after-action report of the incident, which he wrote in May 1963. "It appeared the Circle was full of people and the street on which we were to drive was a sea of people. The only lights were from the Lyceum and the glow from a burning automobile. As we passed the Geology building and the Confederate Statue, a two-by-six piece of lumber was thrown at my jeep. Fortunately it missed its target! From here to the Lyceum building was absolute Hell! People would not move out of the street. They threw bricks, concrete, everything and anything they could find—including words.

"If there had been any doubt as to whether the men would follow me," recalled Falkner, "there was none now. I was indubitably sure I had their support. A person loose in that mob, wearing a uniform, would have been dead. Now we were all concerned with a matter of self-preservation." Falkner later quipped, "It's hard to feel brotherly love toward someone who is trying to kill you." . . .

Word rippled through some people in the mob that the incoming troops were Mississippi Guardsmen, but this did nothing to dent the crowd's fury. Voices called out, "Leave it to the marshals, Mississippi boys!" and "Go back to the Armory!" As rocks and bricks showered the convoy, a gas-masked Guardsman popped his head out of a truck and called out desperately, "Hey, we're Mississippi National Guard!" Among the replies from the crowd were "Fuck the Guard!" and "Nigger-lovin' son of a bitches!" . . .

As they approached the Lyceum, one of Falkner's men popped his head out of the truck, and, in a frantic attempt to identify themselves, called out the locally famous Ole Miss "Hotty Toddy" football cheer. Before he could finish the cheer, bricks rained into the sides and back flaps of the truck. When Lieutenant "Bo" Metts stepped out of his Jeep a sniper blasted three rounds through the windshield into the seat where he had just been sitting. . . .

Katzenbach handed Captain Falkner a bullhorn and asked if he would try to reason with the mob. Nursing his shattered arm, Falkner stepped out of the front door of the Lyceum with the battery-powered bullhorn and six volunteers and walked across the street into the Circle, shouting that they were Mississippi National Guardsmen. . . .

"We're from Mississippi," Falkner announced. "We live here. Now y'all get out of here!" But this just made the mob madder. Again they were cursed and stoned by the mob, and the Guardsmen had to return to their lines under a cover of tear gas.

One rioter appeared with a big drum of gasoline and yelled, "Get your gas here, boys!" Teams of rioters lined up to fill their Molotov cocktails, and as they hurled the bombs toward the Lyceum, several of the rioters thought proudly of the newsreel footage of Hungarian students fighting Soviet tanks in 1956. . . .

Like a predator, the mob sensed that the defenders had hurled their last gas and surged forward for the kill. "Here comes the damn mob," remembered Oxford National Guard Specialist Fourth Class Loyd Gunter. . . . "We were standing out there and we didn't have any ammunition. Here they come. They get closer and closer. They start throwing bricks. We were under the streetlights. You couldn't see those bricks coming out of the dark." . . .

The Oxford National Guardsmen were not fighting for segregation or integration, for state's rights or Ross Barnett or John Kennedy. They weren't fighting for James Meredith or the U.S. Marshals. They had a duty to perform, to save lives, to save their school, and to save their city. They stayed on the line because they were now regular U.S. Army troops, and they knew that an American soldier obeys orders and when necessary faces his own death without debating the fine points.

Sergeant Babb looked around for an officer but couldn't see one. He thought, "Well, only one thing to do."

He called out the command, "Fix bayonets!"

The Guardsmen pulled their bayonets out of scabbards and clicked them into the rifles. As they did this, they let out an ear-piercing squall at the top of their voices, a scare tactic they learned during their brief riot training. . . .

They snapped into the long guard position, stomped forward three steps, thrust their steel-tipped weapons out fully extended from their bodies, and let out another bloodcurdling holler. They stood their shoulder to shoulder, less than twenty soldiers facing a force many times their size, their hearts pounding like jackhammers, their bayonets pointing at the mob. . . .

Another wave of armed Mississippians was closing fast on the Lyceum after midnight . . . on direct orders from the president of the United States.

They were 165 fresh National Guard troops of the 108th Cavalry Regiment's Second Squadron, the first units that could get to Oxford fast enough to reinforce the men of Oxford's Troop E. These Guardsmen came from two nearby towns. . . .

A National Guard officer called out, "Soldiers, load and cock your weapons!"

From somewhere in the darkness, deep in the line of the National Guardsmen, came an astonishing call. It was a voice yelling a line from the new state song, a song that until this moment had been automatically connected to support for Ross Barnett and eternal segregation and the defiance of federal law. Loud and clear, the Guardsman's voice said, "Let's go, Mississippi!"

The order rippled around the building, "Forward march." The circle slowly surged out in all directions. Another voice called out, "Charge!" and parts of the line rushed forward in disorganized fragments.

Seeing the wave of advancing soldiers, most of the mob quickly fell back in all directions and melted away from the center of campus. Before he fled, one of the rioters planted a little rebel flag at the base of the Confederate monument. A Mississippi National Guardsman stopped a group of escaping rioters, grabbed a Confederate flag from one, and stomped it into the ground. . . .

Troop E's Loyd Gunter remembered seeing a rioter close by bending over to pick up a brick to throw at the troops. One of his sergeants, Gunter recalled, "double-timed over, took his bayonet, and he stuck that guy right in the ass with that damn bayonet. That guy let out a bloodcurdling yell, and he cut out of there screaming and hollering. He stuck that thing about four inches up his rear end." Explained another man from Troop E. "Hell, we'd been shot at and had bricks thrown at us all night. We was pissed off mad."

Source: William Doyle, *The American Insurrection: The Battle of Oxford, Mississippi, 1962* (New York: Doubleday, 2001), 199–205, 217–18, 223, 244–45. Copyright 2001 by William Doyle. Used by permission of William Doyle.

JAIL AS A TEMPLE OF FREEDOM

A veteran of World War II, Mississippi-born Aaron Henry challenged Mississippi segregationists through the 1950s. Elected state NAACP president, Henry vowed to turn Mississippi jails into "temples of freedom" by filling them with civil rights protesters, and organized a boycott of white merchants. Henry was a grassroots organizer, one of the "local people" like Fannie Lou Hamer and Medgar Evers who first stirred civil rights protest in the Deep South. In 1963 he testified before the House Judiciary Committee on behalf of legislation that would ultimately become the Civil Rights Act of 1964. His testimony documented the pervasive violence white southerners routinely relied on to keep black southerners in a subordinate position.

Aaron Henry's Testimony before the House Judiciary Committee, 1963

. . . I was to have been met here to join me in his testimony by a man that several of you have referred to already, Mr. Medgar Evers.

When I turned on the television set yesterday morning to really see what had happened to Mr. Wallace in Alabama and saw the picture of Mr. Evers in the top of the "Today" screen, I began to wonder what statement has Medgar made now that has hit the national headlines, only to hear Mr. Jack Lescoulie say that, "Mr. [Roy] Wilkins has been invited to this program this morning to go with Miss Lena Horne because of the fact that Mr. Evers has been murdered in Mississippi."

That man was the closest friend I had. We even shared the same birthday. We had worked together in the civil rights struggle for over 5 years.

I want you to know that it is under these conditions that I appear before you.

My name is Aaron E. Henry. I live in Clarksdale, Miss., the county in which I was born July 2, 1922. I want to express my appreciation to this House Judiciary Committee, a committee of the highest governmental body in the world, for this opportunity of appearing before you and acquainting you with some of the conditions under which many Negro and white citizens live in my home State of Mississippi. I am happy also for this opportunity to acquaint you with some of the actions we feel that Congress can and should take to relieve these conditions.

Our chief problems are to be found in these areas: (1) Law enforcement and the courts; (2) employment; (3) education; (4) voting rights; and (5) human dignity.

In listing these problems in the order stated it should not in any way place priority of one over the other. We should take an approach of both and, rather than either/or, in trying to resolve these problems. They all can be brought close to home by citing some examples of deprivation in each category. In the area of law enforcement in the courts, Negroes generally feel that we do not have any chance of successfully defending ourselves when we are charged by the local officials and are tried in the local courts. Neither do we have any defense against police actions directed toward us outside the courtroom.

These are some of my own experiences as president of the Mississippi State Conference of the National Association for the Advancement of Colored People.

On December 7, 1961, I was called to the county attorney's office. The county attorney of my home county, Coahoma, is Mr. T. H. Pearson. Mr. Pearson was concerned about a campaign to withhold patronage that the Negro citizens had launched against the downtown merchants trying to get the merchants to employ Negroes above the menial level and to use courtesy titles when addressing them, instead of such titles as boy, girl, aunt, uncle, preacher, and nigger. Mr. Pearson told me that if I did not agree to use my influence to put a stop to the campaign he was going to put me in jail. When I refused, he called the chief of police, Mr. Ben Collins, whom he already had waiting and told him, "Carry this nigger to jail." I was arrested out of the county attorney's office, without a warrant. While I know this was an illegal arrest, I went peacefully, because there is no defense from a bullet in your head for resisting arrest, legal or illegal. Before the day was over six more leaders of the Negro community were behind bars in the Coahoma County jail on the same charge. . . .

On March 3, 1962, I was arrested from my home at 636 Page Street, while in bed with my wife. A white boy by the name of Sterlin Lee Eilert had complained that I had tried to get him to secure me a white woman. After he was not able to get one he charged I made sexual advances toward him.

I presented witnesses at the trial that substantiated my activities during the day. At the time of the alleged attack, only 10 minutes of my day was unaccounted for. The drive from Memphis, Tenn., to Shelby, Miss., would take at least 2 hours. The boy claimed he was put out of my car at Shelby, Miss. My car had been stored at a car wash rack from 10 a.m. until 5:30 p.m., so attested to by the car wash rack manager. The boy was allegedly picked up at 5 p.m. Visitors and neighbors testified that I was home by 5:30. The affidavit used in the case was dated 11 days after my arrest.

After I had been arrested some 5 hours, the chief of police, Mr. Ben Collins, went out to my home, secured the keys to the car and searched it for "gum paper in the ashtrays, and a faulty cigarette lighter," which he testified at the trial that he found.

The week of June 2 of this year, the case was set aside and overruled and remanded by the Mississippi State supreme court. Upon discussing this case with the Justice Department agent, Mr. John Doar, I was called by the press as someone had been informed that I had made a complaint to the Justice Department. I informed the agent of the press just who I thought was behind this heinous plot. The men suspected were both local law-enforcement agents. I was promptly sued for $40,000 and a judgment against me was rendered in their favor. The men involved were Mr. T. H. Pearson, county attorney, and Mr. Ben Collins, chief of police in my hometown.

March 4, 1963—For the seventh time in 2 years the plate glass windows of the Fourth Street Drugstore, which is owned by me, have been broken and smashed with rocks and bricks. No arrests have been made. The insurance company has canceled the insurance.

On Good Friday, April 5, early in the morning, my family and I, and a guest we had visiting with us, Congressman Charles C. Diggs, Jr., were awakened by broken glass and flames. Our house had been fire-bombed by two white men in the early hours of the morning. We succeeded in getting the family out of the house and then Congressman Diggs and I fought the fire and extinguished it. Our lives were narrowly saved.

On April 20 of this year, a hole was blown through the roof of the drugstore that I own. The Justice Department and local officials are still investigating.

My wife, Mrs. Noelle Henry, who has been employed by the local school system for 11 years, has had her contract revoked because of my activity in the civil rights movement. A suit has been filed to recover her employment. . . .

Saturday morning of last week, three shots were fired into our home around 1 in the morning while my family and I were asleep. General areas of deprivations, the first category, law enforcement and the courts, other cases and other people:

i. March 30, 1961, Jackson, Hinds County: Club swinging police and 2 police dogs chased more than 100 Negroes from a courthouse where 9 Negro students were convicted for staging a sit-in demonstration. Several were struck by the clubs and at least two were bitten by dogs.

ii. August 27 and 29, 1961, McComb, Pike County: Five Negro students from a local high school were convicted of breach of the peace following a sit-in in a variety store and bus terminal. They were sentenced to a $400 fine each and 8 months in jail. One of these students, a girl 15, named Miss Brenda Travis, was subsequently rearrested, and sentenced to 12 months in a State school for delinquents.

iii. August 29, 1961, McComb, Pike County: Two Negro leaders were arrested in McComb as an aftermath of the sit-in protest march on city hall, charged with contributing to the delinquency of minors. They were Curtis C. Bryant, of McComb, president of the McComb Branch of the NAACP, and Cordelle Regan. Each arrest was made on an affidavit signed by Police Chief George Guy, who said he had information that the two "were behind some of this racial trouble."

iv. October 22, 1961, Jackson, Hinds County: Dion Diamond was arrested for "running a stop sign" after having been followed all day. In court the next day, the arresting officer told the Judge, "he is a freedom rider. Throw the book at him." Diamond was refused legal counsel and fined $168.

v. April 12, 1962, Taylorsville, Smith County: Corp. Roman Duckworth, Jr., U.S. Army, a Negro, was shot and killed by Policeman Bill Kelly when, according to witnesses on the bus, "he insisted on his right to sit where he chose on an interstate bus." Policeman Kelly claimed that Duckworth was drunk and started fighting. No charges were brought against Kelly. Duckworth was en route from Camp Ritchie, Md., to see his wife who was ill in a Laurel, Miss. hospital.

vi. June 21, 1962, Clarksdale, Coahoma County: A white lawyer from Jackson,

Miss., named William Higgs, came into Clarksdale working as legal advisor to the Reverend Merrill W. Lindsey, a candidate for Congress on the Democratic ticket. With Mr. Higgs were several students, some Negro and some white. The whole group was jailed upon trying to leave Clarksdale. They reported that they were held nearly 20 hours without permission to use a telephone, and no formal charge has yet been brought against them. . . .

In the area of employment, the question of employment for Negroes can be cataloged in this manner: In the entire employment structure on the State level, except in the department of education, there is not a single Negro employed. . . .

In the field of public school systems—still 100-percent segregated despite legal rulings to the contrary . . . every school that white children attend is accredited . . . [while] in the entire State there are not more than eight schools that Negroes attend that are accredited . . .

We are now in the area of voting rights.

Fewer than 15,000 of 950,000 Negroes in Mississippi are registered voters; here are a few of the reasons why.

1. August 29, 1962, Clarksdale, Coahoma County, Miss.: Seven Negroes were arrested after attending a voter registration meeting. David Dennis was charged with failing to yield the right of way although he was driving on the main highway of the city. Police officers forced him to submit to a long harangue of threats and abuse. The others were forced by Clarksdale police to alight from their car and were charged with loitering in violation of the city curfew. They were in a moving automobile, leaving town. . . .

2. August 30, 1962, Indianola, Sunflower County, Miss.: C. R. McLauren, Albert Garner, J. O. Hodges, Samuel Block and Robert Moses were arrested by Indianola police on charges of distributing literature without a permit. The registration workers had been taking leaflets announcing a registration mass meeting door to door in a Negro community.

3. September 3, 1962, Ruleville, Sunflower County: Because of registration activity, two Negro-owned drycleaning establishments were closed (allegedly for violating city ordinances).

4. September 3, 1962, Clarksdale, Miss., Coahoma County: Miss Willie Griffin was arrested on the streets of downtown Clarksdale as she tried to persuade Negroes seen downtown to go to the courthouse to try to register to vote. She was grabbed from behind and held by a policeman. She jerked herself away from him and was charged with resisting arrest. She was placed in a cell in the city jail without a bed or a chair. She pulled a

pad from the wall and made herself a seat on the floor. She was then charged with destroying public property. She has been fined over $600 in local courts. The judge has given her 6 months to pay another fine and costs of $245.

5. September 3, 1962, Ruleville, Sunflower County: A letter from Mayor Durrough notified the Williams Chapel Missionary Baptist Church that tax exemption and free water were being cut off because the property was being used for purposes other than worship services. The church was a meeting place for voter registration schools and workers.

6. October 29, 1963, Clarksdale, Coahoma County: Charles McLaurin working in the voter education campaign in Coahoma County carried an elderly crippled Negro lady to the Coahoma County Courthouse for the purpose of registering to vote. He stopped the car to let her out as near the courthouse door as possible. Upon getting out of the car the lady went into the courthouse. The chief of police, Mr. Ben Collins, charged McLaurin with stopping in the street, and backing up in the street, and he was fined $102. He decided to forfeit the bond rather than run the risk of a higher fine or incur the legal expense of an appeal.

7. February 28, Greenwood, LaFlore County: Three registration workers were attacked with gunfire on U.S. highway 82, just outside of Greenwood. The shots were fired from a 1962 white Buick, with no license plates. The car in which the workers were riding was punctured by 11 bullets.

There are many more cases that could be cited.
We are now in the area of human dignity:

1. May 7, 1962, Jackson, Hinds County: Several white youths, riding in an open convertible, lassoed 9-year-old Negro Gloria Laverne Floyd with a wire and dragged her along the street. The girl suffered a deep gash in her head that required several stitches, cheek bruises, a laceration of her right shoulder, and burn marks are still on her neck. Police have made no arrest.

2. September 25, Liberty, Amite County: Herbert Lee, a Negro who had been active in a voter registration campaign, was shot and killed by a white member of the Mississippi House of Representatives of the State Legislature, named E. H. Hurst, in downtown Liberty, Miss. No prosecution was undertaken. The authorities explained that the representative had shot in self-defense.

3. Rev. M. W. Lindsey, candidate for Congress from the Second Congressional District in Mississippi, was refused newspaper space for advertisement by the Clarksdale Press Register and radio time over radio station WROX, until this situation was called to the attention of Mr.

Clarence Mitchell, our Washington bureau head of the NAACP, who in turn reported it to the FCC. The Reverend Lindsey was not permitted to have any of his supporters serve as members of the election commission while all other major candidates had this privilege.

4. December 26, 1963, Clarksdale, Coahoma County: Ivanhoe Donaldson and Benjamin Taylor, students from Detroit, brought a truckload of food, clothing, and medicines for distribution to the delta's needy families who had been cut off from receiving Federal surplus commodities. (The medicines had been donated by physicians in Louisville and were consigned to me, a licensed pharmacist.) They were arrested by Clarksdale police and held for investigation. The police did not search the truck until December 27, and found what they described as "a drug to ease the pain of middle-aged women." Donaldson and Taylor were charged with possession of narcotics and bond was set at $15,000 each. Bond was later reduced to $1,500. The grand jury did not indict them after all of this difficulty.

These are a few of the major cases.

The Federal Government can help relieve these cases [by] . . . [e]nacting civil rights legislation that will give the Department of Justice the authority to act when danger is imminent, and not have to wait until an act of violence has been committed.

Source: Hearings Before Subcommittee No. 5 of the Committee on the Judiciary, House of Representatives, 88th Cong., 1st sess., pt. II, pp. 1331–37, 1340–42 (June 13, 1963).

A PRESIDENT SPEAKS IN FAVOR OF CIVIL RIGHTS

After Congress passed the 1964 Civil Rights Act, civil rights leaders began to press for legislation guaranteeing the right to vote. In the Justice Department civil rights lawyers drafted legislation that would outlaw the states' schemes designed to prevent black voting. President Lyndon Johnson doubted Congress could pass another civil rights law so soon after the marathon effort needed to break the southerners' filibuster in 1964. On January 18, 1965, Martin Luther King and his Southern Christian Leadership Conference began to dramatize their demands for voting rights by staging protests and demonstrations in Selma, Alabama. At first state authorities tried to avoid violence and confrontations with the demonstrators, and King feared he would lose his national audience.

On March 7 some six hundred demonstrators began a march from Selma to Montgomery. Feeling he had neglected his congregation, King was in Atlanta, and Hosea Williams led the march. As the crowd crossed over Selma's Edmund Pettus Bridge, the demonstrators could see a mass of Alabama state troopers, armed with billy clubs. The troopers charged into the marchers, firing tear gas. As the demonstrators scattered in panic, mounted men on horseback swept into the crowd. The television networks inter-

rupted their regular programming to broadcast live pictures of the peaceful marchers scrambling to escape the state troopers and horsemen. Viewers could see clubs rising from the clouds of tear gas, furiously beating the demonstrators. The episode came to be called "Bloody Sunday."

Once again white violence turned the nation against the segregationists. Johnson, sensing that shift, addressed a joint session of Congress on March 15, calling for a new law protecting voting rights. Alabama whites had tried to violently protect their rule but had instead sparked such a public outcry that it actually shrank states' rights. Johnson's proposed law would send federal officers into the states to register minorities to vote in state-managed elections. Many Americans found Johnson's speech deeply moving, particularly when he adopted what had become the slogan of the civil rights movement: "We shall overcome." And Johnson endorsed the slogan as a way of making the demonstrators' program truly national, the cause of all Americans. "Really," he said, "it is all of us who must overcome the crippling legacy of bigotry and injustice."

President Lyndon B. Johnson Calls for an End to Racist Violence, 1965

Mr. Speaker, Mr. President, Members of the Congress:

I speak tonight for the dignity of man and the destiny of democracy.

I urge every member of both parties, Americans of all religions and of all colors, from every section of this country, to join me in that cause.

At times history and fate meet at a single time in a single place to shape a turning point in man's unending search for freedom. So it was at Lexington and Concord. So it was a century ago at Appomattox. So it was last week in Selma, Alabama.

There, long-suffering men and women peacefully protested the denial of their rights as Americans. Many were brutally assaulted. One good man, a man of God, was killed.

There is no cause for pride in what has happened in Selma. There is no cause for self-satisfaction in the long denial of equal rights of millions of Americans. But there is cause for hope and for faith in our democracy in what is happening here tonight.

For the cries of pain and the hymns of protests of oppressed people have summoned into convocation all the majesty of this great government—the Government of the greatest Nation on earth.

Our mission is at once the oldest and the most basic of this country: to right wrongs and to do justice, to serve man. . . .

Wednesday I will send to Congress a law designed to eliminate illegal barriers to the right to vote. . . .

This bill will strike down restrictions to voting in all elections—Federal, State, and local—which have been used to deny Negroes the right to vote.

This bill will establish a simple, uniform standard which cannot be used, however ingenious the effort, to flout our Constitution.

It will provide for citizens to be registered by officials of the United States Government if the State officials refuse to register them. . . .

But even if we pass this bill, the battle will not be over. What happened in Selma is part of a far larger movement which reaches into every section and State of America. It is the effort of American Negroes to secure for themselves the full blessings of American life.

Their cause must be our cause too. Because it is not just Negroes, but really it is all of us, who must overcome the crippling legacy of bigotry and injustice.

And we shall overcome.

As a man whose roots go deeply into Southern soil I know how agonizing racial feelings are. I know how difficult it is to reshape the attitudes and the structure of our society.

But a century has passed, more than a hundred years, since the Negro was freed. And he is not fully free tonight. . . .

A century has passed since the day of promise. And the promise is unkept.

The time of justice has now come. I tell you that I believe sincerely that no force can hold it back. It is right in the eyes of man and God that it should come. And when it does, I think that day will brighten the lives of every American. . . .

The real hero of this struggle is the American Negro. His actions and protests, his courage to risk safety and even to risk his life, have awakened the conscience of this Nation. His demonstrations have been designed to call attention to injustice, designed to provoke change, designed to stir reform.

He has called upon us to make good the promise of America. And who among us can say that we would have made the same progress were it not for his persistent bravery, and his faith in American democracy.

For at the real heart of battle for equality is a deep-seated belief in the democratic process. Equality depends not on the force of arms or tear gas but upon the force of moral right; not on recourse to violence but on respect for law and order.

. . . I pledge you tonight that we intend to fight this battle where it should be fought: in the courts, and in the Congress, and in the hearts of men. . . .

In Selma as elsewhere we seek and pray for peace. We seek order. We seek unity. But we will not accept the peace of stifled rights, or the order imposed

by fear, or the unity that stifles protest. For peace cannot be purchased at the
cost of liberty.

Source: *Public Papers of the Presidents of the United States: Lyndon B. Johnson, Containing the
Public Messages, Speeches, and Statements of the President, 1965,* 2 vols. (Washington, DC: Government Printing Office, 1966), 1:281–85.

THE SUPREME COURT PLACES CIVIL RIGHTS
ABOVE STATES' RIGHTS

*In the summer of 1964, college students converged on Mississippi. They called their project
Freedom Summer. They set up makeshift schools to make potential black voters literate
so they could vote. In reality, the civil rights workers expected to attract the bigots'
violence. And they did: Mississippi Klansmen murdered Michael Schwerner, Andrew
Goodman, and James Chaney. The Justice Department charged eighteen men with violating the civil rights workers' civil rights by killing them. Even before the eighteen defendants could go on trial, their case went to the Supreme Court so the justices could
determine if the charges passed constitutional muster. Previous generations of justices had
carefully protected the states' power to prosecute crime free of federal interference. In
1967 a federal court convicted seven klansmen of violating the victims' civil rights. But it
was not until 2005 that a state court convicted Edgar Ray Killen of commiting these
murders.*

The Supreme Court on the Murder of Michael Schwerner, James
Goodman, and James Chaney, in *United States v. Price, et al.*, 1966

MR. JUSTICE FORTAS delivered the opinion of the Court. . . .

The events upon which the charges are based, as alleged in the indictments, are as follows: On June 21, 1964, Cecil Ray Price, the Deputy Sheriff of
Neshoba County, Mississippi, detained Michael Henry Schwerner, James Earl
Chaney and Andrew Goodman in the Neshoba County jail located in Philadelphia, Mississippi. He released them in the dark of that night. He then proceeded by automobile on Highway 19 to intercept his erstwhile wards. He removed the three men from their automobile, placed them in an official
automobile of the Neshoba County Sheriff's office, and transported them to
a place on an unpaved road.

These acts, it is alleged, were part of a plan and conspiracy whereby the
three men were intercepted by the 18 defendants, including Deputy Sheriff
Price, Sheriff Rainey and Patrolman Willis of the Philadelphia, Mississippi,
Police Department. The purpose and intent of the release from custody and
the interception, according to the charge, were to "punish" the three men.

The defendants, it is alleged, "did wilfully assault, shoot and kill" each of the three. And, the charge continues, the bodies of the three victims were transported by one of the defendants from the rendezvous on the unpaved road to the vicinity of the construction site of an earthen dam approximately five miles southwest of Philadelphia, Mississippi.

These are federal and not state indictments. They do not charge as crimes the alleged assaults or murders. The indictments are framed to fit the stated federal statutes, and the question before us is whether the attempt of the draftsman for the Grand Jury in Mississippi has been successful: whether the indictments charge offenses against the various defendants which may be prosecuted under the designated federal statutes. . . .

The District Court held these counts of the indictment valid as to the sheriff, deputy sheriff and patrolman. But it dismissed them as against the nonofficial defendants because the counts do not charge that the latter were "officers in fact, or de facto in anything allegedly done by them 'under color of law.' " . . .

But we cannot agree. . . . Private persons, jointly engaged with state officials in the prohibited action, are acting "under color" of law for purposes of the statute. To act "under color" of law does not require that the accused be an officer of the State. It is enough that he is a willful participant in joint activity with the State or its agents.

In the present case, according to the indictment, the brutal joint adventure was made possible by state detention and calculated release of the prisoners by an officer of the State. This action, clearly attributable to the State, was part of the monstrous design described by the indictment. State officers participated in every phase of the alleged venture: the release from jail, the interception, assault and murder. It was a joint activity, from start to finish. Those who took advantage of participation by state officers in accomplishment of the foul purpose alleged must suffer the consequences of that participation. In effect, if the allegations are true, they were participants in official lawlessness, acting in willful concert with state officers and hence under color of law. . . .

The indictment specifically alleges that the sheriff, deputy sheriff and a patrolman participated in the conspiracy; that it was a part of the "plan and purpose of the conspiracy" that Deputy Sheriff Price, "while having [the three victims] . . . in his custody in the Neshoba County Jail . . . would release them from custody at such time that he [and others of the defendants] . . . could and would intercept [the three victims] . . . and threaten, assault, shoot and kill them."

This is an allegation of state action which, beyond dispute, brings the conspiracy within the ambit of the Fourteenth Amendment. It is an allegation of official, state participation in murder, accomplished by and through its officers with the participation of others. It is an allegation that the State, without the semblance of due process of law as required of it by the Fourteenth Amendment, used its sovereign power and office to release the victims from jail so that they were not charged and tried as required by law, but instead could be intercepted and killed. If the Fourteenth Amendment forbids denial of counsel, it clearly denounces denial of any trial at all.

As we have consistently held "The Fourteenth Amendment protects the individual against *state action*, not against wrongs done by *individuals.*" In the present case, the participation by law enforcement officers, as alleged in the indictment, is clearly state action, as we have discussed, and it is therefore within the scope of the Fourteenth Amendment.

Source: 383 U.S. 787 (1966).

FURTHER READINGS

Carl M. Brauer, *John F. Kennedy and the Second Reconstruction* (New York: Columbia University Press, 1977); Harvard Sitkoff, *A New Deal for Blacks: The Emergence of Civil Rights as a National Issue: The Depression Decade* (New York: Oxford University Press, 1978); Michal R. Belknap, *Federal Law and Southern Order: Racial Violence and Constitutional Conflict in the Post-Brown South* (Athens: University of Georgia Press, 1987); Taylor Branch, *Parting the Waters: America in the King Years, 1954–63* (New York: Simon and Schuster, 1988); John Dittmer, *Local People: The Struggle for Civil Rights in Mississippi* (Urbana: University of Illinois Press, 1994); Charles M. Payne, *I've Got the Light of Freedom: The Organizing Traditions and the Mississippi Freedom Struggle* (Berkelery: University of California Press, 1995). Taylor Branch, *Pillar of Fire: America in the King Years, 1963–65* (New York: Simon and Schuster, 1998); William Doyle, *American Insurrection: The Battle of Oxford, Mississippi, 1962* (New York: Doubleday, 2001); Diane McWhorter, *Carry Me Home: Birmingham, Alabama: The Climactic Battle of the Civil Rights Revolution* (New York: Simon and Schuster, 2001); Adam Fairclough, *Race and Democracy: The Civil Rights Struggle in Louisiana, 1915–1972* (Athens: University of Georgia, 1995); *Paul Hendrickson, Sons of Mississippi: A Story of Race and Its Legacy* (New York: Knopf, 2003); Nick Kotz, *Judgment Days: Lyndon Baines Johnson, Martin Luther King Jr., and the Laws that Changed America* (Boston: Houghton Mifflin, 2005); John Lewis, *Walking with the Wind: A Memoir of the Movement* (San Diego: Harcourt Brace, 1998); Michael J. Klarman, *From Jim Crow to Civil Rights: The Supreme Court and the Struggle for Racial Equality* (New York: Oxford University Press, 2004). The classic first-person account remains Anne Moody, *Coming of Age in Mississippi* (New York: Dell, 1968).

ELEVEN

LOST TO HISTORY

S cholars have long debated the relative violence of American society. Those arguments have led to the rediscovery of many forgotten pasts that have changed perceptions of every period in American history. Sometimes historians find more violence than had previously been suspected, as was the case with the labor wars of the late nineteenth century; at other times, most famously with the Wild West, the reality is far calmer than the mythology allowed. But one historical constant has largely eluded historians, mostly because it is so difficult to document: domestic abuse.

Abigail Adams vividly framed the issue when she wrote to her husband, John, at the end of March 1776. Abigail wrote John, who was a Massachusetts delegate at the Continental Congress, that she longed for America to declare its independence. When it did so, Congress would need to frame a new legal code. Abigail urged John to "remember the ladies and be more generous and favorable to them than your ancestors." Of particular concern was that the new nation's laws "not put such unlimited power into the hands of the husbands. Remember, all men would be tyrants if they could." "Why," she asked, "not put it out of the power of the vicious and lawless to use us with cruelty and indignity with impunity?" Abigail warned, "If particular care and attention is not paid to the ladies, we are determined to foment a rebellion, and will not hold ourselves bound by any laws in which we have no voice or representation."

John Adams had no patience for his wife's ideas, dismissing them with a curt "I cannot but laugh." He did insist that there was no substance to male authority: "We dare not exert our power in its full latitude." Any move toward legal equality, John complained, "would completely subject us to the despotism of the petticoat."[1] John was in a position to ignore Abigail Adams, but the latter had a better understanding of the law. For it was the law itself that granted men the power to abuse their wives and then, at least for several centuries, made it very difficult for women to seek legal redress.

English common law codified a woman's obedience, first to her father, then to her husband. These were not just religious standards but legal requirements. This system of coverture was graphically defined by William Blackstone in his *Commentaries* of 1765. "By marriage," Blackstone wrote, "the husband and wife are one person in law; that is, the very being or legal existence of the woman is suspended during marriage, or at least is incorporated and consolidated into that of the husband; under whose wing, protection, and cover, she performs everything."[2] The most obvious representation of this incorporation was the woman's loss of her own name, as she took that of her husband. In the eyes of the law, a woman without a man was a relict, a leftover. The consequence was that a woman could not own or acquire property, write a will, or enter a contract; she had no legal identity, being utterly dependent on a male figure. When the husband died, the household was dissolved; the same was not the case when the wife died.

At times, a woman could appear to be little more than a form of property. Thus the law saw adultery and rape as forms of theft. Well into the nineteenth century, courts usually put a male, generally the husband or father of the victim, in the position of plaintiff in such cases, as the party who had suffered injury and loss. The U.S. Constitution changed nothing in terms of women's legal identity, at least for its first eighty years.

But few rape cases ever found their way into the courts. It is difficult to know how many sexual assaults went unreported, though those scholars who have studied the matter most closely generally conclude that there were far fewer rapes prior to 1900 than after. In the seventeenth and eighteenth centuries, the courts in most colonies could pass an entire decade without convicting anyone of rape. For instance, there were no rape convictions in Connecticut between 1693 and 1760. Still, it is difficult to know if there were few prosecutions because there were few sexual crimes or if they went unreported.

Seventeenth-century courts had been more sympathetic to the victims of rape, with almost all men charged with the crime being convicted. But with rape categorized a capital crime, women were often unwilling to bring charges, while juries and judges usually did their best to find a lesser punishment. Thus only twelve rape cases were brought before Connecticut's courts in the seven-

---

1. Charles Francis Adams, ed., *Familiar Letters of John Adams and His Wife Abigail Adams, during the Revolution* (New York, 1876), 148–55.
2. William Blackstone, *Commentaries on the Laws of England*, 4 vols. (1764–69; reprint, Chicago: University of Chicago Press, 1979), 1:430.

teenth century, eleven of which ended in convictions, one of which culminated with the death penalty. It is also worth noting that half of these cases were for attempted rape, a crime that practically vanished in the eighteenth century. The standard of evidence shifted in the early eighteenth century, as courts became more suspicious of women's testimony, fearing that they might be falsely charging men. As a consequence, in the first nine decades of the eighteenth century, Connecticut's courts heard only eighteen rape prosecutions, six of which ended in conviction. It is also notable that eight of the men charged with rape were black. With the death penalty the likely result, juries probably found it easier to convict those seen as not part of the community.[3]

Prior to the medical examinations of the late twentieth century, it was difficult to provide evidence against a specific attacker, and even then it usually came down to the woman's word that sex was nonconsensual. As Giles Jacob's legal dictionary held, "A Woman's positive Oath of a Rape, without concurring Circumstances, is seldom credited."[4] During the eighteenth century, as one scholar wrote, "The rules of evidence [in rape cases] were weighted for the defendant."[5] Courts usually required evidence that the woman had resisted the attacker, often to the point of being called upon to show signs of bodily injury. Even then, until the later twentieth century, defense lawyers were allowed to enter evidence questioning the integrity and propriety of the victim, lessening the man's guilt if the woman had a reputation for flirting or indiscriminate dating. Some rapists were even released because the victim was wearing provocative clothing that, defense attorneys alleged, invited sexual assault. The great exception to this general lack of legal interest in rape cases arose when the accused was black. Antebellum Southern states ordered the death penalty for any black, slave or free, found guilty of raping a white woman—and blacks were often found guilty once accused by a white woman. After the Civil War, the penalty remained death, though unofficially through the actions of lynch mobs. It is difficult to find an instance when courts or the public acted with the same energy in the prosecution of a white or black man accused of raping a black woman.

If the law granted men seemingly unlimited power, communal standards did not always acknowledge such unrestrained authority. There are a few recorded instances in the eighteenth century of communities acting to halt domestic violence. For example, in 1733, the women of Ridgefield, Connecticut, seized William Drinkwater, tied him to a cart, and beat him for physically

3. Cornelia Hughes Dayton, *Women Before the Bar: Gender, Law, and Society in Connecticut, 1639–1789* (Chapel Hill: University of North Carolina Press, 1995), ch. 5.

4. Giles Jacob, *A New Law-Dictionary*, 7th ed. (London, 1756), under "rape."

5. Barbara S. Lindemann, " 'To Ravish and Carnally Know': Rape in Eighteenth-Century Massachusetts," *Signs: Journal of Women in Culture and Society* 10 (1984–85): 68.

mistreating his wife. When Drinkwater complained to the local magistrates, they laughed at him. Apparently this "rough music," as such instances of community action were known, had the desired effect, as one neighbor commented on the "remarkable Reformation [of Drinkwater] arising from the Justice of the good Women!"[6] A more organized effort occurred in New Jersey, where in 1752, a group of twelve people dressed in women's clothes went to the homes of those "reported to have beat their wives," and would "strip him [the alleged abuser], turn up his Posterior, and flog him with Rods most severely, crying out all the Time, Wo to the Men that beat their Wives."[7] What cannot be determined from such accounts is if spousal abuse was therefore so unusual that it evoked such a response, or if the public humiliation of abusers was the unusual event. It is probable that most abused women remained isolated in their struggle to survive an abusive relationship, with the community quietly ignoring any indications that domestic norms were being violated.

With the father and husband exerting such control over the lives of the women in their families, it is not surprising that the law allowed men authority to "discipline" their wives and daughters. For most families prior to the twentieth century, discipline meant coercive force. Children and wives who failed to obey were subject to physical punishment, with the state intervening only in the most extreme cases of violence. As Abigail Adams had noted, the law thus made every man a tyrant, and tyrants tend to do whatever they please. Thomas Jefferson had made the same point in regard to slavery in his *Notes on the State of Virginia*:

> The whole commerce between master and slave is a perpetual exercise of the most boisterous passions, the most unremitting despotism on the one part, and degrading submissions on the other. Our children see this, and learn to imitate it; for man is an imitative animal. This quality is the germ of all education in him. From his cradle to his grave he is learning to do what he sees others do. If a parent could find no motive either in his philanthropy or his self-love, for restraining the intemperance of passion towards his slave, it should always be a sufficient one that his child is present. But generally it is not sufficient. The parent storms, the child looks on, catches the lineaments of wrath, puts on the same airs in the circle of smaller slaves, gives a loose to the worst of passions, and thus nursed, educated, and daily exercised in tyranny, can-

6. Steven J. Stewart, "Skimmington in the Middle and New England Colonies," in William Pencak, Matthew Dennis, and Simon P. Newman, eds., *Riot and Revelry in Early America* (University Park: Pennsylvania State University Press, 2002), 45.
7. Brendan McConville, "The Rise of Rough Music: Reflections on an Ancient Custom in Eighteenth-Century New Jersey," in Pencak et al., *Riot and Revelry in Early America*, 87. For more examples in New Jersey, see pp. 90–95.

not but be stamped by it with odious peculiarities. The man must be a prodigy who can retain his manners and morals undepraved by such circumstances.[8]

That Jefferson knew exactly the extent and nature of that tyranny may be evidenced by his probable relationship with Sally Hemings. Though scholars will never know for certain,[9] there is strong evidence that a great many slave masters took advantage of their near-total control over the body of the slave to coerce sexual pleasures for themselves—rape in modern legal terms. There is some evidence that many husbands and fathers took the same advantage of their control over the bodies of their wives, daughters, and sons.

The difficulty for scholars is not just that American culture has long encouraged people to remain silent about the physical abuses they have suffered within the family, but also that the law itself worked to maintain a deep silence on the subject. For instance, the leading book on American criminal law in the nineteenth century was Francis Wheaton's *Treatise on Criminal Law*. Wheaton struggled for a definition of and standard of evidence for rape. "It is essential that force should have been used" in order to establish that a rape occurred, and there had to be evidence of efforts of "actual resistance" on the part of the woman. But "a husband cannot be convicted of the offense" of rape; the very concept of marital rape did not exist in American statute law until the 1970s. Since so much of a rape charge depended on the woman's word, courts needed to proceed with caution to verify the accuser's accuracy. Evidence of the woman's past sexual conduct could be introduced in court in order to "prejudice her testimony."[10] Rape prosecution hung on the public character of the woman victim. "If she be of evil fame," there was "a strong, but not a conclusive presumption that her testimony is false or feigned." Judges and juries, Wheaton warned, should guard "themselves from the influence of sympathy on her behalf."[11] Such a legal structure could discourage many women from bringing charges for fear of allowing the defendant to rummage through her past in search of damaging personal information. Oddly, the law did not allow the prosecutor the same right to introduce the sexual history of the defendant into evidence.

Victims of domestic violence similarly faced little legal recourse. An old common-law standard allowed the male head of the family to beat any of its

---

8. Thomas Jefferson, *Notes on the State of Virginia* (New York: Harper and Row, 1964), 155.

9. See especially Annette Gordon-Reed, *Thomas Jefferson and Sally Hemings: An American Controversy* (Charlottesville: University Press of Virginia, 1997); Richard B. Bernstein, *Thomas Jefferson* (New York: Oxford University Press, 2003).

10. Francis Wheaton, *A Treatise on the Criminal Law of the United States* (Philadelphia: James Kay, Jr., and Brother, 1846), 293–94.

11. Wheaton, *Treatise on the Criminal Law*, 295–96.

members for purposes of discipline, which is to say for the maintenance of the paternal order or what John Adams called "our masculine systems."[12] As Wheaton summarized this standard: "It is admissible for the defendant to show that the alleged battery was merely the correcting of a child by its parent, the correcting of a servant or scholar [student] by his master, or the punishment of the criminal by a proper officer; but if the parent or master chastising the child exceed the bound of moderation and inflict cruel and merciless punishment, he is a trespasser and liable to be punished by indictment."[13] Of course agreeing on what exactly exceeded the bounds of moderation posed a problem for the courts, with discretion left to the judge and jury.

This male power over dependents extended to the wife. Again, the exact limits of the exercise of that authority lay with the court to determine. "By the ancient common law," Wheaton wrote, "the husband possessed the power of chastising his wife, though the tendency of criminal courts in the present day is to regard the marital relation as no defence to a battery."[14] But a few mid-nineteenth-century American courts felt some dread that lessening the husband's recourse to physical force had gone too far. In 1824 the Mississippi Supreme Court held that "the husband [should still] be permitted to exercise the right of moderate chastisement, in cases of great emergency, and to use salutary restraints in every case of misbehaviour, without subjecting himself [to] vexatious prosecutions, resulting in the discredit and shame of all parties concerned." By the end of the century things had changed. In 1893 Mississippi's Supreme Court overruled its 1824 decision, calling it strangely decided. The 1893 court ridiculed "the fancied right in the husband to chastise the wife in moderation" as prevalent only in "the humbler classes of our colored population."[15]

The abuse of children also rarely appeared in the records, except as a testament to its normalcy. The beating of children has been considered a standard family practice for most of American history. The application and extent of physical punishment was left entirely to the parents, usually the father, to determine. Diaries and memoirs are full of accounts of often brutal beatings inflicted on children, usually for "their own good." Most interestingly, the children themselves seem to have internalized the normality of such beatings, excusing their parents for using violence against them and even praising them for their sense of justice and concern. The law took cognizance of family violence only on those occasions when it became extreme enough to produce serious bodily injury or death. Even then, few such cases captured the attention

---

12. Adams, *Familiar Letters*, 155.
13. Wheaton, *Treatise on the Criminal Law*, 314.
14. Wheaton, *Treatise on the Criminal Law*.
15. Calvin Bradley V. The State, 1 Miss. 156 (1824); Miles Harris v. The State, 71 Miss. 464 (1893).

of the law until the late twentieth century. A few dramatic instances of infanticide horrified communities, often after the press announced that they were
becoming more common. For instance, in the 1750s the Connecticut courts
heard six cases of infanticide, which appeared a veritable epidemic to many
observers. A similar sense of social crisis existed in Pennsylvania in the last
decade of the eighteenth century. Newspapers repeatedly emphasized that such
crimes were not beneath the capacity of the poor, especially Irish and African
American women. And it is true that with few exceptions, women charged with
infanticide were from the lower class. Any middle-class or upper-class women
guilty of infanticide seemingly got away with their crimes. Nearly all the known
acts of infanticide came as part of an effort to conceal an illegitimate childbirth.
But even infanticide found acceptance in one instance: when a white woman
gave birth to a child by a black, especially a slave, father. The children of white
men and slave women became slaves, increasing the capital of the father, but
the child of a white woman and black man was considered too great an affront
to social mores, particularly because such a child would follow the condition
of the mother and be a free person.

Incest has always aroused the deepest feelings of loathing in American society, which may explain why so few cases have been heard in the courts. For
example, just nine cases reached Connecticut's courts between 1666 and 1789,
with not a single case prosecuted in the half century prior to the Revolution.
The evidence in these few cases must have been fairly compelling, since all but
one ended in conviction. We will never know for certain if there were a sizable
number of unreported incest cases, but the example supplied here by Abigail
Abbot never found its way into the courts, which may have been typical.[16]

It is impossible to know if the exercise of what Elizabeth Pleck called "domestic tyranny" lessened as the nineteenth century progressed. All historians
have is the occasional flash of illumination in court records or news accounts
when a particularly notorious case, usually involving murder, caught the public's attention. In 1836 the murder of a New York City prostitute, Helen Jewett,
filled the national press for several weeks. But the daily terror of spousal abuse
escaped public notice and was thought inappropriate for polite discussion. The
ideology of separate spheres, in which women were confined to the domestic
sphere of the home, made the legal system even less likely to intrude in family
matters. The home became not just "a haven in a heartless world" but also a
man's fortress, complete, on occasion, with metaphorical torture chambers for
his wife and daughter. The larger community paid ever less attention to what
went on within the private world of the man's castle. This desire to avoid even
thinking of the possibility that husbands beat their wives or fathers abused

16. Dayton, *Women Before The Bar*, 233.

their children abated only slowly in the twentieth century as social reformers and legal institutions moved cautiously into territory thought to be the sole purview of the head of the family.

Modern social sciences did not at first offer much hope to the victims of family violence. Social service agencies in the Progressive Era did not want to confront the consequences of questioning the nuclear family or the taboo subject of the sexual abuse of children. Even psychiatry tended to dismiss the matter, following Sigmund Freud's lead in treating tales of sexual molestation as "hysteria." Freud noted that many of his women patients reported that they had been sexually assaulted by family members, including their fathers, but Freud felt that these attacks were fantasies rather than realities. One consequence of Freud's theory was the tendency of officials to treat children who reported molestation as liars. From there it was a small step to a suspicion that women who charged rape were also fantasizing. Though that attitude may appear extreme, it became standard legal practice in the 1930s, after the American Bar Association formed a special committee to revise the rules of testimony in rape and sexual abuse cases. This committee, chaired by John Henry Wigmore, recommended that judges order a psychiatric screening of all children and women who charged sexual assault because of their well-known proclivity to make up such charges. Wigmore personally added that it was the man who was usually the victim in sexual assault cases. The committee justified its recommendations by citing recent psychological research.[17]

Psychology also provided the explanation for spousal abuse: women wanted to be beaten. Freud's disciple Helene Deutsch theorized in 1930 that women were masochistic by nature, which was a requirement for childbirth. But in some women that masochism became a necessity, for why else would a woman stay with a man who beat her? Deutsch's thesis found wide acceptance in legal and intellectual circles in the United States in the 1930s, justifying nonintervention by authorities in spousal abuse cases.

The general attitude through the first six decades of the twentieth century was that domestic abuse was a family matter. Critics of all kinds turned a blind eye to any form of psychological abuse that fell short of physical violence, failing to see how such intimate terrorism could be anyone's concern. But even when such terror turned brutally physical, authorities rarely arrested the perpetrator, preferring to persuade the family to reconcile as soon as possible. Police loathed responding to these "family disturbance" calls, as the police officer often became embroiled in bitter fights that led to his injury. Social workers generally held that children needed far more help than adult women, for

17. John Henry Wigmore, *Wigmore's Code of the Rules of Evidence in Trials of Law* (Boston: Little, Brown, 1935).

the woman could always just leave. But even efforts to ameliorate child abuse ran up against popular attitudes that saw "discipline" as the parent's prerogative. And, like rape, it was a subject that most people preferred not to discuss. As Elizabeth Pleck noted, not a single article on family violence appeared in the *Journal of Marriage and the Family* from its first issue in 1939 until 1969.[18]

In the late 1950s some unrelated, quiet changes in two completely different fields helped to shift popular perceptions of child abuse. As head of the Children's Division of the American Humane Association, Vincent DeFrancis worked to persuade social workers to abandon their traditional standard that they should intervene in families only if requested to do so by the parents. As DeFrancis accumulated evidence that this policy of nonintervention fostered child abuse, more social workers came to feel that they needed a more proactive approach to prevent serious injury to children.

Meanwhile, a similar shift was occurring in the medical profession, though from an unusual direction. Doctors had long been loath to call attention to child abuse for fear of alienating patients and becoming embroiled in lawsuits. They tended to blame bruises and broken bones on accidents, usually the result of rough children's games. But in the 1950s radiologists, who had no direct connection to the patients they treated, began calling ever more attention to the hidden and repeated injuries they found on X-rays. They were not as confident that most of these traumas were unintentional. Radiologists' articles in medical journals persuaded many pediatricians that their duty to protect the health and well-being of their young patients demanded that they pay closer attention to the source of serious injuries. In 1962, C. Henry Kempe published his seminal essay "The Battered-Child Syndrome," which quickly caught national attention. At the same time, California became the first state to require hospitals and doctors to report suspected cases of child abuse to the police. Later that year the popular television shows *Dragnet* and *Ben Casey, M.D.* addressed the issue of child abuse for the first time, which in turn persuaded journalists that this issue deserved further inquiry.[19]

Despite all this attention, child protection advocates found it difficult to get around the traditional notion that parents "needed" to discipline their children with force. And neither opponents nor supporters of child protective legislation found it easy to locate the point at which a spanking became sadism, a slap edged over into a stiff uppercut, or locking a child in a closet became torture.

Attitudes toward spousal violence changed in the early 1970s largely as a

18. Elizabeth Pleck, *Domestic Tyranny: The Making of American Social Policy against Family Violence from Colonial Times to the Present* (New York: Oxford University Press, 1987), 182.

19. Pleck, *Domestic Tyranny*, 168.

result of the resurgent feminist movement. The publication in 1968 of Eldridge Cleaver's *Soul on Ice*, in which his raping of white women was seen as an act of political liberation, fired many feminists to insist on the bodily integrity of women. Maya Angelou's *I Know Why the Caged Bird Sings* (1969), with its graphic portrayal of her uncle raping her while she was very young, made clear to tens of thousands of readers that rape was an act of horrific violence, and one that often occurred within the family. Susan Brownmiller's *Against Our Will* (1975) offered a theoretical perspective that viewed rape not so much as a sexual act but as a crime intended to maintain patriarchal authority, with the man seeking dominance over the body of women. Brownmiller aroused further controversy by emphasizing the previously unthinkable notion that rape could occur within marriage. These latter two books were part of a sudden and dramatic increase in public attention to the issue of domestic abuse that led to a "battered women's movement." In the early 1970s, feminists opened shelters as a refuge for women and children fleeing abusive relations. In 1976, *Ms.* magazine listed twenty women's shelters in the United States; in 1982 the magazine reported three hundred shelters. At the same time, feminists pressured police and local authorities to begin responding more constructively to reports of family violence. Police and social service agencies had tended to "mediate" domestic disputes, which usually left women and children at home with the alleged abuser. On this issue, feminists took a staunch law-and-order position, calling for the arrest and prosecution of men who committed acts of violence against women and children.

From local authorities, feminists turned to state legislatures in their efforts to protect women and children from domestic violence. For the first time in American history, state governments interposed themselves in issues of family discipline. In 1973, largely as a result of the commitment of Senator Walter Mondale of Minnesota, Congress passed the Child Abuse Prevention and Treatment Act, granting funds for pilot programs that treated both children and parents. The Carter presidency was the peak period for this movement to protect family members from violence within the home. In the four years Carter held office, from January 1977 to 1981, nearly every state funded family shelters, criminalized spousal abuse, and reformed criminal court procedures to the benefit of the victim. In 1979 President Carter created the Office of Domestic Violence. But the very next year these efforts came to a sudden halt in the face of renewed Republican opposition.

In 1980 Representative Barbara Mikulski of Maryland introduced legislation to grant federal funding to shelters and other agencies devoted to protecting victims of family violence. Conservatives led by Senator Orrin Hatch of Utah warned that this legislation represented a dangerous first step by federal bureaucracies into family life. As champions of the traditional nuclear family, conservatives feared that the true aim of such feminist-inspired legislation was the destruction of the father's authority, which would in turn lead to the collapse of the family as a social institution. Those identified with the Christian Right went further and maintained that feminists sought nothing less than the destruction of the Christian family. Senator Gordon Humphrey of New Hampshire maintained that shelters for battered women were indoctrination centers for radical feminist "missionaries who would war on the traditional family or on local values."[20] In the face of such emotional opposition, Mikulski and her allies withdrew their bill in hopes of a more positive environment in the near future.

Ronald Reagan's victory in the 1980 election marked the end of the first period of significant government response to domestic violence. Shortly after his inauguration, President Reagan closed the short-lived Office of Domestic Violence. In the ensuing years, Republicans proposed legislation that would terminate all federal support for child or spousal abuse prevention, and to specifically exclude parental discipline from the category of child abuse. However, the Republican leadership found that even many of their core constituency felt that some degree of federal participation in responding to domestic violence was appropriate, leading them to support a scaled-down version of Mikulski's bill in 1984, the Family Violence Prevention and Services Act (42 USCS §10401).

The 1990s saw greater public awareness of the dangers of ignoring abused children. A number of notable cases in which children were beaten to death by a parent or a foster child was tortured by his or her guardian led to increased demands for more government oversight of the parent-child relation. But with the advent of the "new feminism," even many defenders of women's rights placed more responsibility on the woman in an abusive relation, holding that there was no longer any excusing a woman who did not leave. Conservatives continued their opposition to government action as an intrusion in family governance. Yet the need for battered women's shelters persisted, with unlisted addresses and tight security to prevent husbands and boyfriends from tracking down their victims. For far too many women, economic and emotional dependence, and the lack of supportive alternatives like a church, close community, or family, left them no place to turn. Sadly, even in the twenty-first century, the state still tends to act only after it is too late. It is difficult to open a newspaper without seeing a story like one headed "Infant Laid to Rest in Colorado." In October 2002, Joseph and Audra Dowler beat their nine-week-old boy, Tanner, to death "because he pulled out his pacifier." The baby had been burned on his feet and face, had two arms broken, and suffered a severe brain injury. Tanner's grandparents claimed to have written "letters to county social

20. Quoted in Pleck, *Domestic Tyranny*, 197.

services warning that the boy's parents needed parenting classes." The Reverend David DeBord, speaking at the child's funeral, said, "Maybe his death might expose a hole in the safety net that needs repairing."[21] The question remained: Who was responsible for the repairs?

DOCUMENTS

LIVING WITH DOMESTIC VIOLENCE

Abigail Abbot was born in 1746 in Concord, New Hampshire, on what was then the northern frontier of New England. In 1763 she moved with her family north to the Connecticut River town of Newbury, where, the following year, she had a conversion experience and joined the local Congregational church. Later that year, the Abbot family crossed the river to Haverhill, New Hampshire, where Abigail met Asa Bailey, who was a year older and had just arrived with his family in this frontier town. As this memoir makes evident, religion played a vital role in Abigail Abbot's life, yet she married an unconverted man in 1767. Though considered a respectable gentleman in the town, Bailey was known for a sharp and even violent temper. Within the first few months of marriage, Asa turned that violent nature against his wife. In addition, he had affairs with other women, attempted to rape a servant—which led to the Bailey family moving to Landaff, New Hampshire—and ultimately sexually abused his daughter Phebe.

Like many wives before and since, Abigail Abbot Bailey endured years of abuse in hopes that she could change her husband. She used religion, persuasion, and social pressure in efforts to end his violence, all of which failed. Asa left several times, Abbot taking him back each time. After twenty-one years of marriage and fourteen children, Abbot finally had enough. By threatening to bring in the courts, she persuaded Asa Bailey to divide their property and leave the state. But as is described in this chapter, in 1792 Asa tricked Abbot into traveling with him to New York, where the laws were far more favorable to the man's patriarchal authority. Abbot fled her husband and returned to New Hampshire, where her community rallied to her support and she won a legal divorce from Asa Bailey. Abigail Abbot settled in Haverhill and died in 1815. Her minister during the period when she had finally divorced her husband, the Reverend Ethan Smith, published these memoirs, extracted from her diaries, later that year.

Much of Abigail Abbot's memoir carries the flavor of her age, with its restrictive gender legislation, a tendency to cast all woes in religious tones, and a careful avoidance of upsetting language. But much else seems common to many women through the years

21. P. Solomon Banda, "Infant Laid to Rest in Colorado," Associated Press, October 21, 2002.

who have suffered an abusive relationship, most particularly her willingness to blame herself for the man's violence.

Abigail Bailey Describes Her Husband's Violent Ways, 1767–1789

April 15, 1767 I was married to Asa Bailey, just after having entered the 22nd year of my age. I now left my dear parents;—hoping to find in my husband a true hearted and constant friend. My desires and hopes were, that we might live together in peace and friendship; seeking each other's true happiness till death. I did earnestly look to God for his blessing upon this solemn undertaking;—sensible, that "Except the Lord build the house, they labor in vain that build it." As, while I lived with my parents, I esteemed it my happiness to be in subjection to them; so now I thought it must be a still greater benefit to be under the aid of a judicious companion, who would rule well his own house.

It had been my hope to find a companion of a meek, peaceable temper; a lover of truth; discreet and pleasant.... But the allwise God, who has made all things for himself, has a right, and knows how, to govern all things for his own glory; and often to disappoint the purposes of his creatures....

Relative to my new companion, though I had found no evidence that he was a subject of true religion; yet I did hope and expect, from my acquaintance with him, that he would wish for good regulations in his family, and would have its external order accord with the word of God. But I met with sore disappointment.—I soon found that my new friend was naturally of a hard, uneven, rash temper; and was capable of being very unreasonable. My conviction of this was indeed grievous, and caused me many a sorrowful hour. For such were my feelings and habits, that I knew not how to endure a hard word, or a frowning look from any one; much less from a companion. I now began to learn, with trembling, that it was the sovereign pleasure of the allwise God to try me with afflictions in that relation, from which I had hoped to receive the greatest of my earthly comforts. I had placed my highest worldly happiness in the love, tenderness, and peace of relatives and friends. But before one month, from my marriage day, had passed, I learned that I must expect hard and cruel treatment in my new habitation, and from my new friend.

... For some years I thought his repeated instances of hard treatment of me arose,—not from any settled ill will, or real want of kind affection toward me;—but from the usual depravity of the human heart; and from a want of self-government. I still confided in him, as my real friend, and loved him with increasing affection.

After about three years—alas what shall I say? My heart was torn with grief, and my eyes flowed with tears, while I learned, from time to time, the *inconstancy* of a husband! In September, 1770, we hired a young woman to live with us. She had been a stranger to me, I found her rude, and full of vanity. Her ways were to me disagreeable. But to my grief I saw they were pleasing to Mr. B. Their whole attention seemed to be toward each other; and their impertinent conduct very aggravating to me, and (I was sensible) provoking to God. I learned to my full satisfaction, that there was very improper conduct between them. . . .

I kept my troubles to myself as much as I could. But I most earnestly pleaded with Mr. B. from time to time to consider the evil of his ways; and to forsake the foolish and live. But he turned a deaf ear to all my entreaties, and he regarded neither my sorrows, nor the ruin of his family, and of himself, for time and eternity.

In my distress, my only refuge was in God my Saviour. . . .

Soon after this, through the mercy of God, I prevailed to send away the vile young woman from our family. After this Mr. B. became again more regular, and seemed friendly. But alas, my confidence in him was destroyed in a great measure. . . .

July, 1773, Alas, I must again resume my lonely pen, and write grievous things against the husband of my youth! Another young woman was living with us. And I was grieved and astonished to learn that the conduct of Mr. B. with her was unseemly. After my return home from an absence of several days visiting my friends, I was convinced that all had not been right at home. Mr. B. perceived my trouble upon the subject. In the afternoon (the young woman being then absent) he fell into a passion with me. He was so overcome with anger, that he was unable to set up. He took his bed, and remained there till night. Just before evening he said to me, "I never saw such a woman as you. You can be so calm; while I feel so disturbed."

. . . He then took hold of my hand, and said, I am not angry with you now; nor had I ever any reason to be angry with you, since you lived with me. He added, I never knew till now what a sinner I have been. I have broken all God's holy laws, and my life has been one continued course of rebellion against God. I deserve his eternal wrath; and wonder I am out of hell.

. . . I hoped, though with much fear, that God had plucked him as a brand from the burning, and made him a vessel of mercy. I now lived in peace and comfort with my husband;—willing to forgive all that was past, if he might but behave well in future.

In 1774 I again experienced a scene of mortification and trial. The young woman, of whom I last spake, who had lived with us, was induced to go before a grand jury, and to declare under oath that while she lived at our house, and while I was absent, as I before noted, Mr. B. in the night went to her apartment; and after flatteries used in vain, made violent attempts upon her; but was repulsed. All but the violence used, Mr. B. acknowledged. . . .

[The family moved to Landaff.] *Aug.* 7, 1774. . . . The smiles of God attended us in kind providences, of which I would take a grateful notice. Though Mr. B. had done so much to blot his name, and to injure his family; and though his character for some time was low; yet he seemed, after a while, strangely to surmount all those difficulties. In a few years he seemed to be generally and highly esteemed. He was indeed a man of abilities. And as he grew in years, he seemed to advance in prospects of usefulness in society. He became a leading man in the town. . . . He was honored with a major's commission. For a course of years he served in this office; and was celebrated as an active and good officer at the head of his regiment. I perceived the hand of God in trying Mr. B. with prosperity, to see if he would become and remain a regular and good man. . . .

December, 1788. . . . One night, soon after we had retired to bed; he began to talk very familiarly, and seemed pleasant. He said, now I will tell you what I have been studying upon all this while: I have been planning to sell our farm, and to take our family and interest, and move to the westward, over toward the Ohio country, five or six hundred miles; I think that is a much better country than this; and I have planned out the whole matter. . . .

He proceeded to say, that he would take one of our sons, and one daughter, to go first with him on this tour, to wait on him; and that he probably should not return to take the rest of the family under a year from the time he should set out. He said he would put his affairs in order, so that it should be as easy and comfortable for me as possible, during his absence.

Soon after, Mr. B. laid this his pretended plan before the children; and after a while he obtained their consent to move to the westward. They were not pleased with the idea, but wished to be obedient, and to honor their father. Thus we all consented, at last, to follow our head and guide, wherever he should think best; for our family had ever been in the habit of obedience: and perhaps never were more pains taken to please the head of a family, than had ever been taken in our domestic circle.

But alas! words fail to set forth the things which followed! All this pretended *plan* was but a specious cover to infernal designs. . . . Mr. B. . . . said he had altered his plan; he would leave his son, and take only his daughter: he would hire what men's help he needed: his daughter must go and cook for him. He now commenced a new series of conduct in relation to this daughter. . . . A great part of the time he now spent in the room where she was spinning. . . . He seemed to have forgotten his age, his honor, and all decency, as well as all virtue. He would spend his time with this daughter, in telling

idle stories, and foolish riddles, and singing songs to her. . . . He had ever
been sovereign, severe and hard with his children, and they stood in the
greatest fear of him. His whole conduct, toward this daughter especially, was
now changed, and became most disagreeable.

. . . His daily conduct forced a conviction upon my alarmed and tortured
mind, that his designs were the most vile. All his tender affections were withdrawn from the wife of his youth, the mother of his children. My room was
deserted, and left lonely. His care for the rest of his family seemed abandoned, as well as all his attention to his large circle of worldly business. Everything must lie neglected, while this one daughter engrossed all his attention.

Though all the conduct of Mr. B, from day to day, seemed to demonstrate to my apprehension, that he was determined, and was continually plotting, to ruin this poor young daughter, yet it was so intolerably crossing to
every feeling of my soul to admit such a thought, that I strove with all my
might to banish it from my mind, and to disbelieve the possibility of such a
thing. I felt terrified at my own thoughts upon the subject; and shocked that
such a thing should enter my mind, But the more I labored to banish those
things from my mind, the more I found it impossible to annihilate evident
facts. . . . And such were my infirmities, weakness and fears, (my circumstances being very difficult) that I did not dare to hint any thing of my fears
to him, or to any creature. This may to some appear strange; but with me it
was then a reality. I labored to divert his mind from his follies, and to turn
his attention to things of the greatest importance. But I had the mortification
to find that my endeavors were unsuccessful.

I soon perceived that his strange conduct toward this daughter was to her
very disagreeable. And she shewed as much unwillingness to be in the room
with him, as she dared. I often saw her cheeks bedewed with tears, on account of his new and astonishing behaviour. But as his will had ever been
the law of the family, she saw no way to deliver herself from her cruel father.
Such were her fears of him, that she did not dare to talk with me, or any
other person, upon her situation: for he was exceedingly jealous of my con-
versing with her, and cautioning her. If I ever dropped words, which I hoped
would put her upon her guard, or inquired the cause of her troubles, or what
business her father had so much with her? if I was ever so cautious, he
would find it out, and be very angry. He watched her and me most narrowly;
and by his subtle questions with her, he would find out what I had said, during his absence. He would make her think I had informed him what I had
said, and then would be very angry with me: so that at times I feared for my
life. I queried with myself which way I could turn. How could I caution a
young daughter in such a case? My thoughts flew to God for relief, that the

Father of mercies would protect a poor helpless creature marked out for a prey; and turn the heart of a cruel father from every wicked purpose.

After a while Mr. B's conduct toward this daughter was strangely altered. Instead of idle songs, fawning and flattery, he grew very angry with her; and would wish her dead, and buried: and he would correct her very severely. It seems, that when he found his first line of conduct ineffectual, he changed his behaviour, felt his vile indignation moved, and was determined to see what he could effect by tyranny and cruelty. He most cautiously guarded her against having any free conversation with me, or any of the family, at any time; lest she should expose him. He would forbid any of the children going with her to milking. If, at any time, any went with her, it must be a number; so that nothing could be said concerning him. He would not suffer her to go from home: I might not send her abroad on any occasion. Never before had Mr. B. thus confined her, or any of his children. None but an eye witness can conceive of the strangeness of his conduct from day to day, and of his plans to conceal his wickedness, and to secure himself from the light of evidence.

. . . I clearly saw that Mr. B. entertained the most vile intentions relative to his own daughter. Whatever difficulty attended the obtaining of legal proof, yet no remaining doubt existed in my mind, relative to the existence of his wickedness: and I had no doubt remaining of the violence, which he had used; and that hence arose his rage against her. . . . Sometimes he corrected her with a rod; and sometimes with a beach stick, large enough for the driving of a team; and with such sternness and anger sparkling in his eyes, that his visage seemed to resemble an infern[o]; declaring, that if she attempted to run from him again, she should never want but one correction more; for he would whip her to death! . . . It seemed as though the poor girl must now be destroyed under his furious hand. She was abashed, and could look no one in the face. . . .

It may appear surprising that such wickedness was not checked by legal restraints. But great difficulties attend in such a case. While I was fully convinced of the wickedness, yet I knew not that I could make legal proof. I could not prevail upon this daughter to make known to me her troubles; or to testify against the author of them. Fear, shame, youthful inexperience, and the terrible peculiarities of her case, all conspired to close her mouth against affording me, or any one, proper information. My soul was moved with pity for her wretched case: and yet I cannot say I did not feel a degree of resentment, that she would not, as she ought, expose the wickedness of her father, that she might be relieved from him, and he brought to due punishment. But no doubt his intrigues, insinuations, commands, threats, and parental influence, led her to feel that it was in vain for her to seek redress.

[September 1789] . . . The next morning I took an opportunity with Mr. B. alone to have solemn conversation. My health being now restored, I thought it high time, and had determined, to adopt a new mode of treatment with Mr. B. I calmly introduced the subject, and told him, plainly and solemnly, all my views of his wicked conduct, in which he had long lived with his daughter. He flew into a passion, was high, and seemed to imagine, he could at once frighten me out of my object. But I was carried equally above fear, and above temper. . . . I told him I should no longer be turned off in this manner; but should pursue my object with firmness, and with whatever wisdom and ability God might give me; and that God would plead my cause. . . .

. . . I told Mr. B. . . . I would not suffer him to go on any longer as he had done. I would now soon adopt measures to put a stop to his abominable wickedness and cruelties. For this could and ought to be done. . . .

By this time Mr. B. had become silent. He appeared struck with some degree of fear. He, by and by, asked me what I intended or expected to do, to bring about such a revolution as I had intimated? whether I knew what an awful crime I had laid to his charge? which he said could not be proved. He wished to know whether I had considered how difficult it would be for me to do any such thing against him? as I was under his legal control; and he could overrule all my plans as he pleased. . . . I told Mr. B. he *knew* he had violated his marriage covenant; and hence had forfeited all legal and just right and authority over me; and I should convince him that I well knew it. I told him I was not in any passion. I acted on principle, and from long and mature consideration. And though it had ever been my greatest care and pleasure (among my earthly comforts) to obey and please him; yet by his most wicked and cruel conduct, he had compelled me to undertake this most undesirable business—of stopping him in his mad career; and that I now felt strength, courage and zeal to pursue my resolution. . . .

As to what I could prove against him, I told Mr. B. he knew not how much evidence I had of his unnatural crimes, of which I had accused him, and of which *he knew he was guilty.* . . .

Mr. B. seeing me thus bold and determinate, soon changed his countenance and conduct. He appeared panic-struck; and he soon became mild, sociable and pleasant. He now made an attempt, with all his usual subtlety, and flatteries, to induce me to relinquish my design. He pretended to deny the charge of incest. But I told him I had no confidence in his denial of it; it was therefore in vain! Upon this he said, he really did not blame, or think hard of me, for believing him guilty of this sin. He said, he knew he had behaved foolishly; and had given me full reason to be jealous of him. . . . He then took the Bible, and said, he would lay his hand on it, and swear that he was not guilty of the crime laid to his charge. Knowing what I did, I was surprised and disgusted at this impious attempt. I stepped towards him, and in a resolute and solemn manner begged of him to forbear! assuring him, that such an oath could not undo or alter real facts, of which he was conscious. And this proceeding, I assured him, would be so far from giving me any satisfaction, that it would greatly increase the distress of my soul for him in his wickedness. Upon this he forbore, and laid his Bible aside.

He then begged of me to forgive all that was past; and he promised that he would ever be kind and faithful to me in future, and never more give me reason to complain of him for any such conduct. I told him, if I had but evidence of his real reformation, I could readily forgive him as a fellow creature, and could plead with God to forgive him. But as to my living with him in the most endearing relation any longer, after such horrid crimes, I did not see that I *could*, or *ought* to do it! . . . He now pretended to feel much tenderness, and said he was very sorry for all his sins.

I was too well acquainted with Mr. B. to suppose that I now discovered any real evidence of a penitent heart, or to be much deceived by his flatteries. But I did entertain some hopes that he would now reform from his gross abominations. And as I was sensible of the difficulty of proving, to legal conviction, the crimes I had alleged against him, (the daughter never yet having consented to testify against him,) also the consequences of such a process seemed to me of the most terrible kind; I seemed to feel constrained to let those things rest, for the present, as they were; feeling a confidence in God, that if Mr. B. did not reform, or if it were best I should part from him for his past wickedness, God would render my path of duty plain.

Thus upon the many promises Mr. B. had made, I gave encouragement, that I would suffer him to have one season more of trial; that if he would indeed reform, and take the word of God for the guide of his heart and life, and would treat his family as he ought, I might overlook all that was past; and submit to him again, as my head and husband.

Joy and gladness beamed in his countenance. He said he never should be able to express suitable thanks to me for my condescension, in that I had thus far overlooked his ill and unreasonable treatment of me. Mr. B. then took my right hand in his, and said, I call God and angels to witness, that I, from this time, will be to you a loving, kind, and faithful friend and husband. As to that daughter, I will never more do any thing, that shall grieve or trouble you. Nor will I ever more give you cause of uneasiness with me, on account of any female on earth. And I will henceforth take the holy word of God for my guide, and the rule of my life. . . .

For several weeks nothing more was said upon the subject. And Mr. B.'s conduct towards me and the family was pleasant and agreeable. . . .

I again clearly perceived that the same wicked passions, as before, were in operation in Mr. B.'s heart. . . . Upon a certain Sabbath, I went to meeting. Mr. B. did not go. Before I reached home at night, I met with evidence, which convinced me, that the same horrid conduct had on this holy day been repeated in my family! . . .

The next day, I took him alone, and told him of what he had again been guilty, even after all his vows, and fair promises of fidelity. He started, and seemed very angry, that I should think such a thing [of] him. I told him I charged him only with facts; and hence I was not worthy of his censure! . . .

Mr. B. now attempted again to flatter me. He renewed the most solemn promises of amendment. And earnestly begged that I would once more pardon him. He now again seemed cautious as to an acknowledgement of the alleged offence; and yet implicitly acknowledged it; and urged me to bury all that was amiss; and most solemnly engaged that if I would do it, I should find him a true and faithful friend in future. . . . I said that I thought it would now be abominable for me ever to live with him any more. For it was impossible for me to feel the least confidence in his word. . . .

Our unhappy daughter now became eighteen years of age, and thus legally free from her father. She immediately left us, and returned no more. As she was going, I had solemn conversation with her relative to her father's conduct. She gave me to understand that it had been most abominable. But I could not induce her to consent to become an evidence against him. I plead with her the honor and safety of our family; the safety of her young sisters; and her own duty; but she appeared overwhelmed with shame and grief; and nothing effectual could yet be done. . . .

Mr. B. and I parted. I had no expectation, or wish ever to see him again in this life. I petitioned for a bill of divorcement, and readily obtained it. . . .

Source: Ethan Smith, ed., *Memoirs of Mrs. Abigail Bailey, Who Had Been the Wife of Major Asa Bailey* (Boston: Samuel T. Armstrong, 1815), 11–22, 30–35, 38–51, 195.

INCIDENTS IN THE LIFE OF A SLAVE GIRL

Thomas Jefferson was not the only slaveholder to have sexual relations with what he perceived as his property. Slave owners rarely talked about it, though the presence of numerous light-skinned slaves who bore a striking resemblance to a member of the master's family—as Sally Hemings did to her half-sister Martha, Jefferson's wife—testified to these sexual encounters. Many wives of slave owners knew of these relations and tended to blame the victim rather than their husbands. Given the inordinately unequal power relation between master and slave, one in which it is difficult to imagine the woman granting her consent, or even being asked, it seems appropriate to consider these encounters as sexual violence or rape. It is evident that some slaveholders thought of sex as just another form of labor to be exploited. There is very little evidence that these white men ever felt any shame for these sexual liaisons with their slaves, even if they did promote the ideology of slavery as paternalism. After all, at least one notorious slave owner, John James Hammond, recorded in his diary his sexual desire for and encounters with both his slaves and his nieces. He insisted, however, that it was not really his fault, for these females insisted on tempting him; his nieces "permitting my hands to stray unchecked over every part of theirs [bodies] & to rest without the slightest shrinking from it, on the most secret and sacred regions." How, he asked plaintively, is it possible "in flesh and blood to withstand this?" For two years he carried on in this fashion with his four nieces until one of them finally went to her father, Wade Hampton, with the sordid tale. Hammond, who was married and governor of South Carolina at the time, seemed unable to comprehend why his brother-in-law responded with such anger. Hampton exacted political revenge on Hammond, but, as Drew Faust has written, "the father triumphed at his children's expense"; all four of Hampton's daughters "remained single all their lives."[22] But given their experiences with their uncle, that may have preferred to remain single.

The women involved would have told a very different story from Hammond's. Yet few, especially few slave women, ever had the opportunity to testify to the violence and humiliation they suffered at the hands of those claiming to be their protector. One notable exception was Harriet Jacobs. Many slave narratives had appeared in the 1840s and 1850s, but Jacobs's was one of the few written by a woman. Her personal account, published just a few weeks before the start of the Civil War, brought the worst characteristics of slavery to public attention. Writing in the mid–nineteenth century, Jacobs, who published Incidents in the Life of a Slave Girl *under the name Linda Brent, had to mute her language for polite society, probably at the insistence of her publisher. Nonetheless, it is hard to mistake that she is describing the crime of rape, and that the criminal was Dr. James Norcom ("Dr. Flint" in the memoir), the man who called himself her master. It is also clear from Jacobs's telling that she was not Norcom's first victim.*

Jacobs was born to "mulatto" parents in North Carolina in 1813. She stated that she did not know she was a slave until she was six, when her mother died. Jacobs was only fifteen when Norcom began making sexual advances upon her. She gave birth to her first child, Joseph, the following year. Two years later, when she was eighteen, Jacobs had a daughter, Louisa. Though their father was white, these children were slaves.

Unwilling to put up further with Norcom's sexual exploitation, Jacobs went into hiding in 1835. Incredibly, she spent the next seven years in the same town as Norcom, in a small attic room in her grandmother's house. In 1842 Jacobs finally made good her escape north with her daughter, Louisa. They settled first in Brooklyn but were pursued by Norcom's slave catchers, so they moved on to Rochester, joining the abolitionist circle of Fredrick Douglass, who connected her with Maria Child, with whom Jacobs wrote this

---

22. Drew Gilpin Faust, *James Henry Hamond and the Old South* (Baton Rouge: Louisiana State University Press, 1982), 242, 290.

memoir. During the Civil War, Jacobs and Louisa moved to Alexandria, Virginia, where they helped provide medical care for Union troops and refugees. Jacobs also started the Jacobs Free School in Alexandria, which was dedicated to training black teachers for the freedmen. Jacobs spent the next several years helping the freedmen resettle and working to organize the National Association of Colored Women in Washington. Jacobs died in March 1897, after a long life of risking much for freedom.

Harriet Jacobs, a Slave, Is Raped by Her Owner, 1861

. . . I now entered on my fifteenth year—a sad epoch in the life of a slave girl. My master began to whisper foul words in my ear. Young as I was, I could not remain ignorant of their import.

I tried to treat them with indifference or contempt. The master's age, my extreme youth, and the fear that his conduct would be reported to my grandmother, made him bear this treatment for many months. He was a crafty man, and resorted to many means to accomplish his purposes. Sometimes he had stormy, terrific ways, that made his victims tremble; sometimes he assumed a gentleness that he thought must surely subdue. Of the two, I preferred his stormy moods, although they left me trembling. He tried his utmost to corrupt the pure principles my grandmother had instilled. He peopled my young mind with unclean images, such as only a vile monster could think of. I turned from him with disgust and hatred.

But he was my master. I was compelled to live under the same roof with him—where I saw a man forty years my senior daily violating the most sacred commandments of nature. He told me I was his property; that I must be subject to his will in all things. My soul revolted against the mean tyranny. But where could I turn for protection? No matter whether the slave girl be as black as ebony or as fair as her mistress. In either case, there is no shadow of law to protect her from insult, from violence, or even from death; all these are inflicted by fiends who bear the shape of men. The mistress, who ought to protect the helpless victim, has no other feelings towards her but those of jealousy and rage. The degradation, the wrongs, the vices, that grow out of slavery, are more than I can describe. They are greater than you would willingly believe. . . .

Every where the years bring to all enough of sin and sorrow; but in slavery the very dawn of life is darkened by these shadows. Even the little child, who is accustomed to wait on her mistress and her children, will learn, before she is twelve years old, why it is that her mistress hates such and such a one among the slaves. Perhaps the child's own mother is among those hated ones. She listens to violent outbreaks of jealous passion, and cannot help understanding what is the cause. She will become prematurely knowing in evil things. Soon she will learn to tremble when she hears her master's footfall. She will be compelled to realize that she is no longer a child. If God has bestowed beauty upon her, it will prove her greatest curse. That which commands admiration in the white woman only hastens the degradation of the female slave. I know that some are too much brutalized by slavery to feel the humiliation of their position; but many slaves feel it most acutely, and shrink from the memory of it. I cannot tell how much I suffered in the presence of these wrongs, nor how I am still pained by the retrospect.

My master met me at every turn, reminding me that I belonged to him, and swearing by heaven and earth that he would compel me to submit to him. If I went out for a breath of fresh air, after a day of unwearied toil, his footsteps dogged me. If I knelt by my mother's grave, his dark shadow fell on me even there. The light heart which nature had given me became heavy with sad forebodings. The other slaves in my master's house noticed the change. Many of them pitied me; but none dared to ask the cause. They had no need to inquire. They knew too well the guilty practices under that roof; and they were aware that to speak of them was an offense that never went unpunished.

I longed for some one to confide in. I would have given the world to have laid my head on my grandmother's faithful bosom, and told her all my troubles. But Dr. Flint swore he would kill me, if I was not as silent as the grave. . . . I was very young, and felt shamefaced about telling her such impure things, especially as I knew her to be very strict on such subjects. Moreover, she was a woman of a high spirit. She was usually very quiet in her demeanor; but if her indignation was once roused, it was not very easily quelled. I had been told that she once chased a white gentleman with a loaded pistol, because he insulted one of her daughters. I dreaded the consequences of a violent outbreak; and both pride and fear kept me silent. But though I did not confide in my grandmother, and even evaded her vigilant watchfulness and inquiry, her presence in the neighborhood was some protection to me. Though she had been a slave, Dr. Flint was afraid of her. He dreaded her scorching rebukes. Moreover, she was known and patronized by many people; and he did not wish to have his villainy made public. . . .

I would ten thousand times rather that my children should be the half-starved paupers of Ireland than to be the most pampered among the slaves of America. I would rather drudge out my life on a cotton plantation, till the grave opened to give me rest, than to live with an unprincipled master and a jealous mistress. The felon's home in a penitentiary is preferable. He may repent, and turn from the error of his ways, and so find peace; but it is not so with a favorite slave. She is not allowed to have any pride of character. It is deemed a crime in her to wish to be virtuous.

Mrs. Flint possessed the key to her husband's character before I was born. She might have used this knowledge to counsel and to screen the young and the innocent among her slaves; but for them she had no sympathy. They were the objects of her constant suspicion and malevolence. She watched her husband with unceasing vigilance; but he was well practiced in means to evade it. . . .

. . . Sometimes he would complain of the heat of the tea room, and order his supper to be placed on a small table in the piazza. He would seat himself there with a well-satisfied smile, and tell me to stand by and brush away the flies. He would eat very slowly, pausing between the mouthfuls. These intervals were employed in describing the happiness I was so foolishly throwing away, and in threatening me with the penalty that finally awaited my stubborn disobedience. He boasted much of the forbearance he had exercised towards me, and reminded me that there was a limit to his patience. When I succeeded in avoiding opportunities for him to talk to me at home, I was ordered to come to his office, to do some errand. When there, I was obliged to stand and listen to such language as he saw fit to address to me. Sometimes I so openly expressed my contempt for him that he would become violently enraged, and I wondered why he did not strike me. Circumstanced as he was, he probably thought it was better policy to be forbearing. But the state of things grew worse and worse daily. In desperation I told him that I must and would apply to my grandmother for protection. He threatened me with death, and worse than death, if I made any complaint to her. Strange to say, I did not despair. I was naturally of a buoyant disposition, and always I had a hope of somehow getting out of his clutches. Like many a poor, simple slave before me, I trusted that some threads of joy would yet be woven into my dark destiny.

I had entered my sixteenth year, and every day it became more apparent that my presence was intolerable to Mrs. Flint. Angry words frequently passed between her and her husband . . .

After repeated quarrels between the doctor and his wife, he announced his intention to take his youngest daughter, then four years old, to sleep in his apartment. It was necessary that a servant should sleep in the same room, to be on hand if the child stirred. I was selected for that office, and informed for what purpose that arrangement had been made. By managing to keep within sight of people, as much as possible, during the day time, I had hitherto succeeded in eluding my master, though a razor was often held to my throat to force me to change this line of policy. . . . [Now] I was ordered to take my station as nurse the following night. A kind Providence interposed in my favor. During the day Mrs. Flint heard of this new arrangement, and a storm followed. I rejoiced to hear it rage.

After a while my mistress sent for me to come to her room. Her first question was, "Did you know you were to sleep in the doctor's room?"

"Yes, ma'am."

"Who told you?"

"My master."

"Will you answer truly all the questions I ask?"

"Yes, ma'am."

"Tell me, then, as you hope to be forgiven, are you innocent of what I have accused you?"

"I am."

She handed me a Bible, and said, "Lay your hand on your heart, kiss this holy book, and swear before God that you tell me the truth."

I took the oath she required, and I did it with a clear conscience.

"You have taken God's holy word to testify your innocence," said she. "If you have deceived me, beware! Now take this stool, sit down, look me directly in the face, and tell me all that has passed between your master and you."

I did as she ordered. As I went on with my account her color changed frequently, she wept, and sometimes groaned. She spoke in tones so sad, that I was touched by her grief. The tears came to my eyes; but I was soon convinced that her emotions arose from anger and wounded pride. She felt that her marriage vows were desecrated, her dignity insulted; but she had no compassion for the poor victim of her husband's perfidy. She pitied herself as a martyr; but she was incapable of feeling for the condition of shame and misery in which her unfortunate, helpless slave was placed.

Yet perhaps she had some touch of feeling for me; for when the conference was ended, she spoke kindly, and promised to protect me. I should have been much comforted by this assurance if I could have had confidence in it; but my experiences in slavery had filled me with distrust. She was not a very refined woman, and had not much control over her passions. I was an object of her jealousy, and, consequently, of her hatred; and I knew I could not expect kindness or confidence from her under the circumstances in which I was placed. I could not blame her. Slaveholders' wives feel as other women would under similar circumstances. The fire of her temper kindled from small sparks, and now the flame became so intense that the doctor was obliged to give up his intended arrangement.

I knew I had ignited the torch, and I expected to suffer for it afterwards; but I felt too thankful to my mistress for the timely aid she rendered me to care much about that. She now took me to sleep in a room adjoining her own. There I was an object of her especial care, though not of her especial comfort, for she spent many a sleepless night to watch over me. Sometimes I woke up, and found her bending over me. At other times she whispered in my ear, as though it was her husband who was speaking to me, and listened to hear what I would answer. If she startled me, on such occasions, she would glide stealthily away; and the next morning she would tell me I had been talking in my sleep, and ask who I was talking to. At last, I began to be fearful for my life. It had been often threatened; and you can imagine, better than I can describe, what an unpleasant sensation it must produce to wake up in the dead of night and find a jealous woman bending over you. . . .

Why does the slave ever love? Why allow the tendrils of the heart to twine around objects which may at any moment be wrenched away by the hand of violence? . . . I did not reason thus when I was a young girl. Youth will be youth. I loved, and I indulged the hope that the dark clouds around me would turn out a bright lining. I forgot that in the land of my birth the shadows are too dense for light to penetrate. . . .

There was in the neighborhood a young colored carpenter; a free born man. We had been well acquainted in childhood, and frequently met together afterwards. We became mutually attached, and he proposed to marry me. I loved him with all the ardor of a young girl's first love. But when I reflected that I was a slave, and that the laws gave no sanction to the marriage of such, my heart sank within me. My lover wanted to buy me; but I knew that Dr. Flint was too wilful and arbitrary a man to consent to that arrangement. From him, I was sure of experiencing all sorts of opposition, and I had nothing to hope from my mistress. She would have been delighted to have got rid of me, but not in that way. It would have relieved her mind of a burden if she could have seen me sold to some distant state, but if I was married near home I should be just as much in her husband's power as I had previously been,—for the husband of a slave has no power to protect her. Moreover, my mistress, like many others, seemed to think that slaves had no right to any family ties of their own; that they were created merely to wait upon the family of the mistress. I once heard her abuse a young slave girl, who told her that a colored man wanted to make her his wife. "I will have you peeled and pickled, my lady," said she, "if I ever hear you mention that subject again. Do you suppose that I will have you tending my children with the children of that nigger?" The girl to whom she said this had a mulatto child, of course not acknowledged by its father. The poor black man who loved her would have been proud to acknowledge his helpless offspring.

 . . . How I dreaded my master now! Every minute I expected to be summoned to his presence; but the day passed, and I heard nothing from him. The next morning, a message was brought to me: "Master wants you in his study." I found the door ajar and I stood a moment gazing at the hateful man who claimed a right to rule me, body and soul. I entered and tried to appear calm. I did not want him to know how my heart was bleeding. He looked fixedly at me, with an expression which seemed to say, "I have half a mind to kill you on the spot." At last he broke the silence, and that was a relief to both of us.

"So you want to be married, do you?" said he, "and to a free nigger."

"Yes, sir."

"Well, I'll soon convince you whether I am your master, or the nigger fellow you honor so highly. If you *must* have a husband, you may take up with one of my slaves."

What a situation I should be in, as the wife of one of *his* slaves, even if my heart had been interested!

I replied, "Don't you suppose, sir, that a slave can have some preference about marrying? Do you suppose that all men are alike to her?"

"Do you love this nigger?" said he, abruptly.

"Yes, sir."

"How dare you tell me so!" he exclaimed, in great wrath. After a slight pause, he added, "I supposed you thought more of yourself; that you felt above the insults of such puppies."

I replied, "If he is a puppy I am a puppy for we are both of the negro race. It is right and honorable for us to love each other. The man you call a puppy never insulted me, sir; and he would not love me if he did not believe me to be a virtuous woman."

He sprang upon me like a tiger, and gave me a stunning blow. It was the first time he had ever struck me; and fear did not enable me to control my anger. When I had recovered a little from the effects, I exclaimed, "You have struck me for answering you honestly. How I despise you!" . . .

[He answered] ". . . I have wanted to make you happy, and I have been repaid with the basest ingratitude; but though you have proved yourself incapable of appreciating my kindness, I will be lenient towards you, Linda. I will give you one more chance to redeem your character. If you behave yourself and do as I require, I will forgive you and treat you as I always have done; but if you disobey me, I will punish you as I would the meanest slave on my plantation. Never let me hear that fellow's name mentioned again. If I ever know of your speaking to him, I will cowhide you both; and if I catch him lurking about my premises, I will shoot him as soon as I would a dog. Do you hear what I say? I'll teach you a lesson about marriage and free niggers! Now go, and let this be the last time I have occasion to speak to you on this subject."

Reader, did you ever hate? I hope not. I never did but once; and I trust I never shall again. Somebody has called it "the atmosphere of hell"; and I believe it is so.

. . . My lover was an intelligent and religious man. Even if he could have obtained permission to marry me while I was a slave, the marriage would give him no power to protect me from my master. It would have made him miserable to witness the insults I should have been subjected to. And then, if we had children, I knew they must "follow the condition of the mother." What a terrible blight that would be on the heart of a free, intelligent father! For *his* sake, I felt that I ought not to link his fate with my own unhappy destiny. He was going to Savannah to see about a little property left him by an uncle; and hard as it was to bring my feelings to it, I earnestly entreated him not to come back. I advised him to go to the Free States, where his tongue would not be tied, and where his intelligence would be of more avail to him. He left me, still hoping the day would come when I could be bought. With me the lamp of hope had gone out. The dream of my girlhood was over. I felt lonely and desolate.

. . . [Slaveholders] seem to satisfy their consciences with the doctrine that God created the Africans to be slaves. What a libel upon the heavenly Father, who "made of one blood all nations of men!" And then who are Africans? Who can measure the amount of Anglo-Saxon blood coursing in the veins of American slaves? . . .

No pen can give an adequate description of the all-pervading corruption produced by slavery. The slave girl is reared in an atmosphere of licentiousness and fear. The lash and the foul talk of her master and his sons are her teachers. When she is fourteen or fifteen, her owner, or his sons, or the overseer, or perhaps all of them, begin to bribe her with presents. If these fail to accomplish their purpose, she is whipped or starved into submission to their will. She may have had religious principles inculcated by some pious mother or grandmother, or some good mistress; she may have a lover, whose good opinion and peace of mind are dear to her heart; or the profligate men who have power over her may be exceedingly odious to her. But resistance is hopeless. . . .

The slaveholder's sons are, of course, vitiated, even while boys, by the unclean influences every where around them. Nor do the master's daughters always escape. Severe retributions sometimes come upon him for the wrongs he does to the daughters of the slaves. The white daughters early hear their parents quarrelling about some female slave. Their curiosity is excited, and they soon learn the cause. They are attended by the young slave girls whom their father has corrupted; and they hear such talk as should never meet youthful ears, or any other ears. They know that the women slaves are subject to their father's authority in all things; and in some cases they exercise the same authority over the men slaves. I have myself seen the master of such a household whose head was bowed down in shame; for it was known in the neigh-borhood that his daughter had selected one of the meanest slaves on his plantation to be the father of his first grandchild. She did not make her ad-vances to her equals, nor even to her father's more intelligent servants. She selected the most brutalized, over whom her authority could be exercised with less fear of exposure. Her father, half frantic with rage, sought to re-venge himself on the offending black man; but his daughter, foreseeing the storm that would arise, had given him free papers, and sent him out of the state.

In such cases the infant is smothered, or sent where it is never seen by any who know its history. But if the white parent is the *father*, instead of the mother, the offspring are unblushingly reared for the market. If they are girls, I have indicated plainly enough what will be their inevitable destiny.

. . . I can testify, from my own experience and observation, that slavery is a curse to the whites as well as to the blacks. It makes the white fathers cruel and sensual; the sons violent and licentious; it contaminates the daughters, and makes the wives wretched. And as for the colored race, it needs an abler pen than mine to describe the extremity of their sufferings, the depth of their degradation.

Yet few slaveholders seem to be aware of the widespread moral ruin occa-sioned by this wicked system. Their talk is of blighted cotton crops—not of the blight on their children's souls.

Source: Harriet Jacobs with L. Maria Child, *Incidents in the Life of a Slave Girl* (Boston, 1861), 44–47, 49–54, 58–63, 65–69, 79–81.

THE RIGHTS OF THE VICTIM

In 1986, Marla Hanson, a New York City model, angered her landlord, Steve Roth, by refusing to go out with him any longer. He hired two men to slash her face with razors. Incredibly, Ms. Hanson was able to get away from her attackers and seek help. But she needed 150 stitches and suffered immeasurably. Despite efforts at intimidation, and the trial judge's efforts to publicly humiliate her, Ms. Hanson testified against the men who attacked her. The defense attorney attempted to put Ms. Hanson on trial for her lifestyle, which included dating several men and dressing "provocatively." As Hanson said, "In order to prove their guilt, I had to prove my innocence first." The three men received the maximum allowable sentence of five to fifteen years. Many people were outraged by both this light sentence for a first-degree (premeditated) assault, and by the uncaring and even brutal way Ms. Hanson had been treated in court. Others expressed contempt for the way the press attempted to blacken Hanson's reputation before the trial, implying that

*she somehow bore responsibility for the attack as a consequence of her exciting lifestyle.
Such stories reinforced a notion, common to literature and film, that women who stepped
out of traditional roles might deserve a violent fate.*

*After her attack, Hanson became an advocate for the rights of the victims of violence.
In 1990 she appeared before Congress to speak in favor of victims' rights—her statement
is excerpted here. In 1991 a TV movie,* Face Value, *was made of her experiences, and
she went on to serve as a member of the state of New York's Crime Victims Advisory
Board. In 1996, in response to Hanson's committed efforts, New York's governor George
E. Pataki signed a law increasing the penalty for criminal assault and creating a new
crime of "gang assault." In signing the law, Governor Pataki maintained that it would
see that "there will be no more travesties of justice like the Marla Hanson slashing," in
which her attackers received a lighter sentence than if they had been convicted of stealing
her wallet.[23] The testimony of Marla Hanson reminds us that even in the late twentieth
century, many Americans continued to feel that women did not enjoy the same rights as
men, and that sometimes they deserved to be punished for their conduct. Some aspects of
violence do change. Abigail Abbot suffered a private hell, unable to share her anguish
with others for many years. Marla Hanson's abuse was both private and public, her pain
and humiliation repeated in the courts and the press. While her suffering has helped
others victims of gendered assault, it is hard to escape the conclusion that many Americans
are willing to excuse some forms of violence.*

Marla Hanson's Testimony before the Senate Judiciary Committee, 1990

STATEMENT OF MARLA HANSON

Ms. HANSON. Four years ago when I became a victim of an assault, what
puzzled and distressed me most about the whole ordeal was when I realized I
was suffering more from the stigma of victimization than from the actual violation. I am not trying to minimize the attack; it was as horrible as you
might imagine.

My landlord masterminded a razor attack to my face to end my modeling
career. I met him when I moved out of my apartment, I asked for my rent
deposit back. He refused to give it back, and when I pressed him he finally
said he would. I met him after a modeling assignment rather late one night,
around midnight, in a restaurant that occupied the bottom floor of my
building.

He said he had the money for me in cash, but he didn't want to give that
much cash to me in the bar because it might look wrong, so he asked me if I

23. Governor George Pataki, press release, September 19, 1996.

would step outside. So I did, thinking that I would step outside, get the money, go into my building and up to my apartment. Instead, he had two men waiting for me who grabbed me and began to cut my face.

I was lucky. I got away, ran back to the restaurant. The police were there within 2 minutes. They caught the men at the same time and I was able to identify them the same night. They were convicted and sentenced to the maximum, along with my landlord, of 5 to 15 years.

But in the scope of things, those cuts to my face that night became almost insignificant, except as a reference point. They healed, of course, leaving scars, but it wasn't the scars that hindered the continuance of my modeling career so much as what they represented—violence.

And it was not so much the trauma of the attack that night that has haunted me in the end, but, as I said, it is the stigma of victimization. From the moment the press seized upon my story to the trials of my attackers, I felt as though I was caught in a Kafkaesque world beyond any grasp of reason.

It had never occurred to me to feel ashamed at being attacked. I was, I think, at first embarrassed at not being able to control my situation, but it never occurred to me to blame myself for my own attack; that is, until the courts, the press, and society began to insinuate and to question if I were the architect of my own suffering.

The term "victim" implies innocence, but it seems in this society the term "innocence" implies some sort of guilt, and nowhere is that attitude more apparent than in our current judicial system where it has become a common practice for defense lawyers to blame victims for their own assault and suffering, or at least destroy a victim's credibility and dignity before the trial process is over.

Not only do I find this kind of attitude disgraceful and cruel, but also incredibly ignorant because I feel that by blaming the innocent victims for their own suffering, we are, in fact, excusing the crimes, and thus inviting more crime.

. . . [T]he first day in the hospital I started getting hundreds of phone calls from strangers, phone calls like people would call me up and say, well, what were you doing at the bar at 12 at night in the first place? Well, didn't you know that guy was weird? Why are you renting an apartment from a guy that you obviously knew was weird?

That said to me that I was to blame because I was at a bar at 12 at night. I mean, that was subtle, but that continued on. Every press article—they tore across the countryside digging up details about my life, printing them in the paper. Almost every article ended with a question mark. What did she do to deserve this, as if anything I did would merit this kind of attack to my face.

I found that disturbing, but what was most disturbing was the investigation and the court proceedings that followed. The investigation, to me, was
like an interrogation. [Police officers] had done research on me. They confronted me with facts about my life and said, true or false. They demanded
to know intimate details about my sex life, about everything about my life.
They wanted skeletons, they said, out of the closet. And thinking that the
prosecutor was my lawyer and that this was privileged information, I shared
everything I could think of, only to find out later that the prosecutor was not
my lawyer, that this information was not privileged. It was turned over to defense lawyers; that is required by law. And then it was turned over to the
press, and you can imagine how violated I felt at that.

That was only the beginning. During the trial process, and especially in
the second trial, a lawyer named Alton Maddox, whom I think some of you
are familiar with—runs with Al Sharpton—started his opening statement by
saying let me tell you about a woman who preyed on every man in this city,
who preyed on men and their relationships with women; let me tell you
about a girl named Marla Hanson, a girl out of Texas with a lot of racial
hang-ups; let me tell you about—he said something about a 48-hour rule, that
the police, the prosecutor, myself, and the entire New York City Police Department were involved in a massive coverup.

And then at the end of the trial, he went to the press and said before the
end of the trial, I will have Marla Hanson behind bars. Those were his exact
words. I mean, that is obviously blame. He went on throughout the trial to
humiliate me time after time and insinuate that I was some sort of prostitute
and a woman of loose morals.

He made fun of the fact that I thought I was about to be raped, made it
into a racial issue because the two men were black. But he forgot that my
landlord was white and already convicted of master-minding the attack.

Then we spent at least 20 minutes in the trial on the fact that I was wearing a miniskirt, and he opened the question by saying is it true that on that
night you were barely dressed, and, well, isn't it true that you hardly had anything on; well, you were wearing a miniskirt, weren't you, as if that in itself
was inviting the crime.

And then at one point in the trial he stood up and said this here is a
circus and I am the ringmaster and all I need is a whip to bring this "lying
bitch" to order. At that point in the trial, I think that was the first time I
cried throughout the whole proceeding. It seemed that everywhere I turned I
was being blamed for being the architect of my own suffering. . . .

I think the main impact is that I couldn't model again, although I tried.
. . . [I]t wasn't even the scars that hindered my modeling career. It was what
they represented, which was violence. All my big accounts canceled me.

You know, the scars don't show up in pictures, but when people see me, my face represents violent crime and people don't want to see that; they don't want to deal with that. So I couldn't model after that, and it wasn't really the crime; it was the press and everything surrounding it that caused the most suffering to me.

I have flashbacks sometimes. I think it has changed the way I look at the world forever. It is not a safe place any more, and I think that I have gained a lot of perspective on it in the last four years. But it is one of those things that you never get over. It is always there, and you never know when something is going to trigger a memory and cause you to be, I guess, paralyzed.

Source: Hearing Before the Committee on the Judiciary, U.S. Senate 101st Cong., 2nd sess., pt. 1 (1990).

FURTHER READINGS

On women and the law, see Cornelia Hughes Dayton, *Women Before the Bar: Gender, Law, and Society in Connecticut, 1639–1789* (Chapel Hill: University of North Carolina Press, 1995); Linda Kerber, *No Constitutional Right to Be Ladies: Women and the Obligations of Citizenship* (New York: Hill and Wong, 1998), Michael Grossberg, *Governing the Hearth: Law and the Family in Nineteenth-Century America* Hendrik Hartog, *Man and Wife in America: A History* (Cambridge, MA: Harvard University Press, 2000); Daniel W. Stowell, ed., *In Tender Consideration: Women, Families, and the Law in Abraham Lincoln's Illinois* (Urbana: University of Illinois Press, 2002); Peter W. Bardaglio. *Reconstructing the Household: Families, Sex and the Law in the Nineteenth Century South* (Chapel Hill: University of North Carolina Press, 1995).

On women and violence, see especially Elizabeth Pleck, *Domestic Tyranny: The Making of American Social Policy against Family Violence from Colonial Times to the Present* (New York: Oxford University Press, 1987); Peter C. Hoffer and N.E.H. Hull, *Murdering Mothers: Infanticide in England and New England, 1558–1803* (New York: New York University Press, 1981); Barbara S. Lindemann, " 'To Ravish and Carnally Know': Rape in Eighteenth-Century Massachusetts," *Signs: Journal of Women in Culture and Society* 10 (1984–85): 63–82; Marybeth Hamilton Arnold, " 'The Life of a Citizen in the Hands of a Woman': Sexual Assault in New York City, 1790 to 1820," in Kathy Peiss and Christina Simmons, eds., *Passion and Power: Sexuality in History* (Philadelphia: Temple University Press, 1989); G. S. Rowe, "Infanticide, Its Judicial Resolution, and Criminal Code Revision in Early Pennsylvania," *American Philosophical Society Proceedings* 135 (1991): 200–232; Patricia Cline Cohen. *The Murder of Helen Jewett: The life and Death of a Prostitute in Nineteenth-Century New York* (New York: Knopf, 1998); Christine Daniels and

Michael V. Kennedy, eds., *Over the Threshold: Intimate Violence in Early America* (New York: Routledge, 1999); Diane Miller Sommerville, *Rape and Race in the Nineteenth-Century South* (Chapel Hill: University of North Carolina Press, 2004).

On hate crimes, see James B. Jacob, *Hate Crimes: Criminal Law and Identity Politics* (New York: Oxford University Press, 1998); Frederick M. Lawrence, *Punishing Hate: Bias Crimes under American Law* (Cambridge, MA: Harvard University Press, 1999); Joyce King, *Hate Crime: The Story of a Dragging in Jasper, Texas* (New York: Pantheon, 2002).

INDEX

Abbot, Abigail, 361, 366–374, 384
Abbott, Elizabeth, 42
Abolitionists, 143, 147, 375
Adams, Abigail, 355–356, 358
Adams, Henry, 245
Adams, John, 80, 109, 355–356, 360
Adams, Samuel, 84, 107
African Americans
  and American Revolution, 80–81, 90, 97
  and Bacon's Rebellion, 52
  battle for rights, 180–186, 319–322, 332–334,
    338, 343–349
  and John Brown, 147
  in Civil War, 156, 160–164, 171
  culture of, 113
  in industrial accidents, 275–281
  and the law, 15, 171, 173–175, 246, 285, 357,
    360, 361
  and opposition to lynching, 322–328
  and perceptions of violence, 11–12, 172, 186–
    188
  praised by President, 351
  targeted by the KKK, 171–172, 177–179, 335–
    338
  targeted by lynch mobs, 189–194, 199–200,
    319–321, 324–326, 330–332
  in unions, 247
  and urban riots, 5–6, 160–164, 175–177, 194–
    198, 200–204, 214, 302–307
  See also Racism and slavery
Against our Will, 364

Alamance, battle of, 78–80
Alamo, 208, 215
Alcaraz, Ramon, 216
Algonquian, 51–52
Allen, James, 205
Allen, Philippa, 276–278
Allison, Samuel, 98
Altgeld, John, 251
Ambrose, Stephen, 210n7, 244
American Revolution, 7
  and battles of Lexington and Concord, 84–
    89
  dissent during, 97–104
  events leading to, 79–84
  logistics, 90, 95–97
  on the frontier, 92–95, 101–104
  opportunities presented by, 90–92
Andersonville, 164–166
Angelou, Maya, 364
Apache, 39, 55, 211
Appier, Janis, 318
Arnold, Marybeth Hamilton, 387
Assassinations, 22, 25, 27, 166–169, 251, 268–
    270, 285
Austin, Stephen, 215
Avrich, Paul, 249n11, 282
Ayers, Edward L., 4n6, 169, 204

Bacon, Nathaniel, 51–54
Bacon's Rebellion, 43, 51–54, 65, 73
Bailey, Asa, 366–374

Bailey, F. Lee, 33–36
Bamberg, Robert D., 36
Bancroft, Hubert Howe, 212, 231–234
Banner, Stuart, 309n8, 318
Bardaglio, Peter W., 387
Barnes, David M., 161–164
Batchelor, Albert, 180–181, 183–184
Batchelor, James Madison, 180–181, 183–184
Bear River Massacre, 209
Beauchamp, Jereboam, 12–14, 17
    confession of, 21–27
Beck, E. M., 205
Belknap, Michal, 354
Berkley, William, 51–53
Bernstein, Richard B., 359n9
Billy the Kid, see Henry McCarty
Black Codes, 173–175
Black Defense Force, 184–186
Blackstone, William, 356
Bland, Sterling L., 141
Block, Alan, 318
Blue Knight, The, 283
Bombings, 251–252, 268–270
Bonney, William H. See Henry McCarty
Booth, John Wilkes, 166–169
Boston Massacre, 79–83
Boston Tea Party, 83–84
Bowdoin, James, 104, 109
Boyer, Paul, 61n16, 68
Bradford, William, 46
Branch, Taylor, 354
Brattle, Thomas, 61–65
Brauer, Carl, 354
Brewer, David, 284, 286–288
Brock, Peter, 98n14
Brooks, Juanita, 210n6
Brown, Dee, 210n8, 211n9
Brown, H. Rap, 7
Brown, John, 71, 145, 147–151
Brown, Richard Maxwell, 6–7, 111, 212, 244
Brownmiller, Suzanne, 364
Bruce, Robert V., 254n18
Brundage, W. Fitzhugh, 205
Buchanan, James, 145
Butte, 214

Caesar, 118–124
California Gold Rush, 207, 208

California Highway Patrol, 308
Calloway, Colin G., 37n4, 92
Cannon, Lou, 307n7, 318
Capeci, Dominic J., Jr., 204
Carnegie, Andrew, 15, 249–250
Carp, E. Wayne, 111
Carr, Clark E., 146n6
Carrollton Massacre, 186–188
Carter, Jimmy, 364
Cashman, John Gordon, 198–200
Castellammarese War, 298
Celebrity, 4, 12–15
Centralia, 214
Chambliss, William, 318
Chaney, Andrew, 352–354
Cherniack, Martin, 281
Cheyenne, 211, 220–225
Chicago Tribune, 221–223, 249
Child, Maria, 375
Child Abuse Prevention and Treatment Act,
    364
Chinese, violence against, 211
Chisum, John S., 226–229
Chivington, John, 211
Christian, William, 102–104
Christianity
    and confession, 18–21
    in conquest of America, 39–40, 43, 46, 47,
        55
    and domestic abuse, 365–374
    and national expansion, 215
    and slave rebellion, 125–127
    and violence, 13, 43, 65–66, 68, 97–98, 254,
        365
Christopher, Warren, 302–309
Civil rights, 172, 184
    and the federal government, 319–330, 349–
        354
    movement opposed, 335–343
    organized movement for, 332–334
Civil War, 210, 212, 245, 319, 375, 376
    background of, 143–150
    effects of, 160–164, 166–169, 171–173
    nature of, 146, 151–160, 164
    POWs in, 164–166
Clark, George Rogers, 92–95
Clark, Jonas, 84–86
Clark, Marcia, 15–16, 17n13, 33–36

Class
  and industrialization, 246, 264–268
  and the law, 288–292, 361
  and lynch mobs, 212–213
  and race, 51–52, 160–161, 173–175, 194
  and traditional conflicts, 72–73, 78
Cleveland, Grover, 250, 251
Clymer, Jeffory, 3n3, 282
Cochran, Johnnie, 15, 33
Coeur d'Alene, 214–268
Cohen, Daniel, 36
Cohen, Patricia Cline, 382
Coleman, J. Winston, 36
Columbus, Christopher, 38, 40–41
Commager, Henry Steele, 216n20
Communism, 253–255
Conestoga Massacre, 65–68
Congress on Racial Equality, 332–337
Connor, Patrick, 210
Constitution of the United States
  and civil rights, 184, 319–321, 327–330, 332
  and death penalty, 309–317
  and gender, 356
  origins of, 109–110
  and slavery, 143–44, 211
  and use of troops, 251
Cook, Ann, 13, 17, 21–27
Cooper, William J., 169
Cornwallis, Charles, 97
Coronado, Francisco, 39
Cortés, Hernando, 43
Costello, James, 162
Cotton, John, 40
Cotton, Joshua, 131–133
Countryman, Edward, 111
Courtwright, David, 16, 318
Crazy Horse, 220–221, 223, 224
Cresey, Donald R., 318
Crime literature, 13–14
Cripple Creek, 214
Crook, George, 222, 223
Crow, Walter J., 213
Crowd action, tradition of, 71–73, 78, 80, 83–84, 104, 109
Cummings, Homer, 320, 322–324
Custer, George A., 211, 220–225
Cutler, James, 205
Czolgosz, Leon, 151

Daniels, Christine, 387
Darden, Christopher, 16, 33–36
David, Henry, 248n9, 282
Davis, Jefferson, 133, 145, 167
Davis, Joseph, 133–135
Dayton, Cornelia Hughes, 357n3, 387
Death penalty,
  in colonial period, 4, 13, 42–45, 61, 63, 65, 356–357
  and DNA evidence, 16, 313
  and lethal injection, 313
  as political weapon, 288–292
  and race, 357
  restored by Supreme Court, 312–317
  and slavery, 116–117, 124, 147
  and use of electric chair, 309–312
De Bernicre, Henry, 86–89
DeBord, David, 366
Debs, Eugene V., 246, 250–251, 288
DeFrancis, Vincent, 363
Demos, John, 68
Dennis, Matthew, 111
Derrickson, Ann, 164
Deutsch, Helene, 362
De Vries, David, 48–51
Dinnerstein, Leonard, 204
Dittmer, John, 354
DNA testing, 33, 313
Domestic violence, 5, 9, 15, 32, 41–42, 362–383
Dosch, Arno, 246n5
Douglas, Stephen, 144–146
Douglass, Frederick, 113, 135–140, 141, 147, 375
Douglass, William A., 3n3
Downey, Dennis, 204
Doyle, William, 354
Drago, Harry S., 244
Dray, Philip, 205
Drug abuse, 285, 298–302
Dubofsky, Melvyn, 282
Dueling, 114, 133–135
Due process, 286–288
Duster, Alfreda, 205
Dykstra, Robert R., 244

Edelman, Murray, 3n3
Edison, Thomas, 309

Electric chair, 309–312
Ellsworth, Scott, 205
England
    and Civil War, 160
    and colonial struggles, 48, 52, 74, 80, 83–84, 90
    and the conquest of America, 38–41, 43–44
    heritage of crowd action in, 71–73
    See also American Revolution
Escobar, Edward J., 318
Everett, 214
Evers, Medgar, 343–344
Exceptionalism, American, 4, 6, 8–9
Executions. *See* death penalty and lynching
Execution sermons, 14

Fairclough, Adam, 354
Falkner, Murry, 339–343
Family Violence Prevention and Services Act, 365
Fanning, Edward, 74, 77–78
Faragher, John Mack, 244
Farmer, James, 321, 332–334
Farrell, Harry, 204
Faulk, Odie B., 211n9
Faust, Drew, 375
Federal Bureau of Investigation, 11, 322, 333, 335–338
Finch, John W., 276–278, 281
Finkelman, Paul, 140
Fogelson, Robert M., 317
Foley, Michael A., 318
Follmer, Claude, 298–302
Foner, Eric, 204
Foner, Philip, 282
Fort Sumter, 146
Fortune, T. Thomas, 184–186
Fox, Stephen, 318
France and conquest of America, 41
Frankfurter, Felix, 288
Franklin, Abraham, 162
Franklin, Benjamin, 65–68, 92
Franklin, John Hope, 4n6
Freedom Rides, 321, 332–338
Freedom Summer, 352–354
Fremantle, James A. L., 157–160
Freud, Sigmund, 362

Frick, Henry Clay, 249–259
Friedman, Lawrence M., 69, 317–318
Fries Rebellion, 109
Frisch, Michael, 282
Frontier as source of violence, 8, 38, 65, 67–68
Fuhrman, Mark, 16, 33–36
Furman, William Henry, 312–317

Gage, Thomas, 84, 86–87
Gandhi, Mahatma, 321, 332
Garland, Hamin, 223–225
Garrett, Pat, 226–230
Gary, Joseph, 261
Gender
    and the law, 355–366, 373, 383–387
    in murder cases, 12, 16–36
    and race, 172–173, 177–179, 200
    and slavery, 113, 135–40, 358–359, 374–383
    and witchcraft trials, 42–43
    See also domestic violence
Genovese, Eugene D., 141
George, Henry, 246
Gettysburg, battle of, 156–160
Ghost Dance Religion, 238–239, 241
Gilje, Paul, 282
Gilmore, Glenda Elizabeth, 204
Gilpin, Thomas, 98n15
Gladstone, Thomas H., 144n4
Goble, Danney, 201–204
Godbeer, Richard, 68
Godkin, Edwin L., 254
Goldberg, Hank, 16, 36
Goldman, Ron, 15, 32–36
Gompers, Samuel, 248, 252
Goodman, Andrew, 352–354
Gordon-Reed, Annette, 359
Gould, Jay, 248
Graham, Hugh Davis, 6
Grant, Ulysses, 164, 167–168, 171, 210, 216, 220, 287
Grattan, John L., 210
Gray, Thomas R., 124
Graydon, Alexander, 90
Green, Ben, 204
Greene, Nathanael, 95–97
Griffith, Paddy, 169
Grimsted, David, 143

Grinnell, Julius, 261-262, 264
Grossberg, Michael, 387
Grossman, Dave, 37n3
Gunplay, 213-214
Gurr, Ted Robert, 6
Gutiérez, Ramón A., 68

Hahn, Steven, 282
Hall, Robert, 320
Halttunen, Karen, 4n4, 36
Hamilton, Henry, 93-95
Hampton, Wade, 375
Hancock, John, 84, 109
Hanson, Marla, 383-387
Harding, John Wesley, 212
Harpers Ferry, 147-151
Hartog, Hendrik, 387
Hatch, Orrin, 364
Hawk's Nest Tunnel, 275-281
Hayes, Rutherford B., 253-254
Haymarket, 249, 261-264
Hemings, Sally, 359, 374
Henderson, Richard, 76-78
Hendrickson, Paul, 354
Hening, William W., 42n13
Henry, Aaron, 343-349
Heuston, Peter, 163
Heyrman, Christine L., 41n10
Hinton, Elias, 42
Hirsch, James S., 205
Hispanics, 211-214, 285. See Mexican War
Hockett, Homer C., 216n22
Hoffer, Peter C., 387
Hofstadter, Richard, 7-9, 15n4
Hollon, W. Eugene, 213n17, 244
Holmes, Oliver Wendell, 151-156
Holt, Michael, 169
Holt, Rush Dew, 276-281
Homestead Strike, 250
Homicides
    declining in United States, 11-12, 245
    and gender, 12, 16-17
    individual acts of, 4, 5, 17, 361
    See also Beauchamp, Jereboam; McCarty,
        Henry; Simpson, O. J.; Stone, Hugh;
        Thaw, Harry
Honor culture, 12, 22, 114, 285
Hoover, Herbert, 284

Horowitz, Donald, 3n2
Huebner, Timothy, 140
Huie, William Bradford, 330-332
Hull, N. E. H., 387
Humphrey, Gordon, 365
Hurtado, Albert L., 211n9, 244
Husband, Herman, 75
Hyser, Raymond, 204

I Know Why the Caged Bird Sings, 364
Incest, 361, 362, 366, 369-374
Indentured servitude, 42-44, 114-115
Indians. *See* Native Americans and
    individual nations
Industrialization, 4-5, 214
    and industrial accidents, 246-247, 252-253,
        275-281
    and use of force, 246-261, 264-268, 270-
        275
Infanticide, 361
Insanity and homicide, 27, 32, 147, 212
Ito, Lance, 12, 16, 33-36

Jackson, Frederick, 38
Jackson, Jesse, 11
Jacob, Giles, 357
Jacob, James B., 388
Jacobs, Harriet, 113, 141, 375-383
Jacobs, Margaret, 61
Jamestown, 38, 43-44, 52-53
Jamieson, Perry D., 146n7, 169
Jefferson, Thomas, 97
    on the need for revolution, 109-111
    slavery and, 102, 109, 144, 358-359, 374
Jennings, Francis, 37n4, 68
Jerome, William Travers, 27, 31
Jewett, Helen, 361
Johnson, Andrew, 173
Johnson, Lyndon, 5, 349-352
Johnson, Raynard, 11-12
Johnson County War, 213
Josephe, 55, 57-58
Journalists and violence, 4, 5, 11-12, 14, 27,
    383-386
Jury nullification, 16

Kadish, Sanford H., 318
Kansas, "Bleeding," 144-145

Kantrowitz, Stephen, 204
Karlsen, Carol F., 68
Kars, Marjoleine, 111
Katzenbach, Nicholas, 338
Kay, Melvin L. Michael, 75n7
Kefauver, Estes, 298-302
Kelly, Robert J., 298n6, 318
Kempe, C. Henry, 363
Kennedy, John F., 166, 338, 340, 342
Kennedy, Michael, 388
Kerber, Linda, 387
Kieft's War, 39, 48-51
King, Joyce, 388
King, Martin Luther, 321, 332, 349
King, Rodney, 5, 16, 214, 285, 307-309
King Philip's War, 41
Klarman, Michael J., 354
Knights of Labor, 247
Kotz, Nick, 354
Ku Klux Klan, 171-172, 177-179, 312, 322, 335-338

Labor unions, 268
    and the law, 251-252, 270, 284-285
    strikes by, 214, 246-247, 250-251, 253-261, 264-265, 270
    in violent conflicts with management, 246, 248-261, 264-268, 270-275
Lamar, Howard R., 210n7, 211n10, 212n11
Lane, Roger, 3n2, 5, 5n7, 245, 298n5, 317
Lange, Fred D., 247n6
Langford, Gerald, 36
Lassard, Suzannah, 17n11, 36
Laurie, Bruce, 282
Lawrence, Frederick M., 388
Leadville, 214
Lee, Robert E., 147, 150, 157-159, 167
Lemerick, Patricia, 208
Leonard, Gerald, 169
Levy, George, 170
Lewis, John, 354
Limerick, Patricia Nelson, 208, 244
Lincoln, Abraham, 152, 215
    and 1860 election, 145
    assassinated, 166-169
    and Civil War, 146, 156-157
Lincoln, Benjamin, 107-108
Lincoln County War, 213, 226-230

Lindbergh Kidnapping Law, 323
Linderman, Barbara S., 357n5, 387
Little Bighorn Massacre, 211, 220-225
Litwack, Leon, 204
Lockhart, Patrick, 102-104
Lockwood, John, 107n19
Longstreet, James, 158-60
Los Angeles, 214, 307-309
Los Angeles Police Department, 32, 214, 283, 302-309
    racism of, 15-16, 33-35, 285, 307
Los Angeles Times, bombed, 251-252
Lowther, Henry, 177-179
Loyalists, 98-104
Luciano, Charles, 298
Ludlow Massacre, 214, 252, 270-275
Lynch, Charles, 101-104
Lynching
    assumed, 11-12
    Ida B. Wells on, 186, 188-194
    justified, 172-173, 231-238, 330-332
    opposed, 9, 198-200, 286-288, 320-330
    origins of, 4, 8, 102-104
    U.S. Supreme Court and, 321, 328-330
    in the West, 211-212

McCarthy, Joseph R., 298
McCarty, Henry (Billy the Kid), 225-230, 231
McCaslin, Richard B., 204
McClellan, George B., 152
McCone, John, 302-307
McConville, Brendan, 358n7
McCurry, Linda O., 205
McFeely, William S., 318
McGovern, James R., 204
McKanna, Clare V., 208
McKinley, William, 251
McNamara, James, 252
McNamara, John J., 252
McPherson, James, 169
McSween, Alexander, 226-227
McWhiney, Grady, 146n7, 169
McWhorter, Diane, 354
Madigan, Tim, 205
Madison, James, 109
Madison County, vigilantes, 128-133
Madison Square Garden, 27-30
Mafia, 285, 298-302

Maier, Pauline, 83n9, 111
Mailer, Norman, 318
Manifest Destiny, 215, 216
Markowitz, Gerald, 281
Martin, Asa Earl, 216n21
Marvel, William, 170
Mason, John, 46-48
Masur, Louis P., 318
Mather, Cotton, 4, 18
May, Karl, 230-231
Meredith, James, 338-343
Mexican War, 208, 214-220
Middlekauff, Robert, 111
Mikulski, Barbara, 364-365
Militia
   African American militia companies, 172,
      180-181
   in American Revolution, 84-86, 90
   and crowd actions, 52, 72, 74-75, 78-79,
      104, 109, 161, 253
   lack of 39, 65
   in service of management, 248-251, 253,
      259-260, 265, 268, 270-275
   Western, 211, 214
Miller, Wilbur, 318
Minutaglio, Bill, 281-282
Mississippi, University of, 338-343
Mobs
   in America, 5, 73-83, 99, 144, 160-164, 172,
      186, 188, 200-204, 333-334, 338-343
   in England, 71-72
   in the West, 211-212, 214
   See also crowd action
Mohawk, 48, 51
Mondale, Walter, 364
Monkkonen, Eric, 3n2, 11, 69, 245, 298n5,
   317
Montgomery, David, 282
Moody, Anne, 354
Mooney, James, 238-243
Mooney, Michael Macdonald, 36
Moore, William Howard, 318
Morgan, Bumper, 283
Morgan, Edmund S., 42n12, 68, 140
Morris, Thomas D., 140
Morrison, Samuel Eliot, 216n20
Mountain Meadows Massacre, 210
Murphy, Frank, 320-321, 328-330

Mussel Slough, 213
Mystic Massacre, 46-48

Narcotics, 285, 298-302
National Association for the Advancement
   of Colored People, 320, 322, 325, 343,
   344, 346, 349
National Commission on the Causes and
   Prevention of Violence, 5-7, 9
National Commission on Law Observance
   and Enforcement, 284, 293-299, 292-297
National Guard
   class structure of, 248-249,
   and labor unrest, 253, 265, 270-275
   in Mississippi, 338-343
Native Americans
   in the American Revolution, 92-94
   and Bacon's Rebellion, 51-53
   battle the United States, 209-211, 220-225,
      238-243
   and European conquest, 37-41, 45-51, 54-
      61, 208
   and Paxton Boys, 65-68
   See also individual native nations
Navajos, 39
Neal, Claude, 320, 324
Nelson, Jill, 318
Nelson, Paul D., 111
Nesbit, Evelyn, 17, 27-36
New Deal, 285
New Netherlands, 43, 48-51
New Orleans Race Riot, 175-177
New York City draft riots, 160-164
Newman, Simon P., 11
Nichols, William Henry, 162
Niebuhr, Reinhold, 321
Nissenbaum, Stephen, 61n16, 68
Nixon, Richard, 312
Norcom, James, 375
North Carolina Regulators, 74-78, 83, 104
Norton, Mary Beth, 69

Oakes, James, 141
O'Brien, H. J., 164-165
O'Connell, J. D., 175-177
Oglesby, Richard, 261
Olney, Richard, 251
Oñate, Juan de, 39

Oney, Steve, 204
Orchard, Harry, 268-270
Osofsky, Gilbert, 141
O'Sullivan, John, 215
Otermín, Antonio de, 55-57
Otis, Harrison Gray, 251-252
Otis, James, 80
Overland Trail, 208, 210
Owen, Andrew, 181-183

Pacifism, 65, 75, 97-98
Paludan, Phillip Shaw, 169
Parris, Samuel, 61
Parsons, Lucy, 249
Pawnee, 210
Paxton Boys, 43, 65-68, 75
Payne, Charles, 354
Pearson, Richmond M., 119-22
Pencak, William, 111
Pequot War, 39, 41, 45-48
Percy, George, 38
Peters, Madison, 30-32
Peterson, Dale, 37n1
Peyton, Arthur, 276-279
Pilgrims, 45
Pinkerton, Allan, 254-261
Pinkerton agents, 213, 248, 250, 264, 268
Piute, 210
Pleck, Elizabeth, 41, 69, 361, 363, 387
Police
  history of, 283-285
  and domestic abuse, 362-364
  violence against, 261-264
  violence by, 175-177, 226, 261, 283-286, 292-297, 302, 307-309, 322, 335-337, 346, 349-350
Political violence, 13-14, 22, 171-172, 175-177, 180-181, 194-198, 214, 261-264. See also American Revolution; assassinations; Civil War; Mexican War
Polk, James K., 215, 216
Popular sovereignty, 144
Popular Tribunals, 230-234
Pornography of pain, 3-4
Potter, David M., 169, 339
Powderly, T. V., 247n7, 249
Powell, Colin, 9
Powhatan, 38

Prassel, Frank R., 207, 244
Preston, William, 102-104
Price, Cecil Ray, 322
Prisoners of war, 164-166
Proctor, John, 42
Prude, Jonathan, 282
Pueblo Uprising, 39, 54-57
Pullman Strike, 250-251
Puritans, 40, 41, 45-46

Quakers, 65, 98

Rable, George, 245n2
Racism
  against Indians, 40, 48
  among scholars, 216
  and civil rights, 319-322, 330-349
  and Civil War, 143, 160-164
  and law enforcement, 15-16, 33-35, 42, 171-177, 307-309, 312, 360, 361
  promoted, 52, 171
  and violence, 73, 114-115, 118-124, 128-131, 171-173, 175-184, 186-204, 319-320, 330-332, 376-384
  in the West, 209-214
  See also Native Americans; slavery
Rademaker, Claes, 49
Rampton, Sheldon, 281
Ransom, John L., 164-166
Rape, 136-37, 172, 200, 211, 286, 356-357, 359, 362-364, 374-383
Raper, Arthur, 205
Reconstruction, 171-184, 210, 246, 319, 321
Reed, Joseph, 163-164
Reid, John Phillip, 208, 244
Reiss, Albert J., Jr., 37n2
Religion and murder, 17-21. See also Christianity
Reno, Marcus, 220-222, 224
Reparations, 200, 203-204
Reynolds, David S., 169
Riley, Bennett, 208
Rivington's Gazette, 99-101
Roberts, David, 244
Robertson, David, 141
Robinson, Jeremiah, 163
Robinson, John, 46, 80
Roosevelt, Eleanor, 322, 324-326

Roosevelt, Franklin D., 320, 322–328
Roosevelt, Theodore, 234
Roscoe, Theodore, 170
Rosner, David, 281
Ross, Don, 200–201
Roth, Jeffrey A., 37n2
Rotnem, Victor, 326–328
Roules, Robert, 41
Rountree, Helen, 68
Rousey, Dennis, 318
Rowe, G. S., 387
Rowe, Gary Thomas, Jr., 335–338
Royster, Charles, 111
Ruffin, Thomas, 119, 122–124
Ryan, George, 313

Sacco, Nicola, 288–292
Salem Witchcraft trials, 42–43, 61–65
Salvatore, Nick, 282
San Sabra County War, 211
Santa Anna, Antonio López de, 208, 215
Saunders, William L., 75n6
Savannahs, 38–39
Sawyer, Lorenzo, 213
Schaack, Michael J., 261–264
Schechter, Patricia A., 205
Schindler, Harold, 210n7
Schlesinger, Arthur M., 216n22
Schlicke, Carl, 210n6
Schultz, Duane P., 211n9, 244
Schwartz, Philip J., 140
Schwerner, Michael, 352–354
Screws, Mack Claude, 320, 328–330
Selma, Alabama, 349–352
Seltzer, Mark, 4n4
Seven Years' War, 39, 73, 74
Sewell, Richard H., 169
Sharp, Solomon, 13–14, 17, 21–27
Sharpless, Isaac, 98n17
Sharpton, Al, 11
Shaw, Lemuel, 252
Shays, Daniel, 104–108
Shays's Rebellion, 104–110
Shephard, William, 104–105, 107
Shipman, Marlin, 318
Siguenza y Gongora, Carlos de, 55, 58–61
Silicosis, 275–281
Simpson, Nicole Brown, 15, 17, 32–36

Simpson, Orenthal James (O. J.), 4, 5, 12, 15, 285
    tried for murder, 32–36, 285
Sioux, 210, 211, 220–225, 238–243
Sitkoff, Harvard, 354
Sitting Bull, 220–222, 224
Sjpsjpme, 209–210
Slaughter, Thomas P., 111
Slave rebellions, 71, 73, 114, 124–133, 147, 150
Slavery, 319
    and Civil War, 143–148, 150, 160–161, 171
    during American Revolution, 97
    law of, 42, 113–124, 361
    and Mexican War, 215
    and Native Americans, 38, 46, 211
    violence of, 4, 42, 113–115, 118–124, 135–140,
        143–144, 358–359, 374–383
Slotkin, Richard, 38n6, 244
Smead, Howard, 204–205
Smith, Henry, 190–194
Smith, Persifor F., 208
Social Darwinism, 15, 234, 247–248
Sommerville, Diane Miller, 388
South Carolina Regulators, 74
Spain and the conquest of America, 39–41,
        43, 54–57, 208
Speer, Lonnie R., 170
Spencer, Herbert, 15
Stamp Act Crisis, 73, 83
Stanford, Leland, 213
State sanctioned violence, 42–45, 72, 115–118,
        213–214, 251, 253–54, 270–275. See also
        Death penalty; slavery; individual wars
States' rights, 352–354
Stauber, John, 281
Steele, Ian K., 68
Steers, Edward, 170
Stephens, Alexander, 143–144
Steuben, Friedrich Wilhelm von, 90–92, 95
Steunenberg, Frank, 251, 268–270
Stewart, Steven J., 358n6
Stone, Charles P., 152
Stone, Hugh, 4, 12, 16, 17
    conversation on murder, 17–21
Stono Rebellion, 73
Storti, Craig, 211n10
Stowell, Daniel, 387
Streib, Victor L., 318

Strike of 1877, 253-261
Strikes. *See* labor unions
Stringfellow, Benjamin, 144
Suicide, 11-12, 245
Sumner, William Graham, 247-248
Surratt, John H., 167
Szatmary, David P., 111

Taino, 40
Telluride, 214
Terrorists, 145, 171-172, 177-179, 189-190, 312
Terry, Alfred, 220
Texas rebellion, 208, 215
Thaw, Harry, 12, 14-15, 17, 30-32
    confession of, 27-30, 36
Thayer, Webster, 288
Third degree, 284, 292-297
Thomas, Emory M., 169
Thompson, E. P., 72
Till, Emmett, 321, 330-332
Tillman, Benjamin, 172-173
Tilly, Charles, 6
Tolnay, Stewart, 205
Toobin, Jeffrey, 15n5, 17n12, 33-36
Torture, 41, 97, 139-40, 190, 193-194, 199-200, 319-320, 363, 365
Townsend, Joseph, 98
Trail of Tears, 209
Tragle, Henry Irving, 141
Trials, criminal, 12, 14-18, 27, 32-36, 173-174, 286-292, 356-357, 359-362, 383
Truman, Harry S, 298
Tryon, William, 74-76, 78-79
Tsai, Shih-Shan Henry, 211n10
Tucher, Andie, 4n5
Tulsa Race Riot, 200-204
Tunstall, John, 226-229
Turner, Frederick Jackson, 38
Turner, Nat, 114, 124-127
Turner, Thomas Reed, 170
Two Moon, 221, 223-225

Underhill, John, 46-48
Union Carbide, 275-281
Unwritten law, 11-36
Utley, Robert M., 37n4, 211n9, 244

Vanzetti, Bartolomeo, 288-292
Vardaman, James K., 186-188
Vargas Zapata, Diego de, 55, 58-60
Vestal, Stanley, 244
Vicksburg Massacre, 180-184
Vigilantism, 6, 114, 128-133, 212-214, 226, 230-234, 286, 319. *See also* Ku Klux Klan; lynching
Victims' rights, 383-387
Violence
    culture of, 38, 113-115, 133-140, 143-144, 356-366
    economic, 213-214, 220, 225-30, 248-261, 264-268, 270-281
    family, 41-42, 357-374
    historical scholarship on, 5-10, 355
    increased levels of, 143-146
    justifications for, 12, 22, 40, 42-43, 109-111, 147-148, 172-173, 186-188, 194-197, 383-386
    and the law, 286-297, 307-317, 319-330, 335-343, 349-354, 356-365, 383-387
    as metaphor, 3-5, 11-12
    and national expansion, 209-211, 214-225, 231, 238-243
    nature and causes of, 3-9, 73, 209-214
    opposition to, 198-200, 321, 332-334
    origins, 37-38, 302-306
    perceptions of, 11-12, 207-209, 212, 225-226, 235-238, 360-364
    as spectacle, 261-264
    thrill of, 183-184, 192-194
    uses of, 4, 6, 8, 171-172, 231-234, 245-246, 283, 345-350
Virginia Gazette, 79
Virginian The, 207, 234-238

Waddell, Alfred M., 194-198
Waldrep, Christopher, 11n1, 204, 205, 282
Walker, David, 7n1
Walkowitz, Daniel, 282
Wallace, Michael, 7
Walpole, Robert, 72
Wambaugh, Joseph, 283
Warren, Robert Penn, 36
Washburn, Wilcomb E., 69
Washington, George, 39, 90, 107, 109
Washita, 211, 220

Watts Riot, 5, 214, 285, 302–306

Waumbaugh, Joseph, 283

Wells, Ida B., 9, 186, 188–194, 205

Western violence

  causes of, 209–214

  images of, 207–209, 225–226, 230–231, 235–238

  in industrial conflicts, 213–214

  and the law, 208, 212–213

  in range wars, 213, 225–30, 246

  and warfare, 214–225, 238–243

Westinghouse, George, 309

Westos, 38–39

Wexler, Laura, 204

Wheatland, 214

Wheaton, Francis, 359, 360

Whiskey Rebellion, 109

White, Richard, 68, 209

White, Stanford, 14–15, 17, 27–36

White, Walter, 205, 320, 322–326

Whitfield, Stephen, 204

Wickersham, George, 284. *See also* National

Commission on Law Observance and Enforcement

Wigmore, John Henry, 362

Williams, Daniel, 36

Williams, Lou Falkner, 204

Williamson, Joel, 4n6, 212

Wilmington Race Riots, 194–198

Wilson, Woodrow, 271

Wirtz, Henry, 165

Wister, Owen, 207, 234–238

Wiyot, 211

Wound culture, 3–4

Wounded Knee, 211, 214, 238–243

Wrangham, Richard, 37n1

Wright, Cleo, 326

Wyatt-Brown, Bertram, 141

Young, Alfred F., 75n7, 83, 111

Zoot Suit Riot, 214

Zuckerman, Michael, 72

Zulaika, Joseba, 3n3